Collins

AF662441

Enhanced

Science Now

Revised Edition

A Science Textbook based on Holistic Learning Theory

8

Name : ....

Grade : .... Section : ....

I am a metal. I might seem lightweight, but don't underestimate me—I'm super strong and can resist corrosion like a champ! That's why they pick me for building satellites.
I help them survive the tough conditions in space while being cost-effective for launches and operations. I'm the metal of choice for out-of-this-world adventures!
What am I? ....

Series Editor | Geetha Iyer

HarperCollins*Publishers*

Publishing operations in 17 countries and 120+ imprints globally

William Collins' dream of knowledge for all began with the publication of his first book in 1819. A self-educated mill worker, he not only enriched millions of lives, but also founded a flourishing publishing house. Today, staying true to this spirit, Collins books are packed with inspiration, innovation and practical expertise. They place you at the centre of a world of possibility and give you exactly what you need to explore it.

Published by Collins Learning
An imprint of HarperCollins*Publishers* India
Building No. 10, Tower A, 4th Floor, DLF Cyber City, Gurugram, Haryana 122002, India

First edition: 2024
Reprint edition:2025
ISBN: 978-93-6213-602-2

Content developed by **Excelsoft Technologies Pvt Ltd.**
Artwork, typesetting and layout by **AptaraCorp Ltd., Mammoth Studioz Ltd, iBook Services**
Printed and bound in India by **Print Plus Pvt Ltd.**

ACKNOWLEDGEMENTS

Title Page: xia yuan

Inside: Page **5:** grafikazpazurem, Enis Aksoy, bsd studio; **6:** Qvasimodo, Qvasimodo; **8:** Aldo Pavan, Dmitry Ageev; **10:** Digital Photo art, AJP, arfo, m.bonotto; **11:** Kriangkrai Thitimakorn; **14:** Pauline P, cmgirl, Joyce Vincent; **22:** m.bonotto, Digital Photo art; **23:** dlewis33, mikroman6; **25:** Kallayanee Naloka; **26:** Ed Reschke; **28:** Grandpa, Damian Herde, Julie Vader; **29:** schankz, librakv, carroteater, absolutimages, Winning7799; **30:** Beneda Miroslav; **35:** Paul Starosta; **40:** Kallayanee Naloka, Ed Reschke; **41:** manoa; **44:** Jethuynh; **45:** vuk8691; **56:** m.malinika; **57:** bgblue, Navinpeep, Rebeca Constantin/500px, Tom Kelley; **64:** benimage, R.Tsubin, nndanko; **70:** AdShooter; **71:** KrimKate, KrimKate, RHJ, author, Oat_Phawat, bagi1998; **74:** benimage, R.Tsubin; **82:** FCG; **88:** Panom Pensawang; **95:** ridvan_celik; **102:** Ed Reschke; **109:** PixelsEffect; **122:** Peter Dazeley; **123:** Ekaterina V. Borisova, tazzymoto, Villiers Steyn; **134:** pikepicture; **136:** szefei, Patryk Kosmider, Leena Robinson, photogearch, aodaodaodaod, alfotokunst; **138:** NagyDodo; **141:** Petr Toman, Jacqueline Abromeit, Ryan M. Bolton; **142:** Nickolay Stanev, **143:** Piyathep, Aditya Singh, neelsky, VenkateshMurthy; **146:** Aditya Singh; **149:** Franz Aberham, Smevins Photography; **151:** David Merron Photography; **159:** alphabetMN, msonick; **160:** dencg; **166:** Matthew Micah Wright; **171:** FancyTapis; **173:** Zhukov Oleg, chris2766; **174:** arka38; **177:** jallfree, Zzvet; **186:** AlexMaster, Jayakumar, Sokolov Sergei; **192:** ttsz; **193:** maxim ibragimov, Somchai Som, VectorMine; **199:** zentilia, Ari N; **205:** invincible_bulldog; **206:** Anna Omelchenko, Prometheus72; **218:** SiberianArt; **223:** Tetiana Lazunova; **227:** rusm; **232:** non-exclusive; **233:** Lonely; **236:** Benjamin Albiach Galan; **240:** CHUYN; **241:** Ricardo Reitmeyer, clearviewstock, clearviewstock; **245:** Vadim Sadovski, 3drenderings; **246:** Tristan3; **247:** Dleonello calvetti; **248:** Michael Rosskothen, Tristan3D, njaj; **249:** Tristan3D, BlueRingMedia, godrick; **252:** a. v. ley; **257:** Feodora Chiosea; **258:** WvdM, Nickolay Khoroshkov, Paolo Bona; **260:** art-pho, Guryanov Andrey; **262:** hxdbzxy; **263:** FedeCandoniPhoto; **265:** Dr. Morley Read; **266:** John Kasawa

Supplementary Booklet: Pia Kolle, Icon_Craft_Studio, Olesia Kononenko, Julia_Sudnitskaya, PrettyVectors, TanawatPontchour, FrankyDeMeyer, non157, elenabs, AlionaManakova, hisa nishiya, sarunyu_foto, eliflamra, sarunyu_foto, AlionaManakova, redmal, nizha2, scisettialfio, anankkml

Preface

Enhanced Science Now, Revised Edition is a transformative three-book series designed for Classes 6 to 8, aiming to provide students with a holistic and forward-looking learning experience. Embracing the principles of the **National Education Policy (NEP) 2020 and National Curriculum Framework (NCF) 2023,** this series goes beyond traditional learning approaches to prepare students for the multifaceted challenges of the 21st century.

In this dynamic era, our students face both unprecedented challenges and opportunities that demand a deeper understanding of their role in shaping the world. As educators, we recognize the need to equip them with essential skills, knowledge and a growth mindset to navigate the complexities of modern life successfully.

Our series is founded on the principles of **Holistic Learning Theory**, guiding students to explore their identities, purpose and connection with the community and the environment. Through a strong core content in science, we foster intellectual, emotional, social, artistic, moral and spiritual development, nurturing well-rounded individuals who contribute positively to society.

Innovative features in the series encourage interdisciplinary projects, instill a scientific temper, promote vocational skills and cultivate regional and cultural sensitivities. The series prioritizes **Global Citizenship Education (GCED)** and emphasizes the value of **India's diverse knowledge systems**.

We extend our heartfelt gratitude to all the teachers and educationists who passionately reviewed our books and offered their invaluable feedback. Their contributions have elevated the quality of our content, which will enhance the overall learning experience for students.

Feedback, comments and suggestions from users are always welcome as we continue to strive for excellence in education and better serve the needs of our young learners. Together, let's shape a brighter future for education.

Authors

About the Series Editor

Dr Geetha Iyer is the Former Head of Sahyadri School KFI, Pune. She is an author, a naturalist and consultant in the twin fields of education and environment. She is a curriculum specialist with many years of experience in concept development and regularly conducts workshops on all aspects of teaching science.

Key Features

Enhanced Science Now Revised Edition aligns with the **National Education Policy (NEP) 2020** and the **National Curriculum Framework (NCF) 2023**, promoting holistic education. It focuses on developing intellectual, physical, cognitive, emotional and social skills. With features such as Cognitive Corner, Life Skills, Worksheets and a Supplementary Booklet that contains STEAM Activities, Skills You Need, Happiness Activity Sheets, Vernacular Names, GCED and Assessments, it fosters experiential learning, innovative thinking and creativity. Additionally, the series raises awareness of the Sustainable Development Goals (SDGs) to address global challenges.

Learn more about SDGs at https://www.un.org/sustainabledevelopment/.

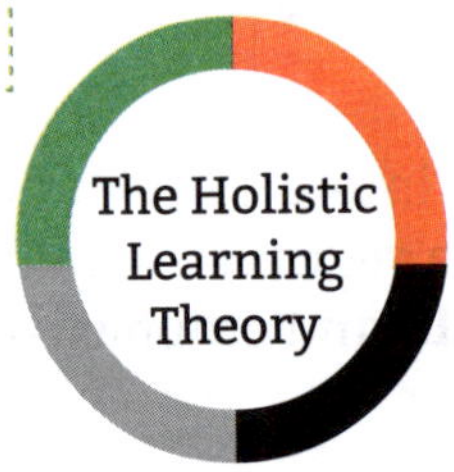

Physical

- Gross motor skills
- Psychomotor skills

→
- Projects
- STEAM Activities

Intellectual

Bloom's Taxonomy
- Remembering
- Understanding
- Applying
- Analysing
- Evaluating
- Creating

Remembering, Understanding →
- Summary
- Exercise

Applying to Creating →
- Cognitive Corner
- Worksheet
- Skills You Need
- STEAM Activities

Social

- Coordination
- Working in a team
- Interaction with others
- Social competencies
- Communication with others

→
- Worksheets
- Vernacular Names
- Life Skills
- STEAM Activities

Emotional

- Empathy
- Self-regulation
- Interpersonal (others)
- Intra-personal (self)

→
- Life Skills
- Happiness Activity Sheets
- GCED

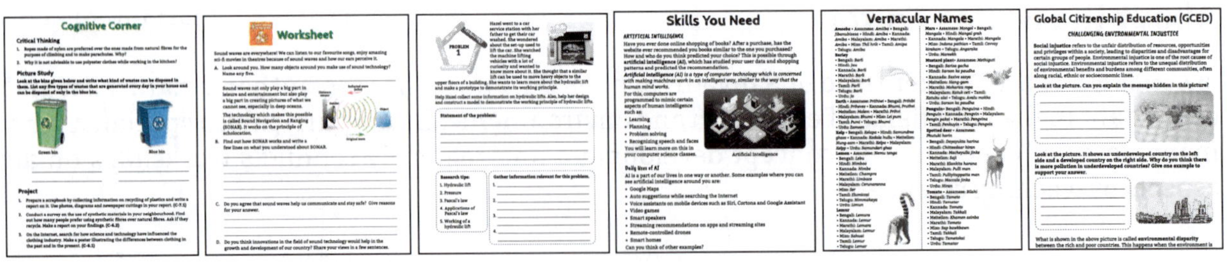

Collins Learning supports the Sustainable Development Goals

Comprehensive Assessment

The assessment papers employ MCQs tagged with icons to indicate competencies such as Difficulty Levels, Bloom's Taxonomy and Science Learning Skills. Each assessment comes along with a scorecard for self-assessment.

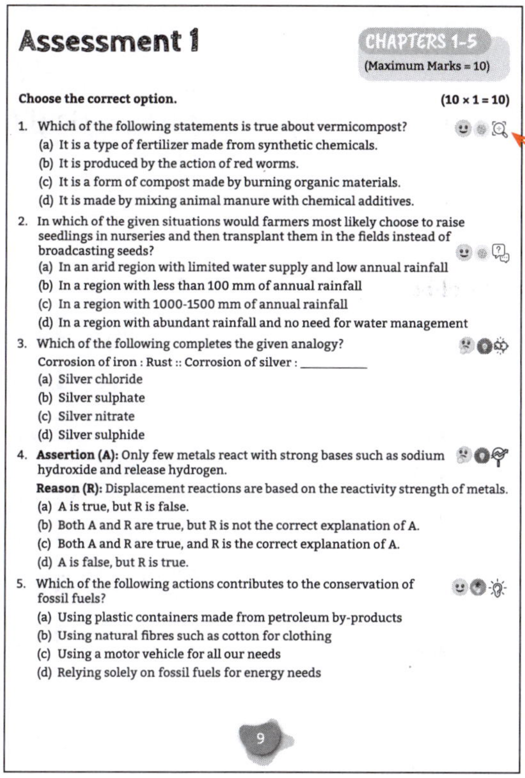

Assessment 1

CHAPTERS 1-5

(Maximum Marks = 10)

Choose the correct option. (10 × 1 = 10)

1. Which of the following statements is true about vermicompost?
   (a) It is a type of fertilizer made from synthetic chemicals.
   (b) It is produced by the action of red worms.
   (c) It is a form of compost made by burning organic materials.
   (d) It is made by mixing animal manure with chemical additives.
2. In which of the given situations would farmers most likely choose to raise seedlings in nurseries and then transplant them in the fields instead of broadcasting seeds?
   (a) In an arid region with limited water supply and low annual rainfall
   (b) In a region with less than 100 mm of annual rainfall
   (c) In a region with 1000-1500 mm of annual rainfall
   (d) In a region with abundant rainfall and no need for water management
3. Which of the following completes the given analogy?
   Corrosion of iron : Rust :: Corrosion of silver : __________
   (a) Silver chloride
   (b) Silver sulphate
   (c) Silver nitrate
   (d) Silver sulphide
4. **Assertion (A):** Only few metals react with strong bases such as sodium hydroxide and release hydrogen.
   Reason (R): Displacement reactions are based on the reactivity strength of metals.
   (a) A is true, but R is false.
   (b) Both A and R are true, but R is not the correct explanation of A.
   (c) Both A and R are true, and R is the correct explanation of A.
   (d) A is false, but R is true.
5. Which of the following actions contributes to the conservation of fossil fuels?
   (a) Using plastic containers made from petroleum by-products
   (b) Using natural fibres such as cotton for clothing
   (c) Using a motor vehicle for all our needs
   (d) Relying solely on fossil fuels for energy needs

9

Icons

Scorecard

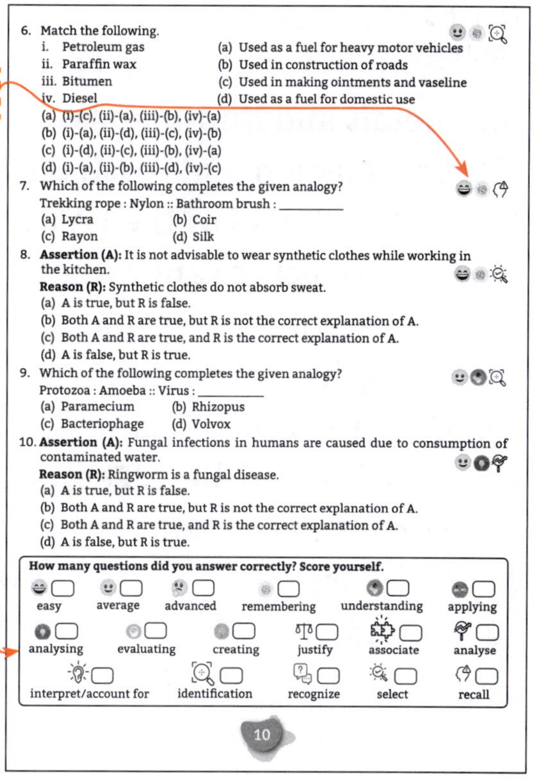

6. Match the following.
   i. Petroleum gas — (a) Used as a fuel for heavy motor vehicles
   ii. Paraffin wax — (b) Used in construction of roads
   iii. Bitumen — (c) Used in making ointments and vaseline
   iv. Diesel — (d) Used as a fuel for domestic use
   (a) (i)-(c), (ii)-(a), (iii)-(b), (iv)-(a)
   (b) (i)-(a), (ii)-(d), (iii)-(c), (iv)-(b)
   (c) (i)-(d), (ii)-(c), (iii)-(b), (iv)-(a)
   (d) (i)-(a), (ii)-(b), (iii)-(d), (iv)-(c)
7. Which of the following completes the given analogy?
   Trekking rope : Nylon :: Bathroom brush : __________
   (a) Lycra (b) Coir
   (c) Rayon (d) Silk
8. **Assertion (A):** It is not advisable to wear synthetic clothes while working in the kitchen.
   Reason (R): Synthetic clothes do not absorb sweat.
   (a) A is true, but R is false.
   (b) Both A and R are true, but R is not the correct explanation of A.
   (c) Both A and R are true, and R is the correct explanation of A.
   (d) A is false, but R is true.
9. Which of the following completes the given analogy?
   Protozoa : Amoeba :: Virus : __________
   (a) Paramecium (b) Rhizopus
   (c) Bacteriophage (d) Volvox
10. **Assertion (A):** Fungal infections in humans are caused due to consumption of contaminated water.
    Reason (R): Ringworm is a fungal disease.
    (a) A is true, but R is false.
    (b) Both A and R are true, but R is not the correct explanation of A.
    (c) Both A and R are true, and R is the correct explanation of A.
    (d) A is false, but R is true.

How many questions did you answer correctly? Score yourself.

easy · average · advanced · remembering · understanding · applying
analysing · evaluating · creating · justify · associate · analyse
interpret/account for · identification · recognize · select · recall

10

Competencies and Icons in Assessment Papers

Difficulty levels	Bloom's Taxonomy	Science Learning Skills
easy	remembering	justify, identification
average	understanding	associate, recognize
advanced	applying	analyse, select
	analysing	interpret/ account for, recall
	evaluating	
	creating	

Contents

Learn Science with a holistic approach...
Become smarter and make more friends...
Understand feelings better...
Understand the world better...
And become a global superhero!

1 Crop Production and Management

Curricular Goals

- Explore the living world in scientific terms **(CG-3)**
- Understand the interface of science, technology and society **(CG-5)**

Competencies

- Distinguish the characteristics of living organisms from non-living things **(C-3.2)**
- Analyse patterns of relationship between living organisms and their environment in terms of dependence on and response to each other **(C-3.3)**
- Explain the conditions suitable for sustaining life on earth **(C-3.4)**
- Illustrate how science and technology can help to improve the quality of human life as well as some of the harmful uses of science in history **(C-5.1)**

Let's Get Started

Hari wants to grow some plants. The pictures given below show him working in his field. Number these practices in the correct sequence.

Sowing seeds

Preparing the land

Watering the field

The above practices are related to agriculture. Agriculture is a fundamental human activity that has shaped civilizations throughout history and continues to play a critical role in our present and future.

AGRICULTURE

*The practice of growing plants and rearing animals for food, fibre and other useful products is called **agriculture**. Plants grown on a large scale for human consumption or use are called **crops**.*

In Northern and Western India, crops are planted in June and harvested in October. These crops are called ***kharif* crops**. Examples: Paddy (rice), maize, bajra, cotton and sugarcane (Fig. 1.1).

Fig. 1.1: Sugarcane, a *kharif* crop

Crops planted in November and harvested in April of the succeeding year are called ***rabi* crops**. Examples: Wheat (Fig. 1.2), barley, peas, gram and mustard.

Fig. 1.2: Wheat, a *rabi* crop

In the southernmost parts of India, the sowing and planting seasons for paddy are April and October, and the harvesting is done in July and January, respectively. These are called *kaar* and *pisanam* crops.

Main Crops Grown in Different Parts of India

India's varied climate and geography allow for the growth of many different crops in different parts of the country, ensuring a rich and abundant food supply for the country. Table 1.1 lists some examples of the main crops grown in different parts of India:

Table 1.1 Main crops grown in different parts of India

Region	States	Crops
North India	Punjab and Haryana	Wheat, rice, maize, sugarcane and mustard
	Uttar Pradesh	Rice, wheat, sugarcane, wheat and pulses
South India	Tamil Nadu	Rice, groundnut, cotton, sugarcane, tea and wheat
	Andhra Pradesh	Rice, pulses, groundnut, oilseeds, cotton, jute and wheat
	Kerala	Rice, tea, coffee and spices
	Karnataka	Cotton, sugarcane, tea, coffee and spices
East India	West Bengal	Rice, wheat, jute, tea and potatoes
	Odisha	Rice, pulses, oilseeds and coconut
	Bihar	Rice, wheat, maize, jute and lentils

Region	States	Crops
West India	Maharashtra	Rice, wheat, sugarcane, cotton and oilseeds
	Gujarat	Cotton, groundnut, sugarcane, oilseeds and tobacco
	Rajasthan	Wheat, cotton, barley, pulses and oilseeds
Northeast India	Assam	Rice, tea, jute and mustard
	Meghalaya	Rice, maize, coffee, potatoes and pineapples
	Manipur	Rice, pulses, oilseeds and vegetables

Horticulture in India

Horticulture is a branch of agriculture that includes growing crops such as fruits, vegetables, flowers and ornamental plants. The word "horticulture" is derived from the Latin terms *Hortus* meaning garden and *cultura* meaning cultivation. In India, it plays a vital role in providing fresh and nutritious food, beautifying surroundings, and creates employment opportunities. It can be practiced on both large and small scales.

Science in Context

Scientists have developed disease-resistant tomato varieties such as **Mountain Magic** and **Defiant**. These varieties ensure a more consistent and plentiful supply of tomatoes. This helps enhance food security by ensuring a steady availability of nutritious food and stabilizing prices in the market.

AGRICULTURAL PRACTICES

a

The activities undertaken during different times of the year for the cultivation of crops are called ***agricultural practices***. The following are the main agricultural practices:

1. Preparation of the agricultural land
2. Providing nutrients
3. Seed selection and sowing
4. Transplantation
5. Irrigation
6. Weeding and pest control
7. Harvesting
8. Storage of crops

Preparation of the Agricultural Land

Before planting crops on agricultural land, the soil is prepared.

The first step is to loosen the soil to improve aeration, which helps plants absorb nutrients and water from the soil.

Ploughing

Ploughing (Fig. 1.3) is done to loosen and turn the soil, and provide aeration. By doing so, the roots can be penetrated easily and weeds can be removed.

Traditionally, ploughing is done with a wooden plough. It has a long wooden rod called the **plough shaft**. There is a handle at one end of the shaft, while the other end is attached to a beam. This beam is placed on the neck of the animals that pull the plough. The plough contains a part called the **ploughshare**, which has an iron strip that digs into the soil and loosens it as the animals pull the plough. Nowadays, ploughing is done using **cultivators** driven by tractors or tillers. This modern technique saves farmers' time and effort.

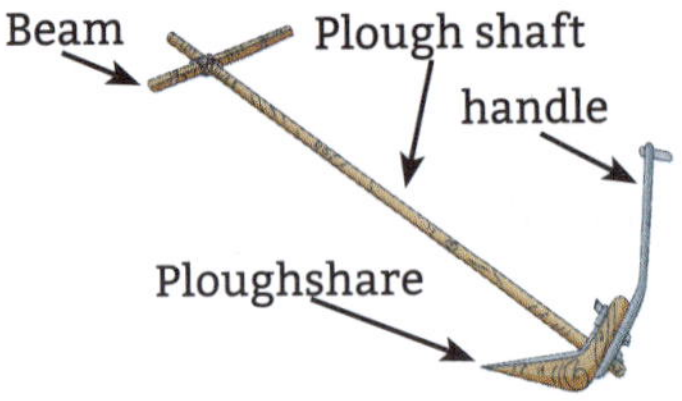

(a) Structure of a plough

(b) Farmer using a wooden plough

(c) Ploughing using a tiller

(d) Ploughing using a tractor

Fig. 1.3: Ploughing

Levelling of the Soil

After ploughing, the moist soil below the topsoil forms clumps. These clumps are crushed using wooden or iron planks or rollers called levellers. The process is called **levelling** (Fig. 1.4).

Fig. 1.4: Farmer levelling a ploughed field

Providing Nutrients

There are 12 essential nutrients (Table 1.2) that plants absorb from the soil.

Table 1.2: Essential nutrients for plant growth (1 ha = 1 hectare = 10,000 m²)

Nutrient	Symbol	Amount Absorbed (kg/ha)	Nutrient	Symbol	Amount Absorbed (kg/ha)
Nitrogen	N	150	Iron	Fe	1.5
Phosphorus	P	60	Manganese	Mn	0.4
Potassium	K	120	Zinc	Zn	0.3
Calcium	Ca	15	Boron	B	0.15
Magnesium	Mg	35	Copper	Cu	0.1
Sulphur	S	17	Molybdenum	Mo	0.01

The required amount of nutrients such as nitrogen, potassium and phosphorus should be added a week or two before sowing the seeds. This can be done by adding materials such as manure or fertilizers to the soil. This increases the nutrient value of the soil.

Natural Methods to Improve Soil Nutrients

Leaving the agricultural land fallow

After a season of crops, the land is left fallow[1]. This provides sufficient time for naturally occurring microbes to decompose plant and animal wastes. This decomposition restores nutrients, making the land fertile.

Word Web

[1]**Fallow:** land that has been dug or ploughed but nothing has been planted in it

Mixed cultivation (Mixed cropping)

*The cultivation of two different crops in the same field is called **mixed cultivation, multiple cultivation** or **mixed cropping**.* A main crop and a legume are grown side-by-side. Legumes increase soil fertility, reducing the requirement of chemical fertilizers. The practice also reduces the chances of infection by pests and the need for chemical pesticides.

Crop rotation

*Cultivation of two crops with different needs grown one after the other in the same field is called **crop rotation**.* The second crop is sowed after the harvest of the first crop. Wheat and paddy absorb most of the nitrogen from the soil. As an alternate crop in the rotation, leguminous plants such as peas, soya beans and green beans are planted. Leguminous plants have nodules in their roots, which contain bacteria that convert gaseous nitrogen in the air into usable nitrogen compounds for easy uptake by plants.

Adding manure/compost

Manures are animal products such as animal dung and urine, where as **compost** is the product of decomposition. Compost can be obtained by the decomposition of organic wastes such as manure, vegetable, plant or food wastes.

Vermicompost is a kind of compost obtained by the action of earthworms. In agricultural fields, earthworms (Fig. 1.5) feed on crop wastes and decompose them, thereby increasing the nutrient level in the soil. Earthworms also help aerate the soil through their movement.

Fig. 1.5: Earthworms in a vermicompost pit

Advantages of manure/compost

- It enhances the fertility of the soil without changing its profile or chemical qualities.
- It increases the water-retention capacity of the soil.
- It is obtained from renewable sources such as cow dung, horse dung and leaf litter.
- It helps in increasing the number of useful soil bacteria.
- It does not alter the pH of the soil.

Disadvantages of manure/compost

- It is required in large amounts.
- It is not nutrient specific.

Go Green

Millicomposting is the process of using millipedes to obtain compost from biodegradable waste.

The quality of millicompost is found to be superior to vermicompost.

Adding Fertilizers

Fertilizers are chemical substances that are rich in nutrients. They are added to increase the fertility of the soil, thereby increasing crop yield. The different types of fertilizers are given below:

- NPK type (Nitrogen, Phosphorus, Potassium, Fig. 1.6)
- Urea
- Ammonium sulphate
- Ammonium nitrate
- Potassium sulphate
- Potassium chloride
- Ammonium phosphate
- Nitrophosphate

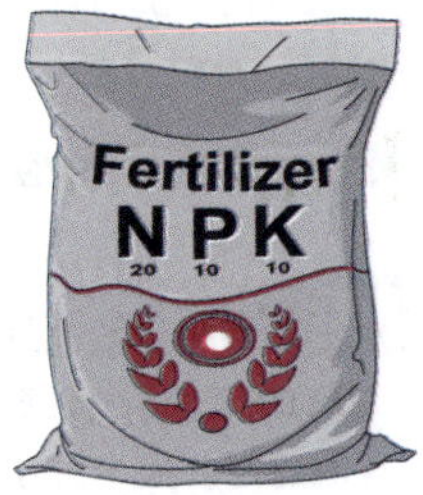

Fig. 1.6: A bag of NPK fertilizer

Advantages of fertilizers

- A small quantity is sufficient and effective.
- These are nutrient specific and can be used for the soil deficient in specific nutrients.
- These provide high yield of crops.
- These are easy to store and transport.

Science in Context

The number that you see on the fertilizer bags, for example, NPK 20 : 10 : 10 denotes the ratio of the amount of Nitrogen, Phosphorus and Potassium present respectively in the chemical fertilizer.

Disadvantages of fertilizers

- These are expensive.
- Excessive usage of fertilizers makes the soil too alkaline or too acidic.
- Fertilizers deplete non-renewable resources as they are manufactured from energy sources such as petroleum and coal, which cannot be renewed quickly.
- Excessive use of fertilizers can wilt the crops if there is inadequate water supply.
- The production of fertilizers (in the factories) causes pollution.
- Fertilizers harm useful soil organisms such as earthworms.

Seed Selection and Sowing

The process of planting seeds is called ***sowing***. Before sowing, selection of healthy seeds is necessary.

- Sowing of seeds should be done at equal and appropriate distances from each other. This gives space to the developing roots to absorb water and nutrients.
- Care should be taken to sow seeds at the right depth. If the seeds are sown at a shallow depth, birds can find and eat them, whereas if they are sown too deep, then the seeds will be deprived of air and will not develop.

(a) Scattering seeds manually (b) Sowing using a seed drill

Fig. 1.7: Sowing of seeds

In the traditional method of broadcasting seeds, the farmer scatters the seeds manually [Fig. 1.7(a)]. However, this method does not distribute the seeds uniformly.

The modern method of sowing seeds involves the use of a seed drill [Fig. 1.7(b)]. It has a tank in which the seeds are stored and a drill to make furrows[1] of the right depth. The tank has a funnel connected to pipes that ensures that the seeds are sown uniformly in rows.

Word Web

[1]**Furrow:** a long narrow cut in the ground

Transplantation

Transplantation *is the technique of moving a seedling from one location to another.*

Farmers sometimes raise seedlings in nurseries and then transplant them in the fields rather than broadcasting seeds. This practice is carried out when water supply is ensured and adequate, where the annual rainfall is 1000–1500 mm. However, shortage of manpower for this process can result in the broadcasting of seeds manually or through seed drills.

Irrigation

Irrigation *is the supply of water to the crops at appropriate intervals.* Indian farmers mainly depend on rainfall, while a few places have a river source for water supply. Some more sources of water for irrigation are wells, tube wells, ponds, lakes, dams and canals.

Traditional Methods of Irrigation

Traditional methods of irrigation are less efficient but cheaper than modern methods. Some of these methods (Fig. 1.8) are pulley system (moat), chain pump, *rahat* (lever system) and *dhekli*. Nowadays, these traditional methods have been replaced by pump sets that need electricity or diesel to function.

(a) Moat (Pulley system) (b) Chain pump (c) *Rahat* (Lever system) (d) *Dhekli*

Fig. 1.8: Traditional methods of irrigation

Modern Methods of Irrigation

Sprinkler system

In this method [Fig. 1.9(a)], water is distributed systematically by pumping through a set of perpendicular pipes that have rotating nozzles at the top. This method is very effective in places where there is an unequal distribution of water.

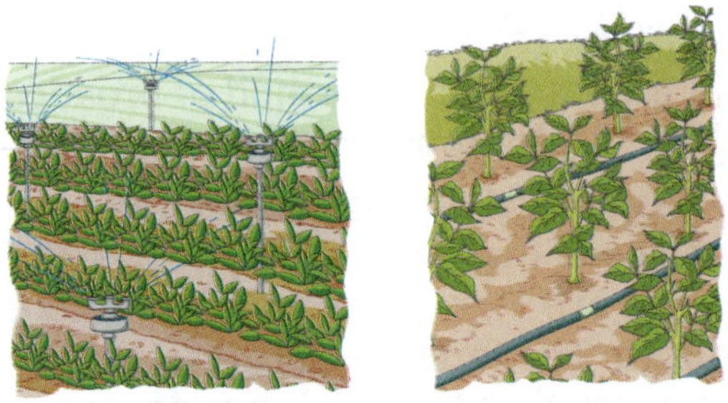

(a) Sprinkler (b) Drip irrigation pipes

Fig. 1.9: Modern irrigation methods

Drip system

This method [Fig. 1.9(b)] is also called **micro-irrigation**. No water is wasted in this method because it allows water to drip slowly to the roots of the plants. It is the best method of irrigation for gardens, trees and fruit plants.

Weeding and Pest Control

Weeds are the unwanted plants that grow naturally along with the crops. Weeds use the nutrients, water, space and light of crop plants and hamper their growth. Some weeds are poisonous for human beings and animals, and cause infections. Weeds act as a host for many insects and pests that cause various diseases in humans.

The process of removal of weeds is called ***weeding***. This can be done manually or by using chemicals called **weedicides**. A few examples of weeds are *Amaranthus*, wild oat and grass (Fig. 1.10).

(a) *Amaranthus* (b) Wild oat (c) Grass

Fig. 1.10: Weeds

Pests are the organisms that destroy crops by causing diseases or eating the plant parts before or after the harvest of crops. They include microorganisms, rodents (rats and squirrels), birds and insects. These are controlled by using chemicals called **pesticides** that kill these pests (Fig. 1.11).

Fig. 1.11: Application of pesticides using a sprayer

Revise and Recall

A. Sort the given crops into Rabi or Kharif crops.

Paddy, Maize, Pea, Sugarcane, Mustard, Barley, Cotton

B. What are *kaar* and *pisanam* crops?

Science in Context

Biopesticides are environment-friendly pest control products derived from natural sources such as plants, microorganisms or beneficial insects. These can be used to manage pests in agriculture while minimizing harm to the environment and human health.

Harvesting

The process of cutting crops after they mature or ripen is called ***harvesting***. Harvesting is done manually by using a sickle [Fig. 1.12(a)] or by a machine called harvester. After harvesting, threshing and winnowing are done.

Threshing

After harvesting, the grains or seeds are separated from the husk or straw through a process called ***threshing***. Traditionally, the process of threshing involves beating the crops on a threshing floor to separate the grains [Fig. 1.12(b)].

The process of threshing is also done with the help of a machine called **combine** [Fig. 1.12(c) is a combined harvester and thresher].

(a) Manual harvesting

(b) Threshing

(c) Combine

(d) Wheat after threshing by a combine

Fig. 1.12: Methods of harvesting

Winnowing, Hulling and Milling

After threshing, the loosened chaff is separated from the grains. This process is called **winnowing**. It can be done manually (Fig. 1.13) or with the help of a winnowing machine.

Fig. 1.13: Winnowing

The process of removing the outer covering of the fruit/seed/grain is called ***hulling***. This can be done by using machines called huller machines.

The process of grinding grains into flour is called ***milling***. This is done by using milling machines.

Storage of Crops

After all the hard work, if the crops are destroyed due to improper storage, it leads to a huge loss for the farmer. The purpose of storage is the protection of crops from rodents (rats and squirrels), birds, insects and microorganisms.
Storage is also important because the crops need to be distributed at many places without being spoiled.

The storehouses (Fig. 1.14) should be away from chemical factories and garbage dumps. To prevent insects and rodents from entering the storehouses, cracks and holes in the walls and ceilings should be sealed properly. The storage areas should be free of dust, dirt and germs.

The process of storing food materials at room temperature is called **dry storage**. Food grains are stored in granaries [Fig. 1.14(a)] and silos [Fig. 1.14(b)]. The grains should be dried in the sun properly to reduce the moisture content. The use of fumigants[1] helps kill pests without affecting the stored food grains. Vegetables get spoiled in a few days; so, they are kept in refrigerated warehouses or containers before and during transportation.

(a) Granaries (b) Silos

Fig. 1.14: Storage of agricultural produce

Word Web

[1]**Fumigants:** chemicals that exist in gaseous state

Revise and Recall

Fill in the blanks.

ia

1. Urea is a ________. (fertilizer/manure)
2. Tilling or ploughing of the soil is done by a ________. (plough/tractor)
3. The levelling of soil is done with the help of a ________. (leveller/cultivator)
4. The big pieces of soil formed after ploughing are called ________. (crumbs/clumps)
5. Moving a seedling from one location to another is called ________. (transplantation/transportation)

NITROGEN FIXATION AND NITROGEN CYCLE

Nitrogen is one of the most important nutrients required in plant nutrition. Even though it is found in abundance in the atmosphere, plants cannot use it in this form.

The atmospheric nitrogen is converted into usable form of nitrogen compounds; this process is called ***nitrogen fixation***. In nature, nitrogen fixation happens due to lightning, nitrogen-fixing bacteria and blue-green algae. Leguminous plants have nitrogen-fixing bacteria called *Rhizobium* that live in the structures called nodules in the plant roots. The soil too has bacteria that convert atmospheric nitrogen into usable form. Available nitrogen compounds in the soil are absorbed by the crops and stored in plants in the form of proteins. Herbivores feed on the plants; and carnivores, in turn, feed on herbivores. After the death of plants and animals, their remains are decomposed and the nitrogenous compounds are returned to the soil.

These compounds are absorbed by plants or they are converted into nitrogen by denitrifying bacteria and released into the atmosphere. *This process of the movement of nitrogen between the atmosphere, soil and organisms forms a cycle called the* ***nitrogen cycle (Fig. 1.15)***.

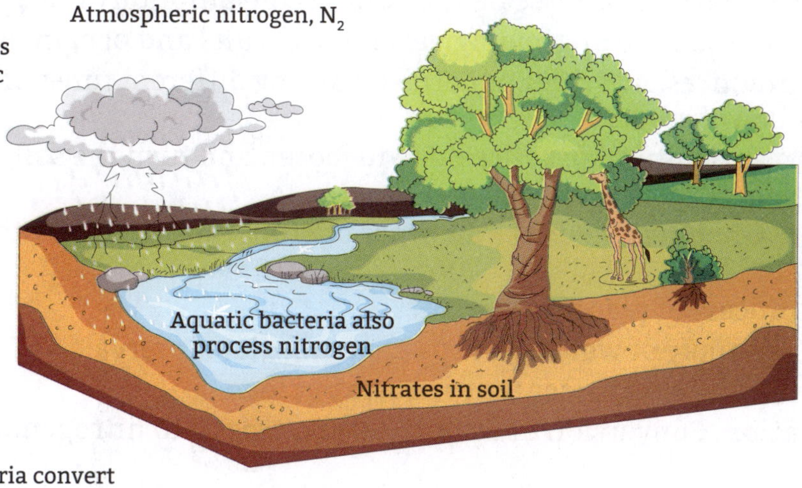

Fig. 1.15: Nitrogen cycle

ANIMAL HUSBANDRY

Apart from plants, animals are also sources of food for human beings. They provide us food rich in protein and fat. *Rearing animals in farms in large numbers to meet our needs of food and other products is called* ***animal husbandry***. Animal husbandry includes **poultry farming** (raising chickens, ducks, and turkeys for meat and egg production), **apiculture** (involves beekeeping for honey production), **pisciculture** (controlled breeding and rearing of fish for commercial purposes) and **dairying** (raising dairy animals such as cows and goats for milk and other dairy products). Table 1.3 gives information about the animals that are reared in farms and the products obtained from these animals.

Table 1.3: Products obtained from different animals

Animal Husbandry	Animals Reared	Food	Other Products
Poultry	Hen, geese, ducks	Eggs, meat	
Rearing	Sheep, goat, silkworm	Milk, meat	Wool, silk
Dairy farming	Cow, buffalo, goat, yak	Milk	Curd, butter, cheese
Aquaculture	Fish, prawns	Meat	Fish liver oil
Apiculture	Honeybees	Honey	Wax

Keywords

Agriculture: The practice of growing plants and rearing animals for food, fibre and other useful products

Crops: Plants grown on a large scale for human consumption or use

Horticulture: The science of growing vegetables, fruits and ornamental plants

Agricultural practices: Activities undertaken during different times of the year for the cultivation of crops

Ploughing: An agricultural practice done to loosen and turn the soil, and provide aeration

Crop rotation: Growing two different types of crops one after the other in the same field

Sowing: The process of planting seeds

Irrigation: The supply of water to crops at appropriate intervals

Harvesting: Cutting crops after they mature or ripen

Nitrogen fixation: Conversion of atmospheric nitrogen to nitrogenous compounds

Summary

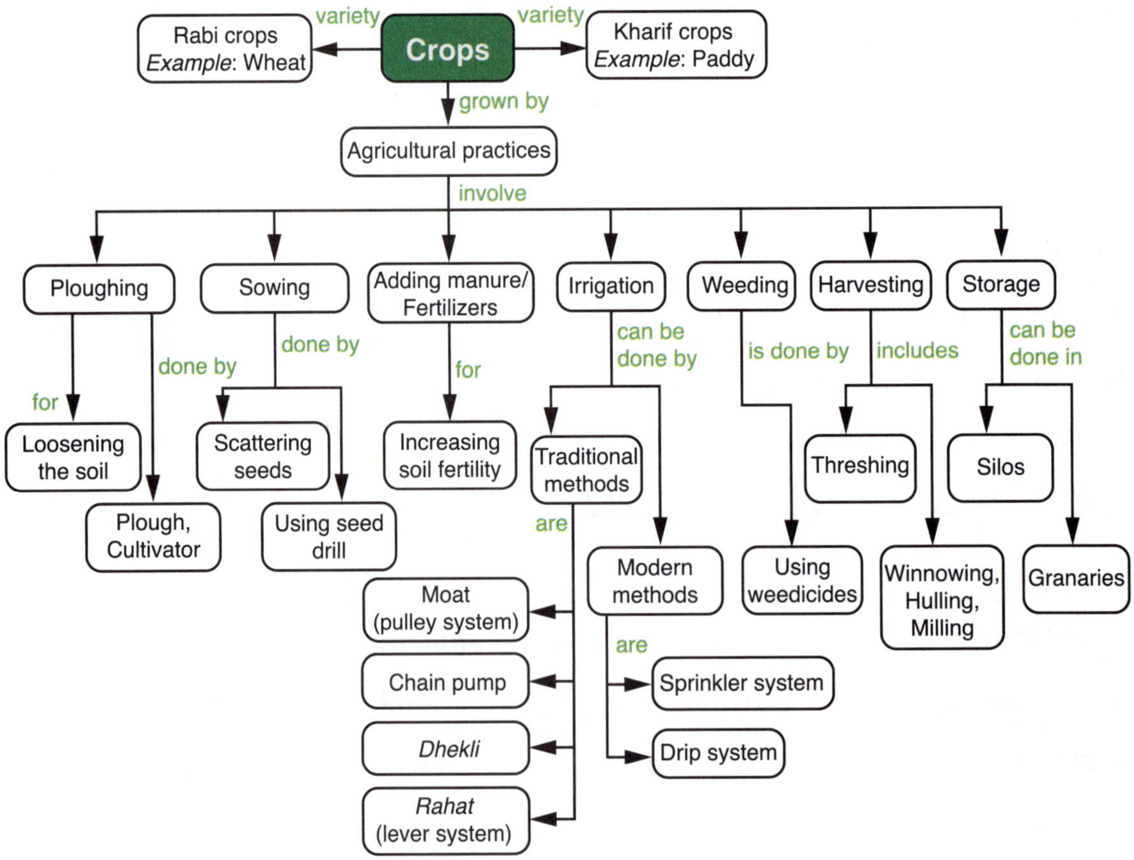

Exercise

A. Choose the correct option.

1. In which month are *kharif* crops harvested?
   (a) March (b) September (c) October (d) April
2. In which month are *Rabi* crops planted?
   (a) June (b) November (c) January (d) April
3. Which of the following is a part of the process of soil preparation?
   (a) Sowing (b) Tilling (c) Threshing (d) Irrigation
4. ________________ is the practice of growing two different crops together in the same field.
   (a) Mixed cropping (b) Ploughing (c) Harvesting (d) Irrigation
5. __________________ is the process of storing food materials at room temperature.
   (a) Dry storage (b) Cold storage (c) Wet storage (d) Hot storage

B. State whether the following statements are true (T) or false (F).

1. Crops are the plants cultivated only for food. ☐
2. Manure is not nutrient specific. ☐
3. Continuous growth of crops in the same field enhances the fertility of the soil. ☐
4. Paddy is a Kharif crop. ☐
5. Seed drill is used to remove excess seeds to avoid overcrowding. ☐
6. Plants can use nitrogen directly from the atmosphere. ☐

C. Give two examples for each of the following.

1. Traditional methods of irrigation
2. Weeds
3. Methods of sowing
4. *Rabi* crops

D. Give reasons for the following.

1. Drip irrigation system is the best way to irrigate crops.
2. Seeds should be sown at appropriate distances and at proper depths.
3. Weeds should be removed from the area of crop plants.
4. Granaries should be away from chemical factories and garbage dumps.
5. Grains should be dried before storage.

E. Answer the following questions briefly.

1. Name two modern irrigation methods and their advantages.
2. What is nitrogen fixation?
3. How do leguminous plants fix nitrogen?
4. What are pests? How are they controlled?
5. What is animal husbandry? Give two examples of animals reared in farms and the products obtained from them.

F. Answer the following questions in detail.

1. Explain the processes that are carried out after the crops mature.
2. Differentiate between fertilizers and manures.
3. Describe the role of nitrogen fixation in agriculture.
4. Mention briefly about the main crops grown in different parts of India.
5. Write a note on Horticulture in India.

Cognitive Corner

Critical Thinking

1. In places such as Kerala, crop rotation is not a common practice. Why?
2. Are there any disadvantages of using tractors for agriculture? Give reasons for your answer.
3. The implementation of a drip irrigation system has a higher initial cost. Still, it is considered a valuable investment despite its higher initial cost.

Picture Study

Label the following diagram to show nitrogen cycle.

Project

1. Meet some farmers and talk to them. Make a report on the crops they grow, the difficulties they face due to factors such as climate change, higher prices of commodities, shortage of labour, unpredictable rainfall, poor irrigation facilities and low procurement price (low price for their produce). **(C-7.3)**
2. Fertilizers and pesticides are used extensively in the Indian agricultural practice in spite of their disadvantages. What measures can be taken to reduce the use of fertilizers and pesticides while promoting eco-friendly alternatives such as manure, compost or biopesticides? Have a discussion in the class on the measures that can be taken to reduce their use. **(C-5.1)**
3. List all the agricultural practices, their purpose and the implements used. Make a chart based on your list. Is there any implement that can be improved or tinkered to achieve more efficiency? Can you innovate an implement that would help in better agricultural practices? **(C-5.2)**

Life Skills

Farmers in our country have been facing many problems, more so with the arrival of the pandemic, COVID-19. This is a story of a farmer called Bansilal who lives with his family in Pandavpura village in Karnataka.

Bansilal (to his wife): I need money to cultivate cotton as it is in demand. But I do not have money to buy the seeds and for other agricultural expenditures.

Parvati (Bansilal's wife): Why don't you ask Muniya Bhai (the moneylender) for help?

Bansilal: No, I already owe him money that I borrowed last year. Moreover, he lends money at a very high rate of interest.

Parvati: Oh! I heard that the bank offers loans at a lower rate of interest.

Bansilal: The bank would be closed due to this COVID-19 lockdown. What do I do?

Bansilal somehow manages to arrange money from his friends' help and starts cultivating the crop. The crop grows well and he is hoping for a good sale.

Bansilal: Aha! Now, I can sell the crops at a very good rate and clear my debts.

Bansilal goes to the market to sell the crops and he returns home in the evening.

Parvati: What happened? Why do you look so sad?

Bansilal: The crops were sold at a very low price as the price of cotton has fallen.

From this story, list down the actual problems faced by farmers in our country. **(C-5.2)**

Natural Problems	Human-made Problems

Worksheet

The major occupation of people in India is agriculture, with farmers playing a crucial role. Around 60% of the country's land is agricultural, and 70% of the population is engaged in farming. The Green Revolution in the mid-1960s transformed Indian agriculture with modern methods such as high-yielding seeds, tractors, pesticides and fertilizers, leading to increased crop production. However, this industrial shift brought pollution-related challenges with significant consequences.

Traditional method of farming

To counter the challenges arising from the Green Revolution's aftermath and encourage sustainable agriculture, we can tap into our ancestral farming wisdom. Embracing traditional practices such as organic farming, agroforestry, water harvesting, diverse cropping and crop-livestock integration can curb pollution and preserve ecosystems.

Modern method of farming

A. Write down the nature of pollution caused by the following modern agricultural practices.

1. Use of fertilizers and pesticides

____

____

2. Excessive use of water for irrigation

____

____

3. Suggest methods by which pollution through these two sources can be reduced or eliminated.

____

____

B. How can the spread of ancient Indian agricultural wisdom among farmers help build a stronger, more resilient and eco-friendly agricultural system in response to the challenges posed by the Green Revolution?

____

____

____

C. How can you leverage the best of both worlds (the ancient agricultural wisdom and technology) to usher in a new era of sustainable and productive agriculture, aligning with the principles of SDG 12? Draw a plan to integrate new technology with ancient wisdom for sustainable agriculture.

____

____

____

2 Microorganisms

Curricular Goals

- Explore the living world in scientific terms **(CG-3)**
- Understand the interface of science, technology and society **(CG-5)**
- Communicate questions, observations and conclusions related to science **(CG-7)**

Competencies

- Describe the diversity of living things observed in the natural surroundings, including at a smaller scale **(C-3.1)**
- Distinguish the characteristics of living organisms from non-living things **(C-3.2)**
- Analyse patterns of relationship between living organisms and their environment in terms of dependence on and response to each other **(C-3.3)**
- Illustrate how science and technology can help to improve the quality of human life as well as some of the harmful uses of science in history **(C-5.1)**

Let's Get Started

Look at the pictures given below. What do you think is growing on the shoes and orange? Have you ever seen such growth on bread?

Very tiny organisms called fungi are growing on these objects. What these pictures show are a large number of fungi living in groups, called **colonies**, and that is the reason they are visible to the naked eye. There are many organisms that are so small that they cannot be seen with the naked eye.

These very small organisms can only be seen through an instrument called microscope. Hence, they are called **microorganisms** or **microbes**.

Microorganisms are found in all kinds of places including extremely cold places such as Siberia and Alaska, hot deserts such as the Atacama Desert, hot water springs, volcanoes, oxygen-deficient environments and even in the gut of humans and animals. In this chapter, we will learn about the different parts of a compound microscope that help us observe different types of microorganisms and then learn about these microorganisms in detail.

MICROSCOPE

Microorganisms can be seen and studied using an instrument called **microscope**. Laboratories generally use simple and compound microscopes. In institutions involved in research, electron microscopes are used.

Figure 2.1 shows the different parts of a compound microscope.

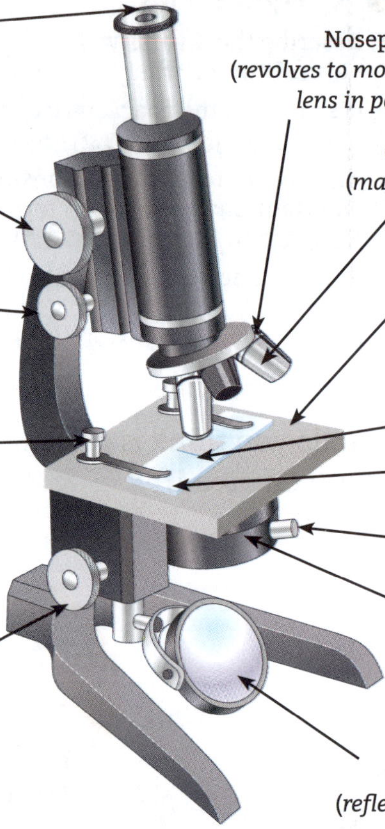

Fig. 2.1: A compound microscope

Recall what you learned about the use of lenses in class 7. Microscopes have a combination of lenses placed in such a manner that they can magnify the objects of study and produce high-resolution images. Thus, not only do they magnify minute objects allowing us to see them clearly, but they also have the power of resolution that allows us to see closely placed parts separately. The lens that we place our eyes to see the object is called the **eyepiece** or **ocular lens**. The lenses mounted on the revolving nosepiece are called **objective lenses**. The extent of magnification and resolution depends on the power of the lenses used.

Try It!

1. Observe the objective lenses of a microscope. Can you decide which of the lenses will give you a higher magnification by merely looking at the lenses (not looking at their power)?
2. If you were observing an object through a 15× eyepiece coupled with 40× objective lenses, what magnification would you get?

TYPES OF MICROORGANISMS

Microorganisms can be divided into five major groups: bacteria, algae, fungi, protozoa and viruses.

- **Bacteria** *(singular: bacterium)*: Bacteria are the most commonly found single-celled or unicellular microorganisms. These can be rod-shaped (bacilli), spherical (cocci), comma-shaped (vibrio) and spiral (spirilla) (Fig. 2.2). These are found everywhere including in the oceans and guts of animals. A few examples of bacteria are *Lactobacillus*, *Escherichia coli*, *Vibrio cholerae* and *Yersinia pestis*.

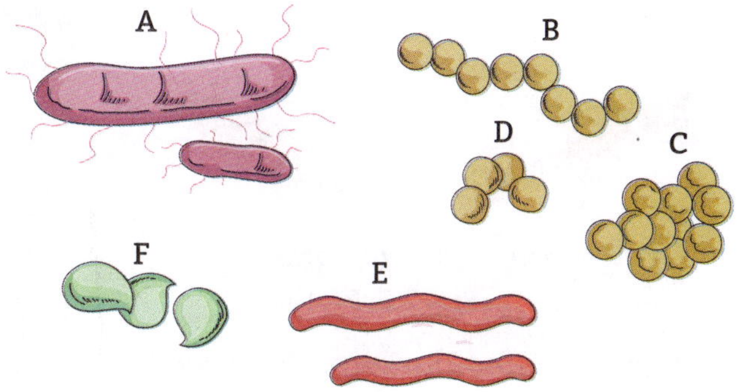

Fig. 2.2: Different shapes of bacteria (A - Bacilli; B, C, D - Cocci; E - Spirilla and F - Vibrio)

- **Algae** *(singular: alga; pronounced*: al·gee): These are autotrophic microorganisms. Like plants, algae have chlorophyll and cell walls in their cells. These can be unicellular or multicellular. Algal cells found attached to each other are called algal colonies. Their habitat may be moist rocks, tree barks, soil and all kinds of water bodies. A few examples of algae are *Nostoc, Polysiphonia* and *Volvox* (Fig. 2.3).

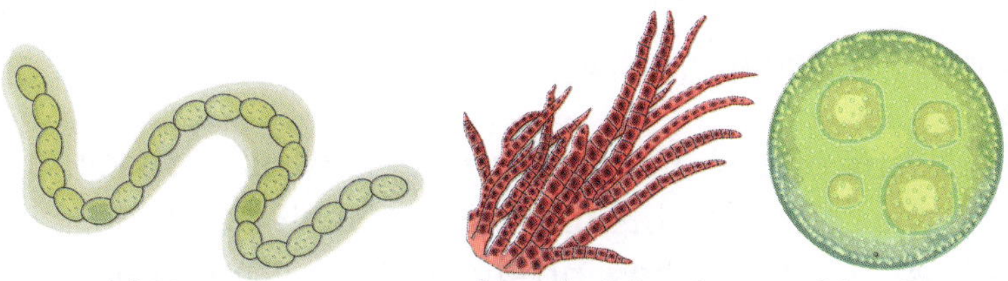

(a) *Nostoc* (b) *Polysiphonia* (c) *Volvox*

Fig. 2.3: Algae

> **Science in Context**
>
> Some forms of algae are large and can be seen with the naked eye. They are found in marine waters and are called seaweeds.

- **Fungi** *(singular: fungus; pronounced*: fuhng·gee): These are the organisms that lack chlorophyll and follow the heterotrophic mode of nutrition. Fungi can be unicellular or multicellular. Some multicellular fungi such as mushrooms are visible to the naked eye. Fungi grow best in dark, humid and moist places. A few examples are *Rhizopus* (bread mould), *Agaricus* and *Penicillium* (Fig. 2.4).

(a) Rhizopus *(b) Agaricus* *(c) Penicillium*

Fig. 2.4: Fungi

- **Protozoa** *(singular: protozoan)*: These are unicellular microorganisms showing animal-like characteristics such as movement and food capture. Their habitats include freshwater or saltwater, soil and bodies of other organisms. A few examples of protozoa are *Amoeba, Paramoecium* (Fig. 2.5) and *Plasmodium* (malarial parasite).

(a) Amoeba *(b) Paramoecium*

Fig. 2.5: Protozoa

Science in Context

Microorganisms are so small that they cannot be seen clearly even under compound microscopes. To enhance visualization and see the various parts of a microorganism clearly, scientists use some dyes or colouring agents called stains. Hence, the colour that is seen while viewing a microorganism under the microscope is is not the colour of the microbe but the of the dye used to stain that microbe.

- **Viruses** *(singular: virus)*: These can be seen only through an electron microscope because they are so small that they need to be magnified up to 2,00,000 times their original size to be observed. A few examples of viruses are bacteriophage[1], adenovirus and influenza virus (Fig. 2.6).

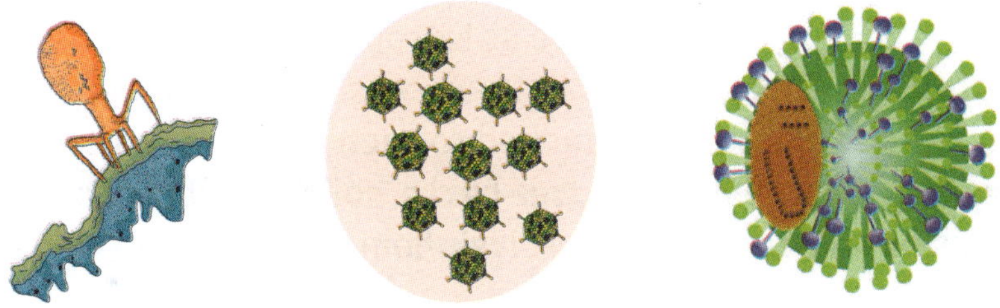

(a) Bacteriophage (b) Adenovirus (c) Influenza virus

Fig. 2.6: Viruses

Word Web

[1]**Bacteriophages:** viruses that infect bacteria

It is difficult to classify viruses as living or non-living microorganisms. Viruses can only grow and multiply inside the cells of living organisms (such as plants, animals and bacteria). Outside a host cell, they show no signs of life. This non-living state of a virus is called **virion**.

Revise and Recall

Fill in the blanks.

1. Algae are found in clumps called ____________ (groups/colonies).
2. Viruses can only be seen through a(n) ____________ (electron/compound) microscope.
3. The microorganisms that show animal-like characteristics are called ____________ (algae/protozoa).
4. The non-living state of a virus is called ____________ (virion/virium).

MICROBIAL HABITAT

Microbes can grow in almost all habitats. They can be found in hot springs, in volcanic rocks beneath the ocean floor, in extremely salty waters of the Great Salt Lake and the Dead Sea, and below the ice caps of Antarctica. They are also found on and inside the bodies of animals and humans.

Activity 1

Aim: To demonstrate that microbes are present everywhere

Materials required: Four nutrient agar Petri dishes, cotton swabs, hot water/distilled water

Procedure:

1. Take four nutrient agar Petri dishes and label them Control, A, B and C, respectively.
2. Collect microbe samples from three different sources: your palm, kitchen sink and bathroom counter.
3. To collect sample from any surface, take a clean cotton swab dipped in boiled or distilled water and rub it several times over that surface. Then, rub the swab gently in a zigzag pattern over the surface of the nutrient agar in without breaking the agar gel.
4. Following the above method, collect microbe samples from your palm, kitchen sink and bathroom counter with three different cotton swabs and then rubbing the swabs in nutrient agar in Petri dishes A, B and C respectively.

5. Place the Petri dishes at room temperature in a dark place for a week. Cover each of the Petri dishes with a lid.
6. After a week, observe the Petri dishes without removing the lids. Record your observations in the given table.

Petri dish	Source	Microbial colonies formed Yes/No
Control	None	
A	Palm	
B	Kitchen sink	
C	Bathroom counter	

Observation: Microbial colonies were formed in Petri dishes ____________________

Conclusion: ____

Some microorganisms cause diseases in plants, animals and human beings. There are also certain microorganisms that are beneficial to us. They are used in the food industry, for the preparation of medicines and in agriculture.

DISEASE-CAUSING MICROORGANISMS

The microorganisms that cause diseases are called **pathogens** or **germs**. Pathogens can enter the body of other organisms through air, food and water, contact, carriers or cuts and wounds. Pathogens can also get transmitted by direct contact with an infected person or carried by an animal.

Microbial diseases that can spread from an infected person to a healthy person by various means such as through air, water, food or physical contact are called **communicable diseases**.

- **Air**: When a person suffering from the common cold coughs or sneezes, he or she releases germs into the air. The germs enter a healthy person's body when this air is inhaled by them. Some other diseases that spread through the air are chickenpox, mumps, tuberculosis and measles. They are called airborne diseases.
- **Food and water**: Diseases such as cholera, diarrhoea and typhoid are caused by eating or drinking contaminated food or water. They are called food and water-borne diseases. The germs enter the body through contaminated food and water and start multiplying, eventually causing the disease. Water and food get contaminated due to unhygienic conditions and a lack of sanitation.
- **Contact**: Direct physical contact with a sick person or contaminated surfaces can transfer pathogens to another individual causing diseases such as ringworm, chickenpox and flu.
- **Carriers**: Insects such as mosquitoes and houseflies carry pathogens from an infected person to a healthy person. Hence, they are called carriers or vectors of diseases. The female *Anopheles* mosquito is a carrier of the malaria-causing protozoan called *Plasmodium*. When it bites a healthy individual, it transfers the pathogen. The pathogen multiplies and grows inside the healthy person's body, causing the disease. In a similar way, dengue fever is caused by a virus spread by the *Aedes* mosquito. Another example of carriers is rats.
- **Cuts and wounds**: When we get a cut, there is a break in the skin. Pathogens enter the body through the cut and cause diseases such as tetanus.

Diseases Caused by Fungi

Some fungal infections in plants are potato blight, corn smut, leaf rust and powdery mildew (Fig. 2.7).

(a) Potato blight (b) Leaf rust (c) Powdery mildew

Fig. 2.7: Fungal diseases in plants

Most fungal infections in humans are caused due to unhygienic living conditions. Some fungal diseases are ringworm, scalp infection, skin infection and Athlete's foot (Fig. 2.8).

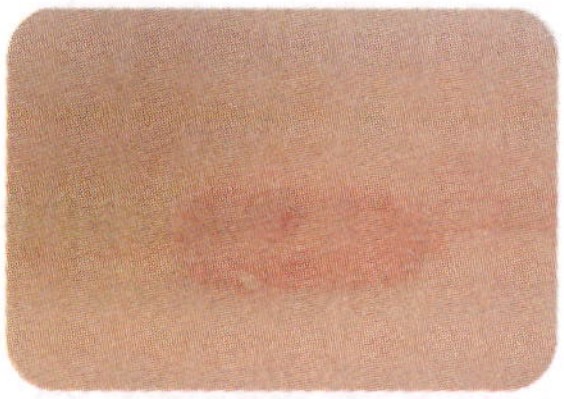

(a) Ringworm

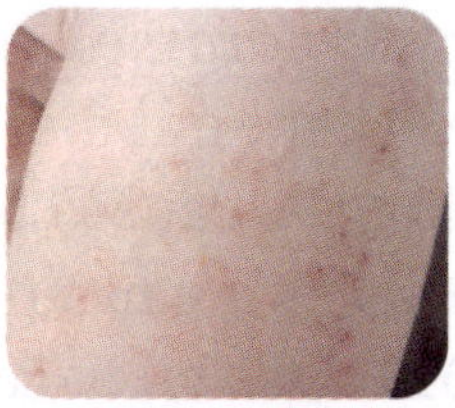

(b) Skin infection

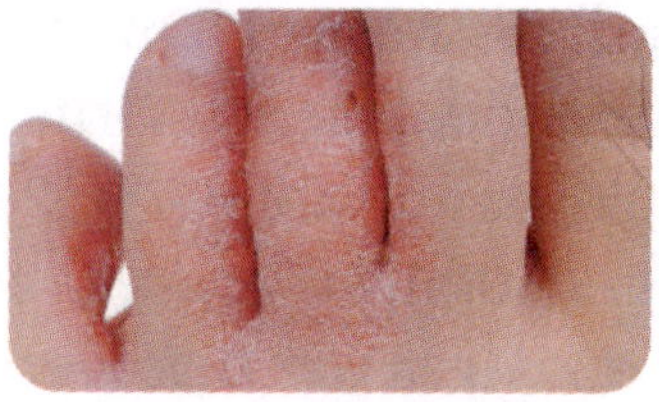

(c) Athlete's foot

Fig. 2.8: Fungal diseases in humans

Diseases Caused by Bacteria

Table 2.1 shows some bacterial diseases, the causative bacteria and the host.

Table 2.1: Bacterial diseases

Disease	Bacteria	Host
Cholera	*Vibrio cholerae*	Human beings
Typhoid	*Salmonella typhi*	Human beings
Gastric ulcer	*Helicobacter pylori*	Human beings
Tetanus	*Clostridium tetani*	Human beings
Tuberculosis	*Mycobacterium tuberculosis*	Human beings
Leprosy	*Mycobacterium leprae*	Human beings
Anthrax	*Bacillus anthracis*	Ruminants
Crown gall	*Agrobacterium tumefaciens*	Plants
Blight disease	*Xanthomonas oryzae*	Rice plant
Leaf spot disease	*Pseudomonas tomato*	Tomato plant
Citrus canker	*Xanthomonas axonopodis*	Lemon tree, orange tree

Some bacterial diseases in plants are shown in Figure 2.9.

(a) *Pseudomonas tomato:* Causes leaf spots in Tomato plant leaf

(b) *Xanthomonas axonopodis:* Causes citrus canker

Fig. 2.9: Bacterial diseases in plants

Diseases Caused by Virus

Viruses cause some diseases that are incurable or difficult to cure. One such fatal disease is **A**cquired **I**mmunodeficiency **S**yndrome (**AIDS**) caused by the **H**uman **I**mmunodeficiency **V**irus (HIV). Some other viral diseases are influenza, rabies, hepatitis and polio [Fig. 2.10(a)]. Smallpox is caused by the *Variola* virus, chickenpox [Fig. 2.10(b)] by *Varicella zoster* and measles is caused by the *Rubeola* virus. A new coronavirus was discovered in late 2019. This virus causes an infectious disease called coronavirus disease or COVID-19.

The yellow vein mosaic virus causes a disease of the same name in vegetable plants.

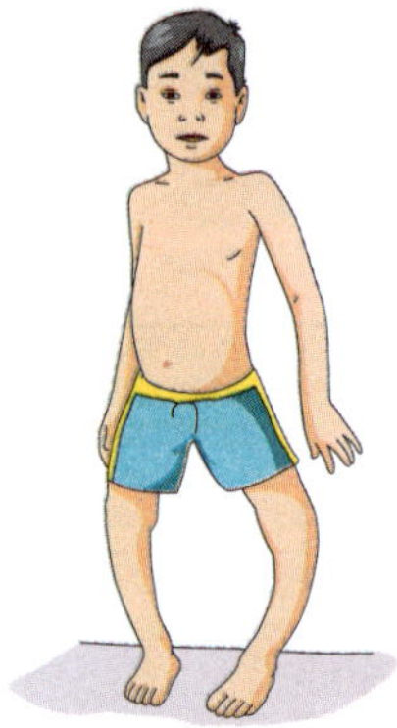

(a) A child infected with polio

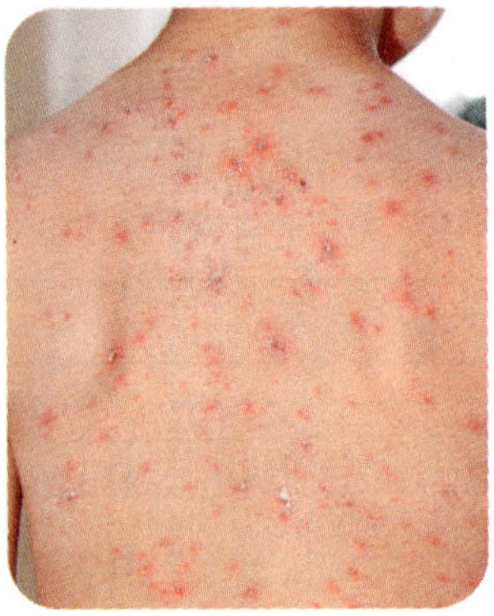

(b) Chickenpox

Fig. 2.10: Viral diseases in humans

Science in Context

Influenza A (H1N1) virus has caused serious respiratory illness (swine flu) and death over the years. The first confirmed case of swine flu H1N1 in India was documented in May 2009, but huge numbers of cases were reported thereafter. In 2015, swine flu outbreak in India had led to significant morbidity and mortality.

Diseases Caused by Protozoa

A list of diseases caused by protozoa in human beings is given below:

Plasmodium vivax causes malaria, *Trypanosoma brucei* causes trypanosomiasis, *Giardia lamblia* causes giardiasis and *Entamoeba hystolytica* causes amoebiasis.

BENEFICIAL MICROORGANISMS

Many microbes are beneficial to us. Some examples are discussed below.

Microorganisms in the Food Industry

Fermentation is a process of the conversion of sugar into acid or alcohol and carbon dioxide by the action of microbes. Fermentation is done by microorganisms such as yeast.

- The baking industry uses the fermentation process effectively in **baking bread** [Fig. 2.11(a)]. Yeast releases carbon dioxide, which gets trapped within the dough, forming small air spaces. This raises the dough and makes the bread light and fluffy.
- In the **preparation of wine** [Fig. 2.11(b)], the process of fermentation is used to turn grape juice into an alcoholic beverage. During fermentation, yeast converts sugar in the juice to create ethanol, commonly called ethyl alcohol, releasing carbon dioxide in the process.
- Some species of mushrooms are edible. Different edible species of mushrooms are cultivated worldwide.
- The bacterium *Lactobacillus* is used in the preparation of **curd from milk**. It converts lactose present in milk into lactic acid. *Acetobacter aceti* helps to convert alcohol into acetic acid or vinegar. Vinegar is a sour liquid made from the oxidation of ethyl alcohol.
- Bacteria such as *Lactobacillus* and *Streptococcus* are used in the preparation of cheese [Fig. 2.11(c)] and *paneer*.

(a) Baking bread (b) Making wine (c) Making cheese

Fig. 2.11: Microorganisms used in food industry

Science in Context

Not all species of mushrooms are edible; some of them are poisonous.

- *Fucus,* kelp and *Gracilaria* (Fig. 2.12) are different kinds of algae used in ice creams and jellies as a thickening agent. In many countries, sea weeds are also used to prepare food items.
- *Spirulina* and *Chlorella* (Fig. 2.13) are single-celled algae used in the production of **single-celled proteins** (SCPs). SCPs are rich sources of proteins and are used as dietary supplements.

(a) *Fucus* (b) Kelp (c) *Gracilaria*

Fig. 2.12: Algae used in ice creams

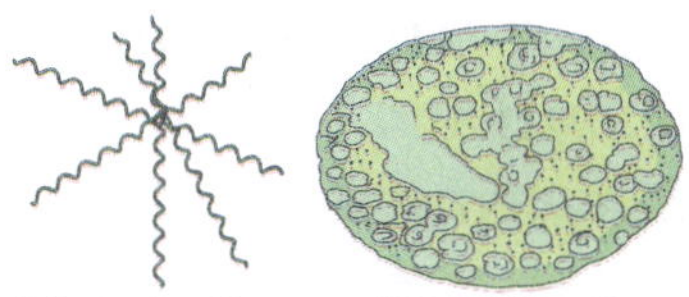

(a) *Spirulina* (b) *Chlorella*

Fig. 2.13: Single-celled algae

- *Acidiothiobacillus ferrooxidans* is a bacterium used for **bioleaching**, a process in which microbes are used to separate metals from mineral deposits. It is the most commonly used bacteria in biomining[1]. More than 30% of the world's copper is extracted through the use of *A. ferrooxidans*.

Word Web

[1]**Biomining:** a process of extracting valuable metals from ores with the assistance of microorganisms

Activity 2

Aim: To observe the presence of *Lactobacillus* in curd

Materials required: Fresh milk (boiled and cooled), fresh homemade curd (that has been diluted well), droppers, water, glass slides, crystal violet stain, spirit lamp, microscope

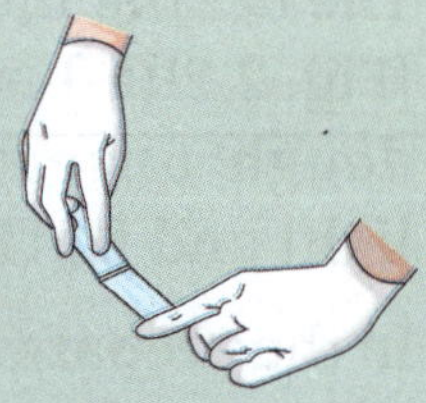

Preparing a smear

Procedure:

1. Take a drop of the diluted curd onto a glass slide with the help of a dropper.
2. Make a smear with the help of another slide by sliding it over the curd sample.
3. Heat-fix the slide by passing it twice or thrice swiftly over a spirit lamp flame.
4. Put a drop of crystal violet stain on the heat-fixed slide and keep it aside for 2 minutes.
5. Rinse the slide very gently with water to remove excess stain.
6. Leave the slide to dry in air for a while and then observe it under the microscope.
7. Repeat the procedure with a drop of milk.

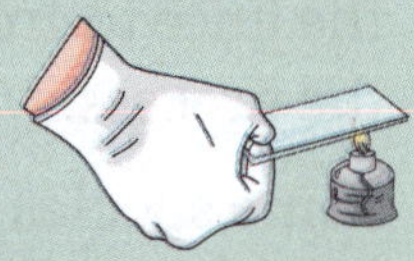

Heat-fix the slide

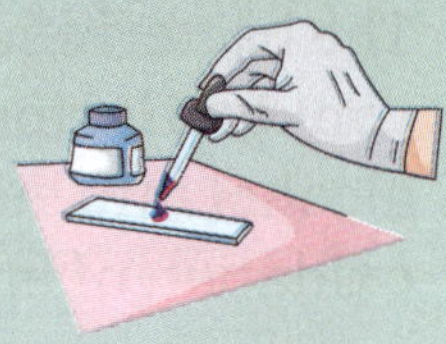

Staining

(Remember to take a clean slide and a clean dropper. Do not reuse the dropper or slide that has been contaminated with curd.)

Observation: Observe the two slides carefully.

Conclusion: The rod-shaped, blue-coloured structures present in curd are *Lactobacillus*.

Note: When observing the slide under the microscope, there are chances that you may also observe yeast, which will appear in round forms. The *Lactobacillus* bacteria will appear as rod-shaped structures stained with crystal violet. Use a sample of freshly prepared curd for observation.

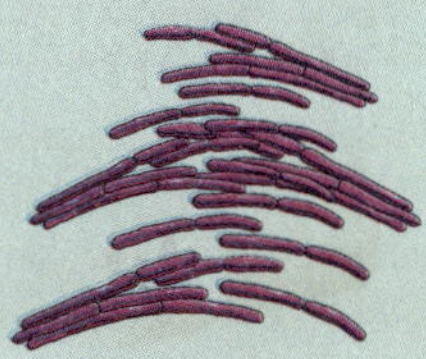

Lactobacillus

Medicinal Uses

- The wonder drug **penicillin** is an antibiotic[1], which is derived from a fungus called *Penicillium*.
- The bacteria *Streptomyces griseus* is used in the preparation of the antibiotic streptomycin. Two other antibiotics obtained from bacteria are tetracycline from *Streptomyces rimosus* and erythromycin from *Streptomyces erythreus*.
- A **vaccine** is a biological preparation that provides immunity against a particular disease. Vaccines can be used to prevent diseases such as typhoid, hepatitis, cholera, chickenpox, measles, polio and smallpox.

Word Web

[1]**Antibiotic:** substance that destroys certain disease-causing microbes

Know the Scientist

Alexander Fleming

Alexander Fleming (1881–1955) discovered the antibiotic penicillin. He won the Nobel Prize in physiology or medicine in 1945 for the discovery of penicillin from the mould *Penicillium notatum*. It saved millions of lives and prevented the need for amputations of limbs that were infected.

Vaccines are of two types. They may contain dead or weakened microorganisms, which on administration induce the body to produce substances called **antibodies**. Antibodies destroy disease-causing microbes and remain in the body to prevent further attacks by the same microbe. Example: vaccines for measles and polio. Some vaccines such as the typhoid vaccine contain readymade antibodies instead of weakened pathogens. While the first type can give long-term immunity, the second type gives short-term immunity. Administration of vaccine can be oral or injected and the process is called **vaccination** or **immunization**.

Agricultural Uses

- *Mycorrhiza* fungi form a symbiotic relationship with the roots of many plant species. The plant provides the fungus nutrition. In return, the plant gains the benefit of the higher absorptive capacity for water and mineral nutrients.
- Nitrogen-fixing leguminous plants live in a symbiotic relationship with nitrogen-fixing bacteria called *Rhizobium*. These bacteria form root nodules in the plant roots (Fig. 2.14) and are capable of fixing the atmospheric nitrogen into the soil in the form that can be used by plants.

Fig. 2.14: Root nodules

- *Bacillus thuringiensis* is used in genetically modified crops to protect them from pests. Bt-toxins present in groundnut leaves protect them from extensive damage caused by European corn borer larvae.

Degradation

***Degradation** is the process of the breakdown of complex materials into simple molecules.*

Materials that can undergo physical and chemical degradation are called **biodegradable materials**. These form simpler molecules by the action of microorganisms such as bacteria and fungi.

Microorganisms and Environment

Organic matter or the dead remains of plant and animals undergo decomposition to form simpler components. The physical and chemical breakdown is brought about by bacteria and saprophytes. This process of degradation by microorganisms is also a part of the nitrogen cycle, in which nitrogen is released by the decomposition of organic matter and is then used by plants as a nutrient. Imagine what would happen if these microorganisms did not act upon the dead remains. The whole earth would be filled with dead and waste materials.

Activity 3

Aim: To study the process of decomposition of organic substances by microorganisms

Materials required: A pot of soil, some fruit peels, small pieces of newspaper, a small polythene cover, a piece of cotton cloth, a few pieces of glass bangles, a thermometer, a hand lens and water

Procedure:

1. Place the soil on a large sheet of newspaper.
2. Observe and record the colour and texture of the fruit peels, pieces of newspaper, polythene cover, pieces of cotton cloth and bangle pieces.
3. Using a small hand shovel, mix the fruit peels, pieces of newspaper, polythene cover, pieces of cotton cloth and bangle pieces into the soil (*do not mix it with your hand as the glass pieces may hurt you*). Put them all inside the pot.
4. Sprinkle a little water on the soil mixture to make it moist. Do this every day for at least 60 days.
5. Make sure that you do not make the soil soggy/soft.
6. Measure the temperature of the soil once a week.
7. Observe and record the changes, if any, in the fruit peels, pieces of newspaper, polythene cover, pieces of cotton cloth and bangle pieces. Do this once a week. What do you conclude?

Decomposition Observation Table

Date	Temperature of the Soil	Changes in Colour, Texture and Smell of:				
		Fruit peels	Newspaper	Polythene	Cotton cloth	Bangles

Soil Fertility and Nitrogen Fixation

Microorganisms play a crucial role in improving soil fertility. Microorganisms such as some algae, bacteria and fungi are present in the soil. Bacteria and fungi present in the soil feed on dead remains of animals and plants and form humus which is rich in nutrients and make the soil fertile.

Microorganisms also convert atmospheric nitrogen into a form that the plants can use and help in nitrogen fixation.

Nitrogen is a critical limiting element for the plant growth and production. It is a major component of chlorophyll, the most important pigment needed for carrying out photosynthesis, as well as amino acids, the key building blocks of proteins. Even though nitrogen is one of the most abundant elements (predominately in the form of nitrogen gas (N_2) present in the Earth's atmosphere), plants cannot absorb nitrogen directly from the atmosphere. Some bacteria are able to combine nitrogen from the atmosphere with oxygen and hydrogen to create usable nitrogen for plants or animals.

These microbes are commonly called **biological nitrogen fixers**. Example: *Rhizobium* bacteria (Fig. 2.15).

Fig. 2.15: *Rhizobium* bacteria in plant root nodules

Spoilage of Food

Microorganisms such as bacteria and fungi can spoil food, particularly the food items containing moisture.

Bacteria: Various bacteria are responsible for the spoilage of products such as milk, cheese, meat, fruits and vegetables. Certain bacteria cause food poisoning in humans.

Fungi: Various fungi are responsible for the spoilage of products such as eggs, meat, fruits and vegetables. Harmful fungi can also grow on bread, wine and beer, if not stored properly.

Revise and Recall

Answer the following questions briefly.

1. What is fermentation?
2. Give an example of the symbiotic relationship between plants and microorganisms.
3. What are antibiotics?
4. How is wine prepared by using microorganisms?
5. Name two algae used in the production of single-celled proteins.
6. Name two food items that get spoiled due to bacteria and two food items that get spoiled due to fungi.

PRESERVATION OF FOOD

Preservation of food is the process of preventing the spoilage of food items that need to be stored for a long period. It includes retaining their colour, taste and nutritive value.

Food is preserved for the following reasons:

- To prevent the contamination of food and hence prevent food poisoning
- To lengthen the shelf life of food by slowing down the spoilage of food caused by microorganisms and to make it available in off-season
- To make transportation and storage of food easier, even to far-off places
- To supply food to hospitals, airlines, trains, defence personnel and astronauts

Techniques for Preservation of Food

Sun drying: The moisture content in food is removed by drying it in the sun. The absence of moisture prevents the multiplication of microorganisms. Most cereals, pulses and spices are stored using this method.

Heating: Boiling water is a basic cooking practice to prevent the spread of diseases due to microorganisms. The same technique is used to store milk. Another technique called the ultra-heat treatment is used to preserve milk, wherein the milk is heated to 135°C for a few seconds and stored in sterile[1] containers.

Word Web

[1]**Sterile:** free from germs

Salting: Fish is mainly preserved using salt. Moisture is absorbed by the salt, keeping the fish dry.

Sugaring: Jams, jellies and fruit squashes are stored using sugar. Sugar inhibits the growth of microorganisms. *Jamun* is preserved for long periods using sugar syrup.

Using oil and vinegar: Pickles, fish, fruits and meat are preserved in oil and vinegar.

Pasteurization: This is a technique used to store milk. It is heated to about 70°C for a minute and cooled quickly. This kills the microorganisms and does not affect the flavour due to heating.

Freezing: Refrigerators are used in all households, restaurants and warehouses for storing vegetables and other food items. The temperature in these is maintained at 5°C. This prevents the growth of microorganisms in the food. Deep-freezing is used to store food for a longer duration of months at temperatures below –18°C.

Canning: After the heating or sterilization of food, it is stored in airtight containers to prevent contamination due to microorganisms.

Using chemical preservatives: Chemicals such as sodium benzoate and sodium meta-bisulphate are used to store jams, ketchups and fruit juices.

Keywords

Microorganisms/microbes: Organisms that are very small and can only be seen through a microscope

Microscope: An instrument used to view microorganisms

Antibiotics: Substances that destroy certain disease-causing microorganisms

Virion: Non-living state of a virus

Fermentation: Conversion of sugar into acid or alcohol by the action of microorganisms

Vaccine: Biological preparation that improves immunity to a particular disease

Degradation: The process of breakdown of complex materials into simple molecules

Pasteurization: Preservation technique, in which milk is boiled to a very high temperature and then quickly cooled to kill microorganisms

Summary

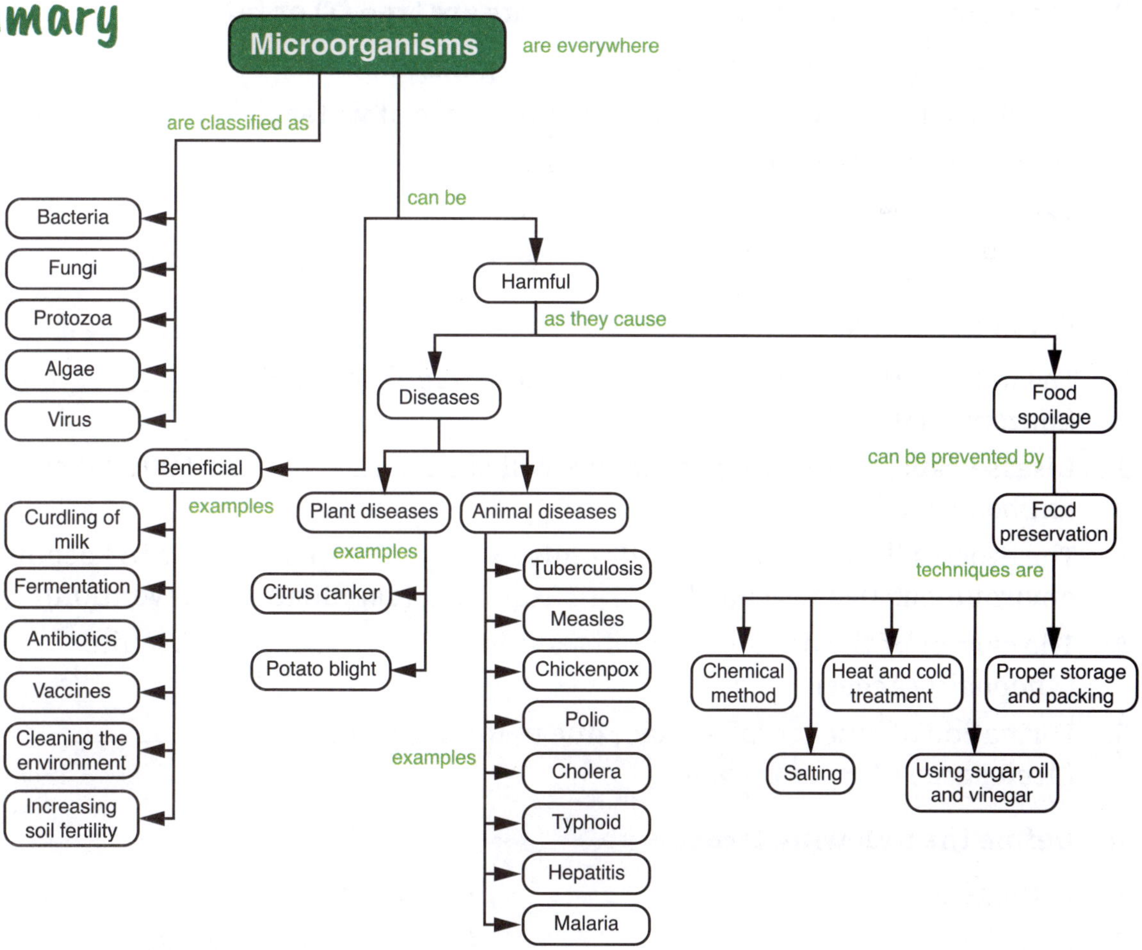

Exercise

W ia

A. Choose the correct option.

1. Which of the following diseases is not caused by a virus?
   (a) Polio (b) Chickenpox (c) Tuberculosis (d) Influenza
2. Bubbles of gas that raise the dough are due to the release of carbon dioxide during ________________.
   (a) fermentation (b) pasteurization (c) vaccination (d) sun drying
3. Which of the following diseases cannot be prevented by vaccination?
   (a) Malaria (b) Smallpox (c) Tuberculosis (d) Hepatitis
4. Which of the following is a nitrogen-fixing bacterium?
   (a) *Lactobacillus* (b) *Rhizobium* (c) Yeast (d) *Acetobacter*
5. Which of the following is not a method of food preservation?
   (a) Vaccination (b) Salting (c) Pasteurization (d) Canning

B. State whether the following statements are true (T) or false (F). ia

1. Viruses reproduce only inside the host organism. ☐
2. The fluffy texture of bread is due to the release of water. ☐
3. Microorganisms are found in volcanoes. ☐
4. Vaccination is also called immunization. ☐
5. Penicillium is an antibiotic drug derived from the fungus penicillin. ☐

C. Fill in the blanks.

1. The bacterium involved in the conversion of milk to curd is ________________. (*Rhizobium*/*Lactobacillus*)
2. Disease-causing microorganisms are called ________________. (pathogens/antibodies)
3. The process in which the microorganisms play an important role in keeping the environment clean is called ________________. (degradation/prevention)
4. The carrier of the dengue fever disease is ________________ mosquito. (*Anopheles*/*Aedes*)
5. Formation of vinegar takes place due to the action of ________________. (*Acetobacter*/*Streptococcus*)

D. Define the following terms.

1. Pathogens
2. Virions
3. Antibiotics
4. Communicable diseases

5. SCPs
6. Canning
7. AIDS and HIV
8. Vaccination

E. Give reasons for the following.

1. We need a microscope to study microorganisms.
2. Not all microorganisms are harmful.
3. Proper hygiene is important for good health.
4. Oil and vinegar are added to pickles.
5. Yeast is used in making bread.

F. Answer the following questions briefly.

1. How does common cold spread?
2. What organisms are used to prepare ice creams and jellies?
3. What are the different shapes of bacteria?
4. Name two diseases in humans and plants caused by fungi.
5. Name one human and one plant disease caused by bacteria.
6. What are carriers? Give examples.
7. What is alcoholic fermentation?
8. Explain the technique of pasteurization.
9. How is freezing used in the preservation of food?
10. How do microrganisms play an important role in keeping the environment clean?

G. Answer the following questions in detail.

1. How do diseases spread? Explain with suitable examples.
2. What are vaccines and how do they prevent diseases?
3. How is fungal fermentation beneficial to human beings?
4. How are bacteria and fungi useful to us? Also, discuss their harmful effects.
5. Write a note on the agricultural uses of microorganisms.

Cognitive Corner

Critical Thinking

1. We eat *Lactobacillus* along with curd! Is it not harmful for us?
2. What do we do to the leather materials infected by fungus or mould?

Picture Study

Identify these microbes and write their names.

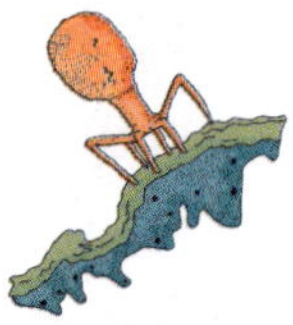

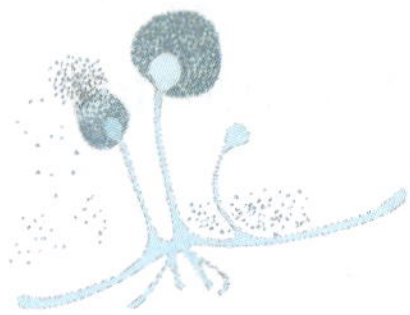

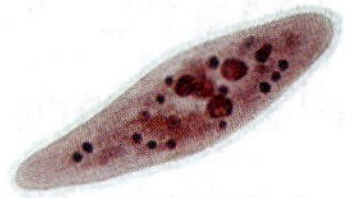

_______________ _______________ _______________

Project

1. It is essential for new-born babies and children to get vaccinated according to a prescribed schedule to prevent various infectious diseases. On the Internet, read about the major vaccines administered to children starting from their birth until they are 10 years old. Also, search for a standard vaccination schedule from the Internet, take its printout and paste it in your notebook. **(C-7.2)**
2. Collect information on the nutritive value of edible mushrooms and the procedure to grow them. If possible, visit the Agriculture Department office to get a demonstration of mushroom cultivation. Follow the procedure to cultivate mushrooms at schools. **(C-7.2)**
3. Read about Louis Pasteur and his contribution to science, the food industry and medicine. Prepare a report about the same and present it in the class. **(C-7.1)**
4. As a health club activity, research how science and technology are used in making bioweapons. **(C-5.1)**

In the Library

Read more about viruses, their unique characteristics and the diseases caused by them. Find out why there are no effective drugs against some viral diseases. **(C-7.1)**

Life Skills

Packaged and preserved food items such as biscuits, fruits, vegetables, jam, noodles and chocolates are available readily in the market. Before you buy your favourite brand of food, do you check the label on the side of the jar or package for the 'Manufactured date' or 'Packaged date', 'Best before' or 'Best if used by' and 'Use by' or 'Expiry date'? Apart from these information, what do the labels contain? What is the advantages or purpose of having these labels? **(C-5.1)**

Worksheet

Polio, a disease spread by a virus, had its first outbreak in 1894. It is transmitted through contaminated water or food or through contact with an infected person. This disease causes paralysis and may result in death. Once polio is contracted, there is no cure. For this dreaded disease, prevention is the best cure. The world has been fighting to eradicate polio for so many years with many polio eradication programmes. Pulse Polio Immunization Programme which was launched in India in 1995 has almost eradicated polio from India. With the fight against polio still on, the world came face-to-face with another deadly disease called COVID-19 in 2019.

This disease outbreak has impacted and disrupted almost everything. The growth and development in every other field has been affected. There has been a chain reaction in almost all sectors of the world, be it education, food industry, small-scale and large-scale industries, and so on. The importance of good health and well-being has become more in focus because of this.

A. How do you think the COVID-19 outbreak has disrupted the world? Identify any five areas where the impact has been massive.

B. Design a solution that would help in restoring the five areas that you have listed above.

3 Synthetic Fibres and Plastics

Curricular Goals

- Explore the world of matter and its constituents, properties and behaviour **(CG-1)**
- Understand the interface of science, technology and society **(CG-5)**
- Explore the nature and processes of science through engaging with the evolution of scientific knowledge and conducting scientific inquiry **(CG-6)**

Competencies

- Classify matter based on observable physical and chemical characteristics **(C-1.1)**
- Illustrate how science and technology can help to improve the quality of human life as well as some of the harmful uses of science in history **(C-5.1)**
- Illustrate how the scientific knowledge and ideas have changed over time and identify the scientific values that are inherent and common across the evolution of scientific knowledge **(C-6.1)**
- Formulate questions using scientific terminology and collect data as evidence **(C-6.2)**

Let's Get Started

Look at the pictures given below and identify the type of season being shown. Also, write the name of the type of fabric worn by the children in these pictures.

In the previous classes, we have learned about the natural fibres and the processes involved in making fabrics from them and the various uses of plastics in our day-to-day life. We have also learned that the texture of fabrics varies depending on the properties of fibres.

In this chapter, let us learn more about synthetic fibres, plastics, their properties and uses.

SYNTHETIC FIBRES

a

Synthetic fibres are obtained by chemical processes. As they are made by human beings, synthetic fibres are also called **human-made fibres.** Before synthetic fibres were manufactured, fibres were obtained from plant and animal sources, also called natural fibres. Natural fibres obtained from cellulose, which comes from plants, are called 'cellulose fibres'. Sir Joseph Swan invented the first synthetic fibre in the 1880s. This fibre was obtained from a cellulose liquid, which was formed by chemically modifying the fibre in tree bark.

What are synthetic fibres made up of?

A synthetic fibre is made up of long chains of small units that are joined together to form the fibre. This long chain of similar kind of small units is called a **polymer**. The name polymer is derived from two Greek words: '*poly*' meaning many and '*mer*' meaning a part or a unit. Each small unit of a polymer is a chemical substance and is called a **monomer**. Thus, a polymer is made up of many repeating units of monomers. *The process in which small monomers link together to form a long chain is called **polymerization.***

The structure of a polymer may be linear or cross-linked. Each coloured hexagon in the structures shown in Figure 3.1 represents a monomer.

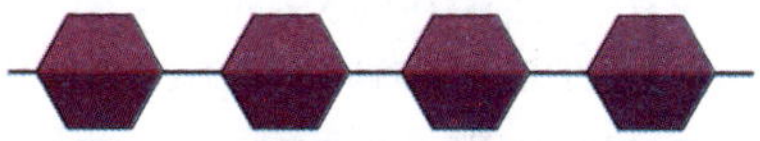
Linear structure

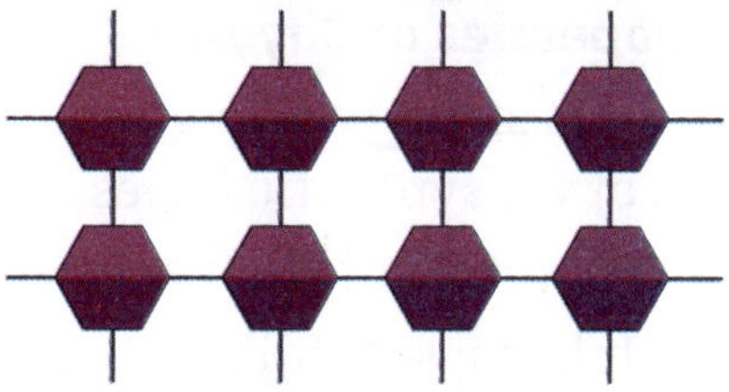
Cross-linked structure

Fig. 3.1: Structure of a polymer

Types of Synthetic Fibres

Nylon

Nylon was produced in the 1930s from coal, water and air by a scientist at the DuPont Company. It derives its name from the cities of New York and London (NY from New York and LON from London), where it was first marketed. It was the first synthetic fibre that was used commercially on a large scale.

Properties of Nylon

- It is more elastic than natural fibres.
- It is stronger than a steel wire.
- It is wrinkle-resistant and wear-resistant, so it lasts for a long time.
- The garments made from nylon dry quickly as it absorbs very little water.
- It is lustrous in appearance.
- It is not attacked by moths and moulds.
- Nylon fibres burn slowly and they shrink away from the flame forming a bead.
- It is thermoplastic in nature.

Uses of Nylon

- It is used in the production of textiles such as sarees and shirts.
- It is used for making fishing nets, tents, parachutes (Fig. 3.2) and ropes.
- Due to its elasticity, it is used to make socks and stockings.
- It is also used to make toothbrush bristles, combs, zip fasteners and machine parts.

Fig. 3.2: A parachute made of nylon

Rayon

It is obtained from the chemical treatment of wood pulp. Rayon resembles silk in appearance, texture and shine. Hence, it is also called **artificial silk.** Rayon is prepared from cellulose that is broken down and then reformed; so, it is also called **regenerated fibre.** It is cheaper than natural silk.

Properties of Rayon

- It is strong and a good absorbent. So, clothes made of rayon are preferred over other synthetic fibres in summer.
- It burns at a high temperature with a smell of burning paper, but does not melt.
- It has a soft, silky touch and drapes well.
- It wrinkles easily and may stretch or shrink when washed.

Uses of Rayon

- It is mixed with cotton (50% each) and used to make dresses, aprons and caps.
- It is used in the medical field for making gauze (for making bandages) and lint (for dressing wounds).
- It is used for making tyre cords.
- It is used in home furnishings such as bedspreads, bedsheets, blankets, curtains, tablecloths and carpets (Fig. 3.3).

Fig. 3.3: A carpet made of rayon

Polyester

It is obtained from petroleum. It is synthesized from repeating units (monomers) of a chemical compound that is chemically described as ester (poly + ester). Examples of polyester fibres are Terylene and Dacron. PET (Polyethene tetraphthalate) is a very common form of ***polyester***. A mixture of polyester and cotton is called **polycot**. A mixture of polyester and wool is called **polywool**. Similarly, a mixture of terylene and cotton is called **terrycot** and a mixture of terylene and wool is called **terrywool**.

Properties of Polyester

- It is light, strong, elastic and wrinkle-resistant.
- It absorbs very little water, so clothes dry quickly.
- It is quite resistant to the action of chemicals.
- It is not attacked by moths and moulds.
- These fibres burn slowly forming a bead.

Know the Scientist

The first synthetic fibre nylon was made by an American chemist **W.H. Carothers**.

A German chemist **Hermann Staudinger** won the Nobel Prize in the year 1953 for his contribution in the development of plastics.

Uses of Polyester

- It is mixed with natural fibres to make fabrics such as suits, jackets, shirts, trousers, sarees and other dress materials.
- PET is used for making bottles, utensils and films.
- It is used for making lightweight sails (Fig. 3.4).
- The water-resistant property makes it ideal for garments and jackets that can be used in wet or damp environments.
- It is also used for making fire hoses and conveyor belts.

Fig. 3.4: A lightweight sail made of polyester

Acrylic

It is made from a chemical substance called acrylonitrile. To be called acrylic, the polymer must contain at least 85% of acrylonitrile monomers. It closely resembles wool in its properties. Orlon, Acrilan and Cashmilon are a few examples of acrylic fibres. Clothes made of acrylic are available in a variety of colours and are cheaper than wool.

Properties of Acrylic

- It is light, soft and warm with a wool-like feeling.
- It is resistant to moths and other insects.
- It is also resistant to shrinkage, wrinkles and the action of chemicals.
- Acrylic fibres shrink from a flame, form a black bead and burn with a sooty flame.

Use of Acrylic

It is widely used for making sweaters, shawls and blankets (Fig. 3.5).

Sweater Shawl

Fig. 3.5: Things made of acrylic

Spandex

It is also called **elastane** due to its unique elastic property. Spandex is popularly known as lycra. It is a polyurethane–polyurea copolymer invented by chemists C. L. Sandquist and Joseph Shivers in 1959.

Property of Spandex

These fibres have unusual ***elastic*** property.

Uses of Spandex

- It is used for making clothes that require stretch and comfort. For example, swimsuits, leggings, gloves, skinny jeans and cycling shorts (Fig. 3.6).
- It is also mixed with other fibres such as polyester and cotton to make stretch fabrics.

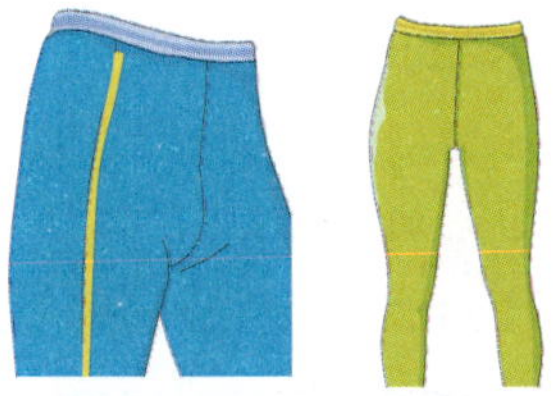

Fig. 3.6: Clothes made of spandex

Some advantages and disadvantages of synthetic fibres are given in Table 3.1.

Table 3.1: Advantages and disadvantages of synthetic fibres

Advantages	Disadvantages
• They are strong and elastic. • They are resistant to moths and moulds. • They dry quickly and are less expensive. • They are wrinkle-resistant. • They can be dyed in a variety of colours. • They are light, durable and easy to wash and maintain.	• They do not absorb sweat like natural fibres do. • They should be ironed carefully as they may get damaged by high temperature. • They catch fire more easily than cotton or wool. • They do not allow air to pass freely through them and stick to the body of the person on sweating. Hence, they are not comfortable for wearing in hot and humid weather.

Activity 1

Aim: To observe the texture of various fabrics

Materials required: Samples of fabric materials (carpet made of rayon, socks made of nylon, shirt made of polyester, shawl made of acrylic)

Procedure: Observe the fibres using a magnifying lens and feel the texture of all these fabrics. Record your observations in the following table. Put a tick (✓) for the suitable option in the table below.

Texture	Carpet	Socks	Shirt	Shawl
Soft				
Rough				
Smooth				
Shiny				
Dull				
Hairy				
Strong				
Preferred fabric (grade them based on the texture)				

Conclusion: The difference in texture is due to the difference in the properties of these fibres.

Activity 2

Aim: To compare the water-absorption capacity of natural and synthetic fibres

Materials required: Two pieces of cloth (cotton and nylon) of equal size, two beakers and water

Procedure:

1. Take half metre square each of a cotton (natural fibre) and a nylon (synthetic fibre) cloth.
2. Take two 250 mℓ glass beakers, both containing the same amount of water.
3. Soak each piece of cloth in a different beaker.
4. After five minutes, take the pieces out of the beaker and compare the volume of water left behind in each beaker.

Observation:

1. Which beaker has less water?
2. What does this indicate?

Conclusion:

Revise and Recall

Fill in the blanks.

1. The synthetic fibre that closely resembles wool is ______________. (polyester/acrylic)
2. Artificial silk is the other name for ______________. (rayon/nylon)
3. Spandex is popularly known as ______________. (polycot/lycra)
4. The first synthetic fibre was made in ______________. (1830s/1930s)
5. A mixture of polyester and wool is called ______________. (polywool/polycot)

PLASTICS

Plastics are also polymers just like synthetic fibres. These are usually synthetic and most commonly derived from petrochemicals. Depending on the nature of plastics with regard to heat, plastics are of two types: thermoplastics and thermosetting plastics.

Types of Plastics

Thermoplastics: The plastics that can be melted easily on heating and can be moulded again and again into different shapes are called **thermoplastics**. Polyethylene, polypropylene, polystyrene and polyvinyl chloride are examples of thermoplastics (Fig. 3.7).

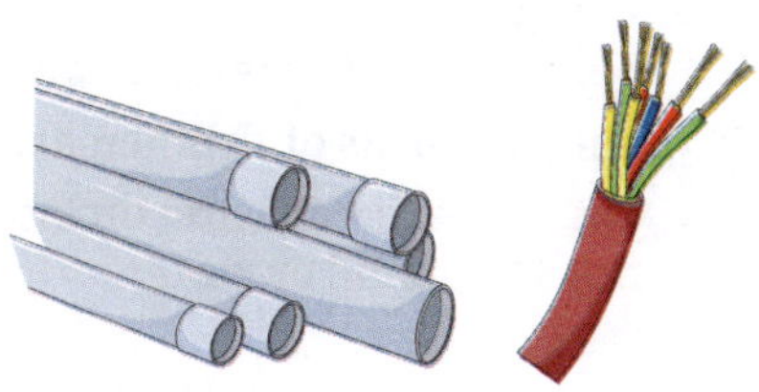

Fig. 3.7: Thermoplastics

Pipes for transporting water, containers for storing food and other items, hand gloves, covering for electric wires and packaging material for delicate and expensive items are made from thermoplastics.

Thermosetting plastics: The plastics that do not soften much on heating and can be moulded only once are called **thermosetting plastics.** Even at high temperatures, these plastics can maintain their shape and size. Bakelite, duroplast, melamine and epoxy resin are examples of thermosetting plastics. They are used to make unbreakable dinnerware, plugs, switches and the handle of tea kettles (Fig. 3.8).

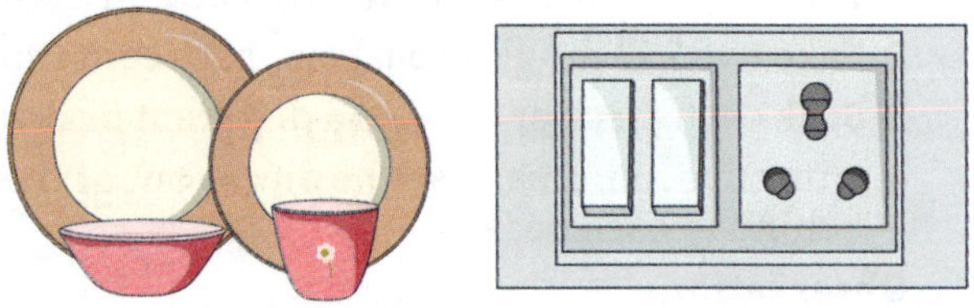

Fig. 3.8: Thermosetting plastics

Properties of Plastics

Plastic articles are durable, light, cheap and strong. Hence, they are widely used in industries and for household purposes. Some common properties of plastics are as follows.

Solubility in water: Plastics are insoluble in water. Hence, buckets and bottles made from plastics are used to store water.

Reactivity: Plastics do not react with water and air; thus, do not corrode or rust easily. So, they are used for storing chemicals and other materials. Since they do not corrode easily, they are also used to make toys.

Effect of flame: Plastics catch fire easily, so they are ***inflammable.***

Thermal conductivity: Plastics are poor conductors of heat. Hence, they are used for making handles of cooking utensils, containers used in microwave ovens and as insulating wool in refrigerators.

Electrical conductivity: Plastics are poor conductors of electricity. So, they are used as a covering for electric wires for making cords of electrical appliances and cables.

Science in Context

- PVC (Polyvinyl Chloride), a type of plastic, is widely used to make ID cards and credit cards because it is flame-resistant.
- The uniforms of firemen are made with flame-resistant material called melamine plastic.
- The non-stick coating on kitchenware is made of a special plastic called Teflon because it does not stick to oil or water.

Uses of Plastics

Plastics are used in many ways in our day-to-day life. Some of the commonly used plastics and their uses are as follows (Tables 3.2 and 3.3).

Table 3.2: Uses of thermoplastics

Plastic	Source	Property	Uses
Polythene	Obtained by the polymerization of ethylene monomers	Strong, insulator, tough, flexible, water- and corrosion-resistant	Used for making containers for storing items and pipes for transporting water, oil and other materials and as waterproofing and packaging material
PVC (Polyvinyl chloride)	Obtained by the polymerization of vinyl chloride	Insulator and stronger than polythene	Used as a covering for making gramophone records, refrigerator linings, electric wires, in the making of handbags and furniture.
Polystyrene	Obtained by the polymerization of styrene monomers	Hard, brittle, cheapest plastic and lighter than polythene	Used as packaging material for fragile objects, such as electronic items, to make thermocol and in the making of disposable cups
Polypropylene	Obtained by the polymerization of propene monomers	Tough and rigid plastic	Used for making different kinds of brushes, bottles, hand gloves, battery casings and fishing nets
Teflon or Polytetra-flouroethene	Obtained by the polymerization of tetrafluoroethylene	Does not react with other substances, not affected by heat and is slippery	Used as a coating material for industrial parts to increase their durability, on pans and other cooking utensils as non-stick coating material
Perspex	Obtained by the polymerization of methyl methacrylate	Transparent and unbreakable	Used in streetlight fittings and telephones, for making windscreens of cars and mostly used as a substitute for glass

Table 3.3: Uses of thermosetting plastics

Plastic	Source	Property	Uses
Bakelite	Obtained by the reaction of phenol with formaldehyde in the presence of a catalyst	Acts as an efficient electrical insulator and is generally harder than other plastics	Used in the making of the handles of tea kettles, sauce pans, pressure cookers, buttons, plugs, switches, telephone cases, radio and television casings
Melamine	Manufactured using urea	Can withstand heat better than other plastics, is hard and resists fire	Used in the making of unbreakable dinnerware, decoration pieces, floor tiles and fireproof fabrics

Environmental Effects of Plastics

Some harmful effects of plastics are given below.

- Burning of plastics releases poisonous gases into the atmosphere causing air pollution.
- Careless disposal of plastic bags blocks the drains, resulting in the overflow of wastewater. This also blocks the percolation of water into the soil and so prevents the renewal of groundwater. Water-logged places become an ideal breeding place for mosquitoes and other disease-causing germs.
- Recycled plastic bags cause health problems if food items are stored in them, as the dyes present in such bags are absorbed into the food materials.
- Plastic bags consumed by animals along with the leftover food cause illness and sometimes lead to their death.

Measures to Prevent Pollution Caused by Plastics

Some ways to minimize plastic pollution are as follows:

- Reduce dependence on plastic bags and on other items made of plastic.
- Encourage reuse and recycling of plastics.
- Buy products with less plastic packaging.
- Plastic wrappings and bags should carry a warning label stating the dangers of plastic pollution, and shoppers should be encouraged to use paper or cloth bags.
- Plastics should not be disposed of in the sewage system, on the streets or on the pavements. Any plastic litter that you see in the vicinity should be picked up and disposed of in a proper place.
- Keep separate garbage bins at home and school for segregating wastes; for example, green bins for **biodegradable** (substances that can be decomposed through natural processes by the action of microorganisms) wastes, and blue bins for **non-biodegradable** (substances that cannot be decomposed by microorganisms) wastes (Fig. 3.9).
- The 5R principle of Reduce, Reuse, Recycle, Refuse and Repurpose to minimize environmental pollution should be followed and practised.

Go Green

Segregating not only plastics, but also other waste materials would lead to better management of wastes and minimize pollution.

Nowadays, besides the standard green and blue garbage bins, additional bins are used to segregate wastes at its source.

Is this waste segregation system used in your locality?

Green bin Blue bin

Fig. 3.9: Types of bins

Keywords

Synthetic fibres: Fibres that are made by humans through chemical processes

Polymerization: The process in which small monomers link together to form a long chain of polymers

Thermoplastics: The plastics that can be melted easily on heating and can be moulded again and again into different shapes

Thermosetting plastics: The plastics that do not soften much on heating and can be moulded only once

Biodegradable: Substances that can be decomposed through natural processes by the action of microorganisms

Non-biodegradable: Substances that cannot be decomposed easily by microorganisms

Summary

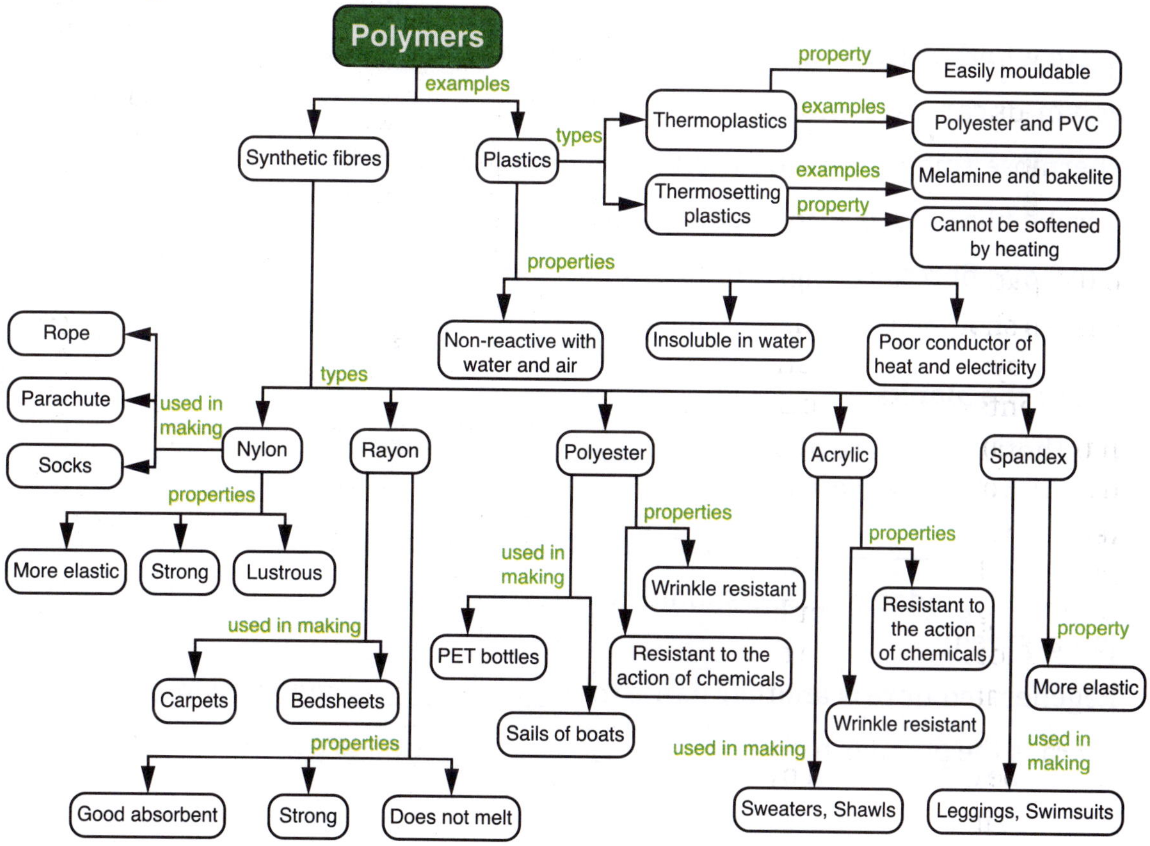

Exercise

W

ia

A. Choose the correct option.

1. _____________ fibre is obtained by the chemical treatment of wood pulp.
   (a) Nylon (b) Rayon (c) Acrylic (d) Polyester
2. _____________ is a synthetic fibre used for making woollen clothes.
   (a) Polyester (b) Acrylic (c) Rayon (d) Polyethylene
3. Which of the following is biodegradable?
   (a) Plastic bags (b) Aluminium sheet (c) Tin (d) Paper bags
4. Which of the following can be used as a substitute for glass?
   (a) Teflon (b) Perspex (c) PVC (d) Melamine
5. Nylon was first prepared from _____________.
   (a) coal, water and air (b) wood pulp
   (c) wool (d) cotton

B. State whether the following statements are true (T) or false (F).

1. Polymers can have only linear structure. ☐
2. Thermosetting plastics are used to make unbreakable dinnerware. ☐
3. Acrylic fibres burn with a sooty flame. ☐
4. Synthetic fibres are resistant to moths and moulds. ☐
5. Plastics are good conductors of electricity. ☐

C. Fill in the blanks.

ia

1. Synthetic fibres are also called _____________ fibres. (natural/human-made)
2. Plastics are _____________. (non-flammable/inflammable)
3. Non-biodegradable wastes should be thrown in the _____________ bins. (blue/green)
4. Regenerated fibre is another name for _____________. (rayon/nylon)
5. Lycra is the popular name for _____________. (spandex/polyester)

D. Match the following.

1.	Polyester	(a)	Blankets
2.	Nylon	(b)	Making disposable cups
3.	Rayon	(c)	PET jars and bottles
4.	Acrylic	(d)	Parachutes
5.	Polystyrene	(e)	Obtained from wood pulp

E. Name the following.

1. The fibre that is also called artificial silk ________________
2. The synthetic fibre that derives its name from two cities ________________
3. This is called the small unit of a polymer ________________
4. A mixture of terylene and cotton ________________
5. Plastics that do not soften much on heating ________________

F. Give reasons for the following.

1. Nylon is used to make fishing nets and parachutes.
2. Rayon is called artificial silk.
3. Thermosetting plastics are used to make the handles of cooking utensils.
4. Burning of plastics is not advised.
5. We should use paper or cloth bag instead of plastic bags.

G. Answer the following questions briefly.

1. What is polymerization?
2. Why is rayon called a regenerated fibre?
3. Write the properties and uses of acrylic.
4. Why do we use containers made of plastic to store water and chemicals?
5. What is PET? Give its two uses.

H. Answer the following questions in detail.

1. List the advantages and disadvantages of synthetic fibres.
2. What are plastics? Write the general properties of plastics.
3. Differentiate between thermoplastics and thermosetting plastics.
4. What are the harmful effects of the excessive use of plastics?
5. Mention a few measures that can be taken to prevent pollution caused by plastics.

Cognitive Corner

Critical Thinking

1. Ropes made of nylon are preferred over the ones made from natural fibres for the purpose of climbing and to make parachutes. Why?
2. Why it is not advisable to use polyester clothes while working in the kitchen?

Picture Study

Look at the bins given below and write what kind of wastes can be disposed in them. List any five types of wastes that are generated every day in your house and can be disposed of only in the blue bin.

Green bin

Blue bin

______________________________ ______________________________

______________________________ ______________________________

______________________________ ______________________________

Project

1. Prepare a scrapbook by collecting information on recycling of plastics and write a report on it. Use photos, diagrams and newspaper cuttings in your report. **(C-7.1)**
2. Conduct a survey on the use of synthetic materials in your neighbourhood. Find out how many people prefer using synthetic fibres over natural fibres. Ask if they recycle. Make a report on your findings. **(C-6.2)**
3. On the Internet, search for how science and technology have influenced the clothing industry. Make a poster illustrating the differences between clothing in the past and in the present. **(C-6.1)**

In the Library

Find information about bioplastics (biodegradable plastics), their composition and the process involved in their synthesis. **(C-5.1)**

In the Laboratory

Aim: To compare the strength of different fibres **(C-7.2)**

Materials required: A laboratory stand, threads of various fibres, a small pan and weights

Procedure:

1. Take a laboratory stand with a clamp.
2. Collect threads of the following fibres: cotton, wool, nylon, silk and polyester (of about the same length and same thickness).
3. Tie one end of the nylon thread to the clamp.
4. Attach a pan at the other end of the thread.
5. Add weight to the pan. Keep on adding weights to the pan until the thread breaks.
6. Record the total weight required to break the thread. This weight gives us the strength of the fibre.
7. Repeat the same procedure with the other threads.
8. Record your observations in the table given below and arrange the threads in the order of their increasing strength.

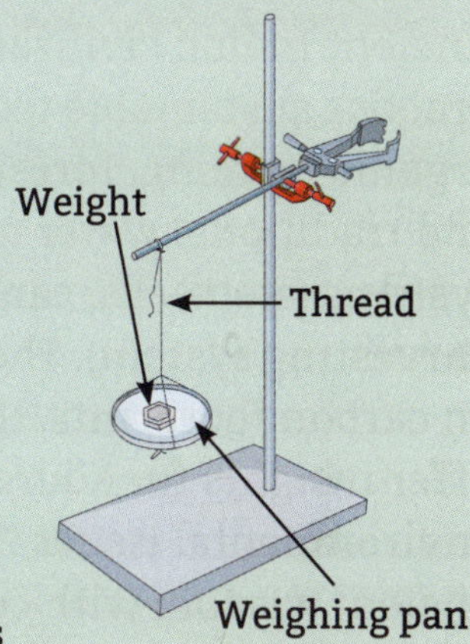

Observation:

S. No.	Type of fibre	Total weight required to break the thread
1	Nylon	
2	Cotton	
3	Wool	
4	Silk	
5	Polyester	

Conclusion: ____________________

Life Skills

Each and every other person on this Earth uses a water bottle made of plastic. Out of these plastic bottles, 80% end up in landfills. What can you do to contribute to reducing the use of plastic by practising the 5R principle? List at least five practises. **(C-6.1)**

Worksheet

A carbon footprint is a measure of the total amount of greenhouse gases, especially carbon dioxide (CO_2), and other equivalent gases emitted directly or indirectly by human activities. Ancient Indian civilizations did practise sustainable techniques such as organic farming, forest conservation and traditional water management systems (stepwells, canals and rainwater harvesting system). Though not focused on carbon footprints, these practices offer insights for addressing modern environmental issues. The integration of ancient wisdom with current knowledge can drive more holistic approaches towards Sustainable Development Goal (SDG) 12 (Responsible Consumption and Production).

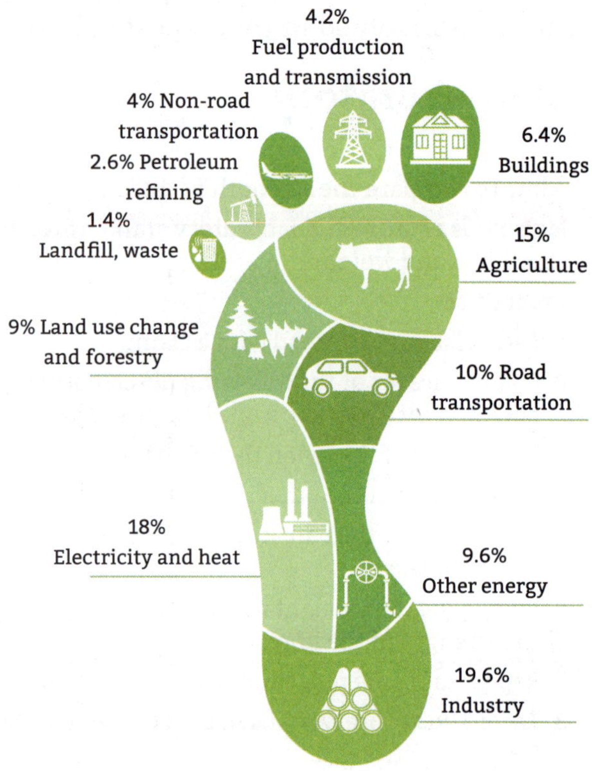

Carbon footprint

A. How can we adapt historical sustainability methods to address today's carbon footprint concerns?

____

____

____

B. How might embracing the holistic wisdom of the past enhance our approach to achieve the objective of SDG 12?

____

____

____

C. Make a poster with catchy slogans to create awareness among people, encouraging them to learn from ancient Indian wisdom and adopt sustainable practices to reduce their carbon footprint and protect the environment.

4 Metals and Non-metals

Curricular Goals

- Explore the world of matter and its constituents, properties and behaviour **(CG-1)**
- Explore the nature and processes of science through engaging with the evolution of scientific knowledge and conducting scientific inquiry **(CG-6)**

Competencies

- Classify matter based on observable physical and chemical characteristics **(C-1.1)**
- Describe changes in matter and use particulate nature to represent the properties of matter and the changes **(C-1.2)**
- Formulate questions using scientific terminology and collect data as evidence **(C-6.2)**

Let's Get Started

Look at the pictures given below. Can you name the element used in making each of these articles? Write down your answers in the space provided.

Pencils

____

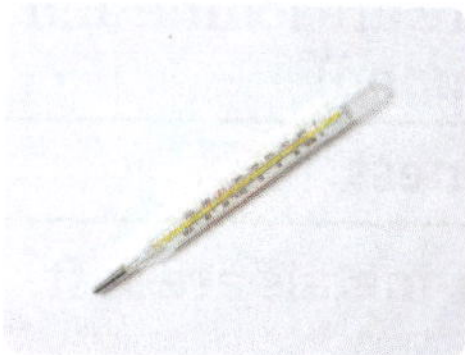

Thermometer

____

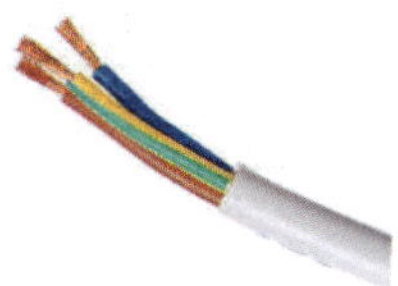

Electric wires

____

Foil paper

____

We have learned in the previous classes that each element has a unique composition. As a result, all elements differ from each other in their properties. Due to their different properties, elements are used in a variety of ways in our daily lives. However, they also possess some common properties. Based on the similarities in their properties, elements can be divided into two broad classes: metals and non-metals.

Metals are mostly solid substances that are hard, lustrous, malleable, ductile, sonorous and good conductors of heat and electricity. Copper, gold, iron and aluminium are some examples of metals.

Non-metals are substances that are soft, lack lustre, non-malleable, non-ductile, non-sonorous and are poor conductors of heat and electricity. Carbon, sulphur and phosphorus are examples of non-metals.

Let us learn about the different properties and uses of metals and non-metals in this chapter.

PHYSICAL PROPERTIES OF METALS AND NON-METALS

Table 4.1 lists the physical properties of metals and non-metals.

Table 4.1: Physical properties of metals and non-metals

<table>
<tr><th>Metals</th><th>Non-metals</th></tr>
<tr><td colspan="2">I. Physical state</td></tr>
<tr><td>They are generally solid at room temperature and crystalline in nature. Examples are magnesium, aluminium, copper and iron.
Exception: Mercury exists in the liquid state at room temperature.</td><td>They generally exist in solid or gaseous state at room temperature. Examples are oxygen, chlorine and hydrogen, which exist in the gaseous state. Solid non-metals are powdery (amorphous) in nature, for example, carbon, and sulphur.
Exception: Bromine exists in the liquid state.</td></tr>
<tr><td colspan="2">II. Lustre</td></tr>
<tr><td>They have lustre, that is, they are shiny in appearance. Examples are gold, silver and platinum.
Sodium loses its lustre when exposed to air.</td><td>They lack lustre, that is, they are not shiny in appearance. Examples are chlorine, hydrogen, sulphur and carbon (charcoal).
Exceptions: The only non-metals that show lustre are iodine and carbon (as graphite and diamond).</td></tr>
<tr><td colspan="2">III. Hardness</td></tr>
<tr><td>Metals are hard.
Exception: Potassium, sodium and calcium are examples of soft metals. Sodium is very soft and can be cut with a knife easily.</td><td>Non-metals are soft.
Exception: Diamond, the hardest known substance, is made of carbon.</td></tr>
<tr><td colspan="2">IV. Malleability and Brittleness
Substances that can be beaten into thin sheets are termed malleable, and the property is called malleability.
Substances that can be broken into thin pieces are defined as brittle substances, and this property is called brittleness.</td></tr>
<tr><td>Most metals are malleable and not very brittle. Examples are gold, silver, aluminium, copper and iron.</td><td>Most non-metals are brittle (break into pieces when hammered) but not malleable. Examples are graphite and coal.</td></tr>
<tr><td colspan="2">V. Ductility
Substances that can be drawn into thin wires are termed ductile and the property is called ductility.</td></tr>
<tr><td>Most metals are ductile. Examples are gold, silver, aluminium and copper.</td><td>Non-metals are non-ductile. Carbon and sulphur break if one attempts to stretch them.</td></tr>
</table>

Metals	Non-metals
VI. Thermal conductivity **Thermal conductivity** is a property of substances that permits heat to pass through them.	
Metals are good conductors of heat. Hence, they are widely used in the making of cooking utensils. Examples are silver and copper.	Most non-metals are bad conductors of heat. Examples are iodine, sulphur and silicon. *Exception*: Diamond is a good conductor of heat.
VII. Electrical conductivity **Electrical conductivity** is a property of substances that permits electric current to pass through them.	
Mostly, metals are good conductors of electricity. Hence, they are widely used for making electrical appliances. Examples are aluminium and copper.	Most non-metals are bad conductors of electricity. *Exception*: Carbon in the form of graphite conducts electricity.
VIII. Sonority **Sonority** is a property of substances that can produce a ringing sound when hit by hard objects.	
Mostly, metals are sonorous. Thus, they are used to make objects such as bells.	Mostly, non-metals are non-sonorous.

Activity 1

Note: *These activities need to be performed carefully in the presence and with the assistance of a teacher.*

Aim: To examine the malleability and electrical conductivity of metals and non-metals

Materials required: Hammer, small pieces of magnesium, copper, graphite and carbon (coal), plastic spoon, iron nail, 9-Volt batteries, insulated copper wires, small transparent light bulbs and crocodile clips

Procedure:

I. To check malleability

1. Take small pieces of magnesium, copper, graphite and carbon (coal) each. With the help of a hammer, strike each of the samples.
2. Observe and note down the change in the shape of these samples.

Observation:

Malleability					
S. No.	**Sample**	**Observation**	**S. No.**	**Sample**	**Observation**
1.	Copper		2.	Graphite	
3.	Magnesium		4.	Carbon (coal)	

Conclusion: ____

____

II. To check electrical conductivity

1. Set up an electrical circuit as shown in the figure given alongside.
2. Take an iron nail and a plastic spoon. Connect the material to be tested separately in the circuit between the terminals as shown in the figures.
3. Observe whether the bulb glows or not.

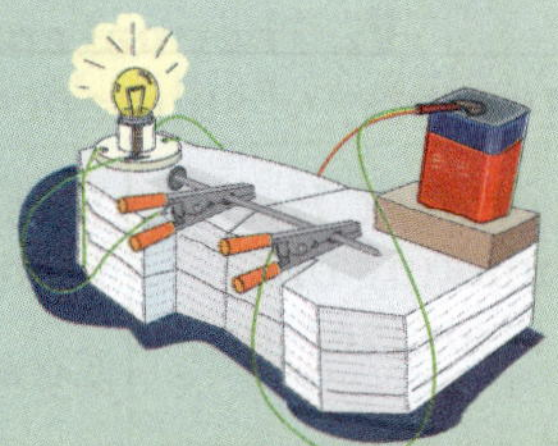

Iron nail

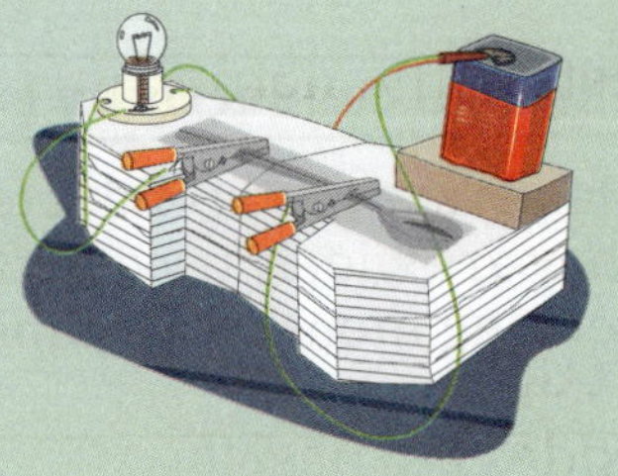

Plastic spoon

Observation:

S. No.	Sample	Observation
1.	Iron nail	
2.	Plastic spoon	

Conclusion: ____________________

____

Activity 2

Note: *This activity needs to be performed carefully in the presence and with the assistance of a teacher.*

Aim: To compare the thermal conductivities of metals and non-metals

Materials required: Copper or aluminium wire, carbon or graphite rod, spirit lamp or Bunsen burner, wax, laboratory stand and needles

Procedure:

1. Take the copper or aluminium wire and fix the wire to a stand. Attach an iron nail to one of the free ends of the wire using wax, as shown in the figure.
2. Start heating the wire from its other free end by using a spirit lamp or a Bunsen burner.
3. Observe whether the wax melts or not and the iron nail falls or not.
4. Repeat the same procedure with a carbon or graphite rod and record your observations.

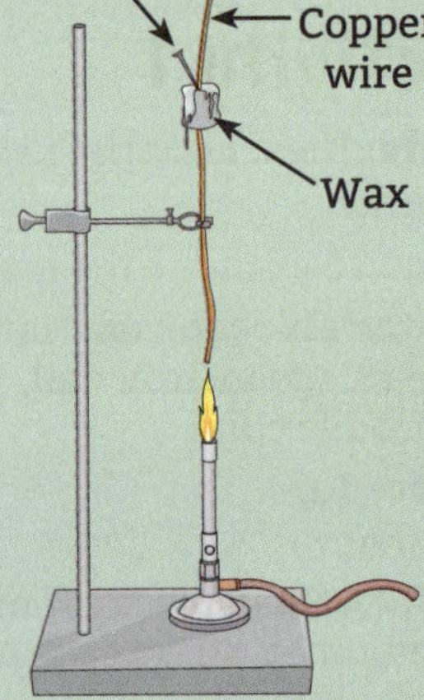

Observation:

S. No.	Sample	Observation
1.	Copper or aluminium wire	
2.	Carbon or graphite rod	

Conclusion: ____________________

CHEMICAL PROPERTIES OF METALS AND NON-METALS

Metals and non-metals exhibit different chemical properties.

Reaction with Oxygen

Metals: Generally, metals react with oxygen to form metallic oxides. These metallic oxides are basic in nature, and thus, they turn red litmus solution to blue.

Metals + Oxygen ⟶ Metallic oxides (basic in nature)

- Magnesium, on heating, burns with a dazzling white flame in the presence of oxygen to form magnesium oxide.

$$\underset{\text{Magnesium}}{2Mg} + \underset{\text{Oxygen}}{O_2} \longrightarrow \underset{\text{Magnesium oxide}}{2MgO}$$

- Metals such as sodium and potassium react vigorously with oxygen at room temperature to form sodium oxide and potassium oxide, respectively. Since these metals burst into flames if left in the open (or in contact with air), they are stored by keeping them immersed in kerosene (Fig. 4.1).

Fig. 4.1: Sodium stored in kerosene

$$\underset{\text{Sodium}}{4Na} + \underset{\text{Oxygen}}{O_2} \longrightarrow \underset{\text{Sodium oxide}}{2Na_2O}$$

Non-Metals: Generally, non-metals react with oxygen to form non-metallic oxides. These non-metallic oxides are acidic in nature, and thus, they turn blue litmus solution to red.

Non-metals + Oxygen ⟶ Non-metallic oxides (acidic in nature)

- Carbon burns in the presence of oxygen to form carbon dioxide.

$$\underset{\text{Carbon}}{C} + \underset{\text{Oxygen}}{O_2} \longrightarrow \underset{\text{Carbon dioxide}}{CO_2}$$

  Non-metallic oxides dissolve in water to form acids.

$$\underset{\text{Carbon dioxide}}{CO_2} + \underset{\text{Water}}{H_2O} \longrightarrow \underset{\text{Carbonic acid}}{H_2CO_3}$$

- Sulphur burns in the presence of oxygen to form sulphur dioxide.

$$\underset{\text{Sulphur}}{S} + \underset{\text{Oxygen}}{O_2} \longrightarrow \underset{\text{Sulphur dioxide}}{SO_2}$$

  Sulphur dioxide dissolves in water to form sulphurous acid.

$$\underset{\text{Sulphur dioxide}}{SO_2} + \underset{\text{Water}}{H_2O} \longrightarrow \underset{\text{Sulphurous acid}}{H_2SO_3}$$

Science in Context

- Oxides that behave as both acidic and basic oxides are called amphoteric oxides.
  Examples: Aluminium oxide (Al_2O_3), Zinc oxide (ZnO)
- Phosphorus, a very reactive non-metal that can catch fire when exposed to air, is usually stored in water as it does not react with water.

Activity 3

Note: *This activity needs to be performed carefully in the presence and with the assistance of a teacher.*

Aim: To examine that metallic oxides are basic in nature

Materials required: Spirit lamp, magnesium ribbon, a pair of tongs, red litmus paper, water and a 100 mℓ glass beaker

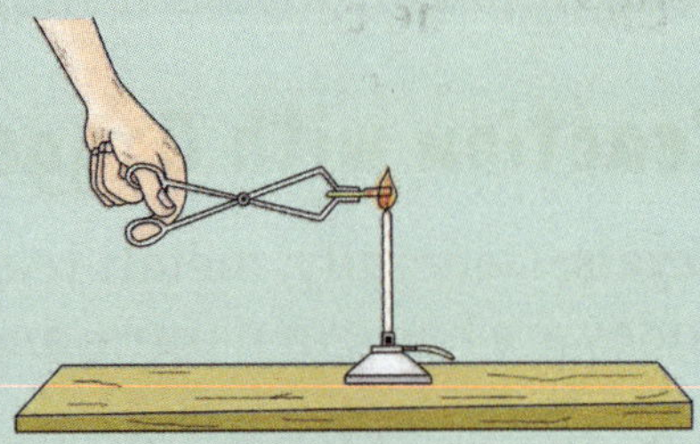

Burning of the magnesium ribbon

Procedure:

1. Take one magnesium ribbon.
2. With the help of a pair of tongs, heat the magnesium ribbon over a spirit lamp flame.
3. You will observe that the magnesium ribbon burns with a dazzling white flame and forms a white powder.
4. Collect this powder in a separate glass beaker containing water and dissolve the powder.
5. Test this solution with a red litmus paper and observe the colour change.

Observation:

Sample	Colour change in the red litmus paper
Magnesium	

Conclusion: ______________________________

Activity 4

Note: *This activity needs to be performed as a teacher demonstration.*

Aim: To examine that non-metallic oxides are acidic in nature

Materials required: Sulphur powder, spirit lamp, deflagrating spoon, gas jar, Petri dish, blue litmus paper and water

Procedure:

1. Take some sulphur powder in a deflagrating spoon and heat it over a spirit lamp flame.
2. Take the gas jar, and as the sulphur starts burning, place the spoon in the jar. Then, cover it with a lid.
3. Remove the spoon once the sulphur stops burning.
4. Add some water into the jar and shake the jar to allow the mixing of the gas produced with the water.
5. Pour some of this solution into a Petri dish and test it with a blue litmus paper.

(a) (b) (c) (d)

Observation:

Sample	Colour change in the blue litmus paper
Sulphur	

Conclusion: ______________________________

Revise and Recall

Choose the correct option.

1. Which of the following elements forms acidic oxide?
   (a) Lithium (b) Sodium (c) Carbon (d) Beryllium
2. Which of the following elements produces basic oxide?
   (a) Sulphur (b) Phosphorus (c) Magnesium (d) Chlorine
3. Which of the following elements is stored in kerosene?
   (a) Potassium (b) Magnesium (c) Sulphur (d) Carbon

Reaction with Water

Metals: Generally, metals react with water to form metal oxides or metal hydroxides and hydrogen gas.

Metals + Water ⟶ Metal oxides or Metal hydroxides + Hydrogen gas

Metals such as potassium, sodium and calcium react vigorously with cold water to form their respective hydroxides and release hydrogen gas. A large amount of heat is also released. Reactions in which heat is released are called **exothermic reactions**.

- Sodium reacts with cold water to form sodium hydroxide and hydrogen gas.

$$\underset{\text{Sodium}}{2Na} + \underset{\text{Water}}{2H_2O} \longrightarrow \underset{\text{Sodium hydroxide}}{2NaOH} + \underset{\text{Hydrogen gas}}{H_2\uparrow}$$

  The release of a large amount of heat in the above reaction makes the hydrogen gas catch fire, as shown in Figure 4.2.

Fig. 4.2: Reaction of sodium with water

- Zinc reacts only with steam to form zinc oxide and release hydrogen gas.

$$\underset{\text{Zinc}}{Zn} + \underset{\text{Steam}}{H_2O(g)} \longrightarrow \underset{\text{Zinc oxide}}{ZnO} + \underset{\text{Hydrogen gas}}{H_2\uparrow}$$

- Magnesium reacts with steam to form magnesium oxide and release hydrogen gas.

$$\underset{\text{Magnesium}}{Mg} + \underset{\text{Steam}}{H_2O(g)} \longrightarrow \underset{\text{Magnesium oxide}}{MgO} + \underset{\text{Hydrogen gas}}{H_2\uparrow}$$

  Metals such as platinum, gold, silver and copper do not react with water at all.

Non-metals: Under any condition, non-metals do not react with water.

Corrosion

The process in which atmospheric moisture and gases slowly eat away the surface of metals is called ***corrosion****.*

Fig. 4.3: Rusted iron objects

Rusting of Iron: Iron reacts with oxygen in the presence of moisture to form **rust** (a brown, flaky substance) (Fig. 4.3). The chemical composition of rust is $Fe_2O_3 \cdot xH_2O$. We have learned about the process of rusting and the conditions necessary for rusting in earlier classes.

Fig. 4.4: Corroded copper coins

Corrosion of Copper: Copper reacts with carbon dioxide in the presence of moisture to form a green substance, which is a mixture of copper hydroxide and copper carbonate (Fig. 4.4).

$$2Cu + H_2O + CO_2 + O_2 \longrightarrow Cu(OH)_2 + CuCO_3$$

2Cu	+ H_2O	+ CO_2	+ O_2	→ $Cu(OH)_2$	+ $CuCO_3$
Copper	Water (moisture)	Carbon dioxide	Oxygen	Copper hydroxide	Copper carbonate

Copper hydroxide + Copper carbonate → Green substance

Fig. 4.5: Corroded silver plate

Corrosion of Silver: Silver reacts with hydrogen sulphide gas present in the atmosphere to form a black-coloured substance called silver sulphide (Fig. 4.5).

Corrosion of Aluminium: Aluminium reacts with oxygen present in the atmosphere to form a thin layer of aluminium oxide on its surface, which acts as a protective barrier against further oxidation.

Corrosion of metal objects can be prevented by oiling, painting, greasing or by coating a layer of another metal on them.

The process of coating iron objects with zinc is called ***galvanization***. For example, the iron pipes used for supplying water in our homes are galvanized to prevent rusting.

Go Green

Measures to reduce atmospheric pollution, such as the usage of biofuels, should be strictly followed because harmful pollutants such as sulphur compounds present in the atmosphere cause corrosion of silver articles. These pollutants also lead to acid rain which causes the corrosion of buildings and monuments.

Science in Context

Alloys are homogeneous mixtures of two or more metals or a combination of metals with a non-metal. For example, cast iron is an alloy made by combining iron with carbon, stainless steel is made by blending iron, chromium, smaller amounts of carbon, nickel, manganese, molybdenum, and other metals, and bronze is made by mixing tin and copper.

Reaction with Acids

Metals: Most metals react with dilute acids to form the corresponding salt and release hydrogen gas (the release of gas is indicated by an upward arrow in the chemical equation). The hydrogen gas produced can be tested by bringing a lighted matchstick near it as the gas burns with a pop sound. Metals react with different acids to form different salts.

$$\text{Metals} + \text{(dil.) Acid} \longrightarrow \text{Salt} + \text{Hydrogen gas}$$

The reaction of sodium and potassium with acids is very fast and vigorous, whereas the reaction of other metals with acids is comparatively slower.

- Sodium reacts with dilute hydrochloric acid to form sodium chloride and hydrogen gas.

$$\underset{\text{Sodium}}{2Na} + \underset{\text{Dilute hydrochloric acid}}{2HCl} \longrightarrow \underset{\text{Sodium chloride}}{2NaCl} + \underset{\text{Hydrogen gas}}{H_2\uparrow}$$

- Magnesium reacts with dilute hydrochloric acid to form magnesium chloride and hydrogen gas.

$$\underset{\text{Magnesium}}{Mg} + \underset{\text{Dilute hydrochloric acid}}{2HCl} \longrightarrow \underset{\text{Magnesium chloride}}{MgCl_2} + \underset{\text{Hydrogen gas}}{H_2\uparrow}$$

- Magnesium reacts with dilute sulphuric acid to form magnesium sulphate and hydrogen gas.

$$\underset{\text{Magnesium}}{Mg} + \underset{\text{Dilute sulphuric acid}}{H_2SO_4} \longrightarrow \underset{\text{Magnesium sulphate}}{MgSO_4} + \underset{\text{Hydrogen gas}}{H_2\uparrow}$$

- Zinc reacts with dilute sulphuric acid to form zinc sulphate and hydrogen gas.

$$\underset{\text{Zinc}}{Zn} + \underset{\text{Dilute sulphuric acid}}{H_2SO_4} \longrightarrow \underset{\text{Zinc sulphate}}{ZnSO_4} + \underset{\text{Hydrogen gas}}{H_2\uparrow}$$

- Aluminium reacts with dilute hydrochloric acid to form aluminium chloride and hydrogen gas.

$$\underset{\text{Aluminium}}{2Al} + \underset{\text{Dilute hydrochloric acid}}{6HCl} \longrightarrow \underset{\text{Aluminium chloride}}{2AlCl_3} + \underset{\text{Hydrogen gas}}{3H_2\uparrow}$$

- Copper and silver do not react with dilute acids, but they react with concentrated sulphuric acid to form their respective sulphates, sulphur dioxide gas and water.

$$\underset{\text{Copper}}{Cu} + \underset{\text{Concentrated sulphuric acid}}{2H_2SO_4} \longrightarrow \underset{\text{Copper sulphate}}{CuSO_4} + \underset{\text{Sulphur dioxide gas}}{SO_2\uparrow} + \underset{\text{Water}}{2H_2O}$$

$$\underset{\text{Silver}}{2Ag} + \underset{\text{Concentrated sulphuric acid}}{2H_2SO_4} \longrightarrow \underset{\text{Silver sulphate}}{Ag_2SO_4} + \underset{\text{Sulphur dioxide gas}}{SO_2\uparrow} + \underset{\text{Water}}{2H_2O}$$

- Gold does not react with acids.

Non-metals: Generally, non-metals do not react with dilute acids. Some non-metals (example, carbon, sulphur and phosphorus) react with concentrated acids to form their respective oxides.

Activity 5

a

Note: *This activity needs to be performed carefully in the presence and with the assistance of a teacher.*

Aim: To determine if metals react with dilute acids and release hydrogen gas

Materials required: 250 mℓ glass beakers, dilute hydrochloric acid, four glass test tubes, spatulas, glass rods, hot water, matchbox, small amounts of magnesium, iron, zinc and aluminium

Procedure:

1. Take four test tubes and label them as 1, 2, 3 and 4.
2. Fill each test tube with 30 mℓ of dilute hydrochloric acid.
3. Take small amounts of the metal samples: magnesium, iron, zinc and aluminium, and place them in separate test tubes.
4. Observe if any gas bubbles are formed in each of the test tubes. If not, slightly warm the test tube in a beaker containing hot water.
5. Bring a burning matchstick near the mouth of each of the test tubes. Record your observations.

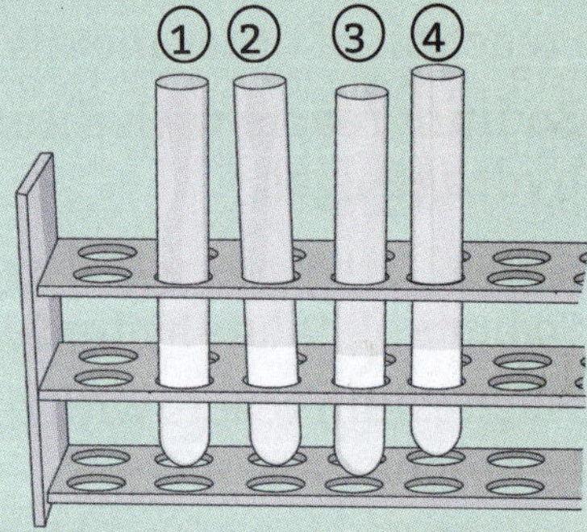

Observation:

S. No.	Sample	Bubble formation	Release of hydrogen gas
1.	Dilute hydrochloric acid + Magnesium		
2.	Dilute hydrochloric acid + Iron		
3.	Dilute hydrochloric acid + Zinc		
4.	Dilute hydrochloric acid + Aluminium		

Conclusion: ______________________________

Revise and Recall

Fill in the blanks.

1. $2Na + 2H_2O \rightarrow$ ________ $+ H_2\uparrow$
2. $Mg +$ ________ $\rightarrow MgO + H_2\uparrow$
3. ________ $+ H_2O + CO_2 +$ ________ $\rightarrow Cu(OH)_2 + CuCO_3$
4. ________ $+ 2HCl \rightarrow 2NaCl + H_2\uparrow$
   (Dilute)
5. $Zn + H_2SO_4 \rightarrow$ ________ $+ H_2\uparrow$
   (Dilute)

Reaction with Bases

Science in Context

Most of the metals do not exist in nature as pure elements. They are found in the form of naturally occurring compounds called **ores**.

Metals: Only a few metals (example, aluminium, zinc and lead) react with strong bases such as sodium hydroxide and release hydrogen gas.

Non-metals: Reactions of non-metals with bases are very complex and will be dealt with in higher classes.

Displacement Reactions

Displacement reactions are those in which one metal reacts with a salt solution, displacing (or replacing) the metal present in the salt solution. These reactions are based on the reactivity strength of metals.

Activity Series and Chemical Reactions

The arrangement of metals in the decreasing order of their reactivity is called the **activity series** (Fig. 4.6).

Although a non-metal, hydrogen is also placed in the activity series, because, like the atoms of metals, its atom also turns into a positively charge ion (H^+) during chemical reactions.

The metals placed higher in the activity series are more reactive than those placed below them. Hence, sodium is more reactive than calcium but less reactive than potassium. Similarly, copper is more reactive than silver but less reactive than zinc, tin or lead.

So, a more reactive metal can displace a less reactive one from its salt solution. However, a less reactive metal cannot displace a more reactive one from its salt solution. The examples given will help you understand this.

Potassium	K	Most reactive
Sodium	Na	↑
Calcium	Ca	
Magnesium	Mg	
Aluminium	Al	
Zinc	Zn	
Iron	Fe	
Tin	Sn	
Lead	Pb	
Hydrogen	H	
Copper	Cu	
Mercury	Hg	
Silver	Ag	
Gold	Au	↓
Platinum	Pt	Least reactive

Fig. 4.6: Activity series

Example: Zinc reacts with copper sulphate to form zinc sulphate and copper.

$$\underset{\text{Zinc}}{Zn} + \underset{\text{Copper sulphate}}{CuSO_4} \longrightarrow \underset{\text{Zinc sulphate}}{ZnSO_4} + \underset{\text{Copper}}{Cu}$$

Zinc is more reactive than copper because it is placed higher than copper in the activity series. So, it can displace copper from its salt solution. The reverse reaction will not take place as copper is less reactive than zinc.

$$\underset{\text{Copper}}{Cu} + \underset{\text{Zinc sulphate}}{ZnSO_4} \longrightarrow \text{No reaction}$$

You can see the positions of copper and zinc in the activity series, as given in Figure 4.6. Thus, the activity series indicates which metals are more reactive as compared to others. Also, by looking at the activity series, we can predict whether a displacement reaction will take place or not.

Activity 6

Note: *This activity needs to be performed carefully in the presence and with the assistance of a teacher.*

Aim: To examine that a more reactive metal can displace a less reactive metal from its salt solution

Materials required: Three 250 mℓ glass beakers, 100 mℓ of copper sulphate solution, 100 mℓ of silver nitrate solution, 100 mℓ of iron sulphate solution, a small piece of zinc metal and two small pieces of copper turnings

Procedure:

1. Take three clean 250 mℓ glass beakers and label them as samples 1, 2 and 3.
2. Take about 100 mℓ of copper sulphate solution in beaker 1, 100 mℓ of silver nitrate in beaker 2 and 100 mℓ of iron sulphate in beaker 3.
3. Add a small piece of zinc metal to beaker 1.
4. Add small pieces of copper turnings to beakers 2 and 3.
5. Keep the beakers undisturbed for a few minutes and record your observations.

Observation:

S. No.	Samples	Observation
1.	Sample 1 (Copper sulphate + Zinc)	
2.	Sample 2 (Silver nitrate + Copper)	
3.	Sample 3 (Iron sulphate + Copper)	

Conclusion:________________________________

Science in Context

- Aluminium does not react with water because as soon as it is exposed to air, it reacts and forms a layer of oxide (aluminium oxide) on its surface and prevents further reaction from taking place.
- Gold and platinum are widely used in jewellery because they do not react with oxygen and water. They do not tarnish or undergo oxidation. Hence, they are extremely durable.

USES OF METALS AND NON-METALS

Uses of some common metals and non-metals are given in Tables 4.2 and 4.3.

Table 4.2: Uses of metals

Metals	Uses
Copper	• It is used in the making of electrical appliances, wires and cables, boiler pipes, car radiators and utensils.
Iron	• It is used in the making of water pipes, railings, nuts, bolts, tools, warships and tanks, and also for preparing ammonia gas.
Aluminium	• It is used for making high-voltage electrical wires and utensils. • Aluminium foil is used for the packaging of food materials and medicines. • It is also used in the manufacturing of aircraft.
Gold and Silver	• They are used for making ornaments and jewellery. They can be moulded into different shapes as they are very soft metals.
Magnesium	• As it is a flammable metal, it is used in fireworks.
Zinc	• It is used to make galvanized iron pipes as it protects iron from corrosion. • It is also used in dry cells.
Lead	• It is highly malleable, flexible and non-reactive. Hence, it is used for making flexible water pipes, X-ray shields and storage batteries.

Table 4.3: Uses of non-metals

Non-metals	Uses
Chlorine	• It is used as a disinfectant to sterilize water. Addition of chlorine tablets to water to kill germs is called chlorination.
Iodine	• It is used in the preparation of tincture iodine and iodized salt.
Helium	• Being lighter than air, helium is used for filling balloons.
Phosphorus	• It is an extremely reactive element and is used in the manufacture of matchsticks, fertilizers, fireworks, smoke screens, phosphoric acid and superphosphate.
Graphite (Carbon)	• It is non-corrosive and cheap. So, it is used for making electrodes in dry cells. • It is also used as lead in pencils and as a dry lubricant.
Sulphur	• It is used in agriculture as an insecticide, fungicide and in skin ointments. • It is also used in the preparation of gunpowder, plastics, detergents, synthetic fibres and explosives.

Non-metals	Uses
Nitrogen	• It is used in food packaging as it removes oxygen and moisture, thus preventing the spoilage of food. • It is also used in the preparation of nitric acid, ammonia and nitrogen fertilizers.
Silicon	• It is used for making integrated chips (ICs) in computer devices. • It is also used as an insulating material in electrical appliances.
Neon	• It is used in fluorescent bulbs that can be used in advertising displays.
Oxygen	• It is used in welding in combination with other gases. • It is essential for respiration.

Revise and Recall

ia

Fill in the blanks.

1. The property by which substances can be beaten into thin sheets is called ________. (ductility/malleability)
2. A property of substances that permits heat to pass through them is known as ________. (thermal conductivity/electrical conductivity)
3. The metal present at the top of the activity series is ________. (gold/potassium)
4. Metallic oxides are ________ in nature. (acidic/basic)
5. The element that does not react with water under any condition is ________. (gold/aluminium)

MINERAL WEALTH OF INDIA

India is blessed with a rich and diverse mineral wealth. The country is home to numerous minerals, found in different regions. India's mineral resources have played a significant role in its economic development and industrial growth. Here are some notable minerals found in India:

Coal: India has abundant coal reserves and has the fourth largest coal reserves in the world. Coal (Fig. 4.7) is used for power generation, steel production and other industrial purposes. It is primarily used for electricity generation, industrial processes and as a fuel for domestic purposes.

Fig. 4.7: Coal

Fig. 4.8: Iron ore

Iron ore: India has the seventh largest iron ore reserves in the world. Iron ore (Fig. 4.8) deposits are found in various states, including Odisha, Chhattisgarh, Karnataka, Jharkhand and Goa. The iron ore is primarily used in the production of steel.

Bauxite: India has the fifth largest bauxite reserves in the world. Bauxite (Fig. 4.9) deposits are found in states such as Odisha, Gujarat, Jharkhand, Maharashtra and Madhya Pradesh. Bauxite is used to produce aluminium.

Fig. 4.9: Bauxite

Fig. 4.10: Manganese ore

Manganese: India has the seventh largest manganese ore reserves in the world. India possesses significant manganese ore reserves, primarily found in Odisha, Madhya Pradesh, Maharashtra, Andhra Pradesh and Karnataka. Manganese (Fig. 4.10) is used in the production of steel, alloys and batteries.

Copper: Copper ore (Fig. 4.11) deposits are found in various parts of India, including Rajasthan, Jharkhand, Madhya Pradesh and Maharashtra. Copper is used in various industries, including electrical wiring, electronics and construction.

Fig. 4.11: Copper

Fig. 4.12: Gold

Gold: India has modest gold reserves, but it has a rich history of gold mining and consumption. Gold (Fig. 4.12) is primarily used for jewellery, investment and as a reserve asset.

Limestone: India has abundant limestone deposits, particularly in states such as Rajasthan, Andhra Pradesh, Madhya Pradesh and Gujarat. Limestone (Fig. 4.13) is a key raw material in cement production and is also used in various industries, including steel, chemicals and construction.

Fig.4.13: Limestone

Zinc: India is one of the largest producers of zinc, with significant reserves found in Rajasthan. Zinc (Fig. 4.14) is primarily used in galvanizing steel, as well as in alloys, batteries and various other applications.

Fig. 4.14: Zinc

Apart from these minerals, India also has reserves of lead, uranium, chromite, titanium, nickel, phosphate, gypsum and many other minerals.

Keywords

Malleability: The property by which substances can be beaten into thin sheets

Brittleness: The property by which substances can be broken into pieces

Ductility: The property by which substances can be drawn into thin wires

Sonority: The property by which substances can produce a ringing sound when they are struck with a hard object

Corrosion: The process in which atmospheric moisture and gases slowly eat away the surface of metals

Activity series: The arrangement of metals in the decreasing order of their reactivity

Displacement reactions: The reactions in which metals react with a salt solution and displace the metal present in the salt solution

Summary

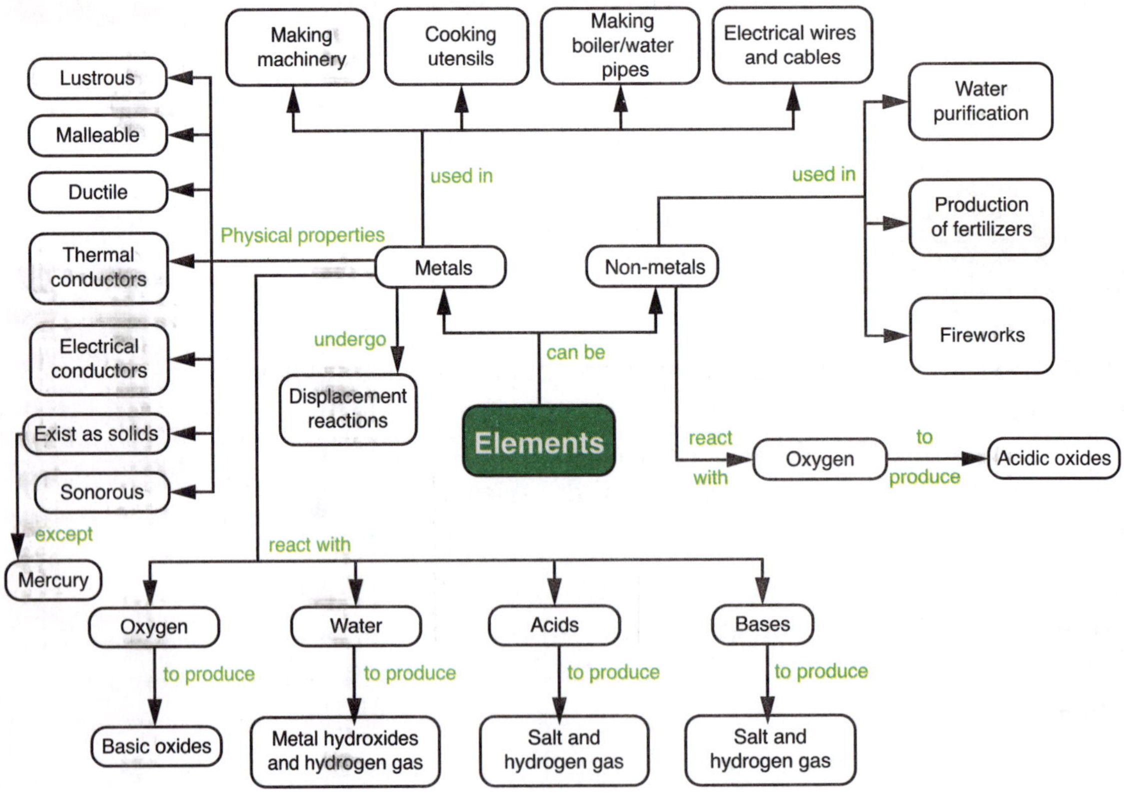

Exercise

A. Choose the correct option.

1. Metal + dilute acids ⟶ Salt + ____________

   (a) Water (b) Hydrogen gas (c) Carbon dioxide (d) Carbon monoxide

2. Identify the correct increasing order of the reactivity of the given metals.

   (a) $Cu < Zn < Mg$ (b) $Mg < Cu < Zn$ (c) $Zn < Mg < Cu$ (d) $Mg < Zn < Cu$

3. ____________ metal is very soft and can be cut with a knife.

   (a) Potassium (b) Iron (c) Copper (d) Carbon

4. ____________ is a non-metal and is a good conductor of electricity.

   (a) Chlorine (b) Nitrogen (c) Graphite (d) Oxygen

5. Which of the following metals reacts vigorously with water?

   (a) Gold (b) Silver (c) Potassium (d) Platinum

B. State whether the following statements are true (T) or false (F).

1. Most metals are not sonorous. ☐
2. Non-metals are generally soft, except diamond. ☐
3. Non-metals are good conductors of electricity, except carbon. ☐
4. Highly reactive metals displace less reactive metals from their salt solutions. ☐
5. Iodine shows lustre. ☐

C. Name the following.

1. A metal that is liquid at room temperature
2. A metal that is stored in kerosene
3. A non-metal used as a disinfectant
4. The process of coating iron objects with zinc
5. The black substance formed due to the corrosion of silver

D. Give reasons for the following.

1. Metallic oxides turn red litmus blue.
2. Nitrogen is used in food packaging.
3. Oiling, painting, greasing or by coating a layer of another metal on a metal prevents corrosion.
4. Copper cannot displace zinc in a chemical reaction.

E. Answer the following questions briefly.

1. Write any two properties of metals.
2. What are displacement reactions?
3. What is corrosion?
4. What is the significance of the activity series of metals?
5. What is the difference between ductility and sonority?

F. Answer the following questions in detail.

1. Distinguish between the physical properties of metals and non-metals.
2. Describe briefly the chemical properties of metals with the help of examples.
3. List the uses of any five metals.
4. Describe the uses of any five non-metals.
5. Write a brief note on mineral wealth of India.

Cognitive Corner

Critical Thinking

Sample A can displace sample B from its salt solution, and sample B can displace sample C, but sample C cannot displace samples A and B. Samples A and B are placed below calcium and above hydrogen in the activity series, whereas sample C is placed between mercury and gold. Sample A can displace tin but not zinc and metals above zinc. Sample B cannot displace tin and metals above it. Find out the names of these samples and arrange them in the decreasing order of their reactivity.

Picture Study

Identify the phenomenon or chemical process shown in the following pictures.

(a)

(b)

__________________ __________________

Project

1. Use a simple word file or an online chart making tool to showcase various objects made of different metals and non-metals. Try and use a variety of pictures to highlight how the design and composition of these objects have changed over time with the advancements in science and technology. **(C-6.1)**
2. As a part of History Club, collect information about the reasons why the Iron Pillar (situated in Delhi) has not rusted even after so many years and effectively communicate your findings with your teacher. **(C-7.3)**

In the Library

1. Look for books or magazines on the history of metallurgy in India. Find out how long ago it started, and how developed it can become now. Write a report on your findings. **(C-8.1)**
2. As a part of chemistry club, collect information about 'electroplating technique' and its usage in the prevention of corrosion. Prepare a chart, discuss it with your teacher and display the same on your class display board. **(C-7.1)**

In the Laboratory

Note: *This activity needs to be performed as a teacher demonstration.* **(C-7.2)**
Aim: To examine that metals react with water, whereas non-metals do not
Materials required: Two 250 mℓ glass beakers, cold water, small pieces of sodium and charcoal, knife and forceps
Procedure:

1. Take a clean 250 mℓ glass beaker and fill it with 100 mℓ of cold water.
2. Cut a small piece of sodium using a knife and dry it with a filter paper.
3. With the help of a tong or forceps, slowly drop the piece of sodium metal into the beaker containing cold water.
4. Try to touch the beaker after the reaction is over. Ensure that the reaction is no longer taking place and touch it from a safe distance.
5. Repeat the same procedure with a charcoal piece in a separate beaker and record your observations.

Reaction of sodium with water

Observation:

S. No.	Sample	Observation
1.	Sodium	
2.	Charcoal piece	

Conclusion:______________________________

Life Skills

Mining of metals and non-metals may be useful for human beings. At the same time, there are many other harmful effects of mining. List out the harmful effects of mining on the environment and on the workers of mining industry. Discuss your views for or against diamond mining with your classmates. **(C-7.3)**

Worksheet

One of the most beautiful and innovative applications of fire is the use of fireworks. All over the world, firework displays are held to celebrate important days and festivals. Fireworks need a source of combustible material such as black powder, which is a mixture of charcoal, sulphur and potassium nitrate. This mixture ignites easily on applying a flame to it. For giving bright colourful sparkling light, metals are added which burn with specific colours.

The main varieties of fireworks are discussed below.

- Sparklers are made with a metal wire coated with black powder, iron filings and glue together with some chemicals which help the black powder to reach high temperature. The iron filings burn, sparkle and flash at that high temperature.
- Rockets are made of cardboard tubes filled with black powder, a chemical to raise the temperature and metals to produce the required colours. In rockets, gases are produced, which propel the rocket upwards.

However, with rising levels of pollution, chemicals that cause lesser pollution are being used to make firecrackers. Children are also opting to burn lesser or no crackers to show that they care for the environment.

A. Find out the colour with which the following metals burn and match the colours with the metals.

1. Sodium	(a) Green
2. Barium	(b) Red
3. Strontium	(c) Blue
4. Copper	(d) White
5. Magnesium	(e) Yellow

B. Innovation should not be at the cost of health and environment. What could be the other challenges of innovation in the metal industry? Brainstorm with your friends and write any five points.

5 Combustion and Fossil Fuels

Curricular Goals

- Explore the world of matter and its constituents, properties and behaviour **(CG-1)**
- Explore the nature and processes of science through engaging with the evolution of scientific knowledge and conducting scientific inquiry **(CG-6)**

Competencies

- Classify matter based on observable physical characteristics **(C-1.1)**
- Describe changes in matter and use particulate nature to represent the properties of matter and the changes **(C-1.2)**
- Formulate questions using scientific terminology and collect data as evidence **(C-6.2)**

Let's Get Started

Look at the picture of the candle.

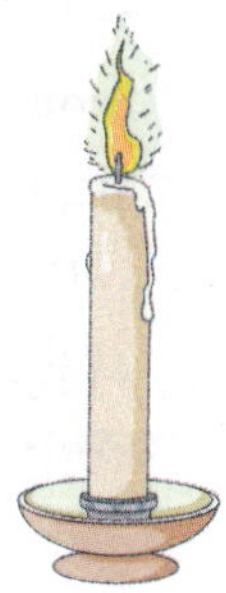

1. Can you name any two substances it produces while burning?

   a. ______________________ b. ______________________

2. What are the similarities and differences between burning of paper and burning of fuels used in our everyday life?

   ____

   ____

3. Do all materials burn with the same intensity?

   ____

   ____

4. What are the conditions required for burning?

   ____

   ____

5. What are the products obtained during burning?

   ____

   ____

In this chapter, let us find out the answers to the above questions and learn in detail about the process of burning and about various types of fuels.

COMBUSTION

Combustion *is a chemical reaction that produces heat and light when a substance burns in the presence of oxygen.*

Substances that undergo the process of combustion (those that catch fire) are called **combustible substances**. Examples are wood, paper (Fig. 5.1), LPG and kerosene.

Fig. 5.1: Combustible substances

Substances that do not undergo the process of combustion (those that do not catch fire even in the presence of oxygen) are called **non-combustible substances**. Examples are water, stone and glass.

Activity 1

Note: *This activity needs to be performed as a teacher demonstration.*

Aim: To prove that some substances are combustible and some are not

Materials required: Paper, spirit (methyl alcohol), water, sand, spatula, deflagrating spoons, Bunsen burner, matchbox or lighter and forceps or a pair of tongs

Procedure:

1. Light a Bunsen burner with a lighter or matchstick.
2. Using a pair of tongs or forceps, hold a piece of paper well above the flame for about a minute.
3. Take one spatula of sand in a deflagrating spoon. Heat it over a Bunsen burner flame for about a minute.
4. Take about 5 mℓ of spirit (methyl alcohol) and 5 mℓ of water separately in a deflagrating spoon. Heat each of them separately over a Bunsen burner flame for about a minute.
5. Observe the changes in each of the substances while heating and record your observations in the following table.

Observation:

S. No	Type of substance	Does the substance burn? (Yes/No)	Combustible/Non-combustible
1.	Paper		
2.	Spirit		
3.	Water		
4.	Sand		

Conclusion: Paper and spirit are combustible, whereas water and sand are not.

Types of Combustion

Spontaneous combustion: The type of combustion in which substances burst into flames without the application of heat is called **spontaneous combustion**. Examples: Burning of phosphorous used in the making of matchsticks. Therefore, phosphorous is stored under water in the laboratory to prevent its exposure to atmospheric oxygen.

Complete combustion: The type of combustion that takes place in a sufficient amount of oxygen (air) is called **complete combustion**. The products obtained during complete combustion are water, carbon dioxide, heat and light.

Incomplete combustion: The type of combustion that takes place in an insufficient amount of oxygen (air) is called **incomplete combustion**. The products obtained during incomplete combustion are soot, water, carbon monoxide, heat and light.

Science in Context

White Phosphorus

For matchsticks, the less active red Phosphorus is used because if there is spontaneous combustion, then matchsticks cannot be stored. White phosphorus is the more active form that catches fire on exposure to air.

Activity 2

Note: *This activity needs to be performed carefully in the presence and with the assistance of a teacher.*

Aim: To differentiate between complete and incomplete combustions

Materials required: Bunsen burner, matchsticks or lighter, small pieces of wood and a pair of tongs

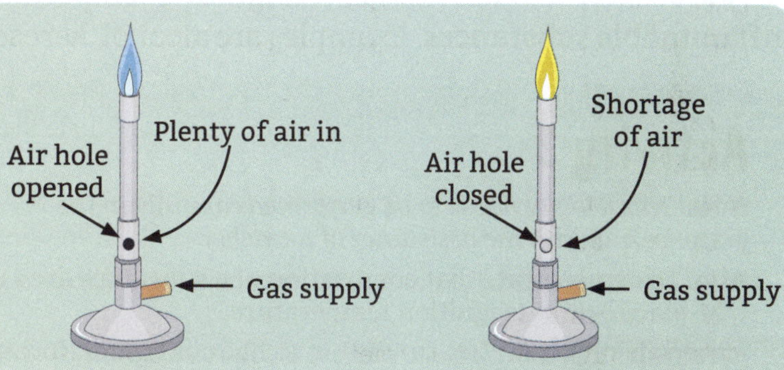

Colour of the flame when collar is open

Colour of the flame when collar is closed

Procedure:

1. Light a Bunsen burner with a lighter or a matchstick.
2. Open the regulating collar (air hole).
3. Observe the colour of the flame.
4. Using a pair of tongs, hold a piece of wood well above the flame for 5–10 seconds. What do you observe?
5. Now, close the regulating collar (air hole) and observe the change in the colour of the flame.
6. Repeat the process of holding the piece of wood above the flame.

Observation:

S. No.	Observation	When the regulating collar is open	When the regulating collar is closed
1.	Colour of the flame		
2.	Residue formation		

Conclusion:

When the regulating collar is closed, there is insufficient amount of air or oxygen available, resulting in incomplete combustion and the formation of soot.

When the regulating collar is open, there is a sufficient amount of oxygen available, resulting in complete combustion and no soot.

Conditions Necessary for Combustion

The following conditions are essential for combustion to take place:

Presence of combustible substances: Combustion takes place only if a combustible substance is present. For example, wood, paper and kerosene are combustible substances.

Presence of oxygen (supporter of combustion): The process of combustion will take place only in the presence of oxygen.

Reaching ignition temperature: Combustible substances must reach a specific temperature before they start burning. *The lowest or minimum temperature at which a combustible substance starts burning, in the presence of air, is called* ***ignition temperature***. The ignition temperature of white phosphorous is 30–35°C and that of wood is 250–300°C.

The substances that have a very low ignition temperature and catch fire easily are called **inflammable substances**. Examples are alcohol, kerosene, LPG, nylon fibres and petrol.

Activity 3

Note: *This activity needs to be performed carefully in the presence and with the assistance of a teacher.*

Aim: To demonstrate that combustion of a substance does not take place below its ignition temperature

Materials required: Two candles, matchbox or lighter, forceps or a pair of tongs, wet filter paper and dry filter paper

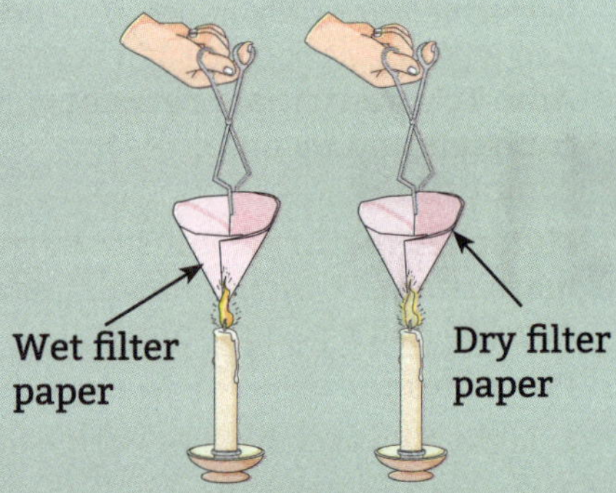

Heating

Procedure:

1. Make two paper funnels, one with the dry filter paper and another with the wet filter paper.
2. Light two candles and place them on a table.
3. Hold the filter papers with forceps/a pair of tongs and heat them over the candle flames one by one.

Observation:

S. No.	Wet filter paper	Dry filter paper

Conclusion:

In the first case, the heat supplied to the wet filter paper funnel is transferred to the moisture. So, the temperature of the paper is not raised by heating. Hence, the paper does not reach its ignition temperature, even though it is held above the candle flame. The paper starts burning only after the moisture from the wet filter paper evaporates completely.

In the second case, the heat provided by the candle raises the temperature of the dry filter paper and when the paper reaches its ignition temperature, it starts burning.

Extinguishing Fire

Fire can be extinguished by controlling any one of the conditions necessary for combustion.

Water, being non-combustible, decreases the ignition temperature of the burning material by absorbing the heat generated by fire, thus lowering the temperature. However, water cannot be used to put out all kinds of fires. For example, it cannot be used to extinguish electrical fires as water is a good conductor of electricity. Water is also not used to put out the fires caused by petrol, kerosene or diesel as they are lighter than water and will not mix but float on water. In such cases, carbon dioxide (CO_2) fire extinguishers are used.

Fig. 5.2: Fire symbol

Carbon dioxide is used in fire extinguishers as it is not a combustible substance and can put off fire. Since it is heavier than air, it restricts the supply of oxygen by forming a layer between the fuel and oxygen. Carbon dioxide fire extinguishers are widely used as they do not damage any electrical equipment. The two commonly used types of fire extinguishers are carbon dioxide and soda–acid fire extinguishers.

Carbon dioxide fire extinguishers (Fig. 5.3) contain carbon dioxide filled under high pressure in cylinders. These fire extinguishers cool down the combustible substance besides cutting off the air supply.

Fig. 5.3: Carbon dioxide fire extinguisher

Soda–acid fire extinguishers (Fig. 5.4) are generally filled with concentrated solutions of sulphuric acid (H_2SO_4) and sodium hydrogen carbonate ($NaHCO_3$). The two solutions mix together and form carbon dioxide that helps in extinguishing fire.

Sand is also used to extinguish fire as it cuts off the oxygen supply for burning by forming a blanket over the burning substance.

Fig. 5.4: Soda–acid fire extinguisher

Activity 4

Note: *This activity needs to be performed as a teacher demonstration.*

Aim: To show whether sand and water can be used as fire extinguishers

Materials required: Sand, papers, enamel tray, matchbox and water in a container

Procedure:

1. Place a few crumpled pieces of paper in the enamel tray and light them with a matchstick.
2. Throw a handful of sand on the burning paper, continue adding sand till the fire stops.
3. Repeat Step 1 and pour water on the burning paper instead of putting sand.

Observation: Fire extinguishes with both sand and water.

Conclusion: Both sand and water can be used to extinguish fires.

FLAME

Flame is the visible gaseous part of a fire.

The colour of the flame (Fig. 5.5) depends on the following parameters:

- Nature of the substance that is burning
- Amount of air (oxygen) available
- Temperature

A blue flame is also called a **non-luminous flame** as complete combustion takes place in this zone, thus, emitting very little light. This occurs when the availability of oxygen is more.

A yellow flame is also called a **luminous flame** as incomplete combustion takes place in this zone. This occurs when the availability of oxygen is very less.

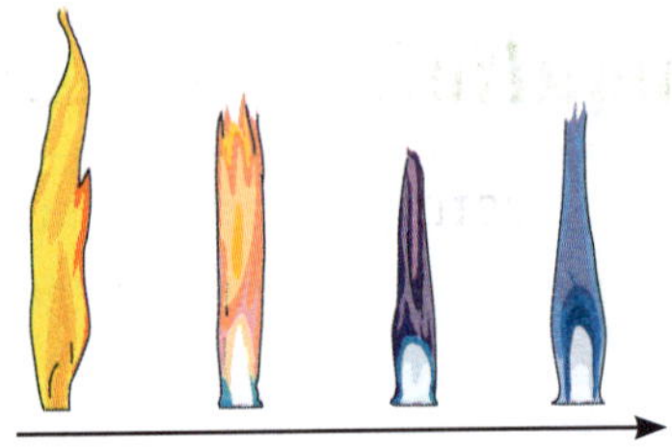

Fig. 5.5: Variation in the colour of the flame of a Bunsen burner with the increase in oxygen supply

Wonder!

Abraham Gesner's 'Kerosene Gaslight Company' was the first to produce wick lamps in 1850 and they replaced the Argand lamp, which had been in widespread use for 70 years. Argand lamp is a type of oil lamp with many wicks.

Structure of a Candle Flame

Depending on the amount of oxygen available, the structure of a candle flame (Fig. 5.6) can be divided into four different zones: outer zone, middle zone, inner zone and blue zone.

The outer zone (non-luminous zone): It is considered as the hottest part of the flame. It is the zone where complete combustion takes place due to the availability of the required amount of oxygen.

The middle zone (yellow or luminous zone): It is a moderately less hot zone than the outer zone. Here, incomplete combustion takes place as the wax particles do not get adequate amount of oxygen supply, resulting in the formation of unburnt carbon particles that glow with a yellow light.

Fig. 5.6: Structure of a candle flame

The inner zone (black or dark zone): It is the innermost and the coolest part of the flame. In this zone, as there is no supply of oxygen, the wax vapours remain unburnt. This zone does not emit any light and is dark in colour. It covers the unburnt vapours produced when the wax around the wick melts.

Blue zone: It is located at the base of the wick. The burning of carbon monoxide gives it a blue colour.

Combustion of a Wax Candle

A candle is composed of two main parts: the paraffin wax that acts as a fuel and the wick that can absorb water or molten wax.

When you observe a candle, you may notice that the wick is burning, but actually the wax vapours also burn along with the wick.

Neither solid wax nor liquid wax will burn. It is only the wax vapours that burn. When we light a candle wick, the heat released from the flame melts the wax in and around the wick. The wick absorbs the molten wax and the heat produced from the flame vaporizes the molten wax in the wick. The wax vapours then burn in the flame. (This is how we are get scented candles. Fragrant materials are added to the wax during the production of the candle.) This process continues until the entire candle is extinguished.

Know the Scientist

Van Helmont

The earliest scientific attempt to explain combustion was made by 'Johann Baptista van Helmont', a Flemish physician and alchemist. He observed the relationship between a burning material, the resulting smoke and the flame it produced.

Activity 5

Aim: To prove that the middle zone of a flame consists of unburnt carbon particles

Materials required: Candle, glass slide and a pair of tongs

Procedure:

1. Hold the glass slide with a pair of tongs and introduce it in the middle zone of the candle flame.
2. Hold it for 10 seconds and observe.

Observation: A black-coloured patch forms on the glass slide. The black colour is due to the formation of unburnt carbon particles as a result of incomplete combustion.

Revise and Recall

State whether the following statements are true (T) or false (F).

1. Substances start burning below their ignition temperature. ☐
2. Burning white phosphorus is an example of complete combustion. ☐
3. A blue flame is a luminous flame. ☐
4. Complete combustion occurs in the outer zone of a flame. ☐
5. There is no flame produced during spontaneous combustion. ☐
6. Inflammable substances have a very low ignition temperature. ☐

FUEL

*Substances that burn to produce energy in the form of heat and light are called **fuels**.* Wood, charcoal, kerosene, cow dung cakes, LPG and petrol are some of the commonly used fuels for producing heat energy.

On the basis of their physical state, fuels are classified into three types: solid fuels, liquid fuels and gaseous fuels.

Solid Fuels

These are the fuels that exist in the solid state at room temperature.

Examples: Coal, wood, dung cakes and agricultural waste

Liquid Fuels

These are the fuels that exist in the liquid state at room temperature.

Examples: Petrol, diesel, kerosene, LPG and fuel oils

Gaseous Fuels

These are the fuels that exist in the gaseous state at room temperature.

Examples: Biogas, coal gas, petroleum gas and natural gas

*The amount of heat energy released when one gram of a fuel is completely burnt is called the **calorific value** of that fuel.* The heat released is measured in kilojoules (kJ). The unit for calorific value is kilojoule/kilogram (kJ/kg). If the calorific value of a fuel (Table 5.1) is high, then it is an efficient fuel, which means it releases more heat.

Table 5.1: Calorific value of some fuels

Fuel	Calorific value (kJ/kg)	Fuel	Calorific value (kJ/kg)
Petrol	44000–46000	Cow dung	6000–8000
Diesel	42000–46000	Wood	17000–22000
Kerosene	43000–46000	Coal	14000–33000
Methane	50000–55000	Alcohol	22700–29000
CNG	50000	Biogas	20000–26000
LPG	46000–51000	Hydrogen gas	120000–142000

Characteristics of a Good Fuel

A good fuel should have the following characteristics:

- low ignition temperature (but well above the room temperature)
- moderate rate of combustion
- easily available
- no residue after burning
- high calorific value
- pollution free
- inexpensive
- safe to handle, store and transport

Commonly used fuels:

- LPG and methane (natural gas) are widely used as domestic fuels. They do not lead to any pollution.
- Diesel and petrol are widely used in automobiles, but their availability is very less and they also lead to atmospheric pollution.

Hydrogen as a fuel: Hydrogen has the highest calorific value but it is not considered as the best fuel because it is highly inflammable and difficult to handle, transport and store. It is used as a rocket fuel.

NATURAL RESOURCES

Natural resources are the materials or substances that exist naturally on Earth and are helpful to humans in various purposes. These resources are essential for the survival, development, and to meet human needs. They can be found in the air, water, and land, and they play a crucial role in supporting life on Earth.

Natural resources are classified into two main categories:

- **Renewable resources:** These are the resources that can be replenished or naturally regenerated within a relatively short period of time. Examples include sunlight, wind, water, forest and biomass[1]. Renewable resources are vital for sustaining ecosystems and provide us with energy, food and other essential materials.
- **Non-renewable resources:** These resources exist in limited quantities and take millions of years to form. Once they are depleted, they cannot be readily replenished within a human lifetime. Examples of non-renewable resources include fossil fuels (coal, oil, natural gas), minerals (iron, copper, gold) and precious stones (diamonds, rubies). It is important to manage and use non-renewable resources judiciously to ensure their sustainable use and to explore alternative sources of energy and materials.

Word Web

[1]**biomass:** The total mass of living things in a particular area

Natural resources provide food, water and shelter for humans and other animals. They can be used to produce goods and services such as clothing, furniture, and transportation and to generate energy, which is needed for everything from powering our homes and businesses to running our vehicles.

FOSSIL FUELS

Fossil fuels are formed from the buried remains of animals and plants (organic matter) over a long period of time, about millions of years (Fig. 5.7).

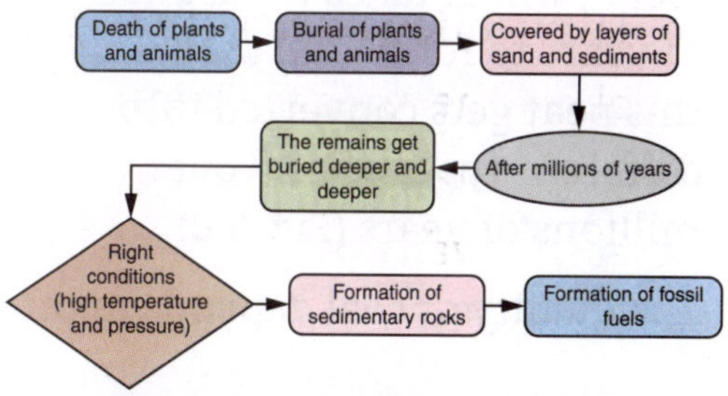

Fig. 5.7: Formation of fossil fuels

These are also called **natural resources** as they are obtained from the nature. Petroleum, coal and natural gas are examples of fossil fuels.

Coal

Coal is a black, hard fossil fuel. The slow chemical process of the conversion of organic matter into coal is called **carbonization**. There are different varieties of coal based on their carbon content.

Anthracite: Anthracite has the highest percentage of carbon content (around 92–96%). It is widely used as a domestic fuel because it burns without giving out much smoke. It is regarded as the best variety of coal.

Bituminous: Bituminous is a type of coal that contains approximately 65–80% of carbon. It is widely used in power generation.

Sub-bituminous: Sub-bituminous is a type of coal that contains approximately 30–35% of carbon. Even though sub-bituminous has a lower heat value, it is widely used because it burns without giving out much smoke.

Lignite: Lignite contains a very low amount of carbon (around 25–35%) and came into existence in very recent periods. It is used in power generation and is the lowest grade of coal.

Peat: Peat is the material formed early in the carbonization process. It consists of partly decayed matter and deposited minerals. Peat is formed in wetlands. It has a low carbon content and a high moisture content. Hence, it has a low heating capacity.

Formation of coal

The remains of dead plants get deposited deep inside the Earth over a period of millions of years. The high pressure combined with heat from the Earth's interior surface transforms this organic matter. First, the organic matter gets converted into 'peat', which takes thousands of years to form, and then, this peat gets converted into different types of coal over millions of years (Fig. 5.8).

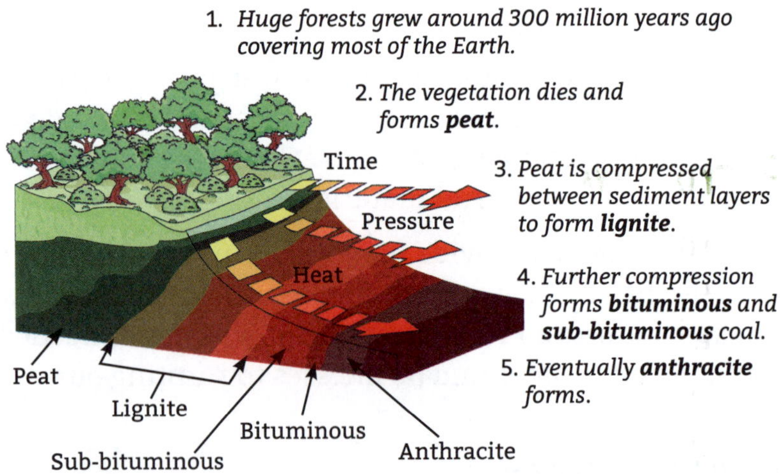

Fig. 5.8: Formation of coal

The quality of coal depends upon the time, pressure and temperature.

Uses of coal

Coal has many significant uses. It was used extensively in the beginning of the industrial revolution. Nowadays, it is used widely in power generation, production of steel, extraction of ores and manufacturing of cement.

The five largest coal users in the world are China, USA, India, Russia and Japan, accounting for nearly 80% of the global coal usage (Fig. 5.9).

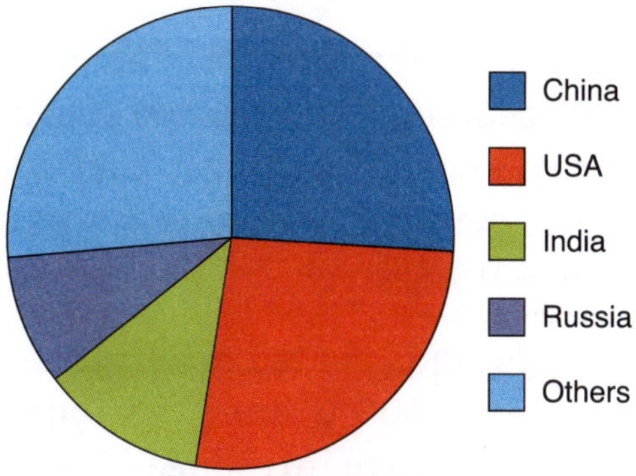

Fig. 5.9: Global coal usage

Products obtained from coal

Coal is processed in industries to obtain various products such as coke, coal tar and coal gas.

Coke: Coke is a tough, porous and grey-coloured substance obtained from bituminous coal. It was first used by Chinese iron workers in the ninth century. It is a high-temperature fuel and was later used as a major source of energy. It is used in the extraction of metals and the manufacturing of steel.

Coal tar: Coal tar is a black or brown liquid with an unpleasant smell. It is obtained as a byproduct when coal is used to make coke. It is used in explosives, perfumes, drugs, roofing materials and synthetic dyes.

Coal gas: Coal gas is also a byproduct formed during the processing of coal to get coke. During the 18th and 19th centuries, coal gas, also known as town gas, gained popularity as a flammable gas produced by heating coal in the absence of air. It was widely used as a fuel for stoves and fireplaces. Nevertheless, with the passage of time, the environmental drawbacks associated with coal gas became increasingly evident and it was eventually replaced by electricity as a cleaner alternative.

Petroleum

Crude oil or petroleum is normally found trapped in underground rocks (*petra* means rock and *oleum* means oil). It is widely used as a fuel.

Formation of Petroleum and Natural Gas

Petroleum and natural gas are formed over millions of years from the remains of organisms that lived in the sea during that time. As these organisms die, their bodies settle at the bottom of the seabed and get covered with layers of sand and clay. Under high temperature, pressure and the absence of air for over millions of years, these remains get transformed into petroleum and natural gas.

Refining of Petroleum

Petroleum is a mixture of solid, liquid and gaseous hydrocarbons. The process of separating these various constituents into useful substances is called **refining**. It is done in a petroleum refinery (Fig. 5.10).

Fig. 5.10: A petroleum refinery

> **Science in Context**
> Petroleum is also called 'black gold' because many useful substances are obtained from it.

Petroleum is heated to a high temperature of around 400°C, and the vapours that are formed are introduced into a tall, cylindrical tower called a *'fractionating column or fractionating tower'*, which contains horizontal trays. The vapours form inside the fractionating column cool and condense at various heights and get collected in different trays. Condensation of the substances depends on their boiling points. The uncondensed hydrocarbons are released from the column.

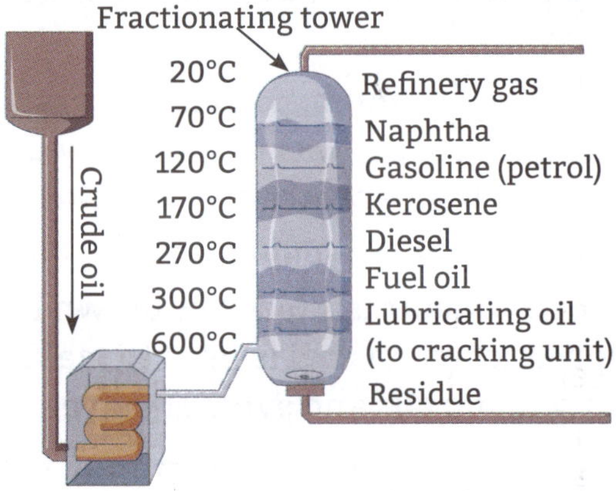

Fig. 5.11: Refining (fractional distillation) of petroleum

The various components with different boiling points are called **fractions**. Therefore, the refining process is also called **fractional distillation** (Fig. 5.11). The constituents of petroleum and their uses are given in Table 5.2.

Table 5.2: Constituents of petroleum and their uses

Products obtained from petroleum	Uses
Petroleum gas	As a fuel in liquified form (LPG) for domestic use and in industries
Petrol	As a fuel in automobiles, aviation fuel and in dry cleaning
Kerosene	As a fuel for lamps, stoves and in jet engines
Diesel	As a fuel for generators and heavy motor vehicles
Fuel oil	As a fuel for ships and power stations
Lubricating oil	In lubrication of machinery
Paraffin wax	In ointments, vaseline and candles
Bitumen (Asphalt)	In paints and building roads

Natural Gas

Large deposits of natural gas are available along with petroleum in reservoirs under the ground. The main constituent of natural gas is methane. It is useful in many ways as given below:

- It is easy for transportation through pipes.
- Compressed natural gas (CNG) is used as a fuel in automobiles.
- It is used in the generation of electricity.
- It is a clean and environment-friendly fuel as it does not emit much harmful gases on combustion.
- It is used in the manufacture of fertilizers and other chemicals.
- It is used in the production of ammonia and hydrogen.

Science in Context

CNG is supplied to homes and factories through pipes and directly used as a fuel in some parts of India. Example: Vadodara (Gujarat) and some parts of Delhi

Limitations of Fossil Fuels

The main limitations of fossil fuels are their limited availability and the air pollution caused by their use.

Limited supply: Fossil fuels need millions of years to form and if we do not manage them properly, all these natural resources will be exhausted soon.

Cause of air pollution: The use of fossil fuels releases many pollutants into the atmosphere. Some of the common air pollutants and their harmful effects are given in Table 5.3.

Table 5.3: Adverse effects of pollutants

Pollutants	Produced during	Adverse effects
Carbon monoxide	Incomplete combustion of fossil fuels	A harmful pollutant that causes dizziness, headache and may lead to coma and death
Carbon dioxide	More combustion of fossil fuels	Main cause for greenhouse effect and global warming
Suspended particulate matter (SPM)	Burning of fuels that contain carbon compounds releases fine particles of unburnt carbon atoms	A dangerous pollutant that leads to respiratory problems
Sulphur dioxide and oxides of nitrogen	Burning of coal, diesel and from the exhausts of vehicle engines	Main cause for acid rains and affects buildings, crops and soil
Soot particles	Incomplete combustion of fossil fuels and wood	Leads to asthma and other respiratory problems

Conservation of Fossil Fuels

Fossil fuels can be conserved in the following ways:

- Usage of alternative sources of energy such as solar energy and wind energy
- Judicious use of the existing resources
- Avoid plastics made from petroleum byproducts
- Usage of public transport such as trains and buses
- Usage of natural fibres such as cotton instead of nylon
- Usage of fuel-efficient vehicles
- Usage of biogas produced from garbage, cattle dung and waste materials

Go Green

Replace the usage of fossil fuels with bio-fuels and CNG to prevent pollution and conserve fossil fuels.

Try to switch off your vehicle engines at traffic lights or at places where you have to wait.

IMPACT OF FOSSIL FUELS ON ENVIRONMENT

Fossil fuels, although a significant energy source worldwide, have a significant impact on the environment. Some of the environmental impacts of fossil fuels are as follows:

- **Climate change:** Fossil fuel combustion releases greenhouse gases such as carbon dioxide, which trap heat in the atmosphere, leading to global warming and climate change. This results in adverse effects such as rising sea levels, altered weather patterns and ecological disruptions.
- **Air pollution:** Burning fossil fuels releases pollutants into the air such as nitrogen oxides, sulphur dioxide, etc. These pollutants can cause respiratory problems, heart disease and cancer.
- **Water pollution:** Fossil fuel extraction and transportation can contaminate water supplies with chemicals, heavy metals, and other pollutants. This can lead to health problems for people who drink the contaminated water, and it can also harm fish and other aquatic life and wildlife.
- **Ecosystem damage:** Fossil fuel extraction and use can damage ecosystems in a number of ways. For example, mining for coal can pollute streams and rivers, and oil spills can contaminate beaches and wetlands. These disruptions can harm plants and animals, and they can also make it difficult for people to live and work in these areas.
- **Resource depletion:** Fossil fuels are non-renewable resources, meaning they are finite and will eventually be depleted. Overreliance on these resources can lead to energy insecurity and economic challenges in the long term.

The environmental impacts of fossil fuels require transitioning to cleaner and more sustainable alternatives. This involves supporting renewable energy sources such as solar and wind power, improving energy efficiency, and advocating for policies that promote clean energy and reduce greenhouse gas emissions.

Keywords

Combustion: A chemical reaction that produces heat and light when a substance burns in the presence of oxygen

Combustible substances: Substances that undergo the process of combustion

Non-combustible substances: Substances that do not undergo the process of combustion

Ignition temperature: The lowest or minimum temperature at which a combustible substance starts burning in the presence of air

Inflammable substances: The substances that have a very low ignition temperature and catch fire easily

Calorific value: The amount of heat energy released when one gram of a fuel is completely burnt

Fossil fuels: The fuels formed from the buried remains of animals and plants over a long period of time

Refining: The process of separating various constituents of petroleum into useful substances

Summary

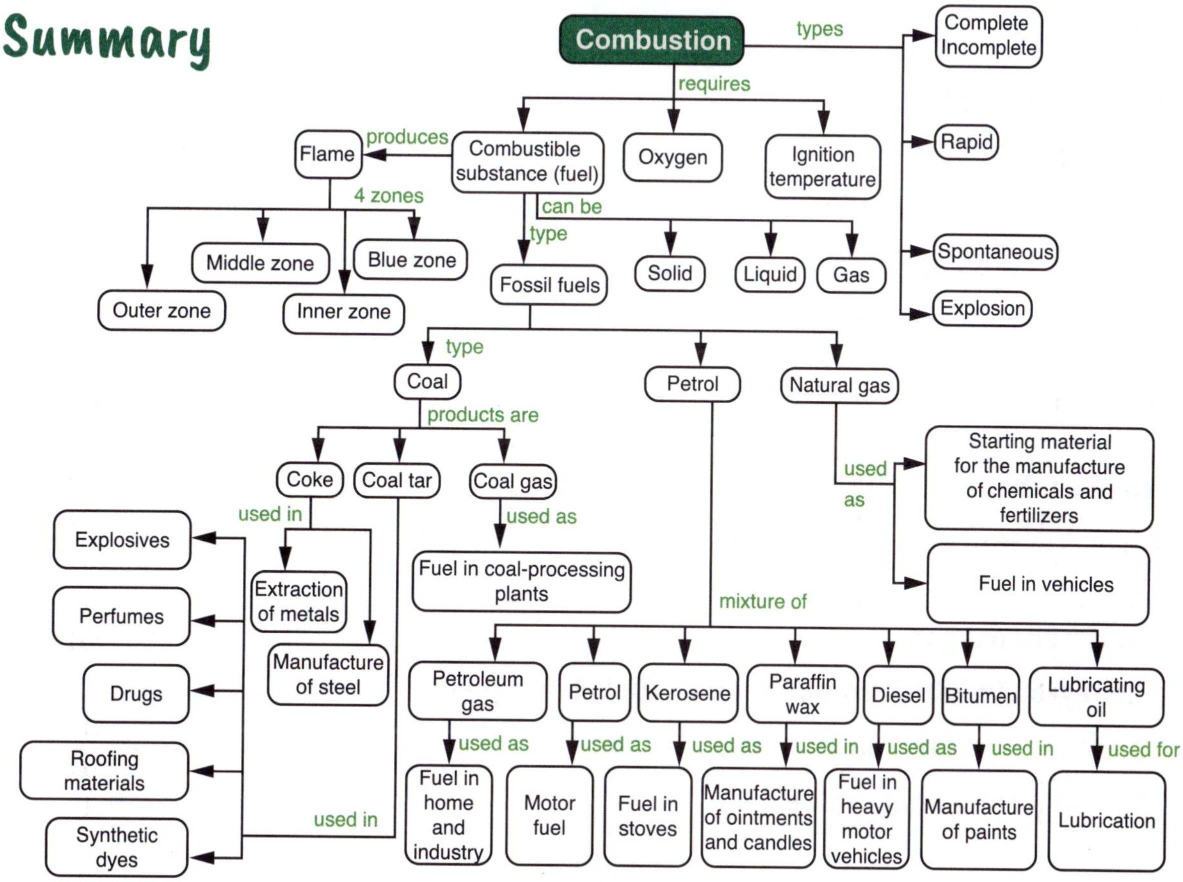

Exercise

W

ia

A. Choose the correct option.

1. Which of the following can be used to extinguish a fire involving petroleum products?
   (a) Water (b) Sand (c) Carbon dioxide (d) Sulphur powder
2. A luminous flame is __________ in colour.
   (a) red (b) yellow (c) blue (d) green
3. Identify the characteristics of a good fuel from the following.
   (a) High ignition temperature (b) High pollution
   (c) High calorific value (d) Both (a) and (c)
4. Identify the petroleum product that is used in ointments.
   (a) Lubricating oil (b) Bitumen
   (c) Paraffin wax (d) Petrol
5. Which of the following products is not obtained during complete combustion?
   (a) Water (b) Carbon dioxide (c) Heat (d) Carbon monoxide

ia

B. Fill in the blanks.

1. Coal and wood are examples of ________________. (solid fuels/liquid fuels)
2. A blue flame is also called ________________ flame. (luminous/non-luminous)
3. Glass and sand are ________________. (non-combustible/combustible)
4. Anthracite is a type of ________________. (petroleum/coal)
5. Refining of petroleum is done by ________________. (fractional distillation/rapid combustion)

C. Answer the following in one word each.

1. An example of combustible substance ________________
2. The type of combustion that takes place in a sufficient amount of oxygen ________________
3. The region in which combustion of fuels takes place ________________
4. The innermost and coolest part of the flame ________________
5. The unit for calorific value ________________

D. Give reasons for the following.

1. Biomass is different from biogas.
2. Our body also undergoes the process of combustion.
3. Combustion lead to global warming and acid rain.
4. Usage of water to extinguish all types of fire is not advisable.
5. The middle zone of a candle is called yellow zone.

E. Answer the following questions briefly.

1. Just by observation, how can you differentiate between incomplete and complete combustion?
2. What are the conditions necessary for combustion?
3. What is a fuel? Name its three types with examples.
4. How are coke, coal tar and coal gas different from each other?
5. What are the limitations of fossil fuels?
6. Write any two ways to conserve fossil fuels.

F. Answer the following questions in detail.

1. Explain the structure of a candle flame with the help of a labelled diagram.
2. What are the characteristics of a good fuel? Why is hydrogen not considered as the best fuel?
3. Draw a flowchart describing the process of the formation of fossil fuels.
4. What is fractional distillation? Explain.
5. Name any five air pollutants. Also, mention the harmful effects of each pollutant.
6. How can promoting sustainable utilization of natural resources, both exhaustible and inexhaustible, ensure long-term environmental benefits?

Cognitive Corner

Critical Thinking

1. During a fire accident, when you are not supported with any fire extinguisher, it is advisable to evacuate the building and close the doors and windows. Why do you think we should close the doors and windows?
2. In today's world, electric vehicles (EVs) are becoming popular. When you compare EVs to regular cars that run on diesel or petrol, how can you figure out which one is a better choice, taking into account factors such as their cost, how far they can travel and their impact on the environment?

Picture Study

In a city, three buildings—Building A, Building B and Building C—have caught fire. The materials present in these buildings are listed in the table given below. Which fire extinguisher can be used in each building?

Fire extinguishers available: Water extinguishers and carbon dioxide extinguishers

Building A	Building B	Building C
• Paper • Wood • Cloth • Non-metals	• Petrol • Kerosene • Oil paint • Other flammable materials	• Electrical equipment • Laboratory materials

Building A: ____________________

Building B: ____________________

Building C: ____________________

Project

As a part of Eco Club, take a survey in your street and your relatives' houses. Find out the percentages of houses that use LPG, wood and kerosene as fuel, and find out whether the consumption of these fuels has increased or decreased over the last 10 years.

Plot graphs to indicate the results of your survey. Prepare a report based on your findings and discuss it in your class. **(C-7.1)**

In the Library

Collect information from library books about the 'history of matchstick'. Discuss with your teacher and give a brief presentation on this topic in your class. **(C-7.1)**

Life Skills

Find out the contact numbers of the fire service. If you come across any fire breaking out in your home or near your surroundings, the first thing to do is to call the fire service.

1. List the various precautions to be taken against fire accidents.
2. List the different ways to reduce the negative effects of combustion.
3. List the merits and demerits of different fuels on a chart. **(C-7.3)**

Worksheet

Coal was first mined in India in 1774 by the East India Company in Ranuganj, West Bengal along the banks of the Damodar River. Its demand greatly increased after the introduction of steam locomotives. India now produces about 18 million kilograms of coal every year. Most of the coal produced is used in the iron and steel industries and production of electricity in thermal power plants.

Coal can be mined by both surface and underground methods. Surface mining or open cast method of mining is carried out when the deposits are closer to the surface. The underground method is suitable when coal is found deeper under the ground.

A miner working at a coal mine

In this industry, the miners face many health hazards from dust, gas, noise, vibration, and in rare cases, collapse of underground mines.

Pollution of both surface water and groundwater by chemicals released during coal mining are the main environmental concerns. Abandoned and active mines ruin huge areas of the countryside. In open cast mining, waste resources are usually stacked as huge dumps in the surroundings, creating an ugly sight.

A. Are you in favour of the continuation of coal mining practice or against it? Choose a side and write about five sentences supporting your choice.

B. Do you think the coal miners have a decent work environment? How can one ensure sustainable growth and development while providing decent work environment to the people employed in coal mining? Share a few of your ideas.

6 Cell: Structure and Function

Curricular Goals

- Explore the living world in scientific terms **(CG-3)**
- Understand the interface of science, technology and society **(CG-5)**

Competencies

- Describe the diversity of living things observed in the natural surroundings, including at a smaller scale **(C-3.1)**
- Explain the conditions suitable for sustaining life on earth **(C-3.4)**
- Illustrate how science and technology can help to improve the quality of human life as well as some of the harmful uses of science in history **(C-5.1)**

Let's Get Started

We know that a group of cells make a tissue, a group of tissues performing the same function make an organ and many organs functioning together make an organ system. Many such organ systems constitute a living organism.

Look at the pictures given below and number them (from 1 to 4) based on the level of organization (moving in order from simple to complex).

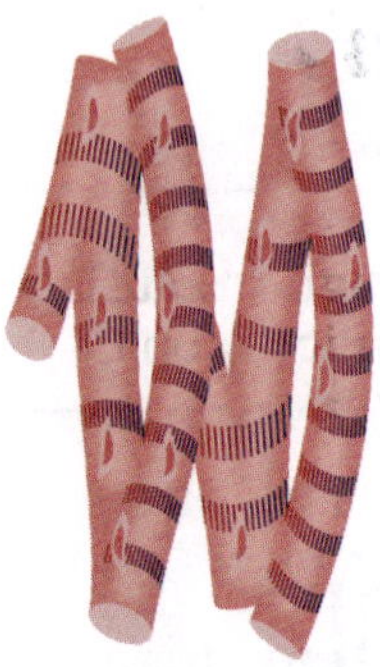

Cardiac muscle ◯

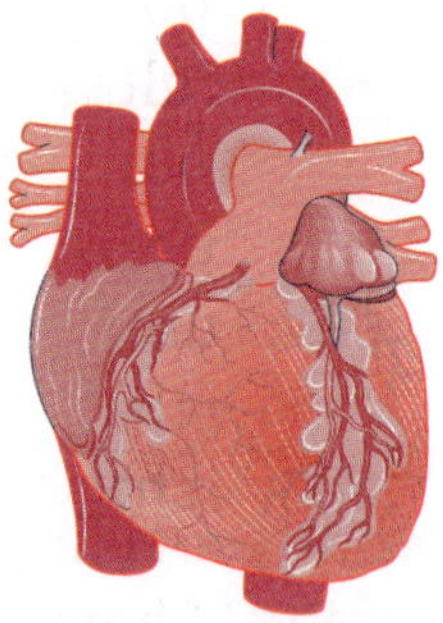

Heart ◯

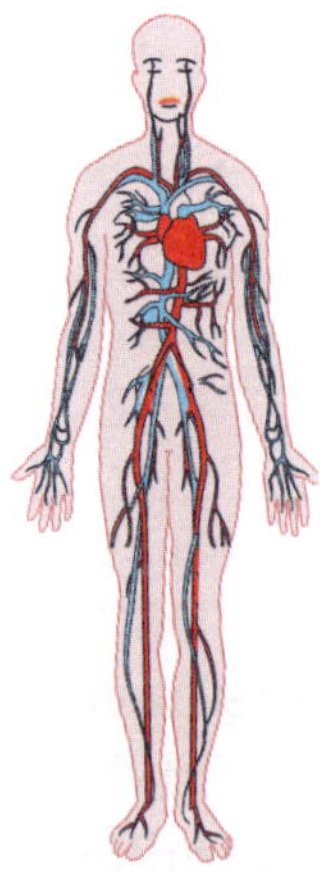

Circulatory system ◯

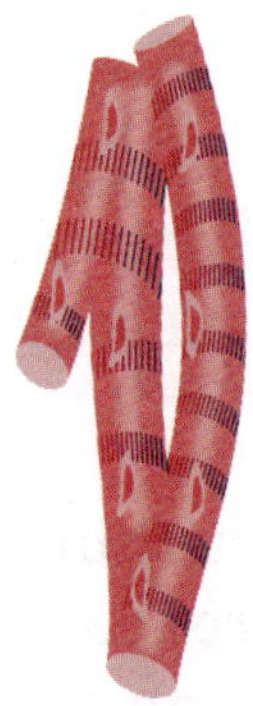

Cardiac muscle cell ◯

CELL AS A BASIC UNIT OF LIFE

The cell is universally recognized as the fundamental unit of life. It serves as the smallest structural and functional component within an organism, responsible for carrying out the essential processes of life. Just as a brick forms the building blocks of a structure, cells are the building blocks of living organisms. Similar to bricks that contribute to the stability and structure of a building, cells possess specific properties and functions that collectively enable the proper functioning of an organism. The human body is made up of trillions of cells, each with its own specialized function. In this chapter, we will learn about the structure of cells and their functions.

DISCOVERY OF CELLS

In 1665, an English scientist named Robert Hooke observed a thin slice of cork (Fig. 6.1) under his basic microscope [Fig. 6.2(a)]. He noticed tiny empty spaces enclosed by walls. He saw that they looked like compartments and named them **cells**.

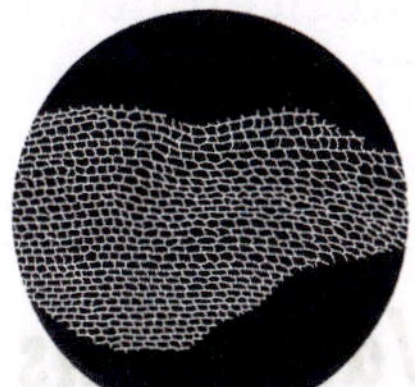

Fig. 6.1: Cork cells observed by Hooke

In 1670, a Dutchman named Antonie Van Leeuwenhoek observed and described the cells in a drop of pond water using a microscope.

In 1838, a German botanist, Matthias Jakob Schleiden, declared that 'the cell is the basic building block of all plant material'.

Theodor Schwann, a German biologist, declared that animal tissues are made up of 'cells' and finally concluded that 'cell is the basic unit of life.'

Scientists observe and study living cells using high-resolution microscopes (Fig. 6.2) as they magnify objects that are difficult to observe through the naked eye. Stains (**dyes**) are used to colour the cells, which helps in getting a detailed look at the structure of the cells (you have learned in Chapter 2 that stains are also used in viewing microorganisms). From such studies, we now know that different living organisms may have a variation in cell size, shape and number.

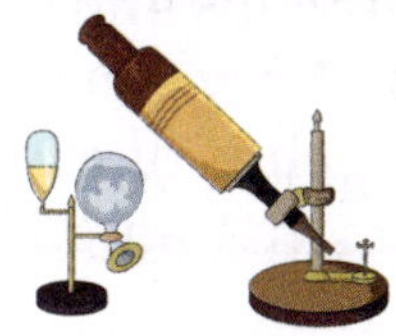

(a) Hooke's microscope

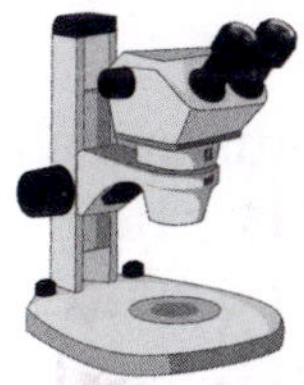

(b) High-resolution microscope

Fig. 6.2: Microscopes

Wonder!

A human body is made up of more than 37 trillion (37,00,000 crores) cells.

DIVERSITY IN CELLS

Cells exhibit remarkable diversity in terms of their number, shape and size. This diversity is crucial for the proper functioning and survival of organisms. Understanding the differences in cell number, shape and size helps us understand how cells work and contribute to the proper functioning of living organisms.

Variations in Cell Number

Living organisms may be made up of a single cell or many cells. *An organism made up of a single cell is called a* ***unicellular*** *organism* ('uni' means 'single' and 'cellular' means 'celled'). Examples of unicellular organisms are *Amoeba* [Fig. 6.3(a)], *Paramoecium, Euglena*, yeast and bacteria. In a unicellular organism, a single cell performs all life functions including feeding, movement, respiration and reproduction.

An organism made up of many cells is called a ***multicellular*** *organism* ('multi' means 'many'). Examples of multicellular organisms are plants [Fig. 6.3(b)] and animals including human beings.

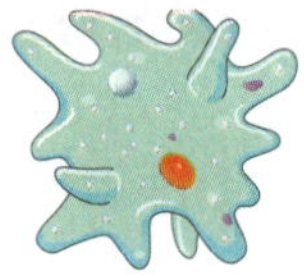

(a) Unicellular organism: *Amoeba*

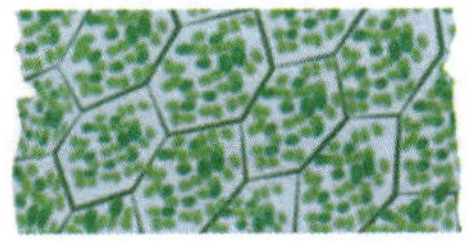

(b) Multicellular organism: Plant (cells in the leaf of a plant)

Fig. 6.3: Unicellular and multicellular organisms

Variations in Cell Shape and Size

Cells become specialized to perform specific functions and exist in different shapes (Fig. 6.4). They can be disc-shaped, polygonal, branched or even without any fixed shape as seen in *Amoeba*.

- Nerve cells are elongated as they need to carry messages to different parts of the body.
- Muscle cells are cylindrical and branched. They help in movement by contracting and relaxing.
- Skin cells are flat in shape to produce a large surface area for covering the body for protection.
- White blood cells (WBC) can change their shape to help in destroying the germs present in the body.

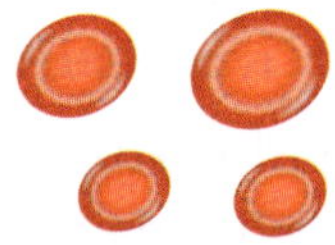

(a) Red blood cells

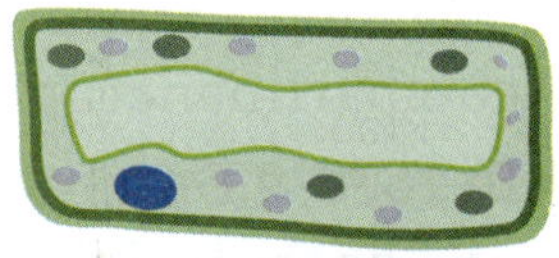

(b) Leaf cell

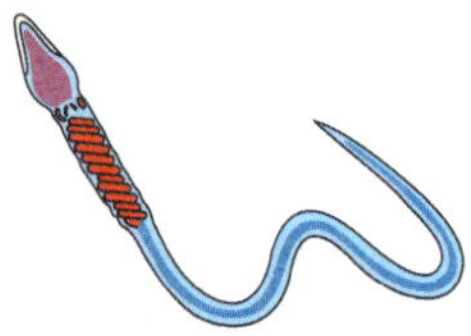

(c) Human sperm cell

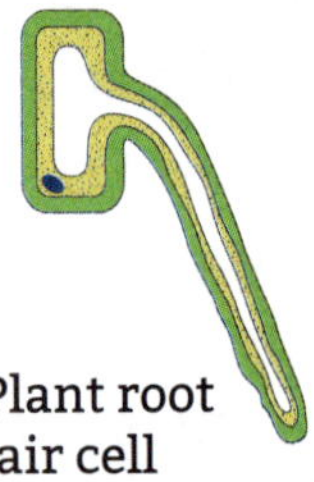

(d) Plant root hair cell

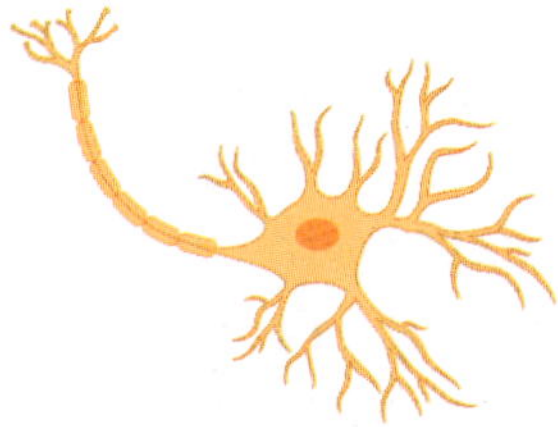

(e) Motor neuron cell

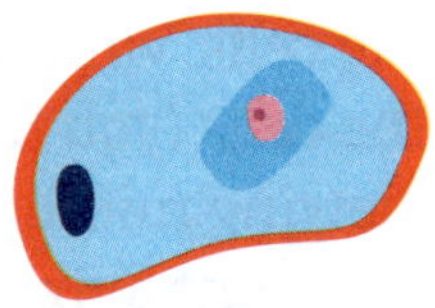

(f) Pollen cell

Fig. 6.4: Variation in cell shape

- Sperm cells need to swim long distances, so they have a wiggly tail to propel themselves.
- Cells in plants may be hexagonal, rectangular or spherical, depending on their functions.

The size of cells may be as small as a **micrometre** or as large as a few **centimetres**.

The smallest living organism is the bacterial cell, which ranges in size from 0.1 to 0.5 micrometre. Human nerve cells are said to be the longest cells.

Science in Context

Gaseous exchange in single-celled organisms takes place through cell membrane.

STRUCTURE OF A CELL

a

A cell has both living and non-living parts. The living parts present in cells have a definite shape, structure and function, and are commonly called **organelles**.

Typically, there are three major parts seen in all cells except bacteria—cell membrane, protoplasm and nucleus. The plant cells have another part called the cell wall, which surrounds the cell membrane but is not found in animal cells.

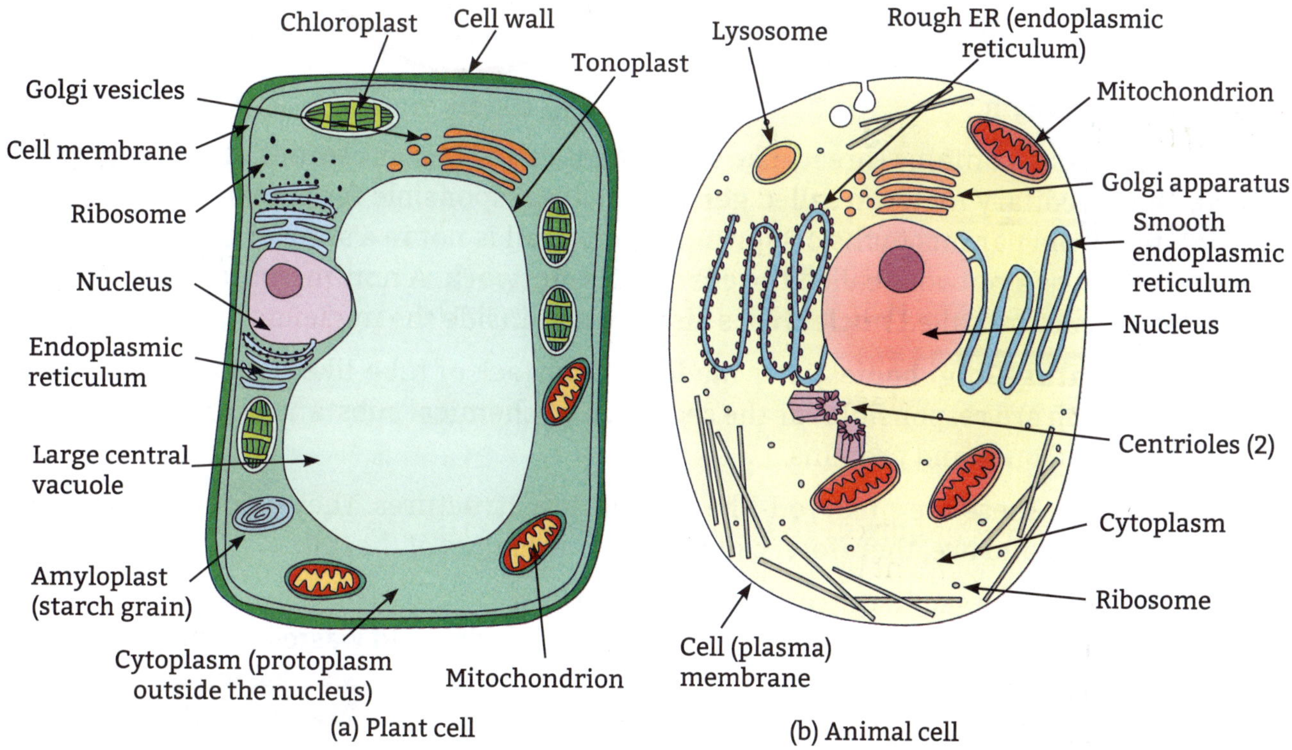

Fig. 6.5: Structure of a plant cell and an animal cell

Observe Figure 6.5 carefully. You will see the cell organelles are embedded in the cytoplasm. Different organelles present in the cell perform different functions.

Let us learn about each of the cell organelles to know their functions.

Cell membrane: A cell is surrounded by a thin covering called the **cell membrane** or the **plasma membrane**. The cell membrane protects the cell and gives it shape. It allows only select materials in and out of the cell. Hence, the cell membrane is also called a selectively permeable membrane. It regulates the movement of selected substances, water and minerals in and out of the cell.

Cell wall: The cell wall is present only in plant cells; animal cells do not have a cell wall. This extra layer provides rigidity and protection to the cells, as plants do not have skeletal support. The cell wall is completely permeable to all substances. The cell wall contains a large amount of cellulose.

Cytoplasm: Cytoplasm is the jelly-like fluid found within the cell membrane. Many organelles are embedded in the cytoplasm.

Some cytoplasmic organelles are discussed below:

Nucleus: The nucleus controls the major functions of the cell. Thus, it is referred to as the **brain of the cell**.

The nucleus (Fig. 6.6) is surrounded by a membrane called the **nuclear membrane**. Protoplasm present inside the nucleus is called **nucleoplasm**.

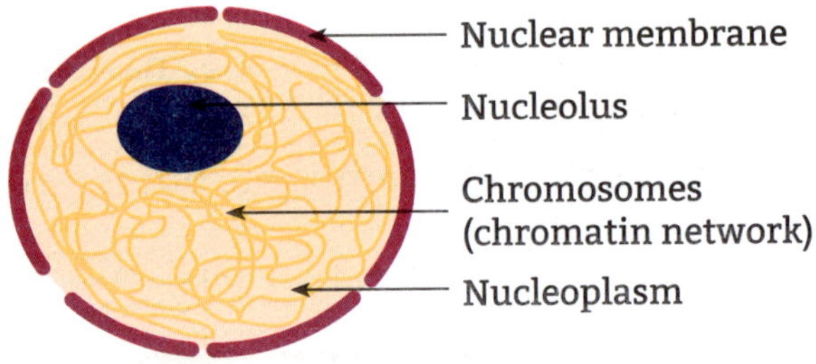

Fig. 6.6: Structure of the nucleus

The nucleoplasm contains thread-like substances called **chromosomes**. Chromosomes carry the hereditary material called **genes** that are responsible for transferring characters from parents to the offspring. When a cell is not in a state of division, they are seen as a network called the **chromatin network**. A non-membrane bound spherical structure called **nucleolus** is also present inside the nucleus.

Golgi apparatus (Golgi bodies): It is made up of a stack of tube-like structures called vesicles, which are responsible for the secretion of chemical substances such as enzymes, hormones and proteins.

Mitochondria: These are small rod-like or spherical structures. They oxidize food to provide energy and are, therefore, called the *powerhouses of the cell.*

Vacuoles: These are sac-like structures enclosed by a membrane called **tonoplast**. They store excess water, food and wastes inside them.

Lysosomes: Lysosomes contain chemical substances called enzymes that can digest cells, and a variety of **intracellular**[1] and **extracellular**[2] materials.

Lysosomes are called the *suicide bags of the cell* as they are capable of bursting and destroying cells during emergency.

Word Web

[1]**Intracellular:** present inside the cell

[2]**Extracellular:** present outside the cell

Ribosomes: These are small granular structures found scattered in the cytoplasm and on the endoplasmic reticulum, and are responsible for protein synthesis.

Endoplasmic reticulum: This is a network of tubules, which are involved in the storage and transportation of substances within the cell. There are two types of endoplasmic reticulum (ER): smooth ER and rough ER. Rough ER has ribosomes attached to its surface, due to which the surface has a grainy appearance. The smooth ER does not have ribosomes.

Centrosomes: These structures are present only in animal cells. Centrosomes mainly function to initiate and regulate cell division.

Plastids: These are present only in plant cells. Plastids contain certain **pigments** that have specific functions. Depending on the pigment colour, plastids are of three kinds: chloroplasts, chromoplasts and leucoplasts.

- **Chloroplasts**: These contain the green pigment called chlorophyll, which helps plants in making food.
- **Chromoplasts**: These contain the non-green pigment, which gives colour to flowers and fruits. Colour attracts insects for pollination and animals for seed dispersal.
- **Leucoplasts**: These do not contain colour-giving pigments. These are colourless and store food in the form of carbohydrates, proteins and fats. They mostly contain starch.

The major differences between plant cells and animal cells are given in Table 6.1.

Table 6.1: Differences and similarities between plant cells and animal cells

Structure	Plant Cell	Animal Cell
Cell wall	Present	Absent
Cell membrane	Present; lies inside the cell wall; encloses the cytoplasm	Present; encloses the cytoplasm
Nucleus	Present; has nuclear membrane, nucleolus, nucleoplasm and chromosomes	Present; has nuclear membrane, nucleolus, nucleoplasm and chromosomes
Vacuole	Several in number; large and prominent	If present, small in size and few in number
Chloroplast (plastids)	Present	Absent
Mitochondria	Present	Present
Centrioles	Absent	Present
Shape	Come in different shapes but shapes are fixed	Generally have fixed shapes, but there are exceptions

Revise and Recall

Match the following.

1. *Amoeba*	(a) Brain of a cell
2. Nerve cells	(b) Unicellular
3. Centrioles	(c) Plant cell
4. Nucleus	(d) Longest cells
5. Plastids	(e) Animal cell

Prokaryotic and Eukaryotic Cells

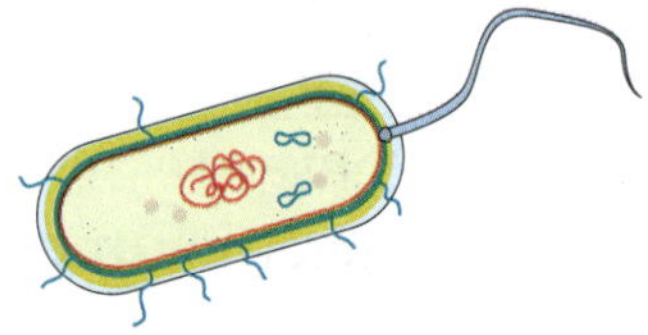

Fig. 6.7: Prokaryotic cell of bacterium *E. coli*

Prokaryotic cells (*Pro: primitive; karyon: nucleus*) are the cells that lack a well-defined membrane-bound nucleus. The genetic material is suspended freely in the cytoplasm. Examples include bacteria (Fig. 6.7) and blue-green algae such as *Nostoc*.

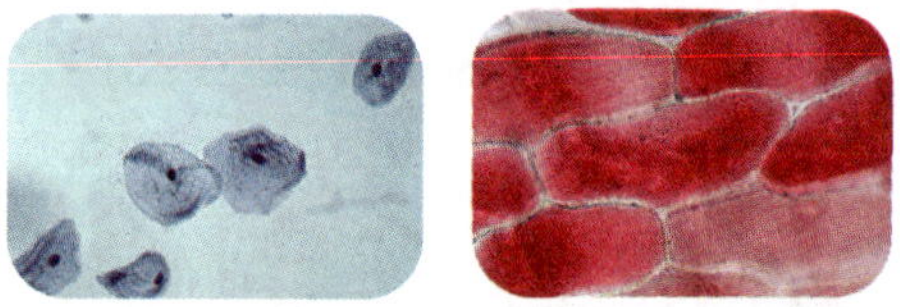

(a) Cheek cells (b) Onion cells

Fig. 6.8: Eukaryotic cells of cheek and onion

Eukaryotic cells (*Eu: true; karyon: nucleus*) are the cells that have a well-defined membrane-bound nucleus. The genetic material is found enclosed within the nucleus. All plants and animals have eukaryotic cells (Fig. 6.8).

CELL DIVISION AND GROWTH

Once a cell is formed, it starts ingesting and digesting food, and grows in size. After reaching a certain size, it divides to form two cells (Fig. 6.9). The new cells formed in this manner are called **daughter cells and are the exact copies of the parent cell**.

New cells are needed not only for the growth of an organism but also to replace dying, damaged or worn-out cells in the body.

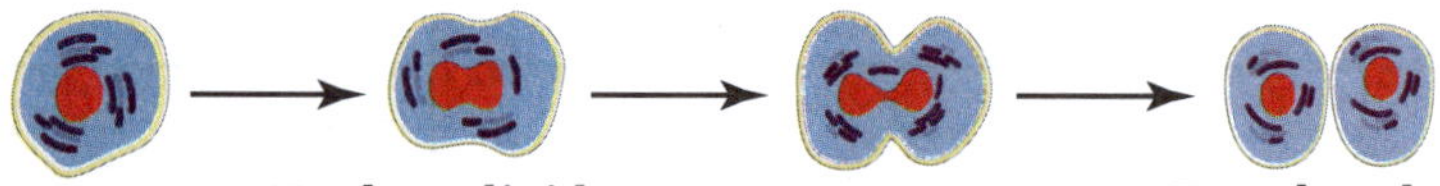

Fig. 6.9: Division of a cell

When a tissue is damaged, the surrounding cells begin to divide to replace the damaged cells. However, in the brain, the spinal cord and nerves, the damage is permanent, because these cells cannot undergo division to replace the damaged cells.

Hence, when there is an injury to a bone, it will heal, but an injury to the spinal cord will not.

Science in Context

Sometimes, during cell division, errors might occur in the division of the genetic material. This results in changes called mutations, which can cause diseases such as cancer and abnormal growth such as moles and non-cancerous tumours.

Preparing a Slide to View Cells

As most living cells are microscopic in nature, they are viewed with the help of a compound microscope. To view a cell under the microscope, the specimen[2] is first placed on a glass slide; this step is called **mounting**.

Word Web

[1]**1 micrometer** = 0.000001 m (1 millionth of a metre), generally written as 10^{-6}.

[2]**Specimen:** sample

[3]**Inanimate:** not alive or dead

Mounting can be carried out in the laboratory in two ways: **dry** mounting or **wet** mounting. Dry mounting does not require water, whereas wet mounting requires water. A dry mount is generally used for viewing **inanimate**[3] objects.

Specimens to be viewed under a microscope are often stained (coloured) using dyes such as methylene blue, safranin or crystal violet. Stains are absorbed by the tissues and organelles present in the cell, which brightens and differentiates them, making it easier for us to view the detailed structure.

Let us carry out the following activity to know how a wet mount is prepared.

Activity 1

Aim: To observe cells under a microscope using the wet mount method

Materials required: Onion, forceps, watchglass, water, dropper, iodine solution or eosin or safranine, cover slip, filter paper, microscope

Procedure:

1. Peel the outermost skin of an onion and take a piece of the fleshy layer from below. When you fold this backwards, that is on its convex side, you will see thin layer of the onion peel jutting out of the margin. Using a forcep, carefully remove a small piece and place it in a petri dish or glass dish containing a few drops of water.
2. Using a dropper, add a drop of iodine solution or eosin or safranine to this water with the onion peel. Let it remain for a minute in this solution.
3. Take a dry glass slide. Gently, using a forcep, remove the peel and place it on the slide. Add a drop of the solution from the petri dish onto the peel.
4. Cover gently with a cover slip.
5. Use a piece of filter paper to remove the excess liquid from the slide.
6. Get your microscope ready for viewing. Place it on a table where light will fall on the mirror. Turn the nose piece so that the objective lens is in line with the eyepiece. Look through the eye piece and adjust the mirror so that the stage is well-lit. If you do not have natural lighting, use a table lamp as the light source.
7. Place the slide on the stage of a microscope and adjust the mirror and the objective lens with the help of your teacher.
8. Observe the slide through the eyepiece.

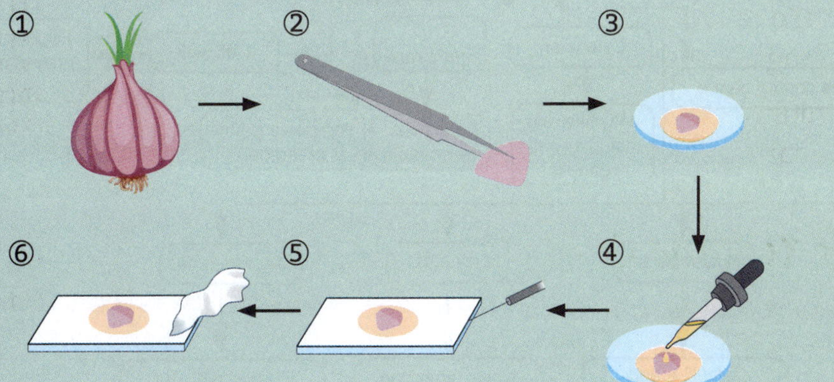

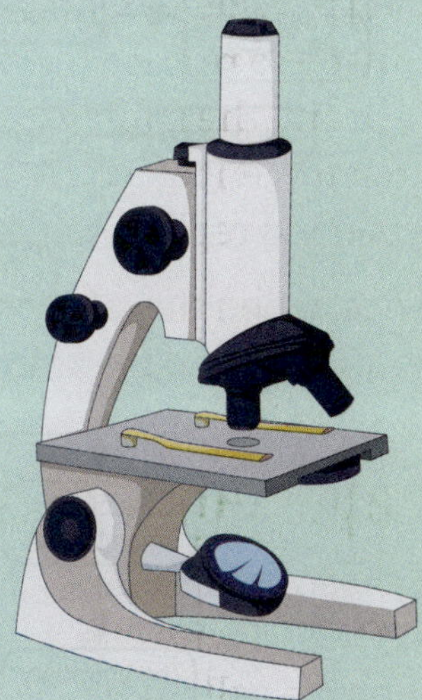

Keywords

Cell: The smallest structural and functional unit of an organism

Organelles: The living parts of a cell that possess a definite shape and structure, and have specific functions

Unicellular organisms: Organisms made up of a single cell

Multicellular organisms: Organisms made up of many cells

Tonoplast: The membrane that surrounds a vacuole

Chloroplast: The cell organelle present only in plants and contains chlorophyll

Gene: That part of a chromosome responsible for the transfer of hereditary characters from parents to the offspring

Pseudopodia: Temporary cytoplasmic projections (also called false feet), used for feeding and movement in *Amoeba*

Prokaryotic cells: Cell that do not have a well-defined membrane-bound nucleus

Eukaryotic cells: Cell that have a well-defined membrane-bound nucleus

Summary

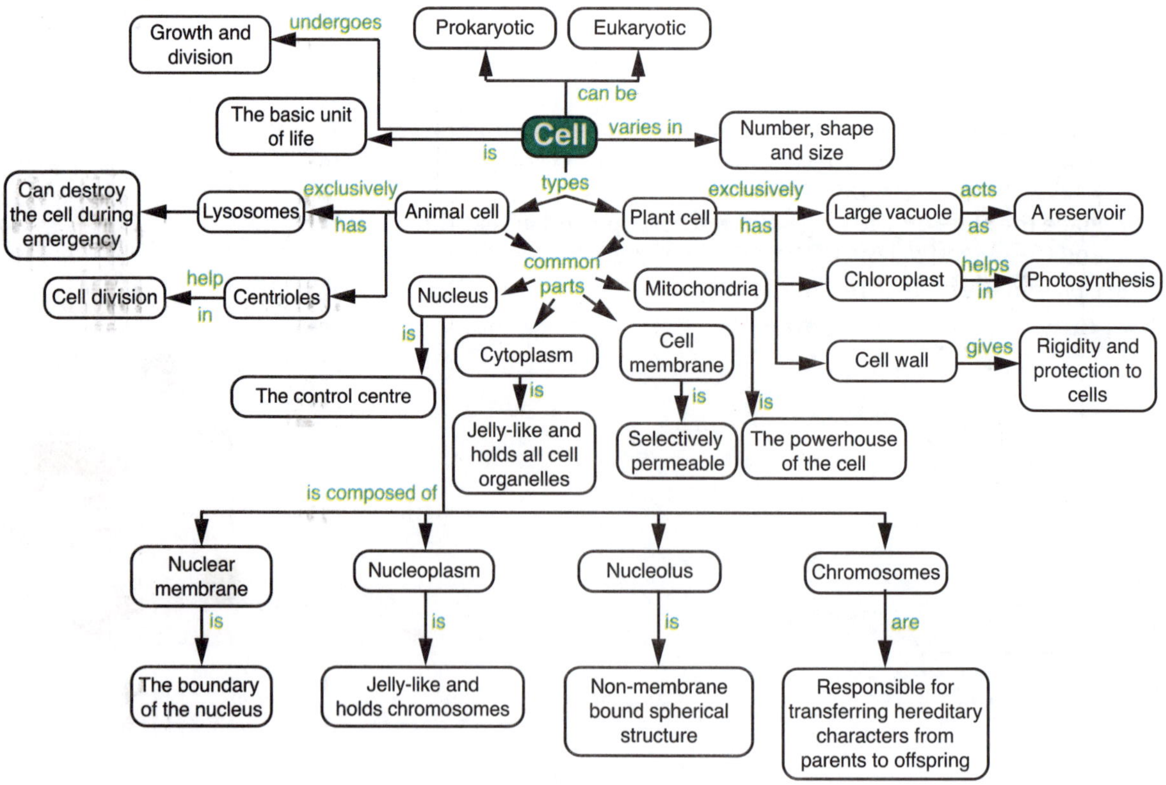

Exercise

w

ia

A. Choose the correct option.

1. Which of the following is a selectively permeable membrane?
   (a) Nuclear membrane (b) Plasma membrane
   (c) Cell wall (d) Both (a) and (b)
2. What is the function of chloroplast?
   (a) Store food (b) Prepare food
   (c) Transport food (d) Break down food
3. ____________ are called the powerhouse of the cell.
   (a) Mitochondria (b) Ribosome (c) Nucleus (d) Cytoplasm
4. Identify the organelle that is found in a plant cell but not in an animal cell.
   (a) Cell membrane (b) Mitochondria (c) Ribosome (d) Chloroplast
5. Who first observed cork cells under a crude microscope?
   (a) Schwann (b) Schleiden (c) Hooke (d) Leeuwenhoek

B. State whether the following statements are true (T) or false (F).

1. Nuclear membrane is absent in plant cells. ☐
2. Leucoplast is a type of plastid. ☐
3. Vacuoles are prominent in plant cells. ☐
4. Size of the cells depends upon the size of the organism. ☐
5. All cells have a clear and definite nucleus. ☐

C. Fill in the blanks.

1. In an animal tissue, one cell is separated from another by a ____________. (plasma membrane/cell wall)
2. Cells without a well-developed nuclear membrane are called ____________. (eukaryotes/prokaryotes)
3. The structures that help in the transfer of characters from the parent to the offspring are ____________. (genes/chromosomes)
4. The jelly-like substance present in between the nuclear membrane and the cell membrane is ____________. (gene/cytoplasm)
5. The term 'cell' was first coined by ____________. (Robert Hooke/ Antonie Van Leeuwenhoek)

D. For the following analogies, compare a plant cell to that of a factory. ia

1. This structure acts as a checkpoint for the entry and exit of the materials.
2. This structure is the office or the control centre of the entire factory.
3. This is the space or the site where all the other components are situated.
4. This structure gives extra support to the plant cell.

E. Give reasons for the following.

1. Chromosomes play an important role in reproduction.
2. Cytoplasm is a jelly-like substance.
3. Cell wall gives extra strength to the plant cells.
4. *Amoeba* has temporary cytoplasmic projections.
5. The nucleus divides first during a cell division.

F. Answer the following questions briefly.

1. What is the function of lysosomes in an animal cell?
2. Differentiate between a unicellular and a multicellular organism with an example each.
3. Define cell. Explain the variation in size that a cell undergoes.
4. How are daughter cells formed?
5. Define prokaryotic and eukaryotic cells with two examples each.

G. Answer the following questions in detail.

1. Differentiate between the organelles present in a plant cell and an animal cell in the form of the given table.

Organelles	Plant Cell	Animal Cell

2. Draw a neat and well-labelled diagram of a generalized cell. Also, explain the components in the nucleus of a cell.
3. Write a brief history on the discovery of cells.
4. Give the steps involved in the preparation of a slide to view cells under a microscope using the wet mount method.
5. Explain how cells vary in shape, size and number.
6. How do cell division and cell growth play a role in the life of a cell?

Cognitive Corner

Critical Thinking

1. Which organism is functionally more effective: a unicellular organism where one single cell performs all the functions, or a multicellular organism where different organs perform different functions? Give reasons for your answer.
2. Name a characteristic feature specific to cells that can be used to classify an organism as a plant.

Picture Study

Name the parts marked by the arrows in the given diagram of an animal cell.

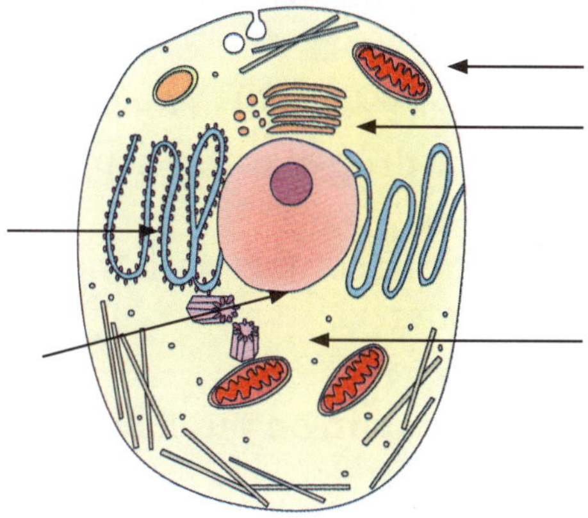

Project

1. Make a chart to show the gradation in size of different cells in different organisms such as bacteria, protozoa, hens, ostriches, humans and so on. **(C-7.2)**
2. Make an edible animal cell model using candy and other edible ingredients as a part of science club. **(C-7.2)**

   Tips: *Prepare a box of gelatin (to represent cytoplasm) according to the package instructions to form the base of your cell. Pour it into a bowl (to represent the cell membrane) when slightly cooled and chill it until it is partially set but still liquid.*

   Once the gelatin has reached a thickened-yet-soft stage, add the candies to the cell. Arrange different candy components (sprinkles for ribosomes, a hard ribbon candy for the golgi body, jelly beans for lysosomes, a gumball for the centrosome, folded fruit roll-ups or gummy worms for the endoplasmic reticulum, chocolate-covered raisins for vacuoles and gumdrops or orange candy slices for mitochondria) and use a fruit cut in half to represent the nucleus (the pit is the nucleolus and the skin is the nuclear membrane).

   Press the candy slowly into the setting gelatin to get a firm model. Finally, let the gelatin set until it becomes firm.

In the Library

1. Read books in your school library or search the Internet to find out about the origin of the first cell, what conditions prevailed during its origin, how different were these cells from the present-day cells. Prepare a powerpoint presentation based on your findings. **(C-7.1)**
2. Do we know everything about how the human brain works? Find out what is the current scientific understanding on how human brain works. What are the latest findings on what happens to the cells of the brain as the body begins to age. Make a report based on your findings. **(C-9.2)**

In the Laboratory

Aim: To observe cheek cells under a microscope **(C-7.2)**

Procedure:

1. Gently scrape the inside of the cheek with a toothpick or swab.
2. Place the scraped material in a drop of water kept on a clean glass slide near an end of the slide.
3. Bring the edge of another slide in contact with the drop and allow the drop to bank evenly behind the spreader.
4. Prepare a thin smear.
5. Place a drop of methylene blue stain on the slide and spread completely throughout the slide.
6. Let the stain stay on the slide for two minutes.
7. Rinse off the excessive stain by washing the slide gently with tap water.
8. Remove the excessive water by using the absorbent paper.
9. Observe the cells under a microscope and verify that they are well stained.
10. If necessary, apply the stain for a few minutes and repeat Steps 7 and 8.
11. Place a coverslip over the stained cells.
12. Observe the slide under the low power of the microscope.

Precautions:

Sterilize the material that you will use to swab. Do not overstain the slide. The smear should be very thin so that crowding of cells can be avoided.

Observation table:

Put a (✓) mark in the appropriate box.

Shape of the cells	Observations
Thin and flat	
Cube shaped	
Ciliated-cells	
Columnar cells (pillar-like)	
Oval	
Round	
Flat and scale-like	

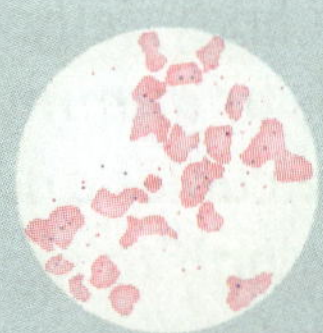

Squamous epithelial cells

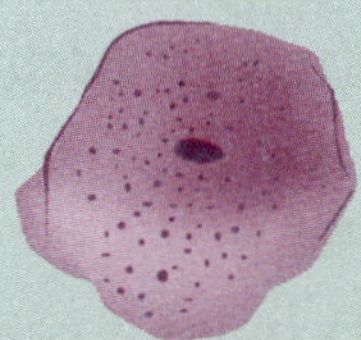

A single squamous epithelium cell

Life Skills

Place a drop of water on a glass slide and observe under a microscope. List the organisms and types of debris found in it. Brainstorm with your classmate and find out a way to remove these tiny debris and microorganisms from water, making it fit for drinking. **(C-7.3)**

3 GOOD HEALTH AND WELL-BEING

Worksheet

Genes are responsible for determining many of our traits and characteristics, and they are contained in our chromosomes. Chromosomes are found in the nucleus of all living beings, and they carry genetic information from parents to their children during reproduction. Each organism has its unique set of chromosomes, and interbreeding is not possible between two distinct groups of organisms due to the differences in their genetic information. This genetic diversity is essential for the survival and adaptation of various species in nature.

Before cells divide, these chromosomes make an exact copy of themselves. During cell division, each daughter cell receives a set of chromosomes.

Sometimes, climate changes or human activities may alter the environment. In response, cell chromosomes do not make exact copies and slight variations develop over time to help organisms adapt to the new habitat. After hundreds of years of evolving variations, new species develop. Giraffes, horses and urangutans are some animals that have evolved into the species we know today.

Not only animals, but germs, insects and pests have also evolved over time.

A. In the medical world, it is becoming more difficult to treat bacterial diseases with antibiotics. What do you think is happening with the bacteria?

____

____

____

B. Do you know household pests have become resistant to pesticides? Name any two such pests.

____

____

____

____

C. Would the use of pesticides also affect human beings? How can we ensure healthy lives and well-being at home?

____

____

____

____

7 Endocrine System and Adolescence

Curricular Goals

- Understand the components of health, hygiene and well-being **(CG-4)**
- Understand the interface of science, technology and society **(CG-5)**

Competencies

- Describe biological changes during adolescence and measures to ensure overall well-being **(C-4.3)**
- Recognize and discuss substance abuse, viewing school as a safe space to raise these concerns **(C-4.4)**
- Illustrate how science and technology can help to improve the quality of human life as well as some of the harmful uses of science in history **(C-5.1)**

Let's Get Started

You may have noticed people (including yourself) responding to situations in a manner as shown in the pictures below. Identify the different reactions and use the words given in the box below to name them.

Fear	Irritation	Happiness

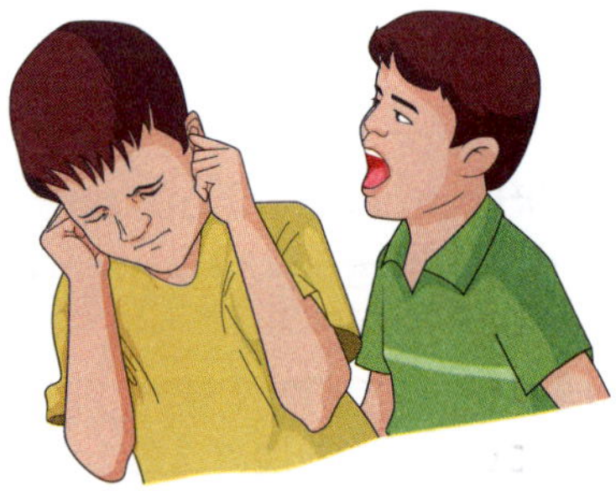

________________ ________________ ________________

These responses are also called **emotions**. An organ system in our body called the **endocrine system** is responsible for causing some of these experiences or emotions.

One of the characteristics of living things is that they grow and then reproduce. Animals, in particular, grow until a particular age and only then begin to reproduce. In human beings, certain changes begin to take place in the body only after which a person becomes capable of reproduction.

The endocrine system also plays a major role in these changes. Let us study more about the endocrine system and how it brings about these changes.

THE ENDOCRINE SYSTEM

a

There are some special structures called **glands** located at specific places inside our body which secrete[1] certain substances. These glands can be of **two types**:

> **Word Web**
> [1]**secrete:** to synthesize and release

Exocrine glands: The liver, sweat glands and salivary glands are **exocrine glands** as they release their secretions to the target site with the help of **ducts** (tubes).

Endocrine glands: These glands directly release their secretions into the blood stream without any ducts.

The chemical substances that the endocrine glands secrete are called ***hormones****, which are circulated in the blood to reach the target sites.* These hormones travel inside our body and act like chemical messengers. Hormones are required in very minute quantities, and they regulate the growth, development, behaviour and reproduction of the organism.

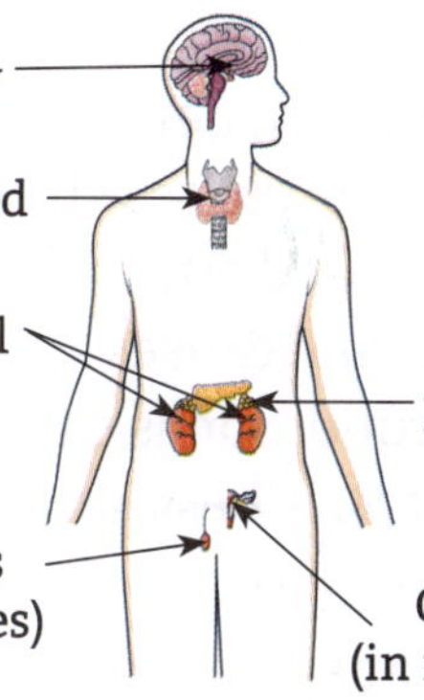

Fig. 7.1: Human endocrine system

The major glands that make up the human endocrine system are shown in Figure 7.1. Let us learn about each of these glands in detail and find out their role in our bodies.

- **Pituitary gland:** Pituitary is a pea-sized gland situated at the base of the brain. It regulates the functioning of most of the other endocrine glands. The pituitary gland in turn is regulated by a structure called the **hypothalamus** (Fig. 7.2) present in the brain. It secretes several hormones; one of the important hormones secreted is the **growth hormone**. This hormone regulates the growth of bones and muscles. A deficiency of this hormone causes **dwarfism**, wherein an individual stops growing early and shows no further growth at all. An excess of growth hormones results in a condition called **gigantism**.

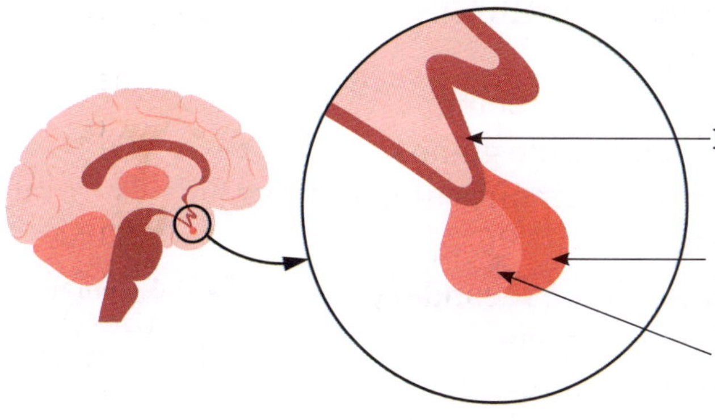

Fig. 7.2: Hypothalamus and pituitary

> **Science in Context**
> Earlier, pituitary used to be called the 'master gland' as it controls the functioning of other endocrine glands. Now we know that pituitary itself is controlled by the hypothalamus. So, hypothalamus is the true master gland, in a way!

Other than the growth hormone, the pituitary gland secretes several other **stimulating hormones** such as the thyroid-stimulating hormone (TSH), follicle-stimulating hormone (FSH) and luteinizing hormone (LH). Follicle-stimulating hormone (FSH) and luteinizing hormone (LH) stimulate the gonads (ovaries and the testes) to release their respective hormones. The thyroid-stimulating hormone (TSH) regulates the secretions of hormones by the thyroid gland.

- **Thyroid gland:** The thyroid gland (Fig. 7.3) is located in the neck region and secretes a hormone called **thyroxine**. Iodine is necessary for the secretion of thyroxine. The thyroid-stimulating hormone from the pituitary gland stimulates the thyroid gland to produce thyroxine.

  Thyroxine regulates the rate of metabolism, physical growth and mental development of an individual. The deficiency of this hormone causes **simple goitre**, wherein the gland gets enlarged. It is caused due to the lack of iodine in the individual's diet. An excess production of thyroxine causes an increase in the rate of heartbeat and respiration and bulging eyes; this condition is called **exophthalmic goitre**. In such a condition, the hands and face show puffiness, and the eyeballs bulge out.

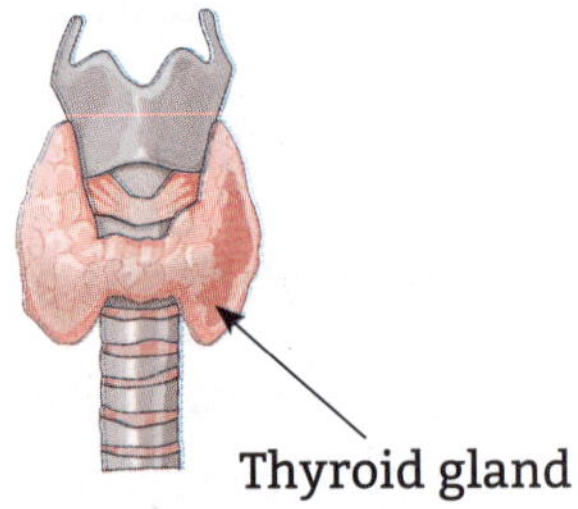

Fig. 7.3: Thyroid gland

- **Adrenal gland:** The adrenal glands (Fig. 7.4) are triangular in shape and situated on top of the two kidneys. They secrete a hormone called **adrenaline,** which prepares the body for action during times of stress. Hence, it is also called the **fright, flight and fight** hormone. This hormone is secreted when the body faces situations of excitement, fear or stress. It regulates the heartbeat, breathing rate and blood pressure. The effect of this hormone is temporary and lasts only for a few minutes.

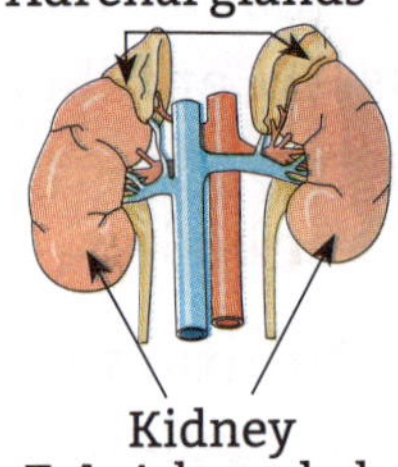

Fig. 7.4: Adrenal glands

- **Pancreas:** Pancreas (Fig. 7.5) acts as both an exocrine and an endocrine gland. It secretes digestive juices as well as hormones. Hence, it is also called a **dual gland**. The pancreas is located in the abdomen region, just below the stomach. Certain special cells in the pancreas secrete the hormone **insulin**. Insulin regulates the metabolism of sugar in the body.

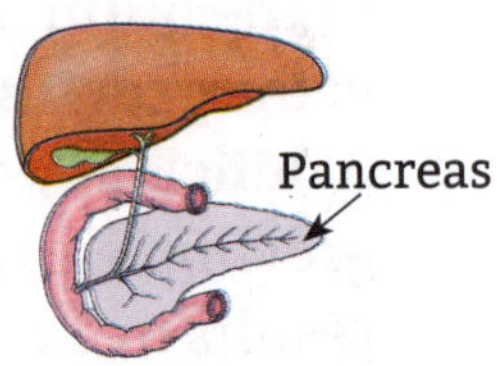

Fig. 7.5: Pancreas

- **Ovaries:** The ovaries (Fig. 7.6) are the egg (ova) producing female reproductive organs. They are also endocrine glands that secrete the **oestrogen** and **progesterone** hormones under the stimulation of the pituitary hormones.

  Oestrogen is responsible for the appearance of the secondary sexual characters in females such as changes in body structures and production of eggs, while progesterone is involved in the changes that take place during the menstrual cycle.

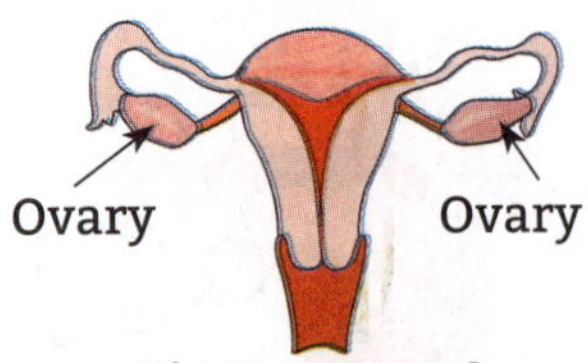

Fig. 7.6: Female reproductive system depicting ovaries

- **Testes:** These are situated inside the scrotal sacs suspended from the lower proximity of a male's body. The testes (Fig. 7.7) are endocrine glands that secrete the hormone **testosterone** under the stimulation by the pituitary hormones.
  Testosterone is responsible for the appearance of the secondary sexual characters in males such as growth of body and facial hair, change in voice and production of sperms.

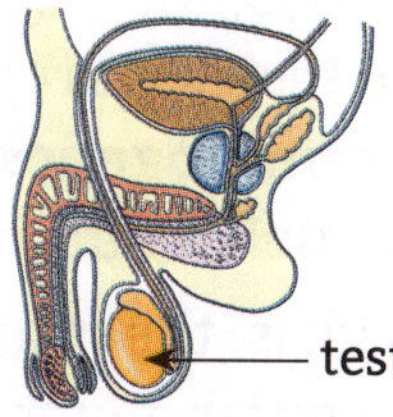

Fig. 7.7: Testis in male's scrotum

PUBERTY AND ADOLESCENCE

As discussed earlier in the chapter, an individual can reproduce only after achieving sexual maturity. *The stage in the life cycle of humans in which the body becomes biologically capable of sexual reproduction is called* **puberty**. It normally occurs between the age of 11–16 years in boys and 10–15 years in girls.

Adolescence *is the transitional period from childhood to adulthood.* The period of adolescence starts at puberty and continues till the age of 18–19 years. Changes that take place during puberty in girls and boys are revealed by external changes to the body, together with the emotional and physiological changes brought about by hormones. Let us learn about some of these changes.

Physical Changes at Puberty

- **Increase in height:** This may happen gradually or sometimes a sudden change in height can take place due to the elongation of the bones in the arms and legs. The rate of growth varies from individual to individual.
- **Activity of sweat and oil glands:** There is an increase in the activity of sweat glands, resulting in body odour. There is also an increased activity of oil glands, resulting in acne and pimples on the face.
- **Development of body hair:** In both boys and girls, hairs develop under armpits and in the pubic region. Boys also develop hair on the face and chest.
- **Voice changes:** In males, the larynx (voice box) increases in size and appears as a protrusion in the throat. This is commonly called the **Adam's apple**. During this stage, the voice cracks and the individual develops a deep voice. Females may develop a high-pitched and shrill voice.
- **Body changes:** In males, the shoulders become broader and the chest becomes wider due to increased muscle development. In females, the waist broadens and deposition of fat around the hips takes place. There is also development and enlargement of the breasts.

Since these features develop as a result of the onset of sexual maturity or puberty, they are called **secondary sexual characters**.

Changes in reproductive organs

In boys, the testes and the penis develop completely and the testes start producing sperms through a process called **spermatogenesis**. The sperm is the male gamete and is motile[1] in nature.

> **Word Web**
>
> [1]**motile:** capable of moving

In girls, the ovaries enlarge. The eggs or ova (singular: ovum), which are the female gametes, begin to mature in ovaries (Fig. 7.8) through a process called **oogenesis**. An ovum is released from an ovary after every 28th day. *The process in which an ovum is released by an ovary is called* ***ovulation***. From the onset of puberty, an ovum is released every 28 days by one of the ovaries. If the left ovary releases an ovum in 28 days, the right ovary will release an ovum in the next 28 days. Before the release of an egg, the uterus prepares itself to receive the egg. The lining of the uterus becomes thick and spongy, and develops a lot of blood vessels. These changes occur due to the production of oesterogen and progesterone under the influence of the pituitary hormone FSH. Once the ovulation takes place, an egg is released, which is sucked into the **fallopian tube**. If the egg meets the sperm cells in the fallopian tube, it may get fertilized. This fertilized egg is called a **zygote**. The zygote then undergoes division and finally implants itself onto the wall of the uterus.

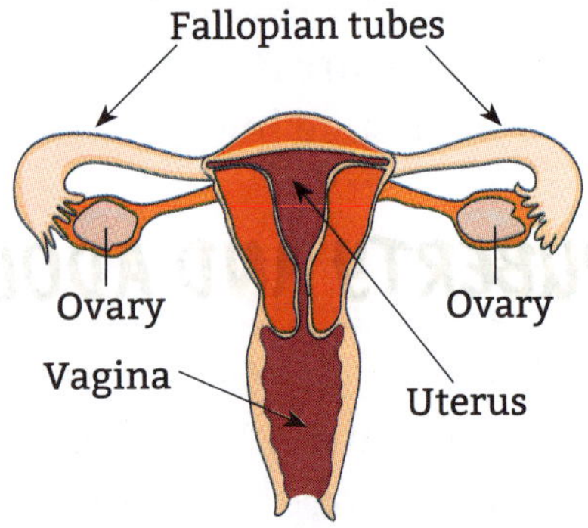

Fig. 7.8: Uterus and ovary in females

If fertilization does not occur, the released egg and the thickened lining of the uterus along with its blood vessels are shed from the body. This is called **menstruation**. The menstrual flow lasts for 4–6 days. *This entire hormone-regulated cycle of events, resulting in the production and release of the unfertilized egg, is called the* ***menstrual cycle***. Menstrual cycle lasts approximately 28 days. It can be broken down into the phases (Table 7.1) during which certain changes take place inside the uterus.

Table 7.1: Phases of a menstrual cycle

Phases	Description
Phase 1 (Day 1–4)	The uterus lining breaks, and the egg and uterine lining are expelled out of the body.
Phase 2 (Day 4–12)	New lining of uterus starts forming and it becomes thick.
Phase 3 (Day 12–14)	Ovulation—the egg is released from the ovary.
Phase 4 (Day 20–24)	The spongy layer remains thick, waiting for the implantation of the fertilized egg. If this does not happen, then it is shed away between days 25 and 28 of the cycle.

The first menstrual flow begins at puberty and is termed as ***menarche****. At about 40–50 years of age, the menstrual cycle stops and is termed as* ***menopause****.*

Science in Context

A girl is born with all the eggs that she will release in her lifetime. The release of eggs starts at menarche and stops around menopause.

However, a boy starts producing sperms only once he attains puberty and continues to produce new sperms every day throughout his lifetime.

Determination of the sex of a baby

Inside the fertilized egg is the information for determining the sex of the baby. This information is present in thread-like structures called **chromosomes**. All human beings have 23 pairs of chromosomes in the nuclei of their cells. Out of these, the 23rd pair of chromosomes are called the **sex chromosomes**. There are two types of sex chromosomes: X chromosome and Y chromosome.

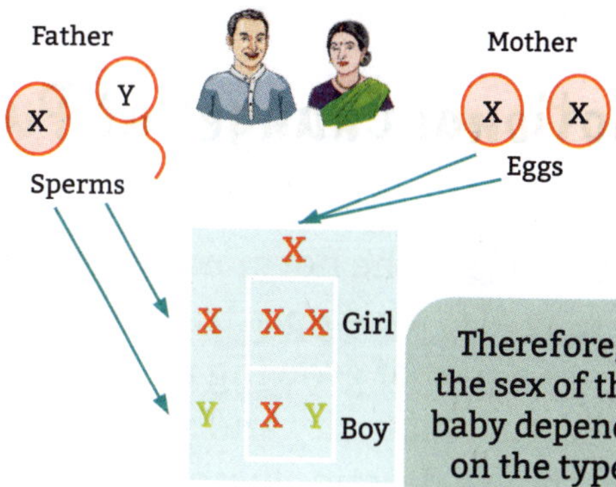

Therefore, the sex of the baby depends on the type of sperm that fuses with the egg.

The 23rd pair of chromosomes in females has two X chromosomes, while males have one X chromosome and one Y chromosome.

(Female— XX; Male— XY).

When gametes are formed, each gamete gets only one chromosome from the parent. As females have only XX chromosomes, in the female gamete, that is the ovum, the sex chromosome is always X. In the male gamete, that is the sperm, the sex chromosome present can be either X or Y. Thus, the type of chromosome present in the male gamete or the sperm determines the sex of the baby.

If a sperm carrying the sex chromosome X fertilizes the egg, then the chromosomes in the zygote formed will be 44 + XX (one X chromosome from the mother and the other X chromosome from the father). The foetus will be a girl since the sex chromosomes are XX.

If a sperm carrying the sex chromosome Y fertilizes the egg, then the chromosomes in the zygote formed will be 44 + XY (one X chromosome from the mother and the Y chromosome from the father). The foetus will be a boy since the sex chromosomes are XY.

Revise and Recall

Fill in the blanks.

1. Glands that release their secretions directly into the blood are called ____________ glands. (endocrine/exocrine)
2. Deficiency of __________ causes dwarfism. (growth hormone/adrenaline)
3. __________ regulates the rate of metabolism. (Thyroxine/Insulin)
4. Oestrogen and progesterone are secreted by the_________ . (ovary/testis)
5. Release of ovum by the ovaries is called _________ . (menstruation/ovulation)

Emotional Changes at Puberty

Emotional changes are experienced in the early stages of puberty. This is because of an increase in the hormonal levels, leading to sudden mood swings. During this phase, one may also develop attraction towards the opposite sex. These changes are normal and are a part of growing up in an individual's life. Individuals attain a certain level of intellectual maturity and start analysing, evaluating and exchanging views and ideas. They show a drastic change in their behaviour and preoccupation with the self is a common feature observed.

Nutritional Requirements and Personal Hygiene

There is a need for extra care on nutrition, fitness and hygiene during adolescence.

Nutritional requirements: Every individual needs a balanced diet to stay healthy. Irregular eating habits may lead to deficiency disorders, while eating in excess can lead to obesity. Some of the suggested dietary requirements and practices for adolescents are given below:

- Calorie-rich and protein-rich foods such as grains, nuts, pulses, meat, milk and milk products help meet the growing demands of the body.
- Calcium and iron-rich foods such as milk, leafy vegetables and meat help to increase bone density and prevent anaemia.
- A balanced diet should also include a variety of fruits and vegetables, which are a rich source of vitamins and minerals. A lack of such food can affect vital functions.
- Having meals at the right time is also very important; skipping meals must be avoided.
- Eating packed or tinned food items should never replace the regular meals as such foods lack nutritional value.
- Eating stale or exposed food must be avoided for the same reason.

Body fitness: Fitness of the body is also required to maintain proper health.

- Food consumption has to be balanced with the amount of physical activity the individual is involved in. In most cases, adolescents are involved in studies, which involves minimal physical activity, and this may lead to obesity.
- Adolescents can engage in activities such as brisk walking, running, jogging, cycling, skipping, swimming, dancing or any sort of outdoor games.
- Exercising helps in burning excess calories, strengthening the muscles, increasing metabolism, and helps keep the body fit and healthy.

Personal hygiene: Hygienic conditions have to be maintained in order to prevent infections as well as to stay healthy.

- During adolescence, there is an excess secretion of sweat and bodily fluids, which leads to body odour. Hence, it is important to bathe daily and keep the body clean.
- Clothes must be changed every day as unhygienic conditions may lead to bacterial or fungal infections.
- Girls should maintain proper hygiene during menstruation and keep track of their menstrual cycle.

Drug Abuse and AIDS

Drugs are the chemical substances that, if taken without a doctor's prescription or in excessive amount, can cause serious damage to the body and affect one's mental health. **Drug abuse** (or substance abuse) is a common problem among adolescents. It generally refers to the excessive use of and dependence on a variety of substances. These substances include *paan* (betel leaf), tobacco, alcohol, sleeping tablets, painkillers, as well as other mind-altering chemicals, or even cough syrups.

Adolescents may indulge in drug abuse for a variety of reasons: peer pressure, to seek attention or to experience a short-term excitement or 'high', to calm one's feelings.

Addiction can lead to a lack of concentration, inability to work, abandoning family and friends or stealing to pay for drugs out of desperation. Some addictive substances are injected directly into the bloodstream. Addicts who share needles to inject the drug into their body face the danger of getting infected with the human immunodeficiency virus (HIV). HIV can cause the acquired immunodeficiency syndrome (AIDS), a fatal disease that has no cure so far.

Drug abuse can seriously damage health and one must never be tempted to use drugs. If you are tempted or know anyone who is involved in drug abuse, discuss the issue with an elder who you think can help. Remember, your life is precious, do not spoil it by abusing drugs!

Keywords

Puberty: The time in the life of human beings when they become sexually mature

Adolescence: The period of transition from childhood to adulthood

Endocrine glands: Glands that secrete substances called hormones directly into the blood stream

Hormones: Chemicals secreted by the glands of the endocrine system that coordinate several life processes

Ovulation: The process of release of an ovum from the ovary

Fertilization: Fusion of the male and the female gametes

Menstrual cycle: The cycle of the production and release of a matured egg (ova)

Menarche: Onset of puberty in females marked by the first menstrual cycle

Menopause: The period during which a woman's menstrual cycle stops

Drugs: Any substance that can alter the chemical constitution of the body

Drug abuse: Use of drugs for purposes other than medicinal use

Summary

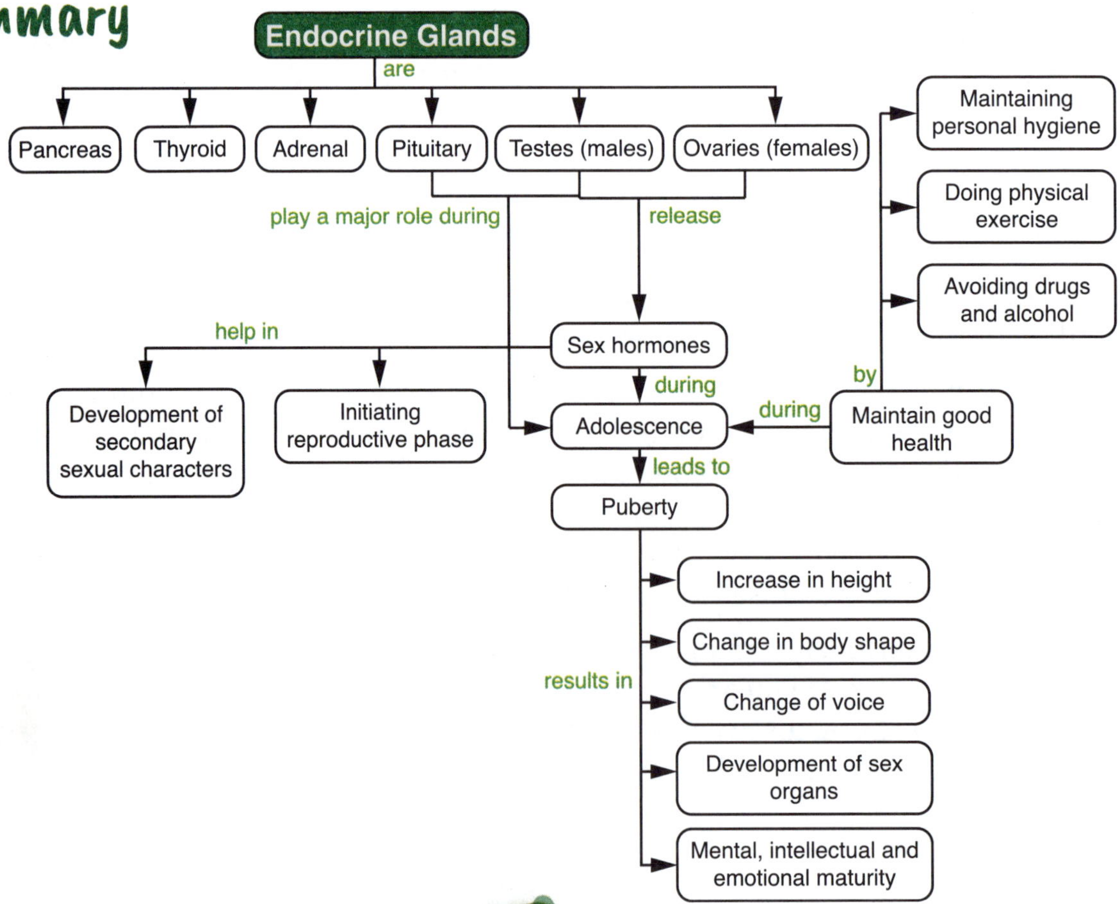

Exercise

W

A. Choose the correct option.

ia

1. ________________ hormone is released under stress or excitement.

   (a) Pituitary (b) Oestrogen (c) Adrenaline (d) Thyroxine

2. ________________ hormone is secreted by the pancreas.

   (a) Insulin (b) Oestrogen (c) Adrenaline (d) Thyroxine

3. ________________ hormone is responsible for the development of secondary sexual characters in males.

   (a) Oestrogen (b) Progesterone (c) Testosterone (d) Adrenaline

4. The fusion of male and female gametes is called ________________.

   (a) implantation (b) gestation (c) fertilization (d) menstruation

5. ________________ is a secondary sexual character in females.

   (a) Enlarged breasts (b) Chest hair

   (c) Deep voice (d) Growth of facial hair

B. State whether the following statements are true (T) or false (F).

1. The female gamete is motile. ☐
2. The release of an ovum from the ovaries is called ovulation. ☐
3. Males develop a deep voice during puberty. ☐
4. The menstrual cycle in females is not regulated by hormones. ☐
5. All parts of the human body grow at the same rate. ☐

C. Fill in the blanks.

ia

1. The first menstrual flow that begins at puberty is called ________________. (menopause/menarche)
2. Oestrogen is the ________________ hormone. (female/male)
3. The changes that occur during adolescence are regulated by ________________. (muscles/hormones)
4. The period between childhood and adulthood is referred to as ________________. (adolescence/early adulthood)
5. The male sex hormone is called ________________. (testosterone/oestrogen)

D. Answer the following questions in two or three sentences each.

1. At what ages do girls and boys reach adolescence?
2. List two changes brought about by the release of adrenaline.
3. Define adolescence and puberty.
4. List two important reasons to maintain personal hygiene during puberty.
5. Name the two types of glands found in our body and state where they are situated.

E. Give reasons for the following.

1. Hypothalamus is called the master gland.
2. Pancreas is essential to maintain blood sugar levels.
3. Glands are of two types: endocrine and exocrine.
4. Follicle stimulating hormone is present only in females.
5. Ovulation occurs once in a month in a female's body.

F. Answer the following questions briefly.

1. Differentiate between a gland and a hormone.
2. Explain why people experience mood swings during adolescence.
3. What is the role of growth hormones?
4. What is the role of the testes and ovaries in the human body?
5. What is menstruation and when does it occur?

G. Answer the following questions in detail.

1. Write a short note on any three endocrine glands. Also, state where they are located in the body and the hormone they release. Write about the effects of the hormones they secrete.
2. Explain the role of hormones during puberty.
3. List any five consequences of drug abuse.
4. List five dietary requirements and practices for adolescents to stay healthy.
5. What are secondary sexual characters? Explain. Also, list the factors that bring about these changes.
6. Write a short note on sex determination.

Cognitive Corner

Critical Thinking

1. Sometimes children may grow taller than both the parents, whereas some may not grow as tall as either of the parents. Why and how?
2. A person is able to control his rapid heart rate, can withstand pain, does not feel tense and does not shiver when confronted with dangerous situations. Another person is unable to control none of these, and suffers from panic attacks. What could be the reason behind this?

Picture Study

Identify and label the endocrine glands shown in the given diagrams.

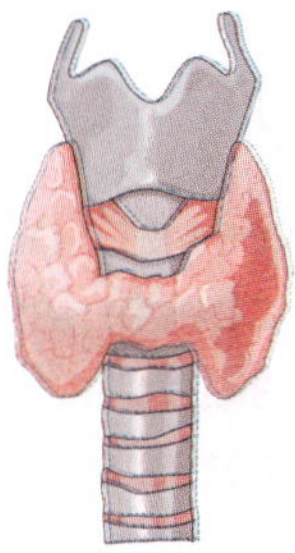

(a)

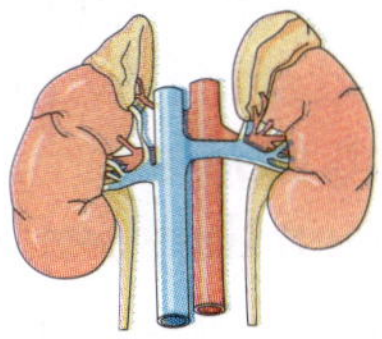

(b)

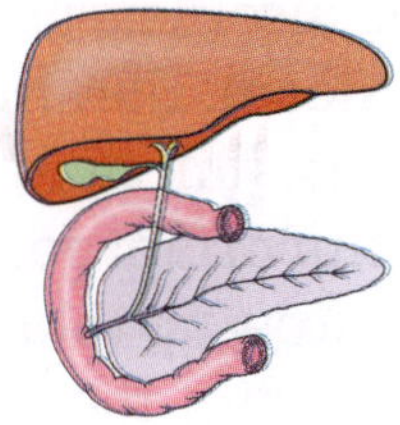

(c)

Project

1. As a part of Health and Wellness club, write an article about the ill-effects of alcohol and drug abuse, and send it to a local newspaper. **(C-7.1)**
2. As a part of School Guidance and Counseling Club, write a case study about the importance of emotional balance during puberty. **(C-7.1)**
3. As a part of Health and Wellness club, make a poster on hygiene practices that should be followed on a regular basis to maintain good health. **(C-7.1)**

In the Library

Read about the role of insulin in treating diabetes, and make a short report. Prepare a power-point presentation based on your findings. **(C-7.1)**

Life Skills

Along with your friends, make a poster with catchy slogans to create awareness about drug addiction. Display the posters on the class noticeboard. **(C-4.4)**

Worksheet

Read the sentences given below. Mark the ones that you feel apply to you.

1. I eat regular meals with my family.
2. I skip meals frequently because I think I am gaining weight.
3. I constantly check my weight to see whether I have gained any since the last time I checked.
4. I am happy with how much I weigh.
5. I am happy with my body's image in the mirror.
6. I always think I am over-weight when I see myself in the mirror.
7. I sometimes secretly throw up my food after meals because I think I have eaten too much.

If you have ticked points 1, 4 and 5, you are a healthy teenager. However, if you have ticked any one or more of the others, there is a chance you are suffering from an eating disorder.

Eating disorders usually show up at adolescence because a person might have low self-esteem. They might not be happy with their bodies, comparing themselves with other students, film stars or models. Looking good and having a perfectly slim body becomes the most important goal in life. To achieve that, a person might eat very little, or skip meals or even throw up voluntarily after eating. When they see themselves in the mirror, even if they are slim, they think they look over-weight. This problem is called *Anorexia nervosa.*

Anorexia is a serious, potentially life-threatening disorder that affects a person's emotional and physical health.

A. Is there anyone around you who seem to be suffering from this disorder? If yes, how would you help them? Remember, the disorder starts in the mind. Give four suggestions on how you will help someone you know is suffering from Anorexia.

____

____

B. Is there any other disorder that you know of? Find out and write a few sentences on it.

____

____

C. How would you tackle any disorder while being sensitive to the emotional well-being of others?

____

____

8 Reproduction in Animals

Curricular Goals

- Explore the living world in scientific terms **(CG-3)**
- Understand the components of health, hygiene and well-being **(CG-4)**
- Understand the interface of science, technology and society **(CG-5)**

Competencies

- Describe the diversity of living things observed in the natural surroundings, including at a smaller scale **(C-3.1)**
- Describe biological changes during adolescence and measures to ensure overall well-being **(C-4.3)**
- Illustrate how science and technology can help to improve the quality of human life as well as some of the harmful uses of science in history **(C-5.1)**

Let's Get Started

All living organisms produce young ones of their own kind. Some animals give birth to babies, while some animals reproduce by laying eggs. In the pictures given below, identify which animals lay eggs and which give birth to their babies.

________________ ________________ ________________

The process by which living organisms produce young ones of their own kind is called **reproduction**. Reproduction is not necessary for the survival of organisms, but it is essential for the continuation of species. In other words, organisms of a particular species will become extinct if they do not reproduce.

TYPES OF REPRODUCTION

Two types of reproduction are seen among living organisms—asexual and sexual.

Asexual Reproduction

Asexual reproduction is the simplest form of reproduction where a new offspring is formed from the cells of a single organism. It is most commonly observed in organisms such as *Amoeba*, *Hydra*, yeast, sponges, starfish and worms. Some examples of asexual reproduction are discussed below.

Binary fission

Binary fission (Fig. 8.1) is seen in organisms such as *Amoeba* and *Paramoecium*. In this method, the nucleus divides, and then the parent cell divides into two daughter cells of roughly equal sizes. The daughter cells are identical to the parent cell.

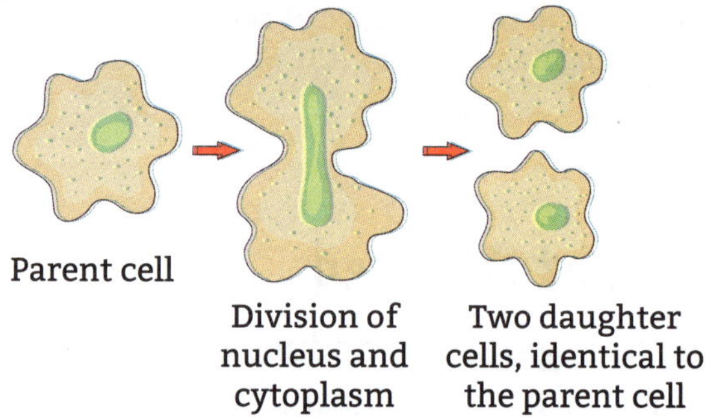

Fig. 8.1: Binary fission in *Amoeba*

Budding

Budding is seen in organisms such as *Hydra* (Fig. 8.2). In this process, a multicellular bulb-like structure develops from the body of a *Hydra* and projects outwards. This projection is called a **bud**. These buds grow and develop and once they mature, they separate from the parent body to live an independent life.

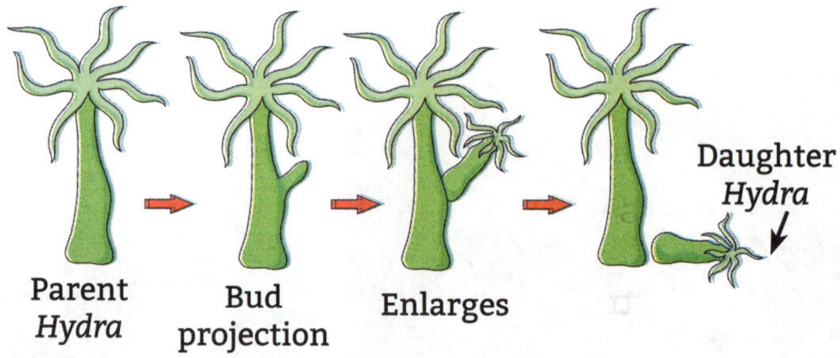

Fig. 8.2: Budding in *Hydra*

Cloning

Cloning is the process of creating a genetically identical copy of a cell or organism. The identical copy of a cell or organism created is known as **clone**. In nature, cloning occurs through asexual reproduction when a cell replicates itself without any changes in its genetic makeup. This can happen naturally in certain organisms, such as bacteria and single-celled organisms, where cells divide and produce genetically identical offspring. This type of cloning maintains the same genetic information without any alteration or recombination.

Case Study: Cloning

Cloning means the production of one or more than one identical offspring. A clone is an organism that is genetically identical to its donor parent.

Cloning involves specialized tools and involves a few basic steps. The steps are listed below:

- Enucleation (removal of nucleus) of the recipient egg
- Transfer of the donor nucleus into the recipient egg
- Fusion of the donor nucleus with the recipient egg
- Growing the resulting cloned embryo under artificial laboratory conditions
- Transfer of the developing embryo into the reproductive tract of a surrogate mother

Sexual Reproduction

Most plants and animals, including human beings, reproduce sexually. Male and female gametes are required for sexual reproduction.

Reproduction in Human Beings

a

In human beings, males and females have different reproductive organs. These organs, called gonads, produce special reproductive cells or **gametes**.

The male gamete [Fig. 8.3(a)] is called a **sperm**. A **sperm cell** is a thin and elongated structure with a head, a middle piece and a tail. These cells are motile and they swim their way to the female gamete. Sperm cells are produced in millions in the testes.

The female gamete [Fig. 8.3(b)] is called an **ovum**. An **ovum (or egg cell)** is round in structure, with thick layers of cells on the outside and abundant cytoplasm. They are immobile[1] structures and very large when compared to the sperm cell.

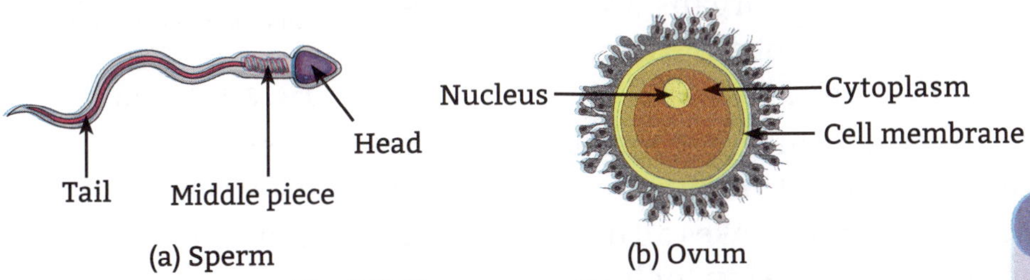

Fig. 8.3: Human gametes

Word Web

[1]**Immobile**: unable to move

Male and Female Reproductive Organs

Let us understand the structure and function of the male (Fig. 8.4) and female reproductive organs (Fig. 8.5).

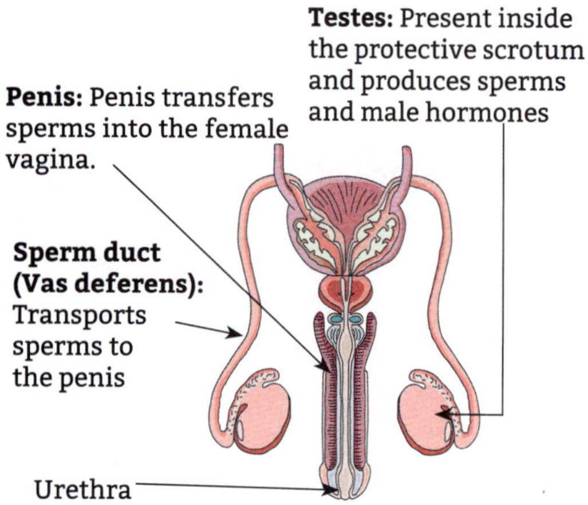

Fig. 8.4: Male reproductive system

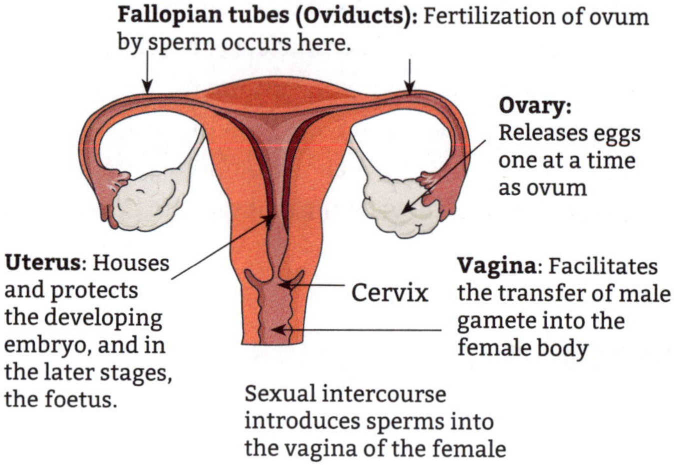

Fig. 8.5: Female reproductive system

Fertilization

The process of the fusion of the two gametes, that is the sperm and the ovum is called **fertilization** (Fig. 8.6). While there are many sperms produced every day in a male, in the female only one ovum is produced in a month.

When the sperms fuse with the ovum, it results in the formation of a zygote. In humans, this process of fertilization occurs in the oviduct or the fallopian tube. The zygote then undergoes repeated division forming two cells, four cells, eight cells and so on till it is a ball of large number of cells ready to differentiate into tissues and organs. As it undergoes division, it moves from the fallopian tube and comes and attaches itself to the walls of the uterus.

Release of a mature egg into the fallopian tube
↓
Sperms travel upwards inside the female reproductive tract
↓
Fusion of sperm with the egg cell in the fallopian tube
↓
Fertilization takes place
↓
Formation of zygote and its downward movement towards the uterus

Fig. 8.6: Fertilization

As the zygote divides it grows to form an embryo with many cells differentiating into tissues. As the tissues develop into organs and organ systems, the zygote is transformed and now called **foetus**. It takes all of 9 months for the zygote to be completely transformed into a baby ready for birth.

If the ovum does not fuse with the sperm, it is expelled from the uterus along with some uterine tissues and blood. This is called **menstruation.**

In human beings, since fertilization takes place inside the female's body, it is called **internal fertilization.** In many other vertebrates, the fertilization takes place outside the body, which is called **external fertilization**.

The differences between these two types of fertilization are given in Table 8.1.

Table 8.1: Difference between internal and external fertilization

	Internal Fertilization	External Fertilization
Meaning	The fusion of the male and female gametes takes place inside the female's body	The fusion of the male and female gametes takes place outside the body
Examples	Mammals (such as human beings and blue whales), birds and reptiles	Fish, frogs
Site of fertilization	Inside the female's body	Outside the body, usually in water/aquatic medium
Number of gametes	Comparatively less, often only one female gamete is produced	More with several female and male gametes

The benefit of internal fertilization is that the number of gametes required is less as fertilization takes place within the body. The female takes sufficient care until the foetus develops within the body, thus ensuring the safety of the foetus. However, in internal fertilization, there are chances of transmission of diseases from the mother to the foetus, in case the mother is suffering from infectious diseases.

In external fertilization, a male can deposit sperms at a slightly different time and location, and the female does not have to incubate the young ones inside the body and bring them up. However, in this type of fertilization, a larger number of gametes is produced by the individuals to ensure reproductive success. This requires extra energy. Several gametes die before fertilization, and even if they make it up to the fertilization stage, the embryo may be destroyed by predators.

Case Study: In Vitro Fertilization

The first success story:

A couple in the UK was unable to conceive even after nine years of their marriage. The woman was diagnosed with a fallopian tube obstruction. The doctor recommended a procedure that involved removing a single mature egg from her ovary to which her husband's sperm was fused under laboratory conditions. This procedure is called in vitro fertilization (IVF). After a few days, the developing embryo was artificially placed into the woman's uterus. After nine months, a baby was born.

About the method:

In vitro in Latin means 'in glass'—a reference to the process taking place in glass containers such as petri dishes and not inside the human body. In vitro fertilization (IVF) is the process of fertilization of an ovum with a sperm in a petri dish under laboratory conditions. IVF is mainly performed to treat infertility. This technique is used under the following conditions:

- Damaged or blocked fallopian tubes (oviducts) and other clinical conditions
- Low sperm production or low sperm motility
- Male and female infertility

Revise and Recall

State whether the following statements are true (T) or false (F).

1. Asexual reproduction involves two parents. ☐
2. The male gamete is called ovum. ☐
3. Sperms are produced in testes. ☐
4. The fusion of two sperms is called fertilization. ☐
5. External fertilization takes place inside the female's body. ☐

Baby inside the womb

After fertilization, the zygote starts moving down the oviduct.

During the first eight weeks after fertilization, the baby is called the **embryo.** From eight weeks after fertilization till birth, the developing baby is called the **foetus.** The baby stays and grows inside the mother's womb (uterus) for about 40 weeks to develop fully (Fig. 8.7). This period is called the **gestation period**.

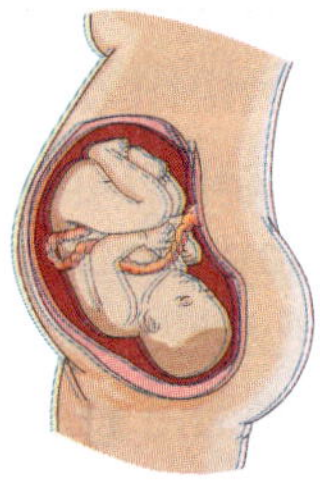

Fig. 8.7: Baby inside the womb

Gestation period is different in different mammals. When the foetus is fully developed, the mother gives birth to the baby. The birth of the baby is called **parturition**.

Care after birth

A newborn baby is very delicate and unable to nourish itself on its own. The mother nurses the baby with her milk, which helps it to grow. Mother's milk is not only nutritious for the developing infant but also it contains substances that develop resistance to diseases as during that stage they are very prone to infections. Hence, a baby needs to be vaccinated against diseases right after birth. A newborn baby depends on the people around it for all its basic needs and, therefore, requires a lot of care.

Viviparous and Oviparous Organisms

Most mammals such as deer, elephant, horse and human beings give birth to babies. Such animals are called **viviparous animals.** Other animals such as birds, snakes and frogs lay eggs that hatch later. Such animals are called **oviparous animals.**

Metamorphosis

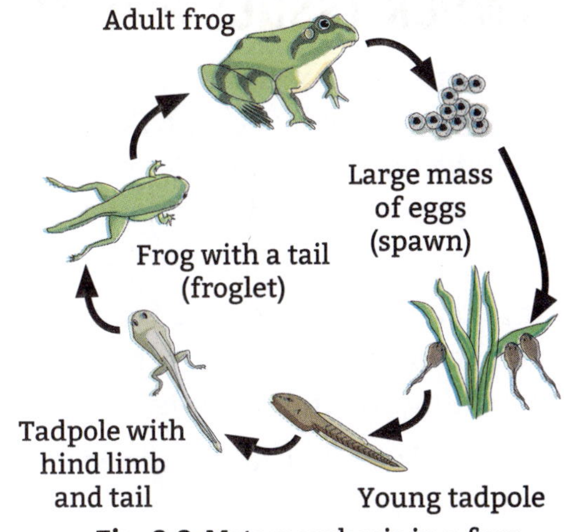

Fig. 8.8: Metamorphosis in a frog

Almost all newborn babies of mammals and hatched chicks of birds resemble their parents. However, in some animals such as insects and frogs, the new hatchlings do not resemble their parents. They undergo a series of changes through different stages, during which they develop into an adult animal. Let us understand this process from the life cycle of a frog and a butterfly.

There are four main stages in the life cycle of a frog (Fig. 8.8).

Egg > Tadpole > Froglet > Adult

An adult female frog lays eggs in water in large numbers. This group of eggs is called a **spawn**. Fertilization happens when the sperms released by the male frog come in contact with these eggs.

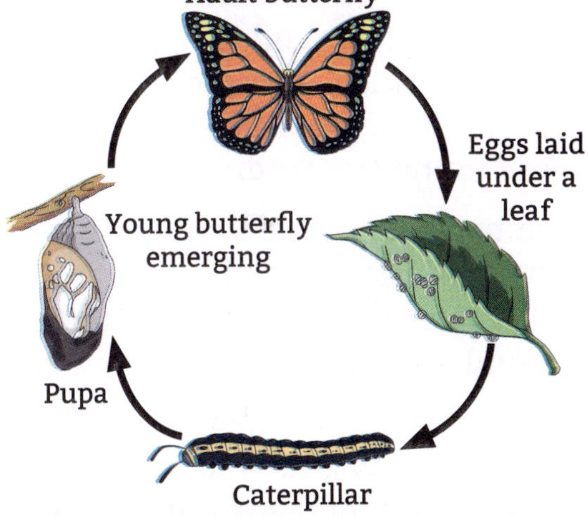

Fig. 8.9: Metamorphosis in a butterfly

The larva that hatches out of the fertilized egg looks different from an adult frog. This soon grows into a tadpole that has no limbs, but a fin to move around. It soon grows and begins to breathe through gills but does not have lungs like an adult frog. The tadpole then undergoes more changes. It grows limbs and the fin disappears to finally become a frog.

The process in which a young one undergoes several changes to finally resemble its adult is called **metamorphosis**.

Butterflies also undergo metamorphosis (Fig. 8.9). The adult butterfly lays eggs. The larva comes out when the eggs hatch. The larva of a butterfly grows to form a caterpillar, which eats, grows to form the pupa. This is called the pupa or the pupal stage. The pupa undergoes changes and after a fixed period, the adult butterfly emerges out of the pupa.

Egg > Larva > Pupa > Adult

Science in Context

Many butterflies can taste with their feet to find out whether the leaf they sit on is good to lay eggs or for their caterpillar's food. Most butterflies do not spin a cocoon. Only moths spin a cocoon.

Wonder!

The male frog is the only one who can croak. Every frog species makes its own unique sound, and some do not even croak. Some frogs whistle and some chirp like a bird.

GENDER ISSUES AND MYTHS

In certain parts of India, women are still considered as burdens to their family. Selective abortion[1], female foeticide (killing of female foetuses), as well as female infanticide (killing female infants) are still in practice.

Word Web

[1]**Abortion:** removal of the embryo or the foetus from the womb

Mothers are held responsible for delivering a female child and are harassed for the same reason. Further, the female child is deprived of a nutritious diet, education and even recreation. Even though the government has banned practices such as sex determination in hospitals, the issue still persists.

The sex of a child is determined by the father's sperm, which fertilizes the ovum to form the zygote. The misconception in people's mind to blame the mother for the birth of a girl child can only be removed by educating them and creating awareness. If not, such misconceptions or gender issues and myths will continue to prevail.

Problems of Adolescent Pregnancy

About 16 million children are born to women between the age of 15–19 years each year worldwide. Girls are not physically and mentally prepared for motherhood at such an early age. Therefore, adolescent pregnancy is dangerous to both the mother and the child.

Compared to mothers in older age groups, teenage mothers are at a greater risk of having medical complications and health problems during pregnancy and child birth. These include anaemia, malaria, HIV and other sexually transmitted diseases, and mental disorders such as depression.

Early marriage and motherhood also restrict educational and career opportunities for girls. Many girls who become pregnant have to leave school. This has long-term implications for them as individuals and even on their families and communities.

Revise and Recall

Fill in the blanks.

1. The type of reproduction that involves a single parent is called __________ reproduction. (asexual/sexual)
2. The animals that lay eggs are called _______. (oviparous/viviparous)
3. Reproduction in *Amoeba* results in ________ daughter cells. (two/many)
4. Metamorphosis is observed in the case of ________. (butterflies/fish)

Keywords

Fertilization: The fusion of male and female gametes to produce a new organism (offspring)

Gestation: The period from the time of fertilization to the birth of the young one, during which it develops inside its mother's womb

Implantation: Attachment of the fertilized egg to the walls of the uterus

Metamorphosis: The process of transformation of the larva into an adult through a series of changes

Summary

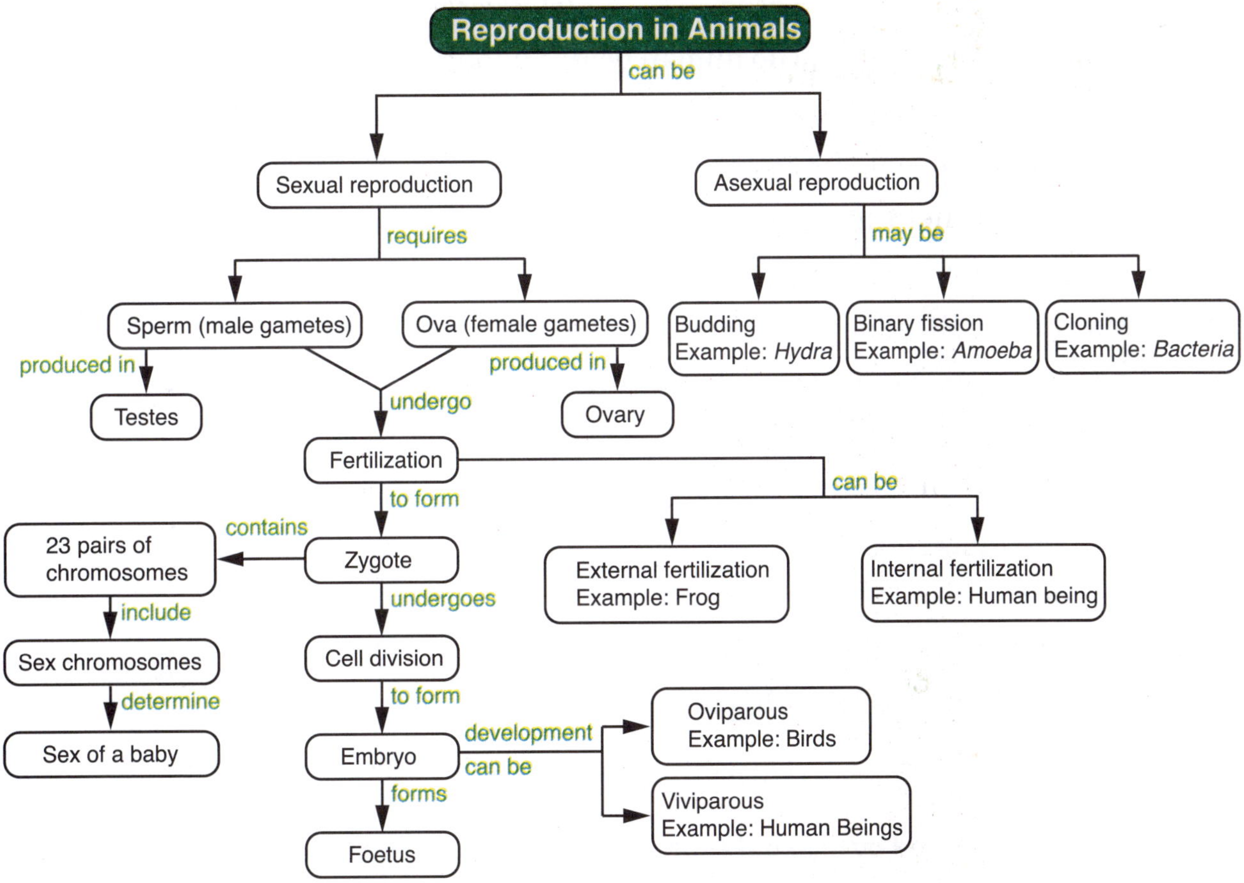

Exercise

A. Choose the correct option.

1. Sexual reproduction involves the fusion of ______________.

   (a) male gametes (b) male and female gametes

   (c) female gametes alone (d) male gametes alone

2. Metamorphosis is the process of transformation of ______________.

   (a) larva into adult (b) new individuals from buds

   (c) eggs to larva (d) eggs to moth

3. Which of the following organisms undergoes internal fertilization?

   (a) Frog (b) Fish (c) Butterfly (d) Hen

4. Which of the following reproduces through binary fission?

   (a) Human beings (b) *Amoeba* (c) *Hydra* (d) Dog

5. Which type of fertilization do human beings undergo?

   (a) External fertilization (b) Internal fertilization

   (c) Both external and internal fertilization (d) None of these

B. State whether the following statements are true (T) or false (F).

1. Fusion of gametes takes place in binary fission. ☐
2. In internal fertilization, the young ones are nourished before birth. ☐
3. All organisms undergo internal fertilization. ☐
4. Zygote is the first stage of human development. ☐
5. Viviparous animals may undergo metamorphosis. ☐

C. Define the following terms.

1. Gestation 2. Gametes 3. Fertilization
4. Sex chromosomes 5. Ovulation 6. Cloning

D. Give reasons for the following.

1. Offspring of oviparous animals are at a greater risk than those of viviparous animals.
2. Offspring produced by asexual reproduction are genetically similar.
3. In human male, testes are situated in the scrotal sac present outside of the abdomen.
4. Teenage mothers are at a greater risk of having medical complications.
5. Internal fertilization will give more promising results when compared to external fertilization.

E. Answer the following questions briefly.

1. List the male and female reproductive organs in humans.
2. What is metamorphosis? List the stages in the metamorphosis of a butterfly.
3. List two problems associated with teenage pregnancy.
4. Give two advantages and one disadvantage of internal fertilization.
5. Differentiate between sexual and asexual reproduction.

F. Answer the following questions in detail.

1. Explain the different parts of a male reproductive organ.
2. With the help of diagrams, explain how *Amoeba* and *Hydra* reproduce.
3. What is cloning? List the basic steps involved in the process.
4. List the gender issues and myths that exist in developing countries.
5. Sequence the steps of fertilization in humans.

Cognitive Corner

Critical Thinking

1. *Hydra* is said to be immortal (not subject to death or decay). What could be the reasons for this?
2. Why do some species of birds and animals become extinct, even though they reproduce and produce young ones?

Picture Study

Label the diagrams given here.

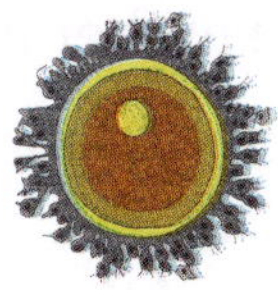

Project

1. Draw the life cycles of a frog and butterfly on a chart paper and display it in your class. **(C-7.2)**
2. Prepare a PowerPoint presentation on cloning, with its advantages and disadvantages. Read books or use the Internet to collect more information. **(C-7.1)**

In the Library

Find out how identical and non-identical twins, triplets and quadruplets are formed. Make a PowerPoint presentation on your findings and present it in your class. **(C-7.1)**

Life Skills

In our society, in this modern era, some families prefer having a son over a daughter. And moreover, the mother is held responsible, blamed and cursed for the birth of a girl child. It is the male parent (the father) whose gamete determines whether the child to be born will be a boy or a girl.

Find out more on this and have a discussion in class about how this social stigma can be eradicated. Base your discussions on scientific facts only. **(C-7.1)**

Worksheet

According to the United Nations, sex ratio is defined as the number of males per 100 females. In India, as per 2011 census, there were 940 females per 1000 males on a national average. What could be the reasons behind this imbalance?

This is because of two main reasons: social and economic factors.

There has been a long-drawn social stigma associated with a girl child:

- the huge cost that parents must bear to get the girl married and custom of dowry
- a deeply rooted superstition that only a son can perform funeral rites

This had led to baby girls being killed at birth in large numbers. After a law banning this was passed, people took another route. As soon as an ultrasound showed that the mother is carrying a girl in her womb, it is aborted. Another law has been passed where it is illegal to inform the parents about the sex of the unborn child during sonography.

India has achieved a literacy rate of 74.04%. It is not a matter of chance that states that have higher literacy rates show a higher sex ratio.

If a mother is educated, she not only contributes to the well-being of her children, she also contributes to the overall development of the country. By not giving a girl child the option of living, we are depriving our families and nation of a lot of talent.

A. Can you state any two reasons for the imbalance of the sex ratio in our country?

B. Suggest at least three ways by which you think the sex ratio can be improved in India.

9 Conservation of Plants and Animals

Curricular Goals

- Explore the living world in scientific terms **(CG-3)**
- Explore the nature and processes of science through engaging with the evolution of scientific knowledge and conducting scientific inquiry **(CG-6)**
- Communicate questions, observations and conclusions related to science **(CG-7)**

Competencies

- Describe the diversity of living things observed in the natural surroundings, including at a smaller scale **(C-3.1)**
- Identify the scientific values that are inherent and common across the evolution of scientific knowledge **(C-6.1)**
- Use scientific vocabulary to communicate science accurately in oral and written forms, and through visual representation **(C-7.1)**

Let's Get Started

Look at the pictures given below and match the animal with its habitat.

Animals

Habitats

In this chapter, we will study about the diversity in plants and animals on Earth, the threats to them and the ways to conserve them.

BIOSPHERE

The part of the Earth where life exists is called ***biosphere***. The atmosphere, land and water bodies such as rivers, ponds, oceans, etc., along with plants and animals that live there, form the biosphere.

The variety in organisms living in a particular region forms the **biodiversity** of that region. Let us learn more about biodiversity.

BIODIVERSITY

Biodiversity (Fig. 9.1) refers to the number, variety and variability of living organisms at a place at a given point of time ('bio' means life and 'diversity' means variety).

Fig. 9.1: Biodiversity

Biodiversity varies, depending on the climatic conditions of a region. Deserts have a different biodiversity compared with the tropical rainforests.

India is a subtropical country with different kinds of habitats such as the Thar desert, the Himalayan region, the Western Ghats and the Sunderbans. Hence, it has a rich biodiversity.

Wonder!

Four biodiversity hotspots have been identified in India because of the unique and diverse species found in these regions: the Himalayas, the Indo–Burma region, the Western Ghats and the Nicobar islands.

Science in Context

Regions with rich biodiversity are called megadiversity centres. There are 12 megadiversity centres in the world. India is one of the twelve megadiversity centres of the world.

Flora and Fauna

The plants found in a region are called **flora**. The flora of a region depends on the climatic conditions of the region.

Animals found in a region are called **fauna**. The density and diversity of flora is closely related to the fauna as plants are the source of food for herbivores, and indirectly for the carnivores. Thus, flora and fauna are interdependent.

Ecosystem

The interactions between organisms and their environment in a given region form the ***ecosystem****. The living elements that form a part of the region are called the* ***biotic factors****,* whereas *the non-living entities are called the* **abiotic factors**.

The **biotic factors** include different kinds of plants and animals. The **abiotic factors** include soil, water, temperature, etc.

The interdependence of biotic and abiotic factors forms an ecosystem. Examples of ecosystems are marine ecosystem, grassland ecosystem and pond ecosystem.

LOSS OF BIODIVERSITY

Different kinds of animals have a specific place in the food chain and food web. If one of them is destroyed, then the food web or the food chain gets disrupted.

In recent times, human interference has resulted in the loss of biodiversity to a great extent. Some human activities that are a threat to biodiversity are given below:

- **Poaching**: Animals are being hunted or trapped to obtain their body parts such as skin, fur, bones, ivory and claws, which are used to make traditional medicines, ornaments, etc.
- **Deforestation**: It is one of the main causes of the loss of biodiversity. When forests are destroyed, animals that live in these forests lose their habitat, which may lead to their extinction.
- **Pollution of air, water and soil** is wiping out many plants and animal species.
- **Invasive species:** The introduction of new species to a particular region leads to the dominance of the new species over the native species.
- **Monoculture:** It is the process of growing only that plant species which is of economic importance, instead of growing the native plant species. During afforestation programmes, monoculture leads to the loss of biodiversity of that particular area.

IMPORTANCE OF FORESTS

One of the most important factors of forests is the production of oxygen by the plants in the forests. For this reason, forests are also called **green lungs**. In our daily lives, we use products such as honey, spices, gums and resins, which come from forests. The timber used for making furniture and building materials also comes from forests.

Forests help in the formation of rain and to control the amount of carbon dioxide in the atmosphere. In rural areas, people depend on forests for firewood, medicines, timber, etc.

Deforestation

a

Fig. 9.2: Deforestation

Deforestation (Fig. 9.2) is the cutting down of trees and destruction of forests on a large scale. The main causes of deforestation are given below:

- The requirement of land for building residential areas, industries and for mining of minerals leads to the clearing of forests.
- Increase in population has led to a high demand for food crops and grazing land for animals, which has resulted in the clearing of forests.
- The rise in population has also led to a higher requirement of timber, wood for fuel and other forest products such as gums, resins, oils, medicines and spices.
- Extreme weather events such as wildfires, droughts, and storm surges destroy millions of hectares of forest land every year. The intensity of such events is increasing with global warming.

Consequences of Deforestation

Human activities leading to deforestation have disturbed the balance of nature and has even caused natural calamities. The main effects of deforestation are given below:

- **Desertification**: Overgrazing, removal of vegetation from soil and deforestation lead to soil erosion. Soil erosion leads to the removal of the fertile topsoil, exposing the soil beneath it. This soil does not support the growth of vegetation, leading to the formation of deserts.
- **Floods**: Due to the removal of vegetation from land, rain does not infiltrate or percolate into the soil. There is excess runoff water that gets collected and leads to flooding. Floods also cause soil erosion.
- **Droughts**: Due to the removal of trees, there is an imbalance in the water cycle causing less rainfall. This eventually leads to the onset of drought.

- **Increased greenhouse gases**: Plants absorb carbon dioxide during photosynthesis. Due to less vegetation, the excess carbon dioxide in the atmosphere absorbs the heat radiated from the land and increases the temperature on Earth. This is called **global warming** due to which the polar icecaps are melting, resulting in an increase in sea levels.
- **Decreased rainfall and water table**: The roots of the plants hold the soil and water percolates into the deeper parts of the soil, creating a water table.
However, when there are fewer trees, the runoff water creates floods.
- **Soil erosion**: Trees check the movement of wind and the flow of water. In their absence, the blowing wind and runoff water carry the topsoil away, making the land infertile.
- **Shortage of food and forest produce:** Forest provides us with a lot of resources such as food, wood, oils and medicines. Deforestation leads to shortage of forest products.
- **Effect on animal and plant life:** Animals and birds are dependent on plants and trees for their survival. Due to loss of forests, their natural habitats and food chain are be disturbed.

Conservation of Forests

Conservation of the existing forests and regeneration of the lost forest cover are the needs of the hour. Some sustainable ways of the use of forests and a few measures for the conservation of forests are given below:

Fig. 9.3: Afforestation

- **Afforestation**: Replanting trees in the deforested areas is a slow and labour-intensive process, but it is an effective method of conservation (Fig. 9.3).
- **Biological control**: Insects or pests cause a lot of damage to the trees in the forests. This is where the natural enemies of the insects and pests are helpful. The rodents, birds, frogs, etc., which feed on insects and pests, can be used as the biological control.
- **Preventing forest fires** during the dry summer months by making fire lines. The forest fires can be extinguished by spraying water/soil.
- Setting up **national parks** and **sanctuaries** where commercial exploitation is prohibited is an effective way to conserve forests.
- **Social forestry** is a concept in which barren and unused land, which is common to the community, is used to grow trees and plants that provide firewood, fodder and timber.

Revise and Recall

Sort the given causes of deforestation into natural or human-made.
(Volcanic eruptions, Urbanization, Floods, Agricultural practices, Soil erosion, Wildfire, Construction of roads and dams)

Natural	Human-made

WILDLIFE AND ITS CONSERVATION

Life in the wild includes all kinds of animals: herbivores, carnivores and omnivores. All animals are directly or indirectly dependent on plants for food. The carnivores are dependent on the herbivores, which depend on plants for their food. If one group of plants or animals is affected, it disturbs the food chain and food web.

Following are some of the major **threats to wildlife**:

- Destruction of habitats by deforestation for the construction of roads, railways, dams, etc.
- Hunting and poaching of animals for their parts such as skin, claws and bones.
- Human encroachments on forestland for commercial and agricultural purposes.
- Destruction of aquatic habitats by pollution and various other means makes the water unfit for fish and other aquatic animals to survive.
- Natural calamities such as floods, epidemics and wildfires.

Following are some measures to **conserve wildlife**:

- Strict wildlife protection laws have to be implemented to prevent hunting and poaching.
- Captive breeding programmes to increase the population of the depleting and endangered species.
- Protection of natural habitats by setting up wildlife sanctuaries and national parks.
- Early identification of population decline by wildlife census will enable us to undertake remedial measures in a timely manner.
- Educating people about the importance and methods of the conservation of wildlife.
- Creating awareness in people to stop purchasing wildlife products such as claws, animal skin, fur and ivory.

International Union for Conservation of Nature and Natural Resources

The International Union for Conservation of Nature and Natural Resources (IUCN) is the world's main authority on the conservation status of species. (A group of individual organisms capable of interbreeding and producing offspring is called **species.**) It periodically lists and gives information about the species of plants and animals that face threats of various kinds. These lists are published through their publications—Red List and the Red Data Book.

Some categories listed by IUCN are as follows:

Extinct (EX) species: Species that do not have any living representative on Earth. Examples are dinosaur and dodo.

Endangered (EN) species: These species are in danger of extinction due to a steep decline in their number. There are 47 critically endangered species in India.

Vulnerable (VU) species: Species that face a high risk of becoming endangered due to adverse factors.

Threatened (T) species: Species whose numbers are fast declining, and which are likely to become endangered or vulnerable in the near future.

Least concern (LC) Species: Species that are widespread and are at a low risk.

Some general classifications are as follows:

Species whose population is small and restricted to only a few regions are called **rare** species. Species of plants and animals that are unique and exclusively found in a particular area are called **endemic** species (Fig. 9.4).

(a) Tapir is endemic to South America and Southeast Asia.

(b) Grey jungle fowl is endemic to India.

(c) Lemur is endemic to Madagascar.

Fig. 9.4: Endemic species

Science in Context

United Nations Educational Scientific and Cultural Organization (UNESCO) conceived the Man and Biosphere (MAB) programme, which encouraged the formation of a group of biosphere reserves representing the main ecosystems of the world.

CONSERVATION OF BIODIVERSITY

As discussed earlier in the chapter, the biodiversity around us is getting destroyed due to deforestation, loss of habitat, hunting and poaching of animals, etc. Replenishment or getting back the lost forests and wildlife will take a lot of time; hence, we need to conserve the forests and wildlife that are left. There are rules and government-issued regulations to help us make informed decisions to safeguard the precious flora and fauna. Specific areas of land have been set aside to protect and safeguard the original habitats and the animals.

Biosphere Reserves

Biosphere reserves are the sites recognized by IUCN's Man and Biosphere (MAB) programme to promote conservation of not only diversity, but also cultural, social and economic development through cooperation and collaboration between people and nature.

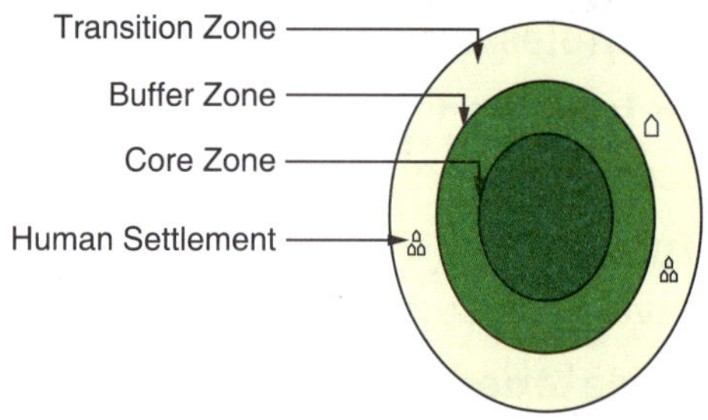

Fig. 9.5: Zones in a biosphere reserve

There are different zones assigned to a biosphere reserve (Fig. 9.5).

The outermost zone of a biosphere reserve is called the **transition zone**. It involves non-destructive human activities such as houses of tribal people, cultivation of crops, etc. The middle zone of a biosphere reserve is called the **buffer zone**, which involves limited human activity. The inner zone of a biosphere reserve is called the **core zone**. It observes the strict protection of wildlife.

Important biosphere reserves in India are Nanda Devi Biosphere Reserve, Sunderbans Biosphere Reserve, Nilgiri Biosphere Reserve (Fig. 9.6), Uttarakhand Biosphere Reserve, etc. India also has marine biosphere reserves such as the Gulf of Mannar and the Rann of Kutch.

Fig. 9.6: Spotted deer at Bandipur National Park under Nilgiri Biosphere Reserve

A biosphere reserve functions to:

- conserve the varied ecosystems of the world.
- provide protection for various species, thereby maintaining diversity.
- develop the economy and cultural aspects of local communities through sustainable use of biodiversity in the region.
- support research, education and the monitoring of local, national and global issues of conservation.

National Parks

National parks are the areas meant to preserve the flora, fauna, landscape and history of regions (Fig. 9.7). People are permitted to enter only the buffer zones or designated areas in the parks for educative, cultural and recreational purposes. No one is allowed inside the core area except the park personnel. There is prohibition on the exploitation of natural resources such as building of dams, sporting events, hunting, fishing, etc. Ranthambhore National Park is an example of a national park in India.

(a) Wild buffalo at Kanha National Park

(b) Tiger at Ranthambhore National Park

Fig. 9.7: Animals in national parks

Science in Context

Yellowstone National Park in the United States of America, set up in 1872, is the first national park of the world.

According to the International Union for Conservation of Nature (IUCN), which monitors the conservation activities in the world, there are 6,555 national parks in the world.

Wildlife Sanctuaries

A **wildlife sanctuary** is a region that is smaller than a national park, set aside for the conservation of wild animals in the natural environment. Sanctuaries help in educating people about the animals being protected there. The public is allowed into the sanctuaries with the forest officials accompanying them. Poaching, fishing and capturing animals are strictly prohibited in the sanctuaries. The region of the sanctuary may have a high population of a particular species of wildlife. The purpose of wildlife sanctuaries is to safeguard the species found in the region.

Examples of wildlife sanctuaries include Ranganathittu Bird Sanctuary in Karnataka, Gir Wildlife Sanctuary for conserving Asiatic Lions and National Chambal Gharial Wildlife Sanctuary (Fig. 9.8).

(a) Asiatic Lion at Gir Wildlife Sanctuary

(b) Birds at Ranganathittu Bird Sanctuary

Fig. 9.8: Animals in wildlife sanctuaries

Science in Context

A sanctuary can also be a temporary home to **migratory birds** from other regions of the world. **Migration** is the movement of birds from their habitats to another region to lay eggs, owing to the unfavourable climate in their habitats. These birds fly long distances to reach favourable places.

The phenomenon of migration is also seen in other major animal groups, including mammals, fish, reptiles and amphibians. Animals migrate mainly in search of food and shelter and to save themselves from harsh climates.

Botanical and Zoological Parks

Botanical or zoological parks are created artificially to house different species in habitats that mimic their original ones. These parks create awareness and educate people about the importance of forests and wildlife. Zoological parks play an important role in breeding and taking care of endangered animals.

National Parks and Sanctuaries in India

On a map of India, mark the location of the national parks and sanctuaries referring to the list given below and mention the animals protected there. How many of them are Tiger Reserves?

- **Kaziranga National Park**: It is situated near Jorhat in the state of Assam. It consists of forest grasslands and swamps that support the Indian one-horned rhinoceros and other wild animals.
- **Chilika Lake Sanctuary**: The Chilika Lake is situated near Bhubaneshwar in the state of Odisha. The fauna includes waterfowl, cranes, sandpipers, flamingos, etc.
- **Mudumalai National Park**: It is located in the north-western part of the Nilgiris in Tamil Nadu. The animals found here are elephants, gaur, pangolins, wild dogs, etc.
- **Keibul Lamjao National Park:** It is located in the state of Manipur. It is known for being the world's only floating national park, and it is situated in the Loktak Lake. The park is unique for its *phumdis*, which are floating islands made of organic matter, vegetation and soil. These *phumdis* are home to various wildlife, including the endangered Manipur brow-antlered deer, also known as the *Sangai*.
- **Bandipur National Park**: It is found in the state of Karnataka, where Project Tiger was started to conserve the depleting population of tigers. The other fauna include chitals, porcupines, langurs, wild dogs, etc.

- **Kanha National Park**: It is situated in the state of Madhya Pradesh. The fauna include tigers, chitals, panthers, black bucks, etc.
- **Sariska National Park**: It is situated in Alwar in the state of Rajastan. The fauna include leopards, tigers, spotted deer, etc.
- **Anamalai Sanctuary**: This sanctuary is in Tamil Nadu. The fauna includes elephants, spotted deer, Nilgiri tahr, lion-tailed macaque, etc.
- **Corbett National Park**: It is situated in Nainital and Garhwal hills in the state of Uttarakhand. It is home to hyenas, tigers, elephants, etc.
- **Periyar National Park**: It is situated in Kerala. It is established around an artificial lake that resulted through the dam built across the river Periyar. The fauna includes sambhars, leopards, sloth bears, etc.

Reforestation

Reforestation can be defined as the process of replanting trees in areas that have been affected by natural disturbances such as wildfires, droughts and disease infestations, and unnatural ones such as logging, mining, agricultural clearing and development.

By planting trees in areas that have been degraded or deforested, reforestation helps the environment by re-establishing healthy forest structure by regrowing the forest canopy and preserving biodiversity within the ecosystem.

The benefits of reforestation are as follows:

- Provides habitat for over 80% of the world's terrestrial biodiversity
- Reduces the impact of global warming and climate change
- Helps to protect endangered species

Recycling of Paper

Paper recycling consists of processes of transforming wastepaper into other forms for reuse. There are several stages to paper recycling such as collecting, sorting, pulping, bleaching, etc. The wastepaper are obtained from paper scraps and paper materials discarded after consumer use including old newspapers and magazines.

The raw material used for the preparation of paper is cellulose, which is extracted from the pulp of trees. Recycling of paper helps to save a lot of trees in the forests.

Biodiversity has been degraded to a large extent, and it is time to save what is left and regenerate the lost forests and wildlife. This will help us save our planet and the various species found on it. Let us pledge to save our forests and wildlife.

Go Green

Follow the rule of 5R—Reduce, Reuse, Recycle, Refuse and Repurpose—to help in the conservation of biodiversity:

- **Reduce** the usage of forest produce or find alternative products for use. Carpooling/public transport/walking/bicycling to school are some of the ways to reduce the use of fossil fuels.
- **Reusable** cloth bags can be carried when one goes shopping rather than getting groceries in polythene bags.
- If wastes from homes are sorted out based on biodegradability, many of the non-biodegradable wastes such as plastic covers and soda cans can be **recycled**.
- **Refuse** unnecessary plastic packaging materials and things that increase waste.
- **Repurpose**, that is, make use of waste objects for a different purpose.

Wonder!

People often think that forests are the only main depositories of biodiversity. However, oceans are equally rich, if not richer, in the number of species that exist in them. Habitats of all kinds including the local ponds or paddy fields contain varieties of organisms, some yet to be discovered, need protection.

Case Study: Project Tiger

At the beginning of the 20th century, the population of the Bengal tiger in India was 40,000. It decreased to 1800 by the year 1972. To stop further decline in the population of the Bengal tiger, the government launched the 'Tiger Conservation Programme' in 1973. This set aside nine tiger reserves in nine states of the country. At present, there are 27 reserves in seven states that endeavour to conserve the Bengal tigers.

The Project Tiger initiative was formed by the government of India in 1973 to stop the depletion of the tiger population and conserve them. A few wildlife sanctuaries such as the Nagarahole National Park, Kanha Tiger Reserve, Sunderbans Tiger Reserve and Biligiri Ranganathaswamy Tiger Reserve have been successful in conserving the tiger population in the country. According to the estimates from the latest tiger census, India is now home to 3,167 tigers.

Keywords

Deforestation: Destruction of trees and wildlife for development purpose

Afforestation: Planting trees where forests have been lost due to human interference

Species: A group of individual organisms capable of interbreeding and producing offspring

Conservation: The judicious use and protection of available natural resources

Monoculture: Growing only that plant species, which is of economic importance instead of native plant species

Biodiversity: The number, variety and variability of living organisms at a given point of time

Indigenous: Originating or occurring naturally in a particular place

Summary

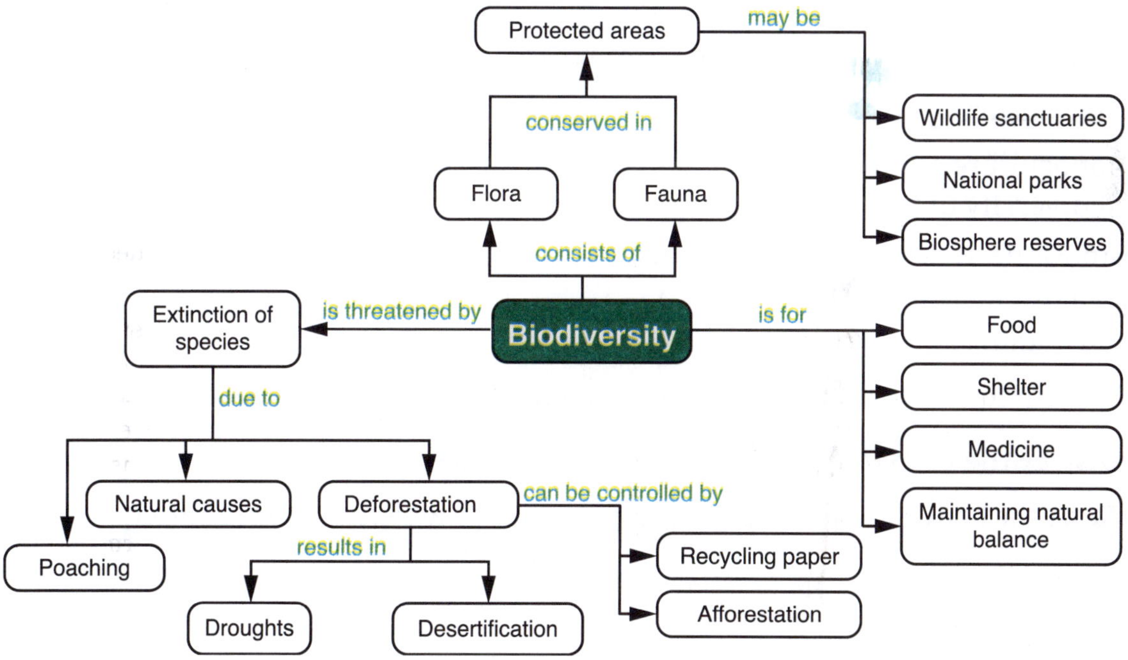

Exercise

W

ia

A. Choose the correct option.

1. One-horned rhinoceros is dwindling in numbers and nearing extinction. Such organisms are categorized as ____________________ species.

   (a) endangered (b) vulnerable (c) rare (d) threatened

2. What is destruction of forests on a large scale called?

   (a) Afforestation (b) Poaching (c) Hunting (d) Deforestation

3. Sanctuaries can be temporary homes for ____________________.

   (a) migratory birds (b) endangered species

   (c) predators (d) herbivores

4. An ecosystem consists of ____________________.

   (a) biotic factors (b) abiotic factors (c) Both (a) and (b) (d) None of these

5. Which of the following is not a reason for deforestation?

   (a) Urbanization (b) Overgrazing of cattle

   (c) Global warming (d) Logging

B. State whether the following statements are true (T) or false (F). ia

1. The non-living elements of an ecosystem are called abiotic factors. ☐
2. Monoculture of an economically important species leads to the loss of biodiversity of that particular area. ☐
3. Dinosaurs are endangered animals. ☐
4. Biodiversity includes only various kinds of animals such as birds, fish and mammals. ☐
5. The core zone of a biosphere reserve can have national parks and sanctuaries. ☐

C. Answer the following in one word or a sentence.

1. Name the body parts in elephants and tigers for which they are hunted.
2. What is IUCN?
3. Define species.
4. Give one example each of flora and fauna found in your neighbourhood.
5. List the different categories of protected areas.
6. What is an ecosystem?
7. What is poaching?

D. Give reasons for the following.

1. Monoculturing of a species of flora affects the native flora of that region.
2. Sanctuaries protect the species inhabiting it.
3. There are various zones in biosphere reserve.
4. One-horned rhinoceros needs to be conserved and protected.
5. Herbal medicine industries affect the biosphere of the forest it depends on.

E. Answer the following questions briefly.

1. How are the flora and fauna of a region dependent on each other?
2. When do species become vulnerable?
3. State the reasons for threat to wildlife.
4. What is a wildlife sanctuary? Give two examples.
5. What are endemic species? Give examples.
6. What are the reasons for deforestation?

F. Answers the following questions in detail.

1. What are the reasons for the loss of biodiversity?
2. Explain the measures taken to conserve wildlife.
3. Briefly explain the consequences of deforestation.
4. What is the Red List? What are the categories of species listed in it?

Cognitive Corner

Critical Thinking

The members of the New Zealand cricket team are fondly called the Kiwis. Kiwi is a bird. Why are the players of that particular country called Kiwis?

Picture Study

Given below are two species endemic to specific regions. Identify the animals and the region they belong to.

Name: ______________

Place: ______________

Name: ______________

Place: ______________

Project

Visit any wildlife sanctuary/national park. Find out which animals are protected there, the year of the park's establishment, the types of animals conserved, successes and failures. Prepare a presentation and present it in your class. **(C-7.1)**

In the Library

The Amazon rainforests represent half of the rainforests in the world. They are found in the South American continent. These tropical forests are species-rich and have an unparalleled biodiversity; that is, they have the largest variety of plants and animals. Some of the species found here are black caimans, jaguars, cougars, anacondas, eels, piranhas and poisonous dart frogs. The Amazon forest territory is found in Peru, Brazil, Colombia, Suriname, Venezuela, Ecuador, Bolivia, Guyana and French Guiana.

Find out more about the Amazon rainforests by reading books from the library and make a case study report. Include the following points in your report. **(C-7.1)**

- The impact of human habitation on the Amazon forest due to

  (a) industrialization (b) agriculture (c) roads (d) timber logging
  (e) mining

- Conservation activities taken up in the Amazon

Life Skills

1. While visiting a zoo or going on a wildlife safari, we need to follow some rules and instructions. Find out the following:

- What are the rules and regulations written on the signboards in a zoo and why?
- When you go on a safari, what are the instructions that need to be followed for safety? **(C-9.1)**

2. Take the following pledge to conserve the nature and its gifts:

Pledge

I, ____________, of Class ____________, pledge to preserve the gifts of nature so that the future generations can enjoy all the comforts that I have been blessed with.

Write three more pledge that can be used to spread awareness on conserving the nature and its gifts. **(C-7.1)**

Worksheet

The Emperor penguin is a majestic animal that spends its entire life on the ice or in the surrounding waters of Antarctica. Every winter, which for the Southern Hemisphere starts from March, emperor penguins travel 80 km across the ice to reach their breeding grounds. After the eggs are laid, the male penguins take care of the eggs and the females travel back to where they had come from.

They feed on krill, squid and fish and travel back to feed their young penguins, who have hatched by now, by **regurgitating** (bringing food back from the stomach before it has been digested) the food for the hatchlings to eat.

Due to global warming, ice caps are melting in the Antarctic at an alarming rate. As their breeding grounds disappear, the number of emperor penguins are decreasing. If the ice disappears, they will have no place to bring up their babies. There will be no more emperor penguins being born on Earth.

A. Number the events, that form a chain, that is causing a scenario where these majestic animals may one day disappear.

- GREENHOUSE EFFECT ☐
- EXTINCTION OF EMPEROR PENGUINS ☐
- INDUSTRIALIZATION ☐
- AIR POLLUTION: EMISSION OF CARBON DIOXIDE ☐
- NO BREEEDING PLACE ☐
- MELTING OF SEA ICE ☐

An Emperor penguin with its chick

B. What are you doing, at your end, to protect and restore the "Life on Land"? Name any three actions you have taken so far. If you have not taken any steps, what do you plan to do?

____

____

____

____

10 Force and Friction

Curricular Goals

- Explore the nature and processes of science through engaging with the evolution of scientific knowledge and conducting scientific inquiry **(CG-6)**
- Communicate questions, observations and conclusions related to science **(CG-7)**

Competencies

- Formulate questions using scientific terminology (to identify possible causes for an event, behaviour of objects) and collect data as evidence (through design of simple experiments) **(C-6.2)**
- Use scientific vocabulary to communicate science accurately in oral and written forms, and through visual representation **(C-7.1)**

Let's Get Started

In the previous classes, we have studied about force and some effects of force. Force is either a push or a pull. In each of the following cases, identify and write if the force is a push or a pull.

1. ________

A bullock cart moving forward

2. ________

A man moving a trolley

3. ________

A man carrying buckets of water

4. ________

A man carrying a heavy load on his head

EFFECTS OF FORCE

Various changes take place when force is applied on a body (Fig. 10.1). Let us learn about these changes.

A force can make a stationary body move or can increase the speed of a moving body

Suppose we are pushing a table in our classroom. What happens to the table? The table starts moving in the direction of the force applied. Thus, we can say that a force can set a body from rest to motion. If we push a trolley, it moves. If we push it harder, it moves faster with a greater speed.

A force can make a moving body stop

Have you seen a fielder in a cricket match stretching out his arms to catch a ball from crossing the boundary? What does he actually do? He applies force with his hands to stop the ball from going further. Similarly, when we apply brakes of a car, we are applying a force to stop it. Thus, we can say that force can make a moving body slow down or stop.

A force can change the direction of a moving body

Consider a moving cricket ball hit by a batsman. The batsman hits the ball and changes the direction of motion of the ball. You must have watched a soccer match. Each player in both teams tries to bring the ball towards their goalpost. If a member of one team kicks the ball in one direction, a player of the opponent team kicks it in the other direction. Here, they are actually applying force to change the direction of the moving ball. This shows that force can change the direction of a moving body.

A force can change the shape of a body

Hold a rubber ball in your hand and press it between both of your palms. What happens to the shape of the ball? The shape of the ball changes. Have you seen your mother making chapattis? She kneads the dough with her hands. Every time she presses into the dough, it changes its shape. Thus, we can say that force can change the shape of the body.

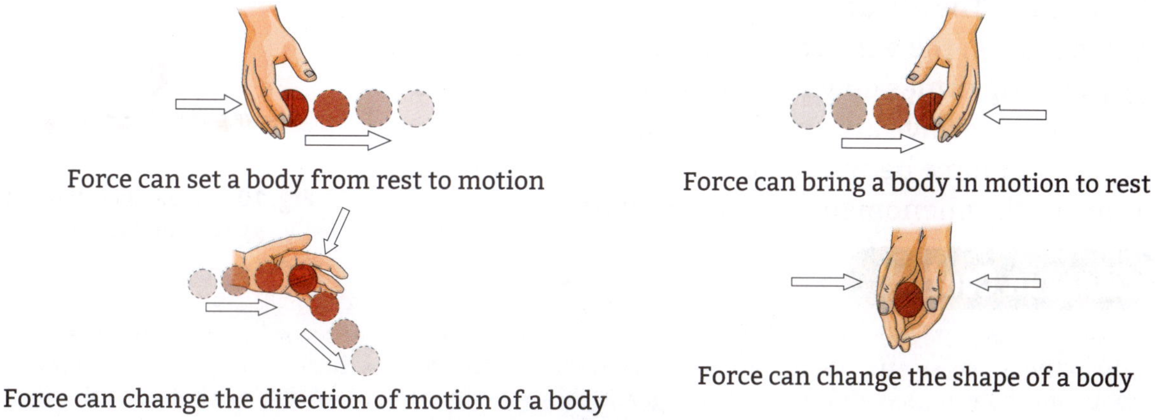

Fig. 10.1: Effects of force

CONTACT FORCES AND NON-CONTACT FORCES

Can we push or pull a chair without touching it? No, we should have physical contact with the chair in order to push or pull it. A force acting between the two bodies that requires a physical contact between them is called a **contact force**. Muscular force and frictional force are examples of contact forces.

Now, consider a body falling towards the Earth. We know that it is falling down because the gravitational force of the Earth is pulling the body down. Is there any physical contact between the Earth and the body? No. A force acting between the two bodies that does not require any physical contact between them is called a **non-contact force**. Gravitational force, electrostatic force and magnetic force are examples of non-contact forces. Let us discuss some contact and non-contact forces one by one.

Muscular Force

Muscular force is the force that is the result of the action of muscles. Lifting a heavy box needs force applied by our hands. A weightlifter (Fig. 10.2) lifts the weight with the force applied by his arms.

Fig. 10.2: Muscular force

Gravitational Force

The force of attraction that pulls objects towards the surface of the Earth is called **gravitational force**. Gravitational force (Fig. 10.3) acts between all the objects in the universe. It plays a very important role in our daily life. Gravitational force of the Earth allows us to walk on its surface. The attraction ensures that the objects on Earth stay on the surface of the Earth. That is why a ball thrown up comes down. Gravitational force causes the planets to revolve around the Sun in their orbits. Gravitational force between the Moon, the Earth and the Sun causes the phenomenon of ocean tides.

Fig. 10.3: Objects fall due to gravitational force

Science in Context

In 1687, Sir Isaac Newton published the Universal Law of Gravitation according to which every body in the universe attracts every other body with a force which is directly proportional to the product of their masses and inversely proportional to the square of the distance between them.

Electrostatic Force

The force acting between charged particles is called **electrostatic force**. It can either be a force of attraction or a force of repulsion between two charged particles. Contact between the charged particles is not required. Unlike gravitational force that causes only attraction, electrostatic force may cause attraction or repulsion between charged particles. The nature of the force depends on the nature of the charges. Like charges repel each other, while unlike charges attract each other. In other words, two positively charged or two negatively charged particles will repel each other; but a negative charge and a positive charge will attract each other (Fig. 10.4).

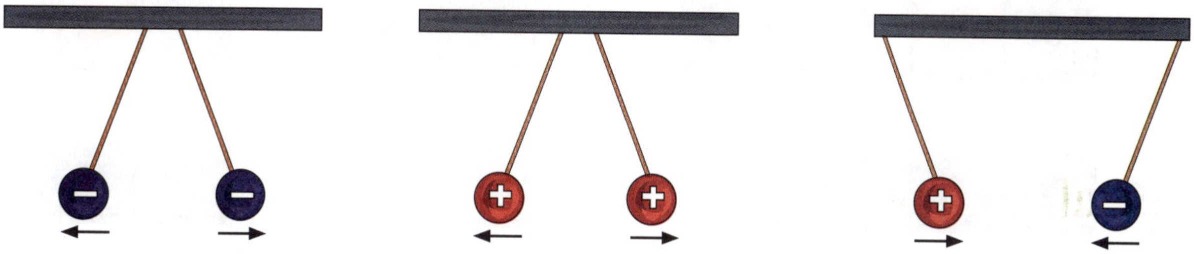

Fig. 10.4: Like charges repel and unlike charges attract each other

Activity 1

Aim: To show that electrostatic force is a non-contact force

Materials required: A small plastic ball, stand, ebonite rod, fur, glass rod and silk

Procedure:

1. Suspend the small plastic ball by the means of a thread on the stand.
2. Rub the ebonite rod with fur and bring it close to the ball. Make sure that the rod does not touch the ball. Observe what happens to the ball. Is there any contact between the ball and the ebonite rod?
3. Rub the glass rod with silk and bring it close to the ball. Make sure that the rod does not touch the ball. Observe what happens to the ball. Is there any contact between the ball and the glass rod?

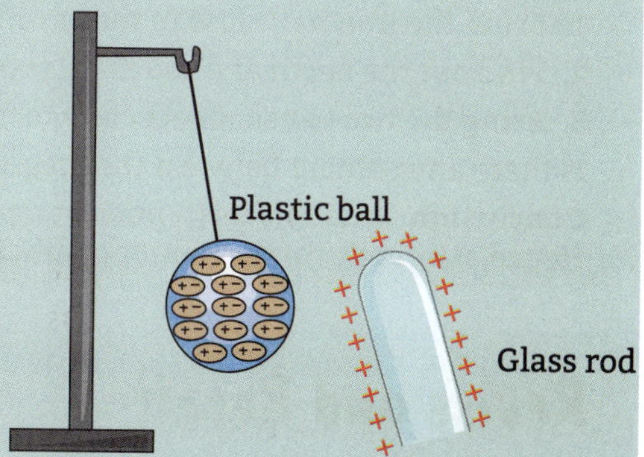

Observation:

1. The plastic ball will move towards the ebonite rod when the ebonite rod is brought close to the ball.
2. The plastic ball will move towards the glass rod when the glass rod is brought close to the ball.

Conclusion: Electrostatic force does not require any contact between the objects. Hence, it is a non-contact force.

In this experiment, why did the plastic ball move towards the ebonite rod? What do you think is likely to happen if both the ball and the ebonite rod were rubbed with fur and then brought next to each other?

Magnetic Force

The force exerted between two magnets or between a magnet and a magnetic material such as iron is called **magnetic force**. Like electrostatic force, magnetic force is either attractive or repulsive (Fig. 10.5). A magnet has two poles—a north pole and a south pole. Two similar poles of two different magnets repel each other, that is, north pole repels north pole and south pole repels south pole. Two opposite poles when brought close to one another attract each other, that is, a north pole attracts a south pole. Magnetic force between two magnets does not require any contact between the magnets, and hence, it is a non-contact force.

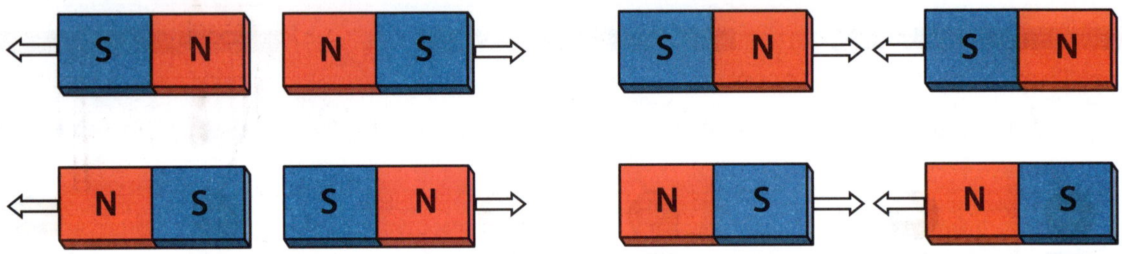

Fig. 10.5: Like poles repel and unlike poles attract each other

Activity 2

Aim: To show that magnetic force is a non-contact force

Materials required: Two bar magnets and one iron nail

Procedure:

1. Bring the iron nail close to the bar magnet. Observe the pull.
2. Find out the north and south poles of the bar magnets.
3. Bring the two bar magnets close to each other. What do you observe? A push or a pull?

Is there any contact between the magnets and the iron nail?

Conclusion: Whether it is a push or a pull that you observed, the two objects are not in contact. Hence, magnetic force is a non-contact force.

Revise and Recall

Fill in the blanks.

1. The force that requires a physical contact between two bodies to act on them is called a ______________ force. (contact/non-contact)
2. When a weightlifter lifts a weight, he uses __________ force. (electrostatic/muscular)
3. Like poles of two magnets __________ each other. (attract/repel)
4. __________ force is always a force of attraction. (Gravitational/Magnetic)

FRICTION

We have seen that a football rolling on the ground comes to rest after some time. If we stop pedalling our cycle, it stops moving after some time. This happens because of a phenomenon that opposes or resists the motion of the football or the cycle over the ground. It is because of a force acting between the ball and the ground or the wheels of the cycle and the ground. This resistive force acting between the two bodies that are in contact and in motion such that it opposes the motion is called **friction** or **frictional force**. Friction exists only if the two surfaces are in contact with each other. Therefore, friction is a contact force.

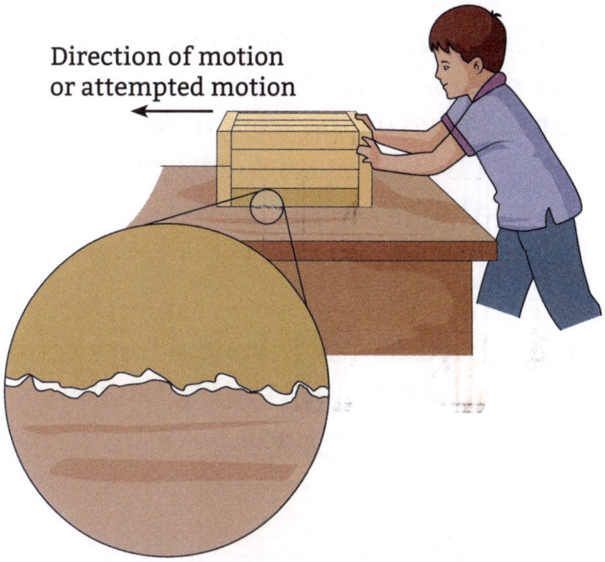

Fig. 10.6: Interlocking of the irregularities of two surfaces in contact causes friction.

If we observe a plane surface through a lens, we will be able to see a lot of irregularities or hills and grooves on the surface. These irregularities exist at the microscopic level even for a fine, smooth surface. These surface irregularities are the cause for friction. When one surface is in contact with another surface, the irregularities on both the surfaces get locked and produce an obstruction to the relative motion between them (Fig. 10.6). When the two surfaces are smooth, the interlocking of the irregularities will be less and the friction between the two surfaces will be less. Therefore, we can reduce the friction by making the surfaces smooth.

Types of Friction

Friction is mainly classified into two categories: static friction and kinetic friction.

Static friction

If we push a table gently, the table does not move. The friction acting between the table and the ground prevents the table from moving. The friction acting between two surfaces in contact when there is no relative motion between them is called **static friction**. If we keep on increasing the applied force on the table, we feel more opposing force and after a limit, the table starts moving. This indicates that the static friction increases with the applied force and reaches a maximum value. The maximum value of static friction just before a body starts to move is called **limiting friction**. If the applied force is increased further, the static friction does not increase beyond this maximum value and the object starts to move.

There are two laws of limiting friction.

1. The limiting friction depends on the nature of the surface (roughness or smoothness) and always acts tangentially to the interface between the two surfaces.
2. The force of limiting friction is independent of the area of contact between the two surfaces.

Kinetic friction

Now, consider a football rolling on the ground. The football comes to rest after moving some distance. This is due to the friction acting between the ball and the ground, while the ball moves on the ground. The frictional force acting between two surfaces when there is a relative motion between them is called **kinetic friction**.

Kinetic friction can be classified into two types: sliding friction (Fig. 10.7) and rolling friction (Fig. 10.8).

The friction acting between the surfaces when an object slides over a surface is called **sliding friction**. The frictional force acting between the surfaces when an object rolls over a surface is called **rolling friction**.

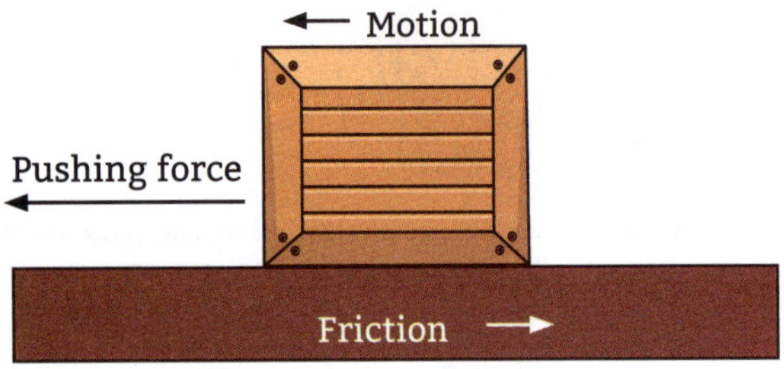

Fig. 10.7: Sliding friction

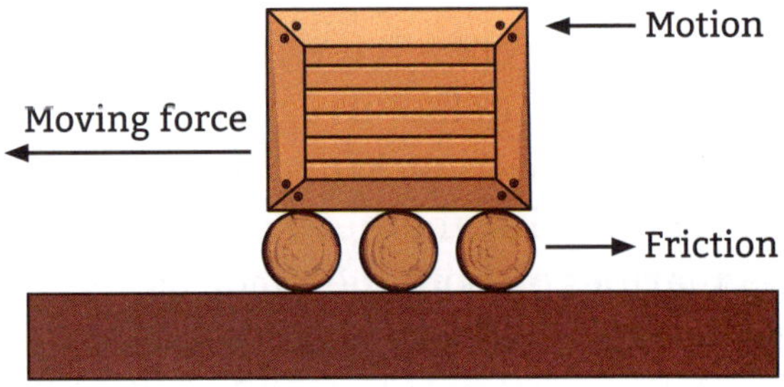

Fig. 10.8: Rolling friction

Activity 3

Aim: To show that the force exerted by sliding friction is greater than the force exerted by rolling friction

Materials required: A flat wooden plank, a small wooden block, a small wooden cylinder and two notebooks

Procedure:

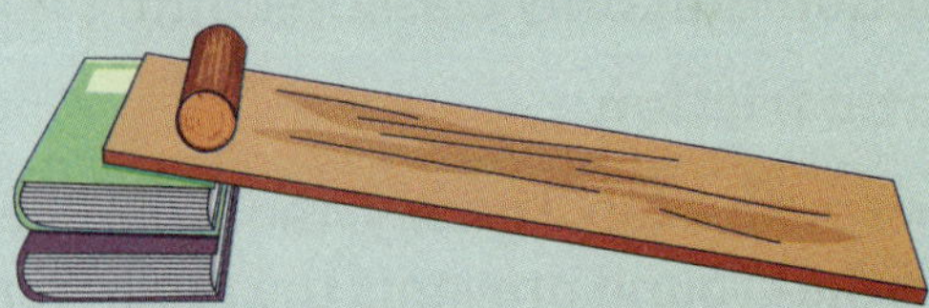

1. Place the wooden plank on the table.
2. Keep one/two notebooks below one end of the wooden plank to make an inclined plane as shown.
3. Place the wooden block at the top of the inclined wooden plank. Does it move down by itself? Push the block gently. Does it move at all or move continuously or move a little and then quickly comes to rest?
4. Next, place the wooden cylinder at the top of the inclined wooden plank. What do you see? Does it roll down on its own? Do you need to push it at all?

Observation: The wooden block remains stationary, whereas the wooden cylinder rolls down.

Conclusion: Sliding friction is greater than rolling friction.

Advantages and disadvantages of friction

- How are we able to walk on the floor? Can we walk easily on an icy road? When we walk on a surface, the friction provided by the surface helps us to walk. Icy road is very smooth and cannot provide sufficient friction to our feet. So, we find it difficult to walk on an icy road (Fig. 10.9).

Fig. 10.9: Friction helps us to walk.

- We are able to hold objects in our hand because of the friction between the skin of our palm and the objects (Fig. 10.10). Without friction, the objects would slip off from our hands.

Fig. 10.10: Friction helps us to hold various objects.

- Friction between the pulleys of a motor and the belt helps to transfer energy from the motor to the required equipment (Fig. 10.11).
- When brakes are applied, friction between the brake pad and the brake disc helps to reduce the speed of vehicle (Fig. 10.12).

Fig. 10.11: Friction between the belt and the pulleys helps to transfer the energy.

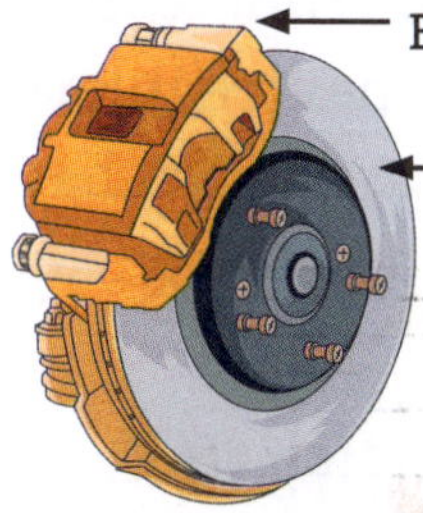

Fig. 10.12: Friction between the brake pad and brake disc helps to slow down the vehicle.

Does friction cause any disadvantage in our daily life? Have you ever observed any machine getting heated when it runs for a long time? Why do machinery parts get worn out when used continuously? It is because of friction. Friction causes unnecessary wastage of energy and reduces the efficiency of the machines.

Friction as a Necessary Evil

Friction is an essential force to carry out our various day-to-day activities. However, as mentioned, friction has its disadvantages too as it causes wear and tear of objects.

- It helps us to walk without slipping but at the same time, it also wears out the soles of our foot-wears.
- It helps us to stop vehicles by applying brakes but at the same time, it also heats up the break-pads and causes it to wear out over time.
- It is necessary to run machines but it also heats up the parts of machines causing wear and tear, thereby increasing the running cost of machines.

Thus, friction is regarded as a necessary evil due to its useful yet destructive nature.

Methods to Minimize Friction

We learned that in many situations in our life, friction is necessary and in many other situations, it causes trouble. Therefore, at times, it is necessary for us to reduce the friction in order to increase efficiency, to save energy and to protect the machines from wear and tear.

We can reduce friction by a number of methods discussed below.

- Friction can be reduced by making the two surfaces in contact smooth. Smoothening reduces the roughness on the two surfaces and further reduces the interlocking between the irregularities, thus decreasing the friction.
- Some materials such as oils, grease, graphite powder, etc., when applied between the two surfaces, help the surfaces to slide easily over one another, minimizing the interlocking of the irregularities on the surfaces. This, in turn, reduces the friction between the surfaces. Such materials used to reduce friction are called **lubricants** (Fig. 10.13).

Fig. 10.13: Lubricants reduce the friction between machine parts.

- We know that rolling friction is less than sliding friction. If the relative motion between the two surfaces is made to roll rather than slide, the friction caused due to sliding can be reduced to friction due to rolling. Usually, ball bearings (Fig. 10.14) are used to minimize the friction by this method to provide the rolling effect.

Fig. 10.14: Ball bearings

Methods to Increase Friction

Friction can be increased by:

- increasing the roughness of surfaces
- increasing the mass of the object in motion

Examples from everyday life:

- Tyres of vehicles are treaded (Fig. 10.15) to provide sufficient friction between the tyres and the roads on which they run. This minimizes the chance of the slipping of the tyres on slippery roads.

Fig. 10.15: Treaded tyre

- Trekking shoes have spikes to give a strong grip.
- Handles of bats and raquets are made of rough materials for a strong grip.
- Playgrounds are made rough so that people would not slip while running or playing.

Friction Due to Fluids

Suppose we drop a feather and a ball from the top floor of a building. We find that the ball reaches the ground first whereas the feather takes longer time. This is because the air exerts a lot more resistance, or friction, to the motion of the feather, thereby slowing it down.

Air is made up of particles and these particles oppose the motion of any object through it. In other words, air exerts a frictional force on the objects moving through it.

All gases and liquids are collectively called **fluids**. The frictional force exerted by fluids on the objects moving through them is called **drag**. The drag acting on an object moving through a fluid depends on the nature of the fluid, the speed of the object and the shape of the object.

Friction caused due to air (drag) can be reduced by making the object (vehicles) in the desired streamlined shape (Fig. 10.16). The body of an aircraft is made such that it reduces the friction provided by air.

Fig. 10.16: Streamlined shape of vehicles helps to reduce friction due to air.

In nature, we can see the streamlined shape of living things that helps them to reduce friction (Fig. 10.17). The shape of a fish helps it to swim easily in water. The shape of a bird minimizes air drag and helps it to fly easily.

Fig. 10.17: Streamlined body shape of living things

Revise and Recall

Fill in the blanks.

1. The force that opposes the motion of a body over a surface is called ____________. (muscular force/friction)
2. Rolling friction is ____________ than sliding friction. (greater/lesser)
3. The ____________ on the surfaces in contact is the cause of friction between them. (irregularities/regularities)
4. Use of lubricants ____________ the friction. (increases/decreases)
5. Streamlined shape of a car ____________ drag due to air. (reduces/enhances)

Keywords

Force: A push or a pull

Electrostatic force: The force acting between charged particles

Magnetic force: The force exerted between two magnets or between magnet and magnetic material

Friction: Force that opposes the relative motion between two surfaces in contact

Static friction: The friction acting between the two surfaces in contact when there is no relative motion between them

Limiting friction: The maximum value of static friction between two surfaces in contact beyond which one surface starts moving over the other

Kinetic friction: The frictional force acting between the two surfaces in contact while there is a relative motion between them

Summary

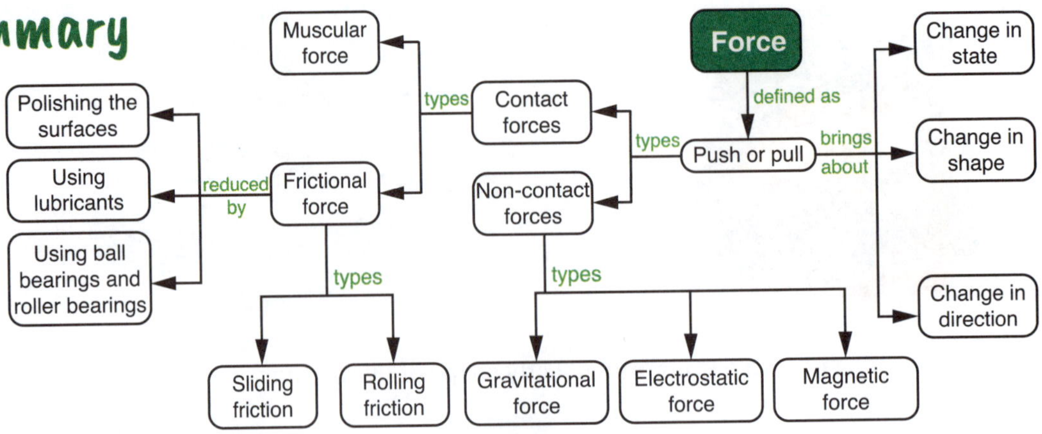

Exercise

w

ia

A. Choose the correct option.

1. Which among the following is an example of a contact force?
   (a) Friction (b) Gravitation (c) Magnetic (d) Electrostatic
2. Force can
   (a) stop a moving body. (b) change the shape of a body.
   (c) change the direction of a moving body. (d) All of these
3. Identify the non-contact force that would best suit in lifting and placing a large amount of iron scraps in a workplace.
   (a) Magnetic (b) Gravitational (c) Electrostatic (d) Muscular
4. Which among the following is not always a disadvantage of friction?
   (a) Friction heats up parts of machines.
   (b) Friction produces wear and tear.
   (c) Friction decreases the speed of a moving body.
   (d) Friction makes movement difficult.
5. Birds have a streamlined body shape that helps them to
   (a) reduce air friction to fly with less effort.
   (b) apply more effort to overcome air friction.
   (c) reduce their speed during flight.
   (d) fly at higher altitudes.

B. State whether the following statements are true (T) or false (F).

1. All contact and non-contact forces exhibit all effects of force. ☐
2. Gravitational force is a contact force. ☐
3. It is not possible to walk in the absence of friction. ☐
4. Electrostatic force is a non-contact force. ☐
5. Friction can be reduced but cannot be eliminated. ☐

C. Fill in the blanks.

ia

1. Gravitational force is always a force of __________. (push/pull)
2. Muscular force is an example of __________. (contact force/non-contact force)
3. A ball thrown upwards comes back; this is due to the __________ of the Earth. (gravitational force/magnetic force)
4. A vehicle slows down when brakes are applied because of __________. (friction/gravitation)
5. Sprinkling a little talcum powder on the carom board helps to __________ the friction.(increase/reduce)

D. Answer the following questions in one sentence each.

1. Give one example of a contact force.
2. Give one example of a non-contact force.
3. Mention one situation in life where friction is necessary.
4. Mention two methods to minimize friction.
5. Mention two methods to increase friction.

E. Give reasons for the following.

1. If we kick a football, it comes to rest after moving for sometime.
2. Wheels of vehicles are made circular in shape.
3. The players sprinkle fine powder on the carrom board before they start playing.
4. The jar of a mixer becomes hot when it is run for few minutes.
5. It is easier to move the box that is already in motion than to move it from rest.

F. Answer the following questions briefly.

1. What are contact forces and non-contact forces?
2. What are sliding friction and rolling friction? Which is more?
3. Mention three disadvantages of friction.
4. What is static friction? What is limiting friction?
5. Mention the two ways of increasing friction.

G. Answer the following questions in detail.

1. Define force. Explain the different effects of force.
2. Explain contact forces and non-contact forces with examples.
3. Describe one activity to show that sliding friction is more than rolling friction.
4. Friction is a necessary evil. Explain.
5. Describe the methods to minimize friction.

Cognitive Corner

Critical Thinking

1. Why is the invention of wheel considered as an important step of development in the history of science?
2. When two balloons rubbed with woollen cloth are brought close to each other, they repel. Why?

Picture Study

Identify which type of friction is depicted in the given pictures.

Project

As a part of Science Club activity, construct a device to study the various factors affecting friction. You need a wooden plank, a small pulley, thread, small pan, weights in grams, wooden blocks of different sizes, and a glass plate of the same length and breadth as the wooden plank.

Arrange the set up as shown in the figure below. Add weights into the pan of the scale, and find out the force at which the block starts moving. Note this value. Now, place the glass plate on the wooden plank. Keep the wooden block on the glass plate and repeat the same experiment. Note down the weight in the pan required to move the wooden block over the glass plate.

Repeat the same experiment using another wooden block of different mass. Compare the results. **(C-7.2)**

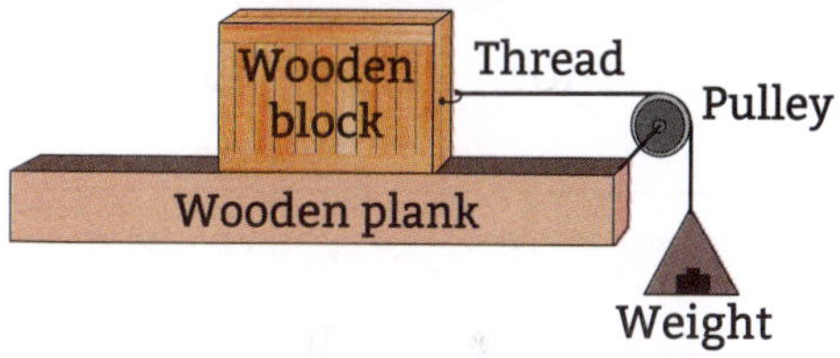

In the Library

The friction between an object and a surface depends on the weight of the object. It does not depend on the area of contact between the object and the surface. Read more about this fact and study what is the coefficient of friction. Make a report on the same. **(C-7.1)**

Life Skills

Friction is often called a necessary evil, but there are many instances in everyday life where friction is necessary and not 'evil'. For example, writing with a pencil requires friction. We would not be able to hold a pencil in our hand if there were no friction. It would slip out every time we try to hold it. The pencil lead (made up of graphite) would also not make a mark on the paper without friction. Similarly, an eraser uses friction to rub off what is written in pencil lead. When we rub an eraser across a pencil mark on the paper, it scratches the surface of the paper. This loosens the graphite particles due to friction. These particles then combine with the small bits of rubber that are left behind and can be brushed off.

Find out and list five more examples where friction is necessary for us. **(C-7.1)**

Worksheet

High mountains, clad in snow, have beckoned mountaineers for centuries. Many human beings yearn to climb up the high slopes and view the amazing world from high above. This is a kind of sport called mountaineering.

There are mountain peaks in Asia, the Americas, Africa and Europe that are covered with snow all the year round and are very popular for this sport. It is also a sport full of risk to life and limbs. That is why mountaineers need rigorous training and first-class equipment.

It is extremely difficult to walk on snow and very easy to slip on ice and fall. To climb steep cliffs, especially snow-covered ones, one needs practice and expertise. Ice axes are used to increase friction, with the help of which climbers can climb up the slopes with less difficulty. Climbers need special mountaineering boots to climb over harsh terrain, soft snow as well as slippery ice. They need to increase the friction between their shoes and the ice.

A. How do you think the soles of such shoes are designed?

____

____

____

B. Special structures called crampons are sometimes added to these boots. How do you think these crampons are helpful?

____

____

____

Crampons

C. Imagine yourself to be an innovator. Design a shoe that would help such mountaineers. Sketch your design below and describe it in a line.

11 Pressure

Curricular Goals

- Explore the nature and processes of science through engaging with the evolution of scientific knowledge and conducting scientific inquiry **(CG-6)**
- Communicate questions, observations and conclusions related to science **(CG-7)**

Competencies

- Formulate questions using scientific terminology (to identify possible causes for an event, patterns, or behaviour of objects), and collect data as evidence (through observation of the natural environment, design of simple experiments or use of simple scientific instruments) **(C-6.2)**
- Use scientific vocabulary to communicate science accurately in oral and written forms, and through visual representation **(C-7.1)**

Let's Get Started

We are familiar with force and the different effects of force. Identify the effect brought about by force in each of the cases given below.

____

____

____

The effects produced by a force on an object depend on the magnitude of the force applied on the body. For example, if we press a ball between both our hands, the shape of the ball changes. If we press the ball with more force, the ball will be compressed more.

Is there any factor on which the effect of a force depends? Let us find out in this chapter.

PRESSURE

Observe Figure 11.1. In both the cases, we use the same hammer to hit the nails with the same force. In which case would it be easy to hammer the nail through the wooden board? Why?

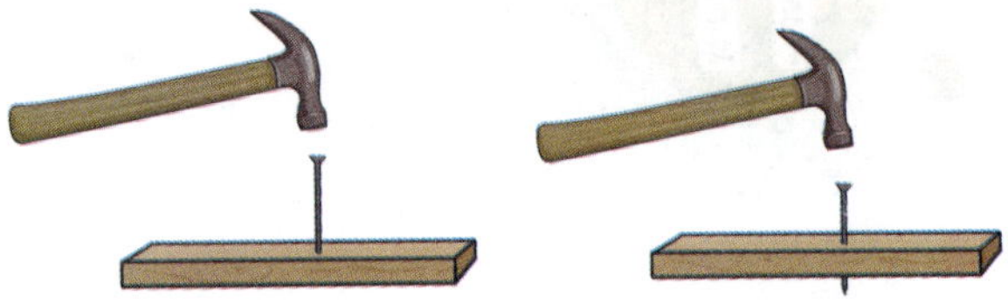

(a) (b)

Fig. 11.1: Hammer hit on a (a) blunt nail and (b) nail with sharp tip

We know that a nail with a sharp tip can be hammered easily. This is because of a quantity known as pressure. *The force acting on the unit area of the surface of an object is called* **pressure**. The pressure on a surface depends on the magnitude of the force acting perpendicular to the surface and the area of the surface. Thus, pressure can be formulated as:

$$\textbf{Pressure} = \frac{\textbf{Force}}{\textbf{Area}}$$

Force is measured in newton (N) and area is measured in square metre (m^2). Hence, the SI unit of pressure is N/m^2, which is also known as pascal (Pa). One pascal is equal to one newton per square metre.

In the figure, the area of the tip of the pointed nail is very small, that is why a hammer exerts a large pressure. However, in the case of blunt nail, pressure exerted is less since the area of the tip is large.

Problem 1:

Calculate the pressure if a force of 600 N is applied on an area of 2 m^2.

Solution:

Force applied = 600 N Area = 2 m^2

$$\text{Pressure} = \frac{\text{Force}}{\text{Area}} = \frac{600}{2} = \textbf{300 Pa}$$

Variation of Pressure with Area

The pressure exerted by a certain force on a surface depends on the area of the surface. If the force is acting on a large area, the pressure exerted is less. If the same force is acting on a small area, then the pressure exerted is more. That is, the smaller the surface area, the greater is the pressure exerted, while the larger the surface area, the lesser is the pressure exerted.

Activity 1

Aim: To show that pressure increases with a decrease in the area

Materials required: A tray of approximately 10 cm height, wet mud and two identical bricks

Procedure:

1. Fill the tray completely with wet mud (in the paste form) till the brim.
2. Take one brick, label it as 'A' and place it gently on the tray of mud horizontally. Do not press the brick hard.
3. Remove the brick gently from the tray and observe the depth of the impression left behind.
4. Take the second brick, label it as 'B' and place it gently on the same tray of mud, vertically this time. Do not press the brick hard.
5. Remove the brick gently from the tray and observe the depth of the impression left behind.

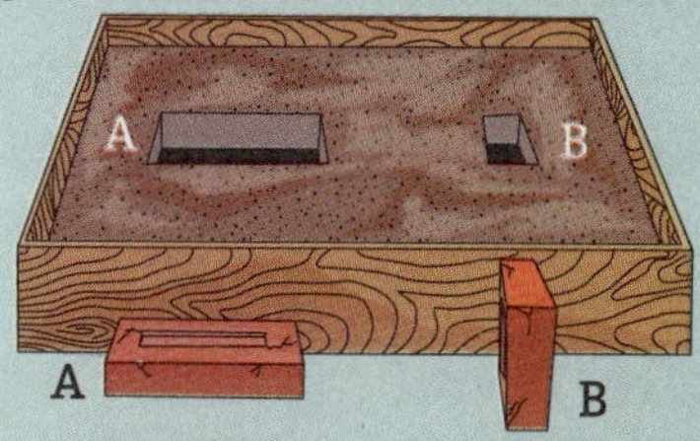

Deeper impression made by the brick with lesser area of contact

Observations: Brick 'B' makes a deeper impression on the mud when compared to brick 'A'.

Conclusion: If the force is constant, the pressure increases with the decrease in area. As the area of the contact between the brick and wet mud is less for brick 'B' than for brick 'A', brick 'B' makes a deeper impression in the mud.

Variation of Pressure with Force

We know that pressure is defined as the force per unit area. As long as the surface area remains unchanged, an increase in the force applied leads to an increase in the pressure or vice versa.

Let us take a look at the following problem. (Force applied in this case is slightly different from the one in Problem 1.)

Problem 2:

Calculate the pressure if a force of 800 N is applied on an area of 2 m^2.

Solution:

Force applied = 800 N   Area = 2 m^2

Pressure $= \frac{\text{Force}}{\text{Area}} = \frac{800}{2} = \mathbf{400\ Pa}$

In this case, the area is constant. When the force is increased, the pressure exerted on the same area also increases.

Find out!

A force of 100 N is acting on a surface of area 4 m^2. If the force is doubled and the area of the surface is made half of the initial area, what would be the difference in the pressure?

Revise and Recall

Fill in the blanks.

1. The force acting on unit area of a surface is called ________. (pressure/push)
2. The unit of pressure in the SI system is ________. (N/Pa)
3. Pressure increases with an increase in the ________. (force applied/ surface area)
4. It is easy to cut vegetables with a ________ knife. (sharp-edged/blunt)

FLUID PRESSURE

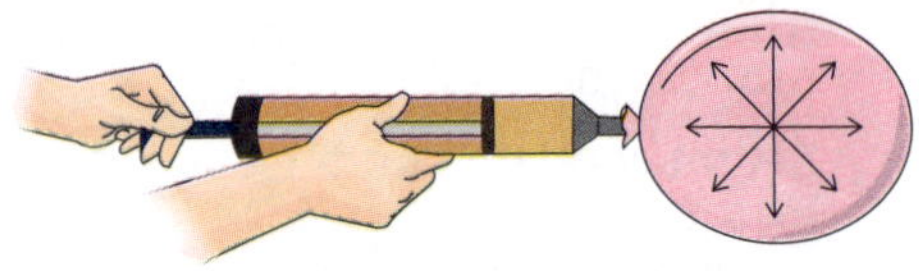

Fig. 11.2: Air exerts pressure on the walls of the balloon.

Liquids and gases are collectively called **fluids** because unlike solids, both liquids and gases can flow. Fluids exert pressure on an object immersed in them and on the walls of the container holding them. This pressure exerted by a fluid is called **fluid pressure**. Therefore, fluid pressure can be classified into two kinds: (1) liquid pressure and (2) gaseous pressure. When air is pumped into a balloon, why does it inflate? The inflation is due to the pressure exerted by the air on the walls of the balloon (Fig. 11.2).

Pressure in Liquids

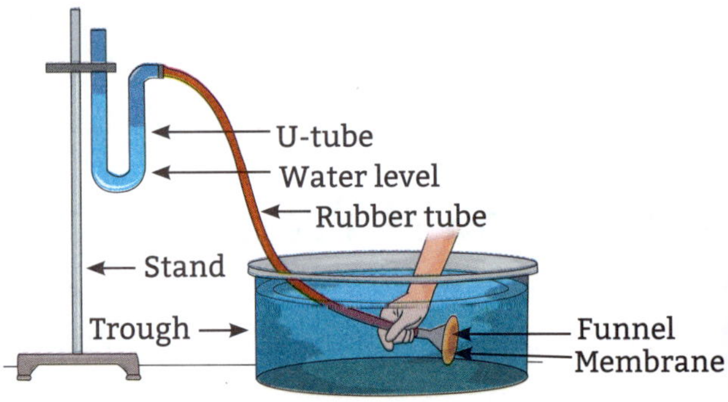

Fig. 11.3: Simple manometer

The pressure exerted by a liquid on an object immersed in it and on the walls of the container is called **liquid pressure**. Liquid pressure is measured using a device called manometer. A simple manometer (Fig. 11.3) consists of a U-shaped tube containing a liquid such as water. One end of the tube is left open to the air and the other end is connected to a trough containing another liquid whose pressure is to be measured. The water level in the U-tube varies as we keep the funnel at different positions inside the liquid. The difference in the liquid level (in the U-tube) determines the liquid pressure.

Properties of liquid pressure

1. Pressure exerted by a liquid increases with the depth from the liquid surface.
2. Pressure exerted by a liquid at the same depth will be the same.
3. Liquids exert pressure in all directions.

Activity 2

Aim: To show that liquid pressure is the same at equal depth

Materials required: Plastic container, water and needle

Procedure:

1. Make three holes on the plastic container at the same level.
2. Fill the container with water.

Observations: You will observe that the water gushes out from the three holes with the same force.

Conclusion: Hence, this proves that pressure is the same at equal depth. This also shows that liquid exerts pressure on all sides.

Activity 3

Aim: To show that the pressure exerted by liquids increases with an increase in depth

Materials required: Transparent plastic bottle or vessel and water

Procedure:

1. Make small holes on the plastic vessel at four different heights as shown in the figure.
2. Place the vessel on a table and then fill it with water. Observe the force with which the water flows out of the three holes. What difference do you find?

Liquid pressure increases with the depth from the surface of the liquid

Observations: The force with which water flows out increases as the depth of the hole from the water surface increases.

Conclusion: Pressure exerted by the liquids increases with depth. The water spouts out of the hole near the bottom with the greatest force as the pressure is more, since depth of the hole from the surface is more. The water flows out of the hole at the top with the least force as the pressure is less since the depth is less.

ATMOSPHERIC PRESSURE

We know that our Earth is surrounded by a blanket of air called the **atmosphere**. This atmosphere exerts pressure on the objects present in it and on the Earth's surface. The pressure exerted by the weight of air on an object on Earth is called **atmospheric pressure**.

Activity 4

Aim: To show the presence of atmospheric pressure

Materials required: Cardboard, glass and water

Procedure:

1. Fill the glass with water up to the brim.
2. Cover the tumbler with a cardboard and press slightly.
3. Turn over the glass quickly, so that it is placed upside down on the palm of your hand.
4. Remove your hand slowly from the cardboard.

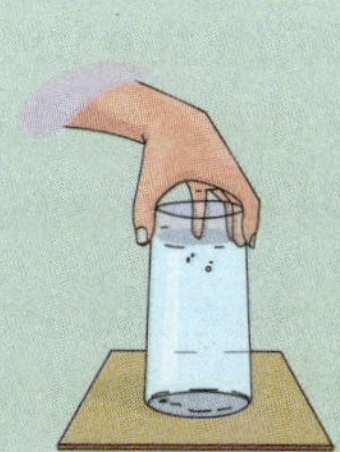

Atmospheric pressure prevents the cardboard from falling down

Observation: Even when you remove your hand, the cardboard remains stuck to the glass and does not fall out, spilling the water.

Conclusion: This happens because the atmospheric pressure acting on the cardboard supports it, preventing the water from spilling out.

Activity 5

Aim: To study the role of atmospheric pressure

Materials required: Rubber sucker and glass sheet

Procedure:

1. Place the rubber sucker on a smooth surface such as the floor or a glass sheet and fix it by pressing it gently.
2. Now, try to remove it. Can you remove it with the same force with which you had fixed it?

Observation: The rubber sucker sticks onto the surface, and we need to apply more force to detach it from the surface.

Conclusion: When the rubber sucker is pressed onto the smooth surface, the air between the sucker and the surface escapes. The pressure inside the rubber sucker becomes less than the atmospheric pressure (pressure of the air from outside) acting on it. Therefore, we find it difficult to remove it as the greater atmospheric pressure pushes it from outside.

Science in Context

A barometer is a device used to measure atmospheric pressure. In 1643, an Italian physicist, Evangelista Torricelli, invented a simple barometer to measure atmospheric pressure. He constructed this device by using a mercury column taken in a long glass tube, inverted over a trough containing mercury. The height of the mercury column, of 76 cm of Hg, is referred to as the normal or standard atmospheric pressure.

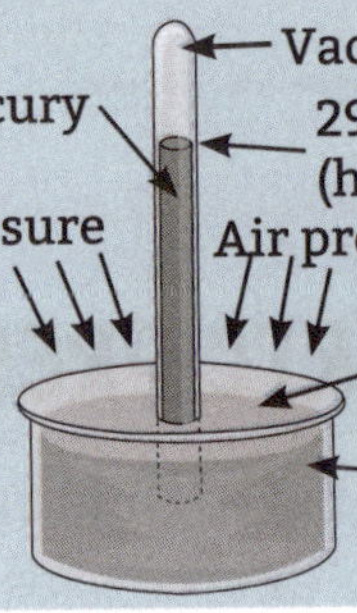

Atmospheric Pressure Varies with Altitude

The altitude is the height of a place from the sea level. As we go higher up, the altitude increases. With the increase in altitude, the atmospheric pressure decreases because the layer of the air column above us becomes thinner. Hence, the pressure exerted by the air on us decreases.

This means that the atmospheric pressure at the sea level is higher as the layer of the air column above us is more. Hence, the pressure exerted by air is more at a lower altitude.

However, this high atmospheric pressure does not affect us because fluids such as blood in our body also exert pressure, which cancels the effect of atmospheric pressure. The value of the atmospheric pressure at the sea level is about 100000 Pa, that is 100 kPa.

Science in Context

People climbing mountains carry oxygen cylinders with them. Otherwise, they may start bleeding from their nose due to low atmospheric pressure at the top of mountains. Moreover, the availability of oxygen is less as we go up to higher altitudes.

Revise and Recall

Match the following.

1. Atmosphere	(a) Measures liquid pressure
2. Barometer	(b) Liquids and gases
3. Fluids	(c) Measures atmospheric pressure
4. Manometer	(d) Blanket of air

APPLICATIONS OF PRESSURE

- It is difficult to cut vegetables if a knife's edge is blunt. A knife with a sharp edge has a small area and exerts more pressure on the vegetables. So, a sharp-edged knife cuts through them easily (Fig. 11.4).

Fig. 11.4: It is easier to cut vegetables with a sharp-edged knife

- It is very easy to fix a sharp pin on a board since the pressure exerted by its sharp tip is high due to the small area it occupies (Fig. 11.5).
- The straps of a school bag are made broad to increase the surface area. With the increase in surface area, the pressure exerted by the bag becomes less. So, broad straps reduce the pressure on shoulders, which makes it easier to carry the school bag.

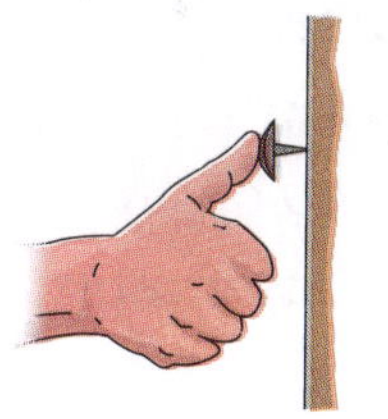

Fig. 11.5: Pushing a pin with a sharp tip

- Skis have broad surface area to reduce the pressure on the snow. This prevents the ice from breaking and the skis from sinking into the snow.
- Camels have flat, broad feet that help them to walk easily on the sand in deserts (Fig. 11.6). Since the area of their feet is more, the pressure exerted by its weight on the sand will be less. Therefore, their feet do not sink into the sand while walking.

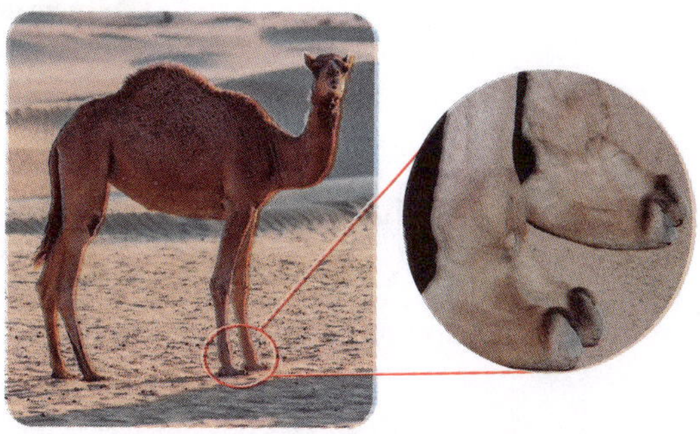

Fig. 11.6: Wide feet of a camel

- When we drink something from a glass by using a straw, the liquid rises through the straw due to the atmospheric pressure acting on the liquid in the glass.

When we suck the liquid upwards, the pressure inside the straw decreases, and the atmospheric pressure acting on the liquid in the glass causes it to rise up through the straw (Fig. 11.7).

- Dams are constructed in such a way that the walls are thicker at the bottom. This is done to withstand liquid pressure, which is highest at the bottom due to greater depth (Fig. 11.8).
- Syringes are used to collect blood from our body. The blood pressure pushes the blood into the syringe as we withdraw the plunger (Fig. 11.9).

Fig. 11.7: Drinking a liquid using a straw

Fig. 11.8: Thicker walls at the bottom to withstand high liquid pressure

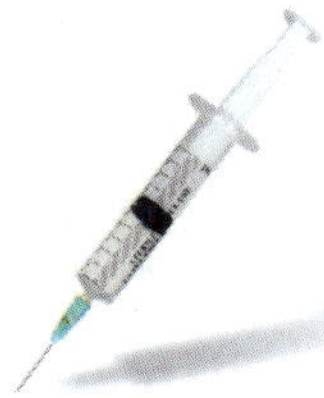

Fig. 11.9: A syringe

Keywords

Pressure: The force acting on the unit area of the surface of an object

Atmospheric pressure: Pressure exerted by the weight of the air on an object on Earth

Barometer: A device used to measure atmospheric pressure

Liquid pressure: The pressure exerted by a liquid on an object immersed in it and on the walls of the container

Manometer: A device used to measure liquid pressure

Summary

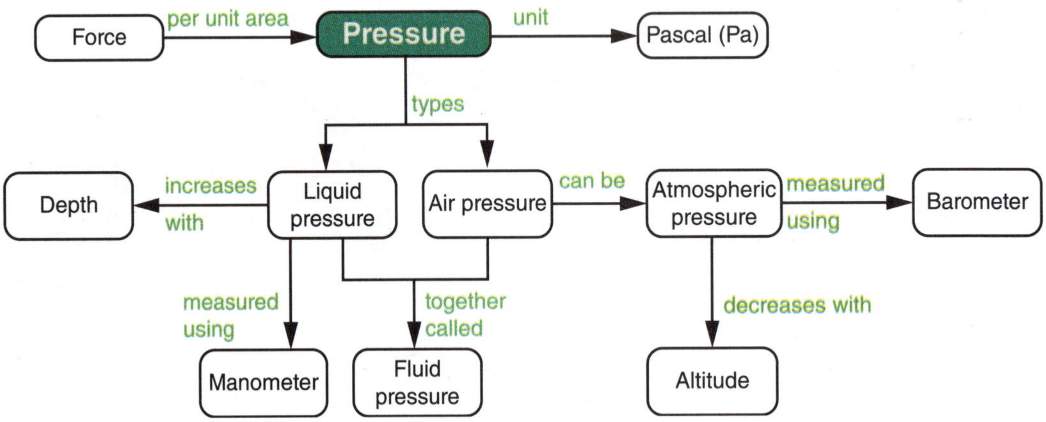

Exercise

W

A. Choose the correct option. ia

1. The straps of a school bag are made broad to increase the ________.
   (a) volume (b) force (c) pressure (d) surface area
2. If the surface area on which a force acts is small, the pressure exerted is ________.
   (a) more (b) less (c) equal (d) None of these
3. The height of a place from the sea level is called ________.
   (a) latitude (b) altitude (c) pressure (d) temperature
4. The value of atmospheric pressure at the sea level is about ________.
   (a) 10 kPa (b) 100 kPa (c) 0 kPa (d) 1000 kPa
5. Liquid pressure is measured using a device called ________.
   (a) barometer (b) manometer (c) thermometer (d) meter

B. State whether the following statements are true (T) or false (F). ia

1. Pressure is the force acting on the unit area of a surface. ☐
2. Air exerts pressure on the walls of a container. ☐
3. All liquids exert equal pressure at all points at the same depth. ☐
4. Pressure exerted by a given force increases with an increase in area. ☐
5. Liquids do not exert pressure on the object immersed in them. ☐

C. Give one word for each of the following. ia

1. This is equal to one newton per square metre
2. Force per unit area
3. The pressure exerted by the weight of air on an object on Earth
4. A device used to measure atmospheric pressure
5. The collective term for liquids and gases

D. Give reasons for the following.

1. It is easier to walk on soft sand if we wear flat shoes rather than shoes with sharp heels.
2. There is a huge amount of atmospheric pressure acting on us. However, we do not experience its effect.
3. Sea divers wear specially designed suits.
4. It is difficult to cut a cloth using a pair of scissors with blunt blades
5. Atmospheric pressure decreases with an increase in altitude.

E. Answer the following questions briefly.

1. Dams are made thicker at the bottom than at the top. Why?
2. What is the relation between pressure, force and area?

3. What is the cause of atmospheric pressure?
4. Mention two situations in our life where atmospheric pressure is helpful.
5. Write any two applications of pressure.

F. Answer the following questions in detail.

1. A carton box exerts a pressure of 40 Pa on a table. Calculate the area of the table if the force exerted by the box is 100 N?
2. Define pressure. Mention any two applications of pressure.
3. What is liquid pressure? Mention the properties of pressure exerted by liquids.
4. Explain one activity to demonstrate that liquid exerts pressure in all directions.
5. Briefly explain how to construct a simple manometer.

Cognitive Corner

Critical Thinking

1. Astronauts wear special suits when on space missions. Why?
2. Trucks meant to carry heavy loads have eight tyres instead of four. Why?

Picture Study

Look at the following pictures and write the kind of pressure that helps us in doing these activities.

____________________ ____________________

Project

As a part of Science Club activity, make a chart on various instruments used to measure pressure, for example, blood pressure, liquid pressure, atmospheric pressure. Collect their pictures, paste them on the chart paper and write a few lines on them. **(C-7.1)**

In the Library

Hydraulic lift is used to lift heavy objects such as vehicles, and it works on the principle of Pascal's law, which says that the pressure applied to any portion of a liquid is transmitted equally in all directions of the walls of the container. Read more about Pascal's law and its applications. **(C-7.1)**

Life Skills

The pressure inside an LPG cylinder is very high. What kind of care should be taken while using LPG cylinders? Make a chart based on this topic. Give an interesting title to your chart. **(C-7.1)**

Worksheet

Have you ever tried opening a can of soda (or a soft drink) after shaking it?

Imagine a huge tank with lots of pressure in it and then exploding like a soda can! If you want to know what happens in such scenarios, read about Deepwater Horizon oil spill.

Pressure plays several important roles in our everyday life. Most of our comfortable life would not have been possible without the innovations and inventions in the field of pressure technology. One of the inventions is the pressure sensor. Pressure sensors are used in modern vehicles, from managing brakes to electric windows, exhaust emissions to power steering which, in turn, help in making our roads safer, lowering pollution and improving our driving experience. In the field of medical science, accurate and stable pressure measurements are done to operate reliably. Many automatic medical devices are used for health monitoring at home.

A. Some more examples of everyday application of pressure are given below. Write an appropriate caption for each of the examples.

1.

____

____

____

2.

____

____

____

B. Do you know why the knowledge of pressure and its application play a key role in industry, innovation and industrialization? Write your views in a few sentences.

____

____

____

____

____

____

____

12 Sound

Curricular Goals

- Explore the nature and processes of science through engaging with the evolution of scientific knowledge and conducting scientific inquiry **(CG-6)**
- Communicate questions, observations and conclusions related to science **(CG-7)**

Competencies

- Formulate questions using scientific terminology and collect data as evidence **(C-6.2)**
- Use scientific vocabulary to communicate science accurately in oral and written forms, and through visual representation **(C-7.1)**
- Design and build simple models to demonstrate scientific concepts **(C-7.2)**

Let's Get Started

Every day we listen to a variety of sounds from our surroundings. Different objects produce different types of sound. Some sounds are pleasant and some are unpleasant. Identify two pleasant and two unpleasant sounds from the picture given below.

To play a mouth organ, we have to blow air into it. We spend some energy to blow the air. If we blow air with more energy, the sound produced will be louder. The energy used by us in blowing is converted into sound. Hence, we can say that sound is a form of energy. It is a sensation that can be felt by the ears. Objects that produce sounds are known as **sources of sound**.

PRODUCTION OF SOUND

a

If we just tap on a table with our hand, we hear a sound. Why is sound produced when we tap on the table?

Sound is produced by the vibration of particles present in objects. The to-and-fro, rapid movement of a particle about its fixed point in an object is called a **vibration**.

Pull a stretched rubber band slightly and then leave it. This will set the rubber band into vibration. Also, we can hear a sound as the rubber band vibrates.

Activity 1

Aim: To show that sound is produced by a vibrating body

Materials required: Tuning fork, rubber pad and a tub filled with water

Procedure:

1. Hold the rubber pad in your left hand and the tuning fork in right hand, and hit the fork on the rubber pad. Bring the tuning fork close to your ear. You can hear the ringing sound.
2. Again strike the tuning fork on the rubber pad. Now, touch the surface of water in the tub with the tuning fork.

Observations: When the tuning fork is hit on the rubber pad, the prongs start to vibrate and sound is produced. When the vibrating prongs are touched in water, they cause ripples across the water surface.

Conclusion: Sound is produced due to the vibration of objects.

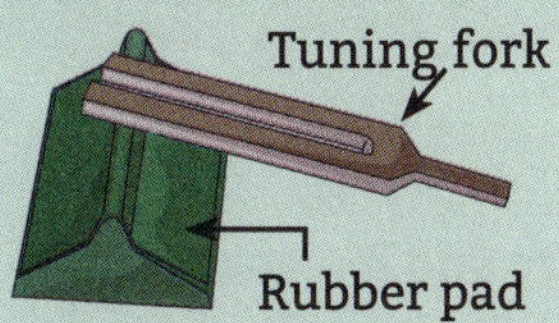

Tuning fork hit on a rubber pad

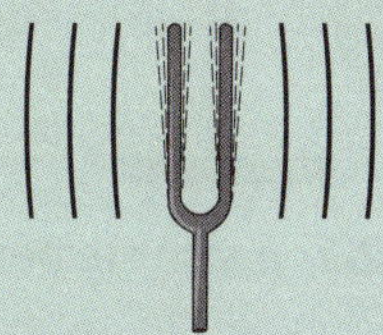

Vibrations in the prongs of the fork

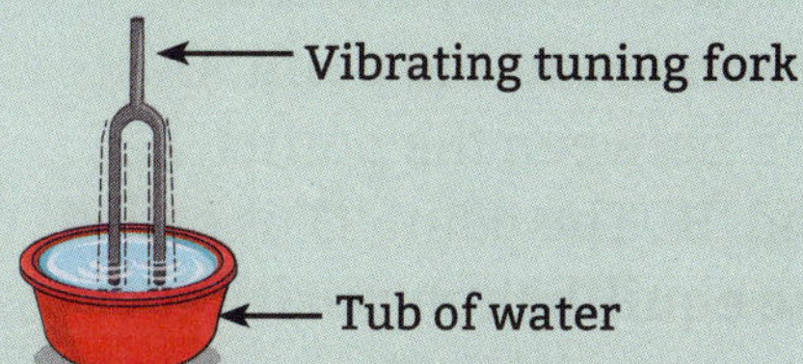

Vibrating prongs dipped in a tub filled with water

How is sound produced when we talk? Keep your fingers on your neck just below the jaws and produce some sound or talk. Do you feel a sensation of vibration? You can feel the vibration produced inside the throat. We human beings have an organ called the **voice box** or **larynx** in the neck region that helps us to produce sound when we talk. It has two membranous tissues called the **vocal cords** with a narrow slit between them for the passage of air. The vocal cords are held together by muscles that control the vibration of the cords (Fig. 12.1). While talking or making a sound, air exits the windpipe. This exhaled air causes the vocal cords to vibrate.

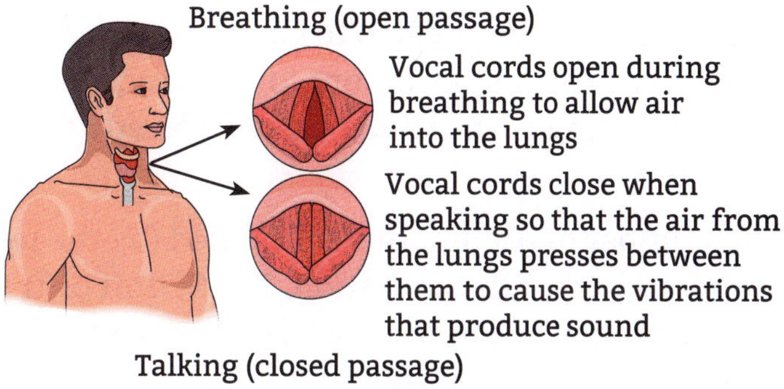

Fig. 12.1: Vocal cords in humans

CHARACTERISTICS OF SOUND

Sound travels in the form of waves. A wave is a disturbance that travels through a medium (a substance or a material) from one location to another. It has three basic quantities: frequency, speed and amplitude.

Let us first understand these quantities, with the help of a simple pendulum, before we discuss the characteristics of sound.

Simple Pendulum

A simple pendulum consists of a metallic bob suspended from a rigid support by means of a flexible string or a thread. Figure 12.2 shows the schematic diagram of a simple pendulum and its motion or oscillation.

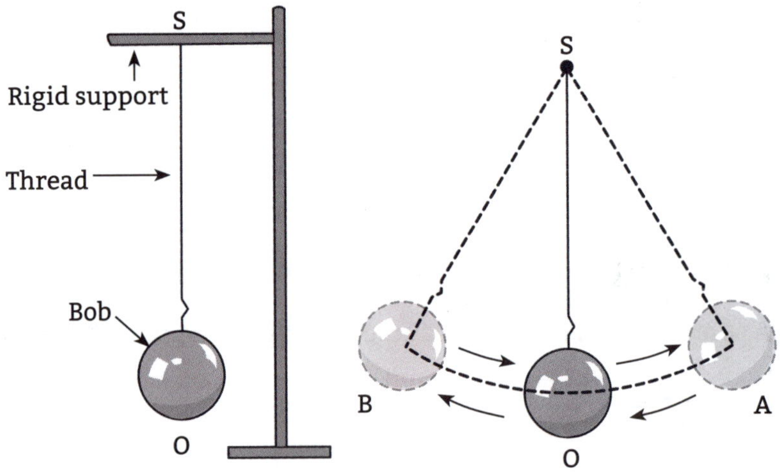

Fig. 12.2: A simple pendulum and its movement

The bob of the pendulum moves about the point 'O', and between the points 'A' and 'B'. The point 'O' is called the **equilibrium position** or **mean position**. The points 'A' and 'B' are called the **extreme positions**.

Now, let us consider the motion of the pendulum bob. Starting from the point O it moves to point A, then it moves from point A to point B, and then from B it comes to O. Now the pendulum is said to have completed one oscillation. *A steady, uninterrupted, backward and forward motion of a body between two points, in regular intervals of time, is called an **oscillation**.*

The time taken by the bob to complete one oscillation is called the **time period (T)**. The maximum displacement (or distance moved) of the pendulum bob from its mean position is the called the **amplitude (A)** of the oscillation. Here, the amplitude is OA or OB.

The number of oscillations completed (by the pendulum) in one second is called the **frequency (f)** of its oscillation. The SI unit of frequency is **hertz (Hz)**. When we say the frequency of a vibrating body is 50 hertz, it means that the object completes 50 oscillations in one second.

The vibrations of a body producing sound is a continuous to-and-fro motion, similar to that of a pendulum. However, the vibrations of a body producing sound move much faster than the motion of a pendulum. A body producing sound vibrates at a higher frequency, that is it completes a large number of vibrations in one second.

When a tuning fork is set into vibration, the prongs of the fork vibrate about the mean position. The continuous to-and-fro motion of the prongs produces continuous sound waves.

The frequency of the sound produced is equal to the frequency of vibration of the body producing sound. When the body completes one vibration, one complete sound wave is formed. The length of one complete wave is called wavelength. A sound wave can be represented by a diagram as shown in Figure 12.3.

Sound waves produced by different sources can be identified by knowing how loud and how sharp they are. Sound is characterized by its loudness, pitch and quality.

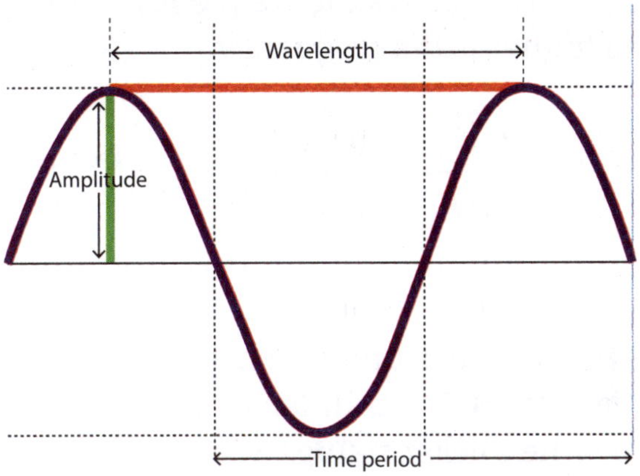

Fig. 12.3: A diagrammatic representation of a sound wave

Loudness of Sound

Are all sounds the same? Some sounds are louder whereas some other sounds are feeble or softer. Human ear can identify whether a sound wave is loud or feeble/soft. This perception of the sound experienced by a listener due to which he can differentiate between loud and soft sounds is called loudness.

Loudness of sound depends on the amplitude of the vibration of the body producing sound. If the body vibrates with more amplitude, then the loudness of the sound produced will be more.

Activity 2

Aim: To show that loudness of sound depends on the amplitude

Materials required: A guitar or a violin

Procedure:

1. Pluck the string of a guitar or violin softly. Observe the sound produced by the string.
2. Now, pluck the same string hard. Observe the sound produced.

Observations: The sound produced when the string is plucked softly is soft sound, and the sound produced when the string is plucked hard is louder.

Conclusion: Loudness of sound increases with amplitude of vibration.

Science in Context

Quality or Timbre of Sound: This characteristic of sound helps us to distinguish one sound from another of the same pitch and loudness. For example, suppose the sounds of the same pitch and loudness are produced from a piano and a guitar, and you are not allowed to see the instruments. You would still be able to distinguish between the sound of a guitar and a piano. This is due to the difference in the timbre or quality of sounds produced by the guitar and the piano.

Pitch

The shrillness of sound experienced by the listener is called the **pitch** of the sound. As the **frequency** of sound increases, its **pitch** also increases. With increase in pitch, the shrillness increases. Since the frequency of female voice is more than that of the male voice, it is shriller than the male voice.

Figure 12.4 shows the frequency of two sound waves. The more the number of waves, the higher is the frequency.

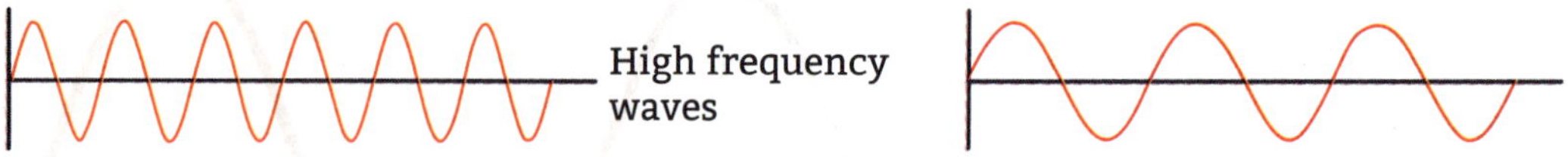

Fig. 12.4: High frequency and low frequency sound waves

In musical instruments such as guitar and violin, we can see strings of different thicknesses. The thinner strings on the instruments can produce shriller sounds than the thicker strings. We can increase the frequency of the vibration of a string by adjusting its tension. If the string is more stretched, it vibrates with more frequency and produces a high-pitch sound. You must have seen musicians tuning the musical instruments by adjusting the tension of the strings of the guitar, violin and tension of the skin of tabla, drums, etc. By tuning these instruments, they ensure that the instruments produce sounds with a desirable pitch. Pitch is important when people sing together in a choir.

PROPAGATION OF SOUND

We know that sound travels in the form of waves. We hear a sound when the waves reach our ears. Sound waves can travel through solids, liquids and gases. Unlike light, sound cannot travel through vacuum. Let us do an activity to understand this.

Activity 3

Aim: To show that sound requires a medium for its propagation

Materials required: Glass bottle, rubber cork with two holes, vacuum pump, wires, small buzzer and battery

Procedure:

1. Connect the two wires to the terminals of the buzzer and insert the other ends of the wires through one hole of the rubber cork. Close the hole by applying some quick fix solution.
2. Put the cork into the neck of the bottle so that the buzzer is inside the bottle.

3. Connect the inlet of a vacuum pump to the other hole of the rubber cork.
4. Now, connect the buzzer to the terminals of a battery. Can you hear the sound produced by the buzzer?
5. Now, switch on the vacuum pump. Observe what happens to the sound.

Observations: Sound produced by the buzzer is heard when there is air inside the bottle. When the air is removed using a vacuum pump, the sound produced by the buzzer is not heard.

Conclusion: Sound requires a medium for its propagation.

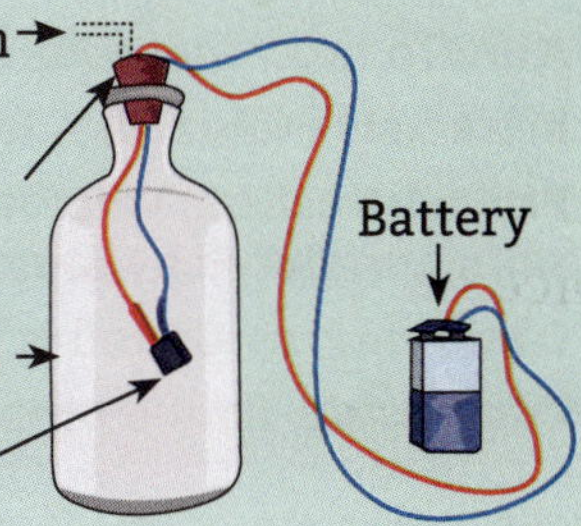

When sound is produced by a vibrating body, it transfers its energy to the molecules of the medium. These air molecules then start vibrating and, in turn, transfer energy to the neighbouring molecules and so on.

When sound waves propagate through a medium, the particles in the medium do not move from one place to another, they just vibrate about a mean position. The method of transfer of sound waves produced by a tuning fork is shown in Figure 12.5.

Fig. 12.5: Compressions and rarefactions

As the prongs of the tuning fork vibrate, they compress the nearby air molecules. This compressed region of the air is called **compression**. The air molecules in the compression region push and transfer their energy to the neighbouring molecules. Hence, the neighbouring region will be compressed and they become a compression. At the same time, the air in the previous compression expands. This region is called as **rarefaction**. In this manner, sound progresses as alternating compressions and rarefactions.

Activity 4

Aim: To show that sound propagates through liquids

Materials required: Two metal rods, tub or bucket and water

Procedure:

1. Take water in a bucket.
2. Hold the metal rods in two hands and immerse them in the water.
3. Strike the two metal rods inside the water. Can you hear the sound produced by the metal rods inside water?

Observations: The sound produced by hitting the metal rods inside the water is heard outside.

Conclusion: Sound propagates through liquids.

Activity 5

Aim: To show that sound propagates through solids

Materials required: A table

Procedure: Keep your ear on the table and tap the table gently with your hand. Can you hear the sound produced by tapping the table?

Observations: Sound is heard when the ear is kept on the table and it is tapped.

Conclusion: Sound propagates through solids.

How do Humans Hear Sound?

a

Ear is the organ in the human body that helps us to hear sound. Figure 12.6 shows the structure of the human ear. We can classify the parts of the ear as (i) outer ear (ii) middle ear and (iii) inner ear.

The **outer ear** consists of an ear flap or external ear called **pinna** and an ear canal or the **auditory canal**, which directs the sound to the eardrum. The eardrum is a stretched membrane like the skin of a drum. It acts as an interface to the outer ear and the middle ear. The eardrum is also called the **tympanum**.

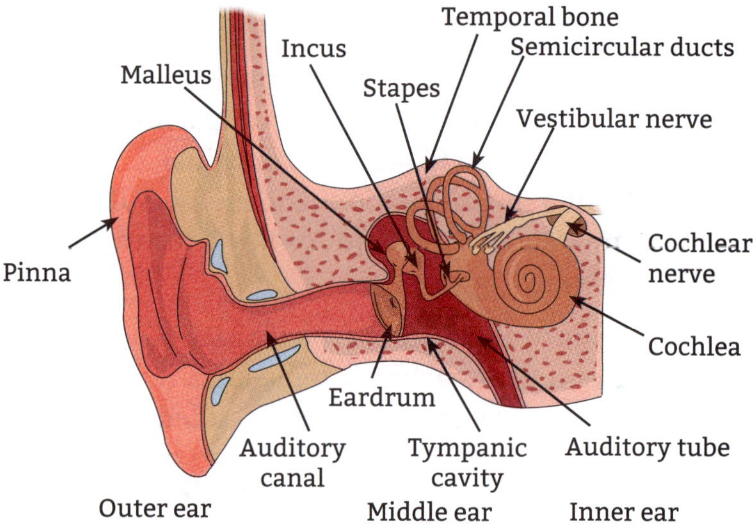

Fig. 12.6: Internal structure of the human ear

Middle ear is an air-filled column with three tiny interconnected bones—incus, malleus and stapes. The **inner ear** has three parts—cochlea, semicircular canals and the auditory nerves.

The pinna collects the sound from outside and channels it to the middle ear. The bones of the middle ear vibrate and amplify the sound, and transfer it to the inner ear. The parts of the inner ear have sound-sensitive cells that receive these amplified vibrations. This causes these specialized cells to vibrate. The vibrations are converted into nerve impulses, which are carried to the brain for interpretation.

Revise and Recall

Fill in the blanks.

1. Sound is produced by the ____________________ of particles present in objects. (vibration/rotation)
2. With an increase in the pitch, the shrillness ____________________. (increases/decreases)
3. The number of oscillations per second is called ____________________. (amplitude/frequency)
4. The SI unit of frequency is ____________________. (hertz/metre)

Speed of Sound

We studied that sound can travel through solids, liquids and gases. Sound travels through these media at different speeds. Of the three media, sound travels the slowest through gases, faster through liquids and fastest through solids. In air, the speed of sound depends on many factors such as temperature, humidity in the air, flow of the wind, etc. For example, the speed of sound in air increases with the increase in temperature.

If an object travels faster than sound, it is said to have **supersonic speed**. Objects travelling with supersonic speed produce shock waves. The sound produced by these shock waves is called **sonic boom**. It is a thunder-like noise heard by a person on the ground when a supersonic aircraft flies in the nearby region.

Reflection of Sound

When sound waves fall on a hard surface, they bounce back from the surface. This phenomenon is called the **reflection of sound**. You must have heard the term 'echo'. **Echo** occurs due to the reflection of sound from the hills or the walls of the building. We hear two sound waves as two distinct sounds only if the time interval between the sound waves is $\frac{1}{10}$th of a second or more than that. Therefore, we can hear the echo of a sound only if the reflected sound reaches our ear after $\frac{1}{10}$th of a second after we hear the first sound. This condition is possible only if there is some minimum distance between the source producing the sound and the surface reflecting the sound (assuming the listener is near to the source).

Let us find the minimum distance required to hear an echo. We know the speed of sound in the air is approximately 340 m/s. Therefore, the distance travelled by the sound in air in a time equal to $\frac{1}{10}$th second is 34 metres. Hence, for the echo of a sound to be heard, the minimum distance travelled by that should be 34 m. This means the surface reflecting the sound from a source should be at least 17 m away from the source.

TYPES OF SOUND

Sound can be classified on the basis of its audibility to humans. The sound of frequency below 20 Hz and above 20,000 Hz cannot be heard by humans. The sound of frequency less than 20 Hz is called **infrasonic sound** and the sound of frequency more than 20,000 Hz is called **ultrasonic sound**. Human ear is sensitive only to sound waves of frequency from 20 Hz to 20,000 Hz. In other words, infrasonic and ultrasonic waves are not audible to us.

Science in Context

Bats use ultrasonic sound and echo for navigation.

Wonder!

Some animals and birds are sensitive to infrasonic and ultrasonic sounds, which are not heard by humans. Bats use ultrasonic sounds to detect their prey.

MUSIC AND NOISE

Are all the sounds we hear from our surroundings pleasant? Some sounds are pleasant, while others are unpleasant. Sounds that give a pleasant feeling are usually called **musical sounds** while the sounds that produce an unpleasant, irritating feeling are called **noises**. In a musical sound, the variation of the amplitude is regular and rhythmic, whereas in noise, the amplitude variation is abrupt and irregular.

Musical Instruments

Musical instruments (Fig. 12.7) can be classified into three categories based on how the sound is produced by them. Instruments such as guitar and violin produce sound through the vibration of the stretched strings. Such instruments are called **string instruments**. Instruments such as flute and trumpet produce sound through the vibration of the air column inside them. Such instruments are called **wind instruments**. Instruments such as drums and tabla produce sound by the vibration of a stretched membrane. Such instruments are termed as **percussion instruments**.

Fig. 12.7: Musical instruments

Noise Pollution and Its Harmful Effects

We know that noise is unwanted, unpleasant, irritating and loud sound. Too much noise in the surrounding is harmful and leads to **noise pollution**. Sounds produced by moving vehicles and their horns, various devices such as vacuum cleaners, drilling machines, mixer and grinder, machines used in the industries, are some of the major sources of noise pollution.

Sound of very high intensity level is much louder. Our ears cannot tolerate such loud sound. Intensity level of sound is expressed in **decibels (dB)**. Any sound of intensity level higher than 120 dB is very loud and can cause pain in the ears.

Table 12.1 shows the intensity level of sounds produced by various sources.

Table 12.1: Sources of sound and their sound levels

Source	Sound level (in dB)
Jet aircraft, 50 m away	140
Threshold of pain	120
Disco, 1 m from speaker	100
Diesel truck, 10 m away	90
Vacuum cleaner at 1 m distance	70
Conversational speech at 1 m	60
At home	50

Long exposure to a noise-polluted environment may lead to some serious health problems. Some of these are given below:

- Long exposure to noise can reduce our concentration and can cause restlessness.
- Exposure to high noise levels may lead to sleep disturbances and discomforts.
- Sudden exposure to very high level noises may lead to temporary or even permanent hearing disability.
- Prolonged exposure to noisy environment leads to frequent headaches, hypertension, high stress levels, behavioural and emotional problems.
- Noise pollution leads to increased heartbeat, constriction of blood vessels and dilation of pupil, etc.

How to Reduce Noise Pollution

If the noise level in our environment is not controlled, it may damage our health. We can take some steps to reduce the noise level around us:

- Avoid very loud music that might hurt our as well as others' ears.
- Plant more trees to help reduce noise levels. The plants and trees have a good ability to absorb the sound.
- Minimize the use of defective machines and engines that produce unwanted sounds.
- Avoid unnecessary use of horns of vehicles while travelling.
- Wear ear plugs to protect the ears while working in a noisy atmosphere.

Keywords

Sound: The form of energy that produces a sensation which can be heard by the ears

Frequency: Number of vibrations completed by a particle in one second

Amplitude: The maximum displacement of a vibrating particle from its mean position to one of the extreme positions

Time period: Time taken by a particle for one complete oscillation or vibration

Infrasonic sound: Sound of frequency less than 20 Hz

Ultrasonic sound: Sound of frequency more than 20,000 Hz

Summary

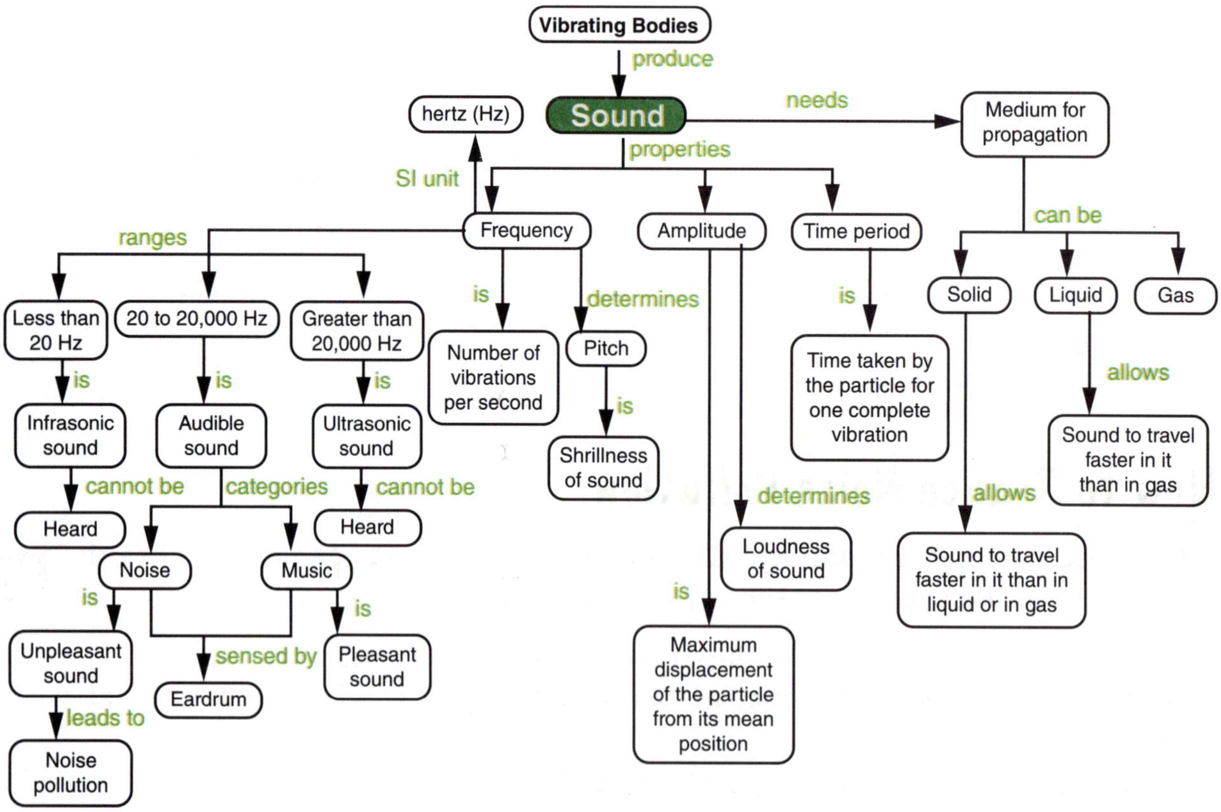

Exercise

W

ia

A. Choose the correct option.

1. Sound cannot travel through ________________.
   (a) solid (b) liquid (c) gas (d) vacuum
2. The audible range of a normal human ear is ________________.
   (a) above 20,000 Hz (b) below 20 Hz
   (c) 20 Hz to 20,000 Hz (d) 2,000 Hz to 20,000 Hz
3. Which of the following is the correct sequence of sound propagation through the human ear?
   (a) Eardrum, inner ear, brain (b) Inner ear, eardrum, brain
   (c) Brain, inner ear, eardrum (d) Brain, eardrum, inner ear
4. Loudness of a sound depends on its ________________.
   (a) amplitude (b) frequency (c) pitch (d) all of these
5. Pitch of a sound is directly proportional to ________________.
   (a) frequency (b) amplitude (c) time period (d) loudness

B. State whether the following statements are true (T) or false (F).

1. A bomb exploding inside a vacuum room does not produce sound. ☐
2. Sound produced by ultrasound equipment creates hearing problems in humans. ☐
3. A loud sound produced inside a liquid medium can be heard in the air medium. ☐
4. Vocal cords vibrate to help humans produce sound. ☐
5. Lower is the frequency of vibration, the higher is the pitch. ☐

C. Fill in the blanks.

1. Loudness of sound depends on ________________ of the sound waves. (frequency/amplitude)
2. Sounds of frequency above 20,000 Hz are called ________________ sounds. (infrasonic/ultrasonic)
3. Time taken by a particle to complete one oscillation is called ________________. (time period/frequency)
4. The SI unit of ________________ is hertz. (frequency/amplitude)
5. Infrasonic waves have a frequency of ________________. (less than 20 Hz/more than 20,000 Hz)

D. Define the following terms.

1. Vibration	2. Amplitude	3. Frequency	4. Pitch
5. Echo	6. Infrasonic sound	7. Music	8. Ultrasonic sound

E. Give reasons for the following.

1. While playing a guitar, if we pull a string gently, we hear a soft sound. If we pull the same string hard, we hear a loud sound.
2. Female voice is shriller than a male voice.
3. The sound produced by a collision or an explosion takes place in the outer space cannot be heard by a space voyager passing by.
4. People living in a city may suffer from health conditions such as headache, hypertension, high stress levels, etc.
5. Planting trees would help to reduce noise pollution.

F. Answer the following questions briefly.

1. Can sound waves produced by a body make another body vibrate?
2. How does the pitch of a sound vary with frequency?
3. Which are the three types of musical instruments? Give one example for each.
4. Mention any two harmful effects of noise pollution.
5. What do you mean by the quality of sound waves?

G. Answer the following questions in detail.

1. Sound is a form of energy. Substantiate this statement with an example.
2. How do sound waves travel in the air medium? Explain.
3. Suggest one experiment to show that sound requires a medium for propagation.
4. Describe an activity to show that sound travels through liquids.
5. What is noise pollution? What are the necessary measures to be taken to reduce it?

Cognitive Corner

Critical Thinking

1. Suppose two objects are colliding in space just above the Earth's atmosphere. Can we hear the sound produced due to the collision? Justify.
2. Will a change in the amplitude change the loudness or pitch of the sound produced? How?
3. We cannot measure the depth of seas using direct methods. Can we use sound waves to find depth of sea? Explain how.
4. 'Bats can catch prey even in the dark'. Do you agree with this statement? Justify your argument.

Picture Study

Label the diagram of the human ear given below.

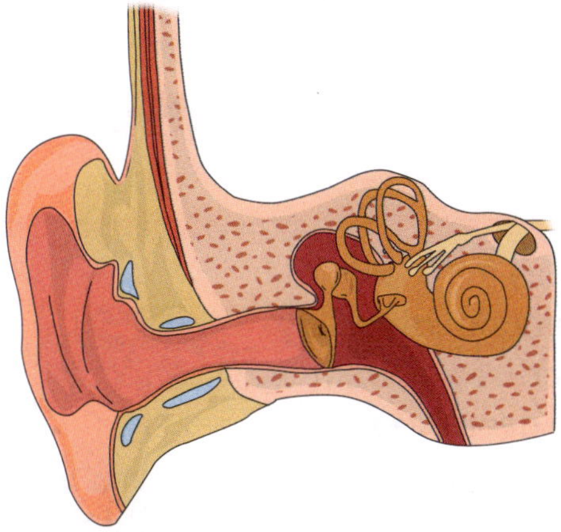

Project

As a part of Science Club activity, make a water bottle *jaltarang*.

When a glass bottle is tapped with a spoon, a sound of a particular pitch is produced. Follow these steps to make your own *jaltarang*.

Materials required: Six glass bottles, water, spoon and marker

1. Fill the water bottles with decreasing levels of water, as shown in the figure, starting from the maximum level.
2. Take the spoon and gently strike the bottles, one after the other.
3. The lesser the water in the bottle, the higher will be the pitch.

Make your own music on your *jaltarang* and play along! **(C-7.2)**

In the Library

1. Read about ultrasound waves. Find out how it is used in our everyday life. **(C-9.1)**
2. People constructing halls for performance of arts and music study the acoustics of the hall. Collect details about acoustics. Make a report on the same. **(C-7.1)**

Life Skills

Playing loudspeakers may cause disturbances to people around us. Using headphones at loud volume may affect our ear drums. Find out other harmful effects of loud sounds. What can you do to not contribute to sound pollution? **(C-7.1)**

Worksheet

Sound waves are everywhere! We can listen to our favourite songs, enjoy amazing sci-fi movies in theatres because of sound waves and how our ears perceive it.

A. Look around you. How many objects around you make use of sound technology? Name any five.

Sound waves not only play a big part in leisure and entertainment but also play a big part in creating pictures of what we cannot see, especially in deep oceans.

The technology which makes this possible is called Sound Navigation and Ranging (SONAR). It works on the principle of echolocation.

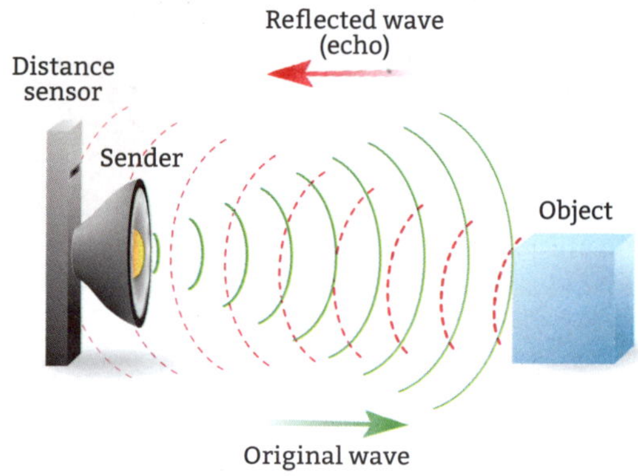

B. Find out how SONAR works and write a few lines on what you understood about SONAR.

C. Do you agree that sound waves help us communicate and stay safe? Give reasons for your answer.

D. Do you think innovations in the field of sound technology would help in the growth and development of our country? Share your views in a few sentences.

13 Chemical Effects of Electric Current

Curricular Goals

- Explore the world of matter, and its constituents, properties and behaviour **(CG-1)**
- Explore the nature and processes of science through engaging with the evolution of scientific knowledge and conducting scientific inquiry **(CG-6)**
- Communicate questions, observations and conclusions related to science **(CG-7)**

Competencies

- Classify matter based on observable physical and chemical characteristics **(C-1.1)**
- Formulate questions using scientific terminology and collect data as evidence **(C-6.2)**
- Use scientific vocabulary to communicate science accurately in oral and written forms, and through visual representation **(C-7.1)**
- Design and build simple models to demonstrate scientific concepts **(C-7.2)**

Let's Get Started

In our previous class, we have studied about electric current and some of its effects. Identify the effects of electric current in order to make each of the following objects work.

____

____

The flow of electric charges through a conductor produces an **electric current**. In most cases, an electric current is produced due to the flow of electrons. Electrons flow from the negative terminal to the positive terminal of a battery through the external circuit. However, conventionally, the direction of electric current is taken as the direction of flow of positive charges, that is from the positive terminal to the negative terminal of the battery.

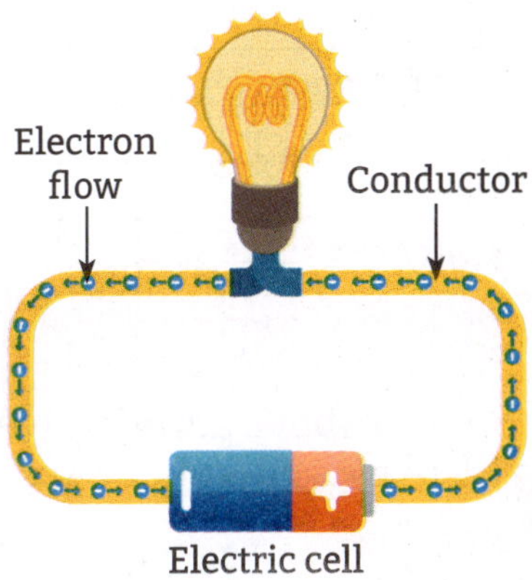

CONDUCTORS AND INSULATORS OF ELECTRICITY

Some metals such as copper, iron and aluminium allow electric current to pass through them. Materials that allow passage of electric current through them are called **conductors** of electric current. Some materials such as rubber, plastic, wood do not allow electric current to pass through them. The materials that do not allow passage of electric current through them are called **insulators** of electric current. We can test whether a material is a conductor or an insulator by using a simple electric circuit consisting of a cell and a bulb connected by wires.

Activity 1

Aim: To test whether a given material is a conductor or an insulator

Materials required: Cells or battery, bulb, bulb holder, insulated copper wires and materials such as pencil, comb, steel spoon, coin, copper rod, iron nail, etc.

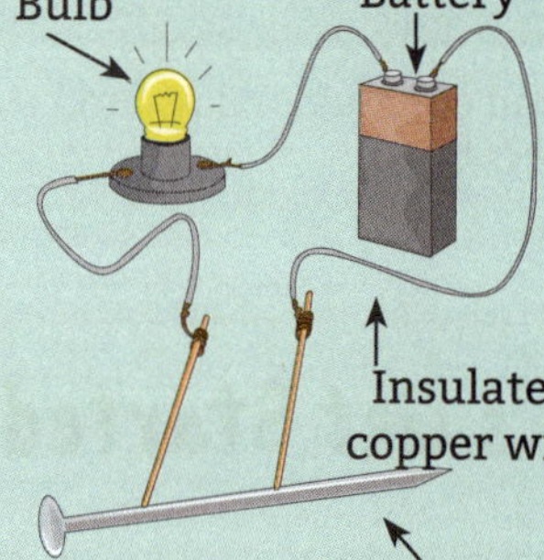

Procedure:

1. Connect the bulb to the battery with the help of copper wires, as shown in the figure alongside. Before setting up the connections, ensure that the insulation at the tip of the wire is removed to expose the copper wire.
2. Keep the materials listed in the table below on a cardboard sheet. Hold the two free ends of the insulated copper wires in your two hands and touch the material that is to be tested (the two ends of the copper wire should touch the material) with the naked copper wire. Repeat the experiment using the other materials listed below.
3. Observe and record what happens to the bulb in the circuit.

Observation: If the bulb glows, the material is a conductor. If the bulb does not glow, the material is an insulator.

Materials	Did the Bulb Glow?	Conductor/Insulator
Metallic paper clip/Iron nail		
Pencil		
Comb		
Steel spoon		
Copper rod		
Coin		

Conclusion: ____

____

From the above activity, we can see that all the materials made up of metals conduct electricity, while the materials made up of wood, rubber, plastic, etc. do not conduct electricity.

Liquids as Conductors of Electricity

Some liquids are good conductors of electricity. Let us perform an activity to find out which liquids conduct electricity and which do not. We can use the same tester circuit used in Activity 1 to test the conductivity of liquids.

Activity 2

Aim: To test whether a given liquid is a conductor or an insulator

Materials required: Cells or battery, bulb, bulb holder, insulated copper wires and small beakers

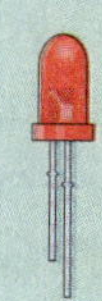

Note: We can also use an LED (light emitting diode) instead of the bulb. An LED will glow even if a very small amount of current flows.

Procedure:

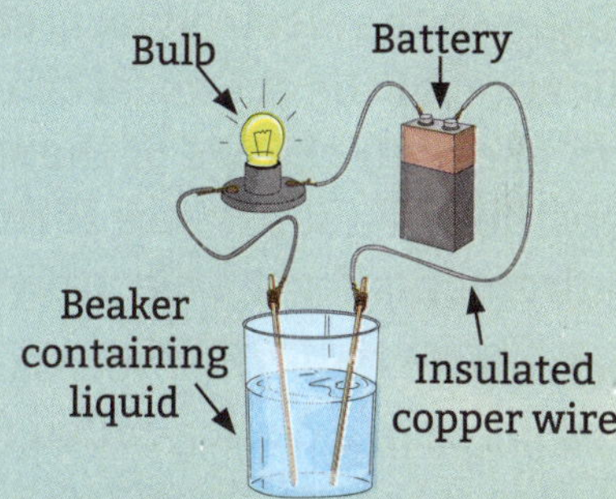

1. Connect the bulb to the battery with the help of copper wires as shown in the figure alongside.
2. Take the liquids mentioned in the observation table given below in different beakers.
3. First, dip the two free ends of the copper wires into one beaker containing one of the liquids (the two ends should not touch each other). Check whether the bulb in the electric circuit is glowing or not. Repeat the experiment with other liquids.

Observation: Tabulate your observations as given below.

Materials	Did the Bulb Glow?	Good Conductor/Poor Conductor
Pure water (distilled water)		
Tap water		
Salt water		
Sugar solution		
Lemon juice		
Vinegar (acid water)		
Castor oil		
Honey		

Conclusion: ____

____

From the above activity, we find that pure water is a poor conductor of electricity, whereas salt water is a good conductor of electricity. Tap water is also a conductor of electricity. This is because tap water is not pure as it contains salts and minerals dissolved in it. When common salt is dissolved in pure water, it becomes a good conductor of electricity. The substances that conduct electricity in their solution or molten state and undergo a chemical change during the process are known as **electrolytes**.

Generally, all **acids** and **bases** are good conductors of electricity. Salts of metals also conduct electricity in their solution or molten state, and they are electrolytes too. Sugar solution, oils, etc. do not conduct electricity, and thus, are poor conductors and non-electrolytes.

ELECTROLYSIS

a

Have you ever noticed any change taking place when electric current is passed through a liquid? If you observe carefully, you can see that gas bubbles are liberated at the two terminals dipped into the solution in Activity 2. What does this indicate? This shows that some chemical changes occur when an electric current flows through liquids. The process of passing an electric current through an electrolyte, to bring about chemical changes in the electrolyte, is called **electrolysis**. Liberation of gases is not the only indication of the chemical changes that occur during electrolysis. It can also be in the form of colour change of the solution, due to the formation of new substances or the deposition of a substance at the electrodes due to decomposition, or other reasons. The requirements for the electrolysis process (Fig. 13.1) to take place are as follows:

Electrolytic Cell: The process of electrolysis takes place in a device called the **electrolytic cell**. It is set up with electrolyte and the electrodes are dipped in it.

Electrolyte: Electrolyte is the solution through which the current passes to carry out the chemical reaction. Strong acids, bases and salts are good electrolytes. In the solution or molten state, the compounds dissociate[1] into ions. The oppositely charged ions flow towards their respective electrodes, which causes the flow of electric current.

Science in Context

An atom gets charged when it gains or loses electrons. The atom becomes positively charged when it loses one or more electrons, and negatively charged when it gains one or more electrons. These charged atoms are called ions.

Word Web

[1]**Dissociate**: to break up or separate

Battery: The electrodes are connected to a battery which provides the current supply.

Electrodes: The two terminals dipped into the solution that make the electrical contact between the solution and the external circuit are called **electrodes**. The electrode connected to the positive terminal of the battery is called an **anode** (positive electrode) and the electrode that is connected to the negative terminal of the battery is called a **cathode** (negative electrode).

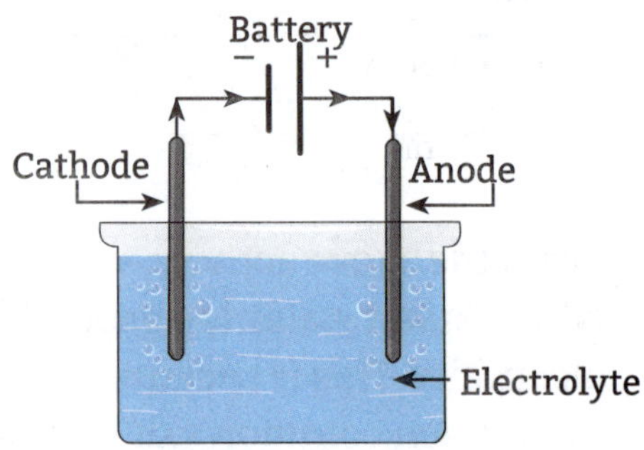

Fig. 13.1: Set-up for electrolysis

When current is passed, the ions in the electrolyte move towards the electrodes. Cations (positive charges) move towards the cathode. Anions (negative charges) move towards the anode.

Electrolysis of Water

In the previous activity, we noticed that tap water and salt water conduct electricity. We know that water is made up of hydrogen and oxygen, combined in the ratio of 2:1. When electric current is passed through water, it decomposes into hydrogen and oxygen.

Activity 3

Aim: To show that water decomposes into hydrogen and oxygen during electrolysis

Materials required: Glass beaker (500 mℓ), two test tubes, two carbon rods, rubber corks with one hole, salt, battery, electric switch and connecting wires

Procedure:

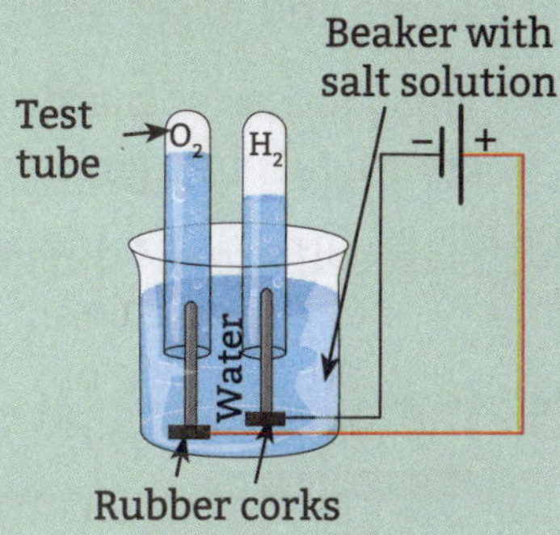

1. Insert a small length of the carbon rod into the rubber cork. Take two pieces of connecting wires and insert a little length of the connecting wires into the rubber cork so that the wire makes contact with the carbon rods. Fix the two rubber corks at the bottom surface of the beaker by using quick fix.
2. Take water in a trough and add a pinch of salt into it. Pour this water into the beaker up to two-thirds of its volume. Fill the two test tubes with water and place them over the two carbon rods, as shown in the figure. Ensure that no air bubbles are trapped inside the test tubes.
3. Connect the free ends of the two wires to a battery through a switch. Switch on the circuit and observe the changes taking place at the two electrodes. Pass the current for 10 to 15 minutes and observe the volume of gases collected in the two test tubes. If you keep the set-up working this way for a long time, you can observe that the volume of the water displaced by the gas in the test tube placed on the cathode will be more than that of the volume of water displaced by the gas in the test tube placed over the anode. This is because hydrogen gas is liberated at the cathode and oxygen gas is liberated at the anode. We can show that the amount of hydrogen gas collected in the test tube in a given time is twice as much as that of the amount of oxygen gas collected in the same time. The ratio of volume of hydrogen to oxygen in water is 2 : 1. Therefore, the volume of hydrogen collected is twice to that of oxygen.

   ***Note:** Narrow test tubes are preferred to easily recognize the volume of gas collected.*

   You can also perform the confirmation test for hydrogen and oxygen gases filled in the two test tubes.
4. Disconnect the wires. Take the test tube from the cathode slowly keeping its mouth closed with your thumb. If the mouth is open, hydrogen gas will escape since it is lighter than air. Light a matchstick and bring it near the mouth of the test tube. You will see that the gas inside the test tube will burn but the flame of the splinter is extinguished with a 'pop' sound. Hydrogen is a combustible gas but not a supporter of combustion. So, it burns but puts off the flame of the matchstick.
5. Now, take the test tube from the anode as described above. While taking the test tube from water, first close the mouth of the test tube with your finger, then turn it upright and remove your finger. If the mouth of the test tube is down, oxygen gas will escape as it is heavier than air. Insert a glowing matchstick (not a burning matchstick) into the test tube. You can see that the glowing matchstick bursts into a flame, but the gas does not burn. Oxygen is a supporter of combustion but is not a combustible gas, its properties are just opposite to that of hydrogen.

Important: *You should take extreme care when you do the above confirmation tests for hydrogen and oxygen. The test tube may break due to the excess heat produced.*

Observations:

(i) Hydrogen gas is liberated at the cathode and oxygen gas is liberated at the anode.

(ii) The volume of the water displaced by the gas in the test tube placed on the cathode is twice that of the volume of water displaced by the gas in the test tube placed over the anode.

From the previous activity, we can see that water decomposes or splits into its constituent gases—hydrogen and oxygen—during electrolysis. It contains hydrogen and oxygen in the ratio 2 : 1 by volume.

Revise and Recall

Fill in the blanks.

1. Pure water is ____________ of electric current. (a conductor/an insulator)
2. Acids and bases are ____________ conductors of electricity. (good/bad)
3. The process of passing electric current through an electrolyte to bring about chemical changes in it is called ____________. (electrolysis/electricity)
4. Gases liberated during the electrolysis of water are ____________ and ____________. (hydrogen, carbon dioxide/hydrogen, oxygen)
5. The substances that conduct electric current in their solution or molten state are called ____________. (electrolytes/electrodes)

Applications of Electrolysis

Electrolysis is used in industries to produce a lot of useful materials from naturally available substances. For example, sodium is manufactured through the electrolysis of molten sodium chloride (common salt). Electrolysis is also used in the purification of metals, coating of one metal over the other metals, etc.

Electroplating

The process of coating a thin layer of metal on another metal or material using electrolysis is called **electroplating.** It is widely used in the industry for coating metals such as nickel, chromium, tin, gold and silver over other metals. It is mainly used to protect corrosive metals from corrosion. For example, iron objects are coated with zinc to prevent rusting. This is called **galvanization**. The metal or material that has to be coated is taken as the cathode and the metal to be coated on another metal or material is taken as the anode. Generally, in electroplating, a solution of the salt of the metal to be coated (taken as anode) is used as the electrolyte. For example, a solution of copper sulphate is used when copper is electroplated on a metal in a laboratory.

Activity 4

Aim: To electroplate copper on another metal

Materials required: Beaker, copper rod, iron key, copper sulphate solution and battery

Procedure:

1. Take the solution of copper sulphate in a beaker.
2. Make connections and set up the experiment as shown below. Let the electric current pass through the copper sulphate solution for 10–15 minutes.
3. Observe the colour of the key. Does the colour change?

Observation: A uniform brown coating forms on the key. Copper gets deposited on the iron key on electroplating.

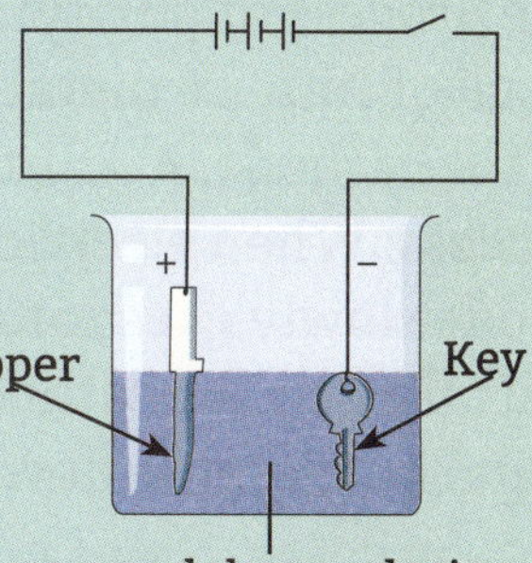

The process of coating gold on other metals is called **gold plating**. If silver is coated on other materials, the process is called **silver plating**.

Some industrial applications of electroplating are as follows:

- Gold and silver platings are used in the jewellery industry for making gold- and silver-coated ornaments (Fig. 13.2).
- Iron parts such as taps, bicycle wheel rims and handle are coated with chromium. Chromium is a hard and shiny metal which protects iron from corrosion. It also protects the surface from scratches and gives a shiny appearance (Fig. 13.3).
- Food cans made up of iron are coated with tin to protect food items from getting spoiled due to the rusting of iron.
- Iron sheets and iron pipes are coated with zinc to protect them from rusting. Coating steel or iron with zinc to prevent rusting is called galvanization.

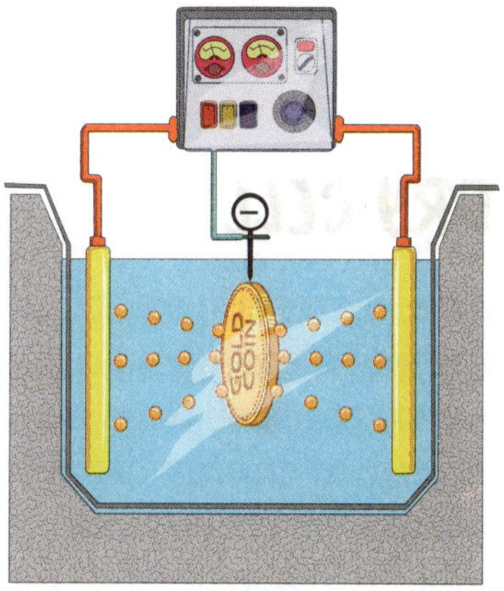

Fig. 13.2: Gold plating a coin

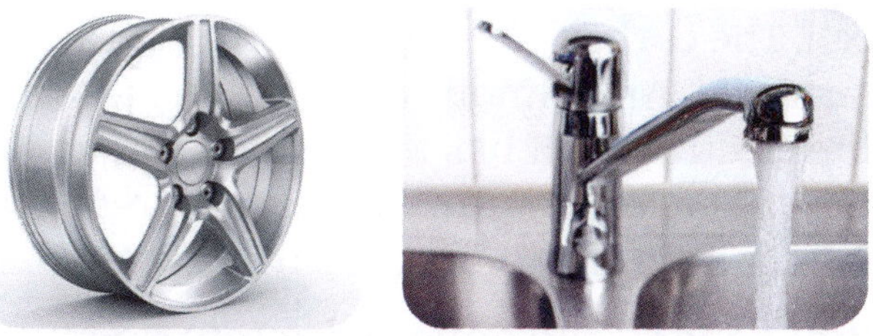

Fig. 13.3: Chromium-plated materials

Science in Context

Galvanization can be done either by the electroplating method or hot-dip galvanization.
In hot-dip galvanization, the iron material to be coated with zinc is submerged in molten zinc and then taken out and dried.

Electrorefining

The process of purifying metals by using electrolysis is called **electrorefining**. A thick block of impure metal is taken as the anode and a thin rod of pure metal is taken as the cathode. A solution of the salt of the metals is used as an electrolyte in this process. When electricity is passed through the solution, the impure metal used as anode slowly goes into the solution and pure metal gets deposited on the thin metal rod taken as the cathode. As the refining process takes place, the impurities in the metal block settle down at the bottom of the container or dissolve in the solution.

Copper is refined industrially by using this process (Fig. 13.4). A thick block of impure copper is used as the anode and a thin copper rod is used as the cathode. Copper sulphate solution is used as electrolyte. When electric current is passed through the solution, impurities go into the solution and pure copper is deposited on the thin copper rod.

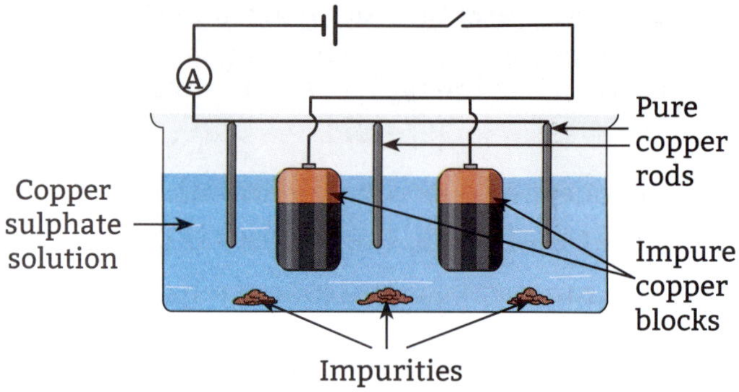

Fig. 13.4: Electrorefining of copper

DRY CELL

An electrolytic cell converts electrical energy into chemical energy (causing chemical changes). A galvanic cell does the opposite. It converts chemical energy into electrical energy. A common example of a galvanic cell is the dry cell. Dry cells (Fig. 13.5) are used in flash lights, radios, clocks, etc.

It consists of a hollow cylindrical container made up of zinc that acts as the negative terminal of the cell. The carbon rod at the centre acts as the positive terminal. An ammonium chloride paste is used as the electrolyte. It has a little moisture to permit the flow of current. A mixture of carbon powder and manganese dioxide is filled in between the anode and cathode.

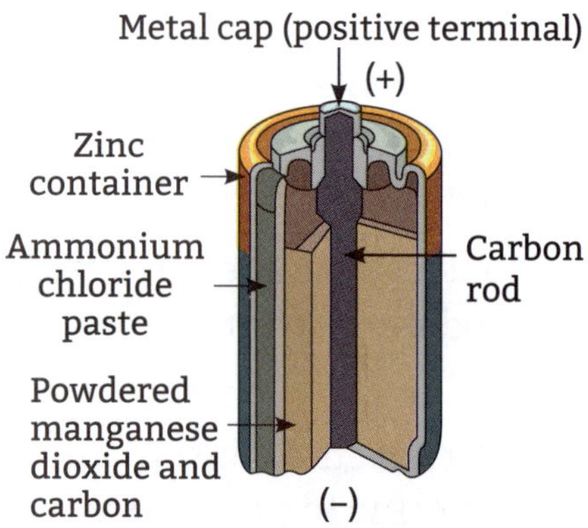

Fig. 13.5: A schematic diagram of a dry cell

When the cell is connected across a circuit, due to the chemical reactions that occur inside, electrons are liberated at the anode (zinc). These electrons pass through the external circuit and reach the cathode (carbon rod).

Unlike a wet cell, a dry cell can be used easily and can be kept in any orientation. It is portable and compact when compared to a wet cell. It is capable of producing a potential difference of 1.5 volts.

Keywords

Electrolyte: A substance that conducts electric current in its solution or molten state

Electrode: The two terminals dipped into the electrolyte that make the electrical contact between the solution and the external circuit

Anode: The electrode connected to the positive terminal of the battery

Cathode: The electrode connected to the negative terminal of the battery

Electrolysis: The process of passing electricity through an electrolyte, thereby causing chemical changes

Electroplating: The process of coating a metal with a layer of another metal using electrolysis

Galvanization: Coating of iron objects with a layer of zinc

Electrolytic cell: A cell consisting of an electrolyte and electrodes to allow for the free passage of electric current from an external source

Electrorefining: The process of purifying a metal using electrolysis

Summary

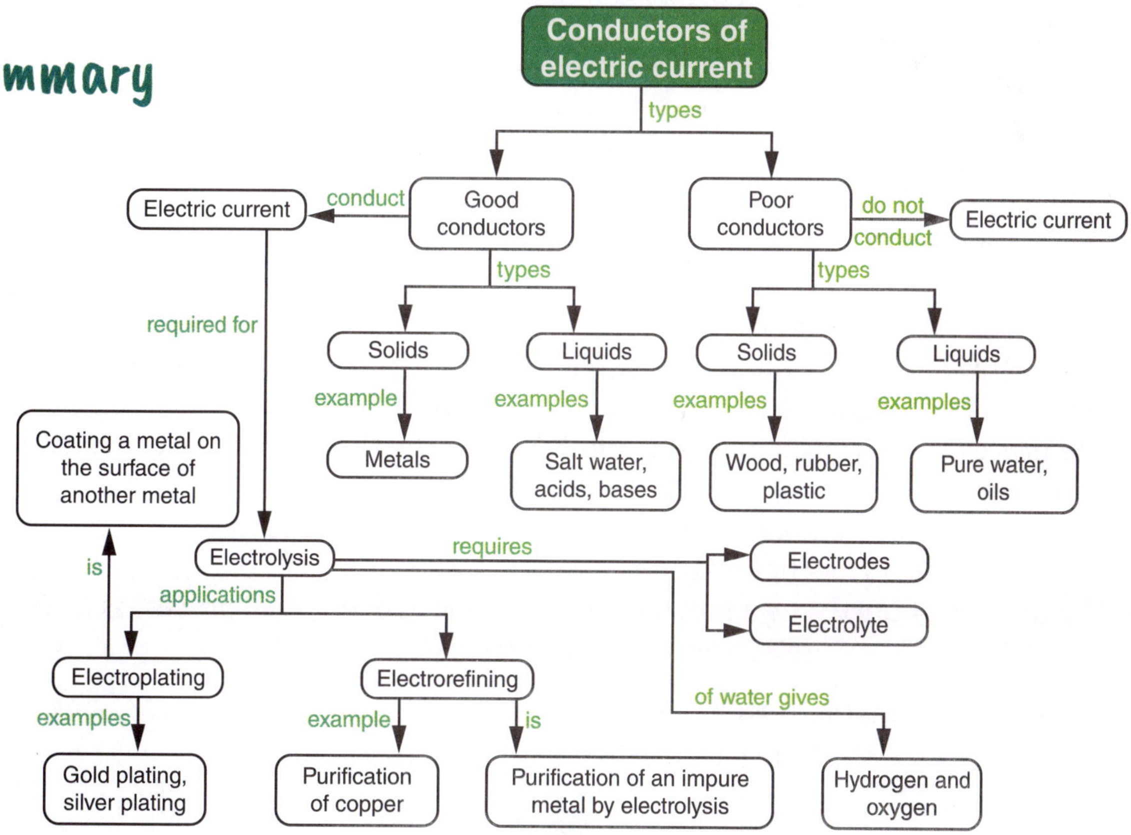

Exercise

A. Choose the correct option.

1. When an electric current passes through salt water, the gas liberated at the positive electrode is ______________.
   (a) chlorine (b) oxygen (c) hydrogen (d) carbon dioxide
2. Which of the following liquids conducts electricity?
   (a) Lemon juice (b) Honey (c) Kerosene (d) Distilled water
3. In which of the following options, the liquids have been arranged in the increasing order of conductivity?
   (a) Salt water, tap water, river water (b) River water, tap water, salt water
   (c) Tap water, river water, salt water (d) Salt water, river water, tap water
4. Iron sheets used for making household articles are usually coated with zinc to prevent ______________.
   (a) rusting (b) electrolysis (c) electroplating (d) none of these
5. Which among the following is not an application of electroplating?
   (a) Coating gold on ornaments (b) Coating silver on ornaments
   (c) Coating chromium on iron objects (d) Coating iron on zinc sheets

B. State whether the following statements are true (T) or false (F).

1. When salt is added to pure water, it reduces the conductivity of water. ☐
2. Electrolyte is a chemical substance that allows electricity to pass through it. ☐
3. Distilled water is a good conductor of electricity. ☐
4. Base water is a bad conductor of electricity. ☐
5. When acid is added to pure water, it becomes a good conductor of electric current. ☐

C. Fill in the blanks.

1. During the electrolysis process, pure metal gets deposited at the ______________. (anode/cathode)
2. For electroplating of copper on iron, the terminal of the battery that is to be connected to the iron is ______________. (negative/positive)
3. The process of coating a metal on another metal by the means of electricity is known as ______________. (electroplating/electrolysis)
4. When electric current passes through a solution, it causes a ______________ effect. (chemical/mechanical)
5. The process of purifying a metal by using an electrochemical process is known as ______________. (electrorefining/electrolysis)

D. Define the following terms.

1. Electrolyte 2. Electroplating 3. Electrorefining
4. Electrolysis 5. Cathode 6. Anode

E. Give reasons for the following.

1. Tin is electroplated on iron to make cans used for storing food.
2. Water obtained from river and lakes conducts electricity, while pure or distilled water does not conduct electricity.
3. An LED is a more efficient device than a normal electric bulb.
4. Electric fires are extinguished by using CO_2 extinguisher and not by using water.
5. Water from taps, hand pumps, wells and ponds can be a good conductor of electricity.

F. Answer the following questions briefly.

1. Mention two applications of electroplating.
2. Seawater is a better conductor of electricity than tap water. Why?
3. Name the gases that are obtained during the electrolysis of water.
4. How do you choose an electrolyte for electroplating a given metal on another metal?
5. What is the advantage of a dry cell over a wet cell?

G. Answer the following questions in detail.

1. Explain the method of copper plating an iron nail.
2. What is an electrolytic cell? Draw its schematic diagram.
3. Draw a schematic diagram of the set-up for electrorefining copper.
4. What are electrodes and how do they function?
5. Explain the working of a dry cell.

Cognitive Corner

Critical Thinking

1. When we dissolve salt in water, it conducts electricity, whereas salt crystals or powder does not conduct electric current. Explain why.
2. In case of a fire, firemen shut off the electricity supply for the area before they use the water hoses to put out the fire. Why?

Picture Study

Identify the chemical process shown in the following diagram and label the set-up.

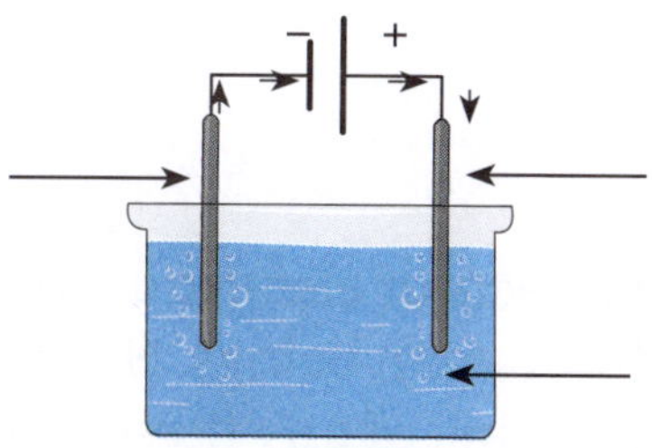

____

Project

As a part of Science Club activity, make a PowerPoint presentation on electroplating, its various uses in different industries and the adverse health effects related to the electroplating of chromium. Present this in your class. Also, identify some items around you that have been electroplated. **(C-7.1)**

In the Library

1. When salt is added to water, the water conducts electric current. When salt is added into water, it makes ions in the water, which help in the conduction of electric current. However, sugar dissolved in water does not conduct electric current as it does not produce ions. Learn more about this process and find out what type of materials ionize in water. **(C-9.1)**
2. Find out more about LEDs and their uses. **(C-6.2)**

In the Laboratory

Aim: To make a simple electric cell **(C-7.2)**

Materials required: A beaker of 500 mℓ capacity, dilute sulphuric acid, water, zinc rod, copper rod, connecting wires and a torch bulb

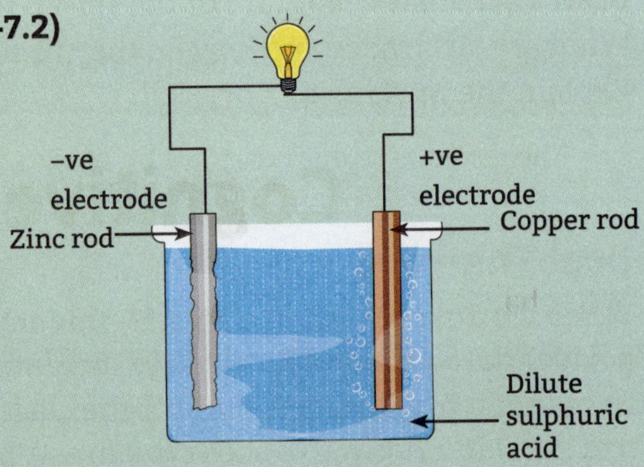

Procedure:

1. Take water in the beaker, about two-thirds of its volume.
2. Add a few drops of sulphuric acid into the water carefully.
3. Dip the zinc rod and copper rod into the solution and connect them to the torch bulb, as shown in the diagram. Observe whether the bulb glows or not.

Life Skills

The application of the chemical effects of electric current may have brought many advancements and inventions for human beings. However, there are negative impacts such as chemical wastes. Can you think of any three other negative impacts? How can these negative impacts be reduced? Make a poster regarding the same. **(C-7.1)**

9 INDUSTRY, INNOVATION AND INFRASTRUCTURE

Worksheet

Iron is a metal that is strong and dependable. It is the very backbone on which a country's progress depends. However, even though iron is used in building practically everything from buildings to bridges, it has a huge disadvantage. It rusts, and with continued rusting, it decays and weakens.

The life of iron can be lengthened by a process called galvanization. Galvanization means coating iron with zinc. Zinc does not react with moisture or air. Zinc and iron layers facing each other bond with each other to form an alloy.

When iron is mixed with carbon, an alloy is formed, which goes by the name steel. Iron and steel industry is one of the most important industries in India. In 2019, India became the 2nd largest steel producer in the world. The industry produced 82.68 million tons of total finished steel and 9.7 million tons of raw iron.

A. Galvanization is a simple process as described below.

1. The iron or steel article is first thoroughly cleaned.

   Tick the correct cleaning agent used.

   a. The dust and grease is cleaned with (soap solution/only water).

   b. The rust stains are removed by dipping the article in (vinegar/hydrochloric acid).

2. The article is then dipped into molten zinc which has been heated to about 450°C for about 4 to 5 minutes.

   What happens during this time?

   ____

   ____

3. The galvanized article is then taken out of the dip and left to cool. The hot zinc layer reacts with air to form a shiny layer of zinc carbonate on the surface. This gives a glazed effect and prevents the inner metal from further reactions; hence, protecting from rusting and decay.

B. Find out how the production of iron and steel impacts programmes such as Make in India, Startup India, Standup India and Skill India. Do these programmes also have an impact on the manufacturing industry?

____

____

____

____

14 Some Natural Phenomena

Curricular Goals

- Explore the nature and processes of science through engaging with the evolution of scientific knowledge and conducting scientific inquiry **(CG-6)**
- Communicate questions, observations and conclusions related to science **(CG-7)**

Competencies

- Formulate questions using scientific terminology and collect data as evidence **(C-6.2)**
- Use scientific vocabulary to communicate science accurately in oral and written forms, and through visual representation **(C-7.1)**
- Design and build simple models to demonstrate scientific concepts **(C-7.2)**

Let's Get Started

Events that occur in nature are called natural phenomena. Some of these natural phenomena cause mass destruction of life and property. They are called **natural disasters**. You may have read in the newspapers about different disasters such as flood, cyclones, earthquake and tsunami, and the damages caused by them. We have studied about some of these in the previous classes. Identify the natural disasters in the pictures given below.

A. ______________________

B. ______________________

Have you ever noticed a flash of lightning in the night sky on a stormy night? It is often accompanied by thunder and rain. Have you ever wondered how lightning occurs? In this chapter, we will learn more about lightning and earthquake. Let us first learn about electric charge and see how it is related to lightning.

ELECTRIC CHARGE

Have you experienced small shocks when you touch metallic door knobs, metallic water taps, etc. during dry days? What could be the reason for such incidents? This happens due to **electric charges** generated through contact. Let us do some activities to understand this.

Activity 1

Aim: To show the presence of static charge on a plastic scale rubbed with hair

Materials required: Plastic scale and bits of paper

Procedure:

1. Rub the scale on your hair.
2. Bring the scale near the pieces of paper.

Observation: The bits of paper stick to the scale.

Conclusion: On rubbing the scale on hair, it becomes **electrically charged**. The charges acquired by the scale are called **static charges** because they are stationary.

Activity 2

Aim: To see if various uncharged objects can be charged by rubbing

Materials required: A balloon, an eraser, an ebonite rod, a glass rod, a plastic ruler, woollen cloth, silk cloth, polythene bag, dry hair and pieces of paper

Procedure and observation: Charge the objects by rubbing with the materials as given in the table below and record your observations.

Object	Rubbed with	Attracts/Does Not Attract Bits of Paper	Charged/Not Charged
Balloon	Polythene bag, dry hair, wool, silk		
Eraser	Wool		
Plastic ruler	Dry hair, wool		
Ebonite rod	Wool		
Glass rod	Silk		

Properties of Electric Charges

Electric charges exhibit some properties when they are brought close to each other. They attract or repel each other according to the nature of the charges.

Activity 3

Aim: To show that like charges repel and unlike charges attract each other

Materials required: Two ebonite rods, two glass rods, wool, silk and thread

Procedure:

1. Hang one ebonite rod by using a thread and rub its ends with wool.
2. Rub one end of the other ebonite rod with wool and bring it near the first one. Observe what happens.
3. Rub one end of the glass rod with silk and bring it near the ebonite rod that is hanging. Observe what happens.
4. Now, remove the ebonite rod and hang the glass rod and rub it with the silk cloth.
5. Rub the other glass rod with the silk cloth and bring it near the glass rod that is hung. Observe what happens.
6. Now, rub an ebonite rod with wool and bring it near the glass rod. Observe what happens.

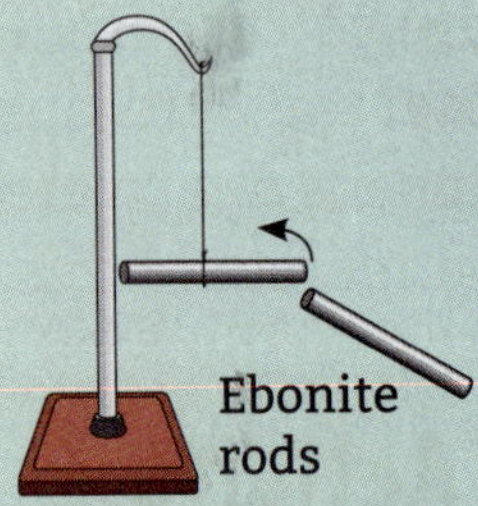

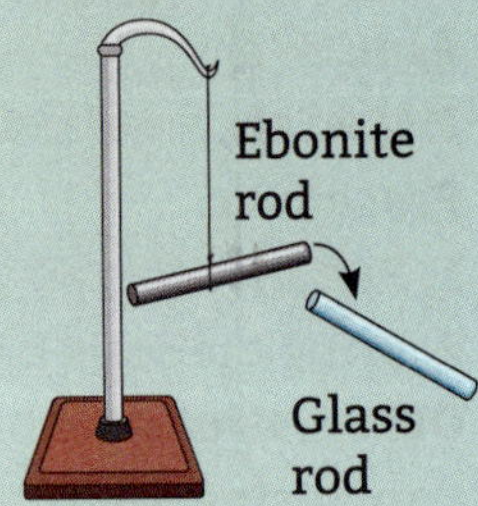

Observation: The charged ebonite rods repelled each other, so did the charged glass rods. However, a charged ebonite rod and a charged glass rod attracted each other.

Conclusion: Like charges repel and unlike charges attract.

In Activity 3, the ebonite rod developed negative charges and the glass rod developed positive charges. The specific names (positive and negative) for these two types of charges were given by the American scientist, Benjamin Franklin.

Like charges repel each other: Two positively charged objects repel each other. Similarly, two negatively charged objects also repel each other.

Unlike charges attract each other: A positively charged object and a negatively charged object attract each other.

Testing Charges

We have seen in the activities that the unlike charges attract each other and like charges repel each other. Moreover, an uncharged object is attracted by both positively and negatively charged objects.

- If the object to be tested is attracted by both positively charged as well as negatively charged objects, then it is uncharged or neutral.
- If the object to be tested is repelled by a positively charged object and attracted by a negatively charged one, then it is positively charged.
- If the object to be tested is repelled by a negatively charged object and attracted by a positively charged one, then it is negatively charged.

Therefore, attraction alone is not a sure shot test for indicating the charge on an object. Repulsion is also an absolute test for indicating the charge on an object.

METHODS OF CHARGING AN OBJECT

Atoms of all substances contain negatively charged particles called electrons and positively charged particles called protons. All uncharged objects have an equal number of protons and electrons. Hence, they are neutral. Objects become charged by gaining or losing electrons. Objects whose atoms lose electrons become positively charged, while those atoms that gain electrons become negatively charged.

An uncharged object can be charged by the following three ways: charging by friction, charging by conduction and charging by induction.

Charging by Friction

From the first two activities, we have seen that some objects can be charged by rubbing against another object. When two objects are rubbed together, some electrons from one object get transferred to the other object. Objects that lose electrons become positively charged, and those that gain the electrons become negatively charged. This method of charging an object by rubbing it with another object is called **charging by friction**.

When a glass rod is rubbed with silk, electrons are transferred from the glass to the silk. This way, the glass rod acquires positive charge and the silk gains electrons, so it acquires negative charge. When an ebonite rod is rubbed with wool/fur, the wool/fur loses electrons which are transferred to the ebonite rod. This way, the wool acquires positive charge and the ebonite rod becomes negatively charged.

Charging by Conduction

When an uncharged object is brought in contact with a charged object, charges flow from the charged object to the uncharged object. This causes the uncharged object to acquire some charge. This method of charging an uncharged object by bringing it in contact with a charged object is called **charging by conduction**. During conduction, the type of charge that the uncharged object acquires is the same as that of the charged object. Figure 14.1 shows the method of charging through conduction.

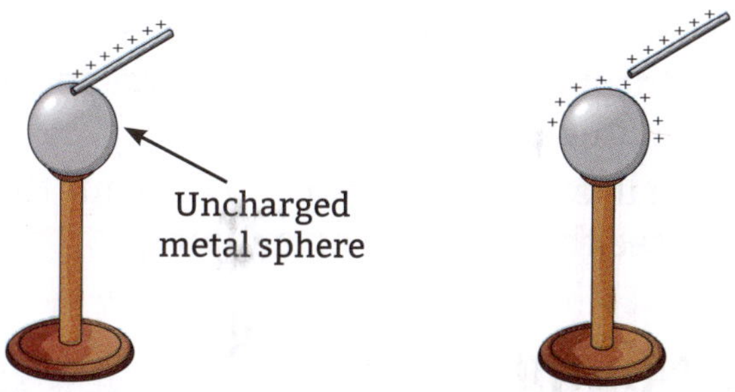

Fig. 14.1: Charging by conduction

When a positively charged glass rod is brought in contact with an uncharged metal sphere, the metal sphere also acquires a positive charge.

Charging by Induction

If an uncharged object is brought near (but not in contact) a charged object, it acquires the charge opposite to that of the charged object. This method of charging an uncharged object by bringing it near a charged object is called **charging by induction**. During induction, the uncharged object acquires the opposite charge. Figure 14.2 shows the steps involved in the method of charging an object by induction.

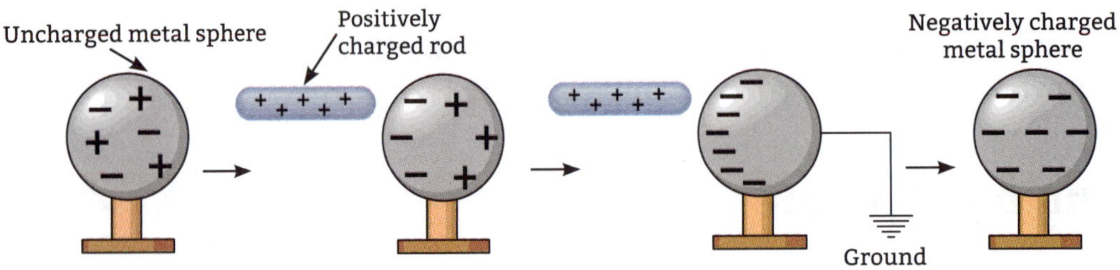

Fig. 14.2: Charging by induction

DETECTION OF CHARGE

Charge on an object can be detected using a device called **electroscope**. Different types of electroscopes such as pith ball electroscope and gold-leaf electroscope are used to detect and measure the amount of charges.

The gold-leaf electroscope (Fig. 14.3) was developed in 1787 by the British physicist Abraham Bennet. It consists of a thick metallic rod kept vertically and a metallic disc or a sphere connected at one end. Two parallel thin and flexible strips of gold (gold leaves) are hung from the bottom end of the rod. To avoid the effect of wind or air, the gold leaves are enclosed in a glass bottle.

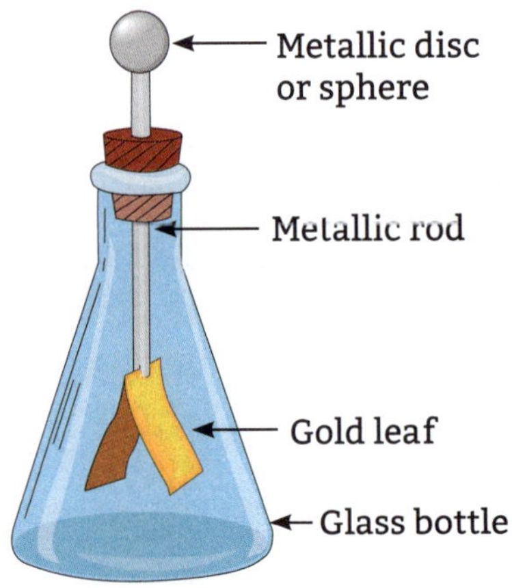

Fig. 14.3: Gold-leaf electroscope

When a charged object is brought close to the metallic sphere, charges are induced on the metallic rod and the gold leaves hanging from the metallic rod move apart. The angle through which the gold leaves move apart gives an approximate measure of the amount of charge.

We can use an electroscope to find out the nature of the charge present on an object. Let us see this through an activity.

Activity 4

Aim: To find out the nature of charge present on an object using a gold-leaf electroscope

Materials required: A negatively charged gold-leaf electroscope and an object with unknown charge

Procedure:

1. Bring the object with unknown charge close to the metallic sphere of the electroscope.
2. Observe the leaves.

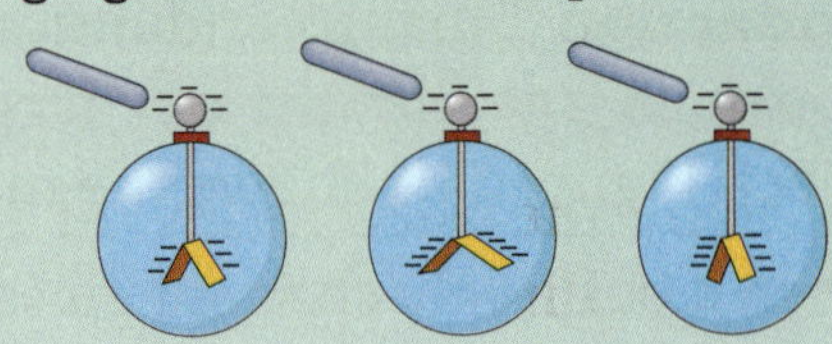

Observation: The two leaves of the electroscope will either move closer or further apart.
Conclusion: If the object is positively charged, the leaves will come closer since the amount of electrons in the leaves will reduce as the positively charged object attracts some electrons towards itself. If the object is negatively charged, the leaves will move further apart since the amount of electrons in the leaves will increase as the negatively charged object repels some electrons from the sphere towards the leaves.

FLOW OF CHARGE

If a charged object is connected to an uncharged object, charges will flow from the charged object to the uncharged object only till their charge densities become equal (you will learn more about charge density in higher classes). However, if we want to maintain the flow of charges continuously, we will have to use an electric cell or a generator.

When charges flow through a material such as a metal, they constitute an electric current. The electric current that we use in our daily life is produced by the flow of charges through metallic wires. For example, if we connect an electric bulb to the terminals of a battery using copper wires, the bulb glows for a long time. This is because a battery can maintain the flow of electric charges for a long time (Fig. 14.4). This is due to the voltage across the terminals of the battery which is maintained by the chemical reactions taking place inside it.

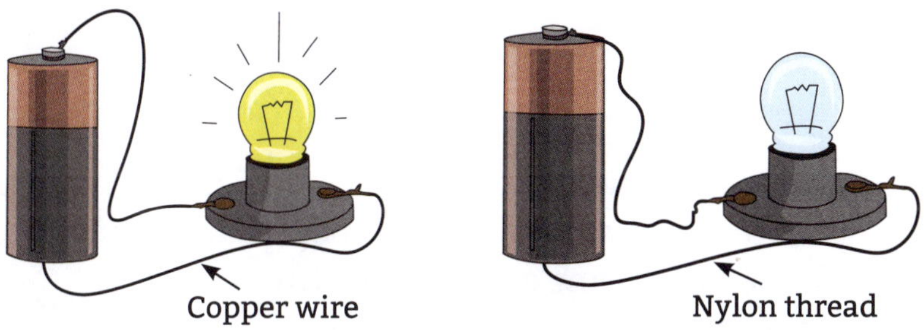

Fig. 14.4: Flow of charges

Now, if we connect the bulb across the terminals of a battery by using a cotton thread or nylon thread, will the bulb glow? The bulb would not glow in these cases because cotton or nylon does not allow electric current to pass through them whereas in the previous case, copper allowed electric current to pass through it.

Materials that allow electric current to pass through them are called **conductors** of electricity. Materials that do not allow electric current to pass through them are called **insulators** of electricity. All metals are good conductors of electricity. Materials such as wood, rubber, plastic and paper are examples of insulators.

The human body is also a conductor of electricity to some extent. Our body provides a path for the electric current to flow to the Earth. That is why we should be careful while handling electrical appliances or we might get a shock. The severity of the shock depends on the amount of current flowing through our body.

To prevent the shock from the electrical appliances while handling them, a connection is made from the main switch in the domestic wiring system to a thick copper rod extending to some depth inside the ground. Any leakage of current will flow through this circuit to the Earth, thereby protecting us from a shock. The process of connecting a charged object to the Earth is called **earthing**.

You may be familiar with three-pin plugs used for household electrical purposes. Have you noticed that one of these pins is bigger as compared to the other two pins? This pin is used for earthing in case of any defect in the electrical appliances so that we do not get an electric shock from the device.

Electric Discharge

Have you ever seen a spark from the electrical sockets and switches when they are plugged in or plugged out? This happens due to a phenomenon called electric discharge. **Electric discharge** is the flow of electric charges through a gas, liquid or a solid. It happens when there is a huge difference in charges between two objects kept in close proximity. An electric discharge through a medium brings about some effects depending on the nature of the medium. Electric discharge through gases produces heat and light in the medium. Lightning is an example of an electrical discharge that occurs in nature.

Lightning

The theory of lightning was explained by the American scientist, Benjamin Franklin, in the 18th century. His kite-flying experiment is a popular and memorable story in science (Fig. 14.5). He flew a kite during a thunderstorm and collected the electric charges in a Leyden jar (a device used to store electric charges) every time the kite was struck by lightning. This enabled him to suggest that lightning is an electrical phenomenon.

Fig. 14.5: Benjamin Franklin's experiment

Lightning is a powerful discharge of electric charges developed in the clouds. Though it is not completely understood how it happens, but charges develop in the clouds during a thunderstorm. It has been found that tiny water droplets in clouds that acquire positive charge become lighter and go to the upper part of the cloud, and the water droplets that acquire negative charge become heavier and occupy the bottom part of the cloud. That is, the top regions of clouds are positively charged and the bottom regions are negatively charged.

This huge amount of charge produces a very high voltage on the cloud with respect to the Earth. This large voltage produces a discharge of the charges through the atmosphere of the Earth (Fig. 14.6). (Note: Difference in charges on two objects creates a potential difference between them which is measured in volts.) This causes a large current to flow through the atmosphere for a very short time. Huge amounts of light and heat are produced during this discharge of current through the air. This is what we see as lightning in the sky. Lightning is accompanied shortly by a loud sound called **thunder**. This is because light travels faster than sound, and so we hear the sound of thunder a bit later than a lightning.

Fig. 14.6: Lightning

Lightning is mainly of three types. The first type is lightning that takes place within the same cloud. The second type is the lightning that takes place between two clouds. The third kind of lightning is the one that takes place between clouds and the Earth.

A lightning between a cloud and the Earth can hit on any object such as tall buildings, trees, etc. on Earth. It is then called a **lightning strike**. A lightning strike can destroy trees, buildings, etc. completely. In hilly areas, the chances of a lightning strike are more as compared to valleys because the distance between the top of hills and clouds is less as compared with the distance between valleys and clouds.

Though lightning causes a lot of damage, it is also beneficial in some ways. During lightning, the heat and light produced enhances the combination of atmospheric nitrogen with oxygen to form oxides of nitrogen. These oxides of nitrogen get dissolved in the rain water and come down as very dilute nitric acid, which reacts with different salts and minerals present in the soil to form nitrogenous compounds. These nitrogenous compounds are required for the growth of plants. Lightning enables the formation of ozone from oxygen, which forms a layer called the **ozone layer**. The ozone layer in the atmosphere protects the Earth from the harmful radiations of the sun by absorbing a part of the ultraviolet radiation.

Lightning Conductor

A specially designed device used to protect buildings, tall towers, etc. from lightning is called a **lightning conductor**. As shown in Figure 14.7, it consists of a thick metal rod with spikes at the top end. The rod is fixed on top of a building such that the spiked ends point upwards. The bottom end of the rod is connected to a copper plate buried deep under the Earth. Lightning conductor was invented by Benjamin Franklin.

Fig. 14.7: Lightning conductor

A lightning conductor provides a low resistance path to the flow of charges. Therefore, during a lightning, electric charges will flow through the lightning conductor to the Earth and not through the building. The study of lightning is called **fulminology**.

Safety and Precautions during Lightning

- Staying inside a building fixed with a lightning conductor is safer than staying in a house without a lightning conductor.
- Do not handle corded devices such as telephone and television with cable during lightning.
- If travelling, do not come out of the vehicle. Staying inside a car is safer than standing in the open space.
- Do not take shelter under a tall tree. There are more chances of a lightning striking a tall tree.
- If you are in an open place, stay away from tall objects such as trees, electric posts, etc.

Revise and Recall

Fill in the blanks.

1. Like charges ________________ each other. (attract/repel)
2. A material that allows the flow of charges through it is called a ________________. (conductor/insulator)
3. The process of connecting a charged object to the Earth is called ________________. (earthing/conduction)
4. The device used to protect buildings from lightning is called a ________________. (lightning conductor/wire)

EARTHQUAKE

An **earthquake** is a sudden movement of the surface of the Earth. Usually, the movement lasts for a few seconds or a few minutes. An earthquake is also known as a **quake**, **tremor** or **temblor**. An earthquake can cause a lot of destruction to life and property on Earth depending on the strength of the quake.

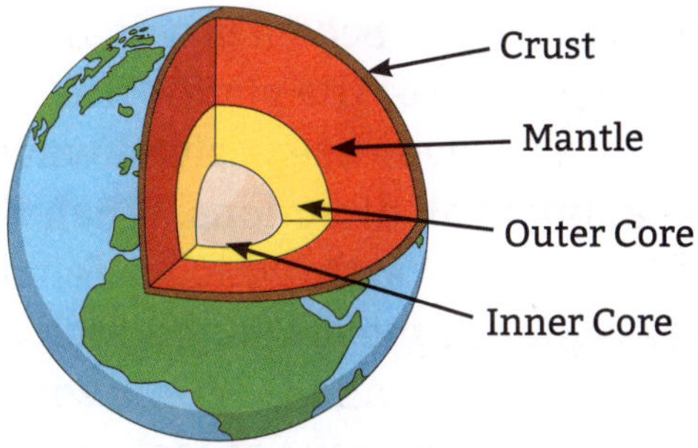

Fig. 14.8: Internal structure of the Earth

To understand how an earthquake occurs, let us first understand the internal structure of the Earth. The internal structure of the Earth consists of different layers. The outermost layer of the Earth is called the **crust**. The crust of the Earth is divided into tectonic plates. Below the crust, is the mantle. The matter in the mantle is in the molten or semisolid state called **magma**. The innermost part is known as the core. The core is divided into inner core and outer core. Figure 14.8 shows the different layers of the interior of the Earth.

Causes of Earthquake

An earthquake occurs due to the sudden movements in the Earth's crust that creates waves travelling through the crust called **seismic waves**. The lithosphere of the Earth is divided into many pieces called **tectonic plates**. There are seven major tectonic plates and several other smaller ones (Fig. 14.9). These plates float on the magma in slow motion (few centimetres per year) with respect to each other. While moving, these plates collide with other plates and one plate may slide over the other gently.

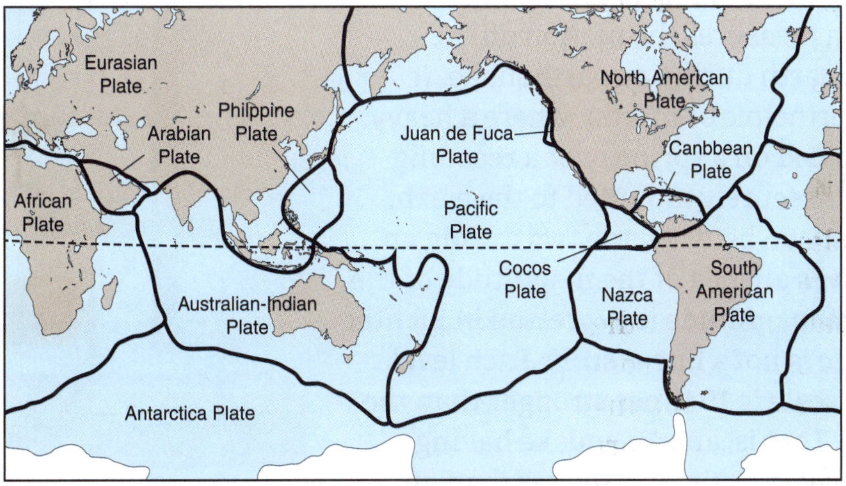

Fig. 14.9: Major tectonic plates of the world

Sometimes, the plate boundaries get interlocked due to the roughness of the edges. This prevents the plates from sliding and leads to an increase in stress or pressure. When the stress becomes very high, it allows a sudden sliding movement over the locked portion of the plates. This sudden movement releases a large amount of stored energy and gives rise to **shockwaves (seismic waves)** with huge amounts of energy travelling in all directions. When these waves reach the crust, it strongly shakes the surface of the Earth, which is felt as an earthquake. The edges of the plates where they collide or move against each other are the sites of intense earthquakes. The plate boundaries are called **seismic zones** or **fault zones**. Places located around these zones are earthquake-prone areas.

The point inside the Earth where the earthquake originates is called the **focus of the quake** (Fig. 14.10). The point on the surface of the Earth vertically from the focus of the earthquake is called the **epicentre**. The effect of a quake is most at the epicentre of the quake.

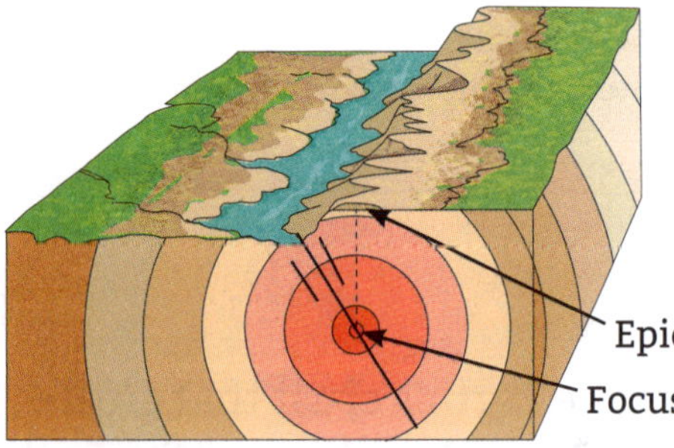

Fig. 14.10: Origin of an earthquake

Science in Context

Plate tectonics is the scientific theory that attempts to explain the movements of the Earth's lithosphere that have formed the landscape features that we see across the globe today.

Measuring Earthquake

The intensity of an earthquake is measured using a device called the **seismograph** (Fig. 14.11). A seismograph measures the motion on the surface of the earth during an earthquake. It works on the principle of inertia, where a heavy mass is suspended on a spring over a recoding device which is securely mounted to the earth. The relative motion between the two during an earthquake gives an idea of the magnitude of the earthquake. Its magnitude is expressed in Richter scale. This scale is not a linear scale. Each level in the Richter scale is 10 times stronger than the previous level. That is, an earthquake having a magnitude of 2 is 10 times stronger than an earthquake of magnitude 1.

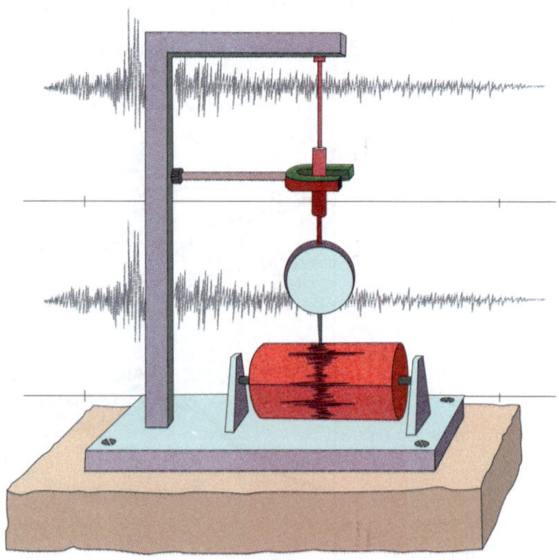
Fig. 14.11: Seismograph

Similarly, an earthquake of magnitude 5 is 10,000 times stronger than that of a magnitude 1 quake. A quake of magnitude 8 is one million times stronger than a quake of magnitude 1.

Earthquakes of magnitude less than 3 are rarely felt by people and do not cause any damage. Earthquakes of magnitude in the range 3 to 3.9 are often felt by people but they rarely cause damage. Shaking of indoor objects is noticeable during the quake of this magnitude. Quakes of magnitude 4 to 4.9 are strong enough to shake indoor objects. It can be felt by most people in the area.

Quakes of this magnitude can cause minimal damage to the affected area. Earthquakes of magnitude 5 to 5.9 on the Richter scale are moderate in strength and can cause severe damage to poorly constructed buildings. The quakes having magnitude of 6 to 6.9 are strong and cause severe damage even to well-constructed buildings. It can be felt in a large area around 100 kilometres from the epicentre. Earthquakes of 7 to 7.9 on the Richter scale belong to the major quake category. They can cause severe damage to most buildings. It can be felt even at a distance of 250 km from the epicentre. Quakes of magnitude 8 to 8.9 are highly destructive. Almost all buildings including earthquake-resistant buildings are completely or partially destroyed. It can be felt in an area of 500 kilometres from the epicentre. Earthquakes of magnitude 9 and above are the most severe. They cause total destruction to the environment. They can cause changes even in the ground structures (ground topography). They can be felt around 1,000 kilometres away from the epicentre.

The branch of science that studies earthquakes and the seismic waves caused by the quake is called **seismology**. The term **seismicity** of an area refers to the frequency, type and size of earthquakes experienced over a period of time.

Know the Scientist

In 1935, Charles Francis Richter, a US seismologist, developed the Richter scale for measuring the magnitude of an earthquake.

Effects of Earthquake on the Earth

The effect of an earthquake on the surface of the Earth varies depending on the intensity of the quake.

Some of the effects caused by strong to major categories of earthquakes are given below:

- Loss of life of humans and animals
- Destruction of towns and cities
- Destruction of buildings and bridges
- Occurrence of landslides

Protection and Safety Precautions

Prediction of the occurrence of an earthquake is very difficult. Some precautions can be taken against an earthquake, especially in the earthquake-prone areas.

- Earthquake-resistant houses and buildings should be built in high seismic areas.
- Houses made up of wood are better than that of concrete and brick buildings in earthquake-prone areas.
- Fire alarm and fire extinguishing devices should be kept ready in high seismic areas.

The following precautions can be taken during an earthquake (Fig. 14.12):

- If trapped inside a building during a quake, take shelter under a table and do not run or move around. Do not touch electrical appliances or running water.
- If possible, move to an open space immediately.
- Do not stay under a tree, electric post or any such tall object.
- If travelling, come out of the car or bus.

Fig. 14.12: Earthquake safety

Revise and Recall

Fill in the blanks.

1. The Earth's crust is divided into ______________ plates. (tectonic/tremor)
2. The device used to measure the intensity of an earthquake is known as ________________. (seismology/seismograph)
3. The scale used to express the magnitude of an earthquake is the ________________. (ruler/Richter scale)
4. The point inside the Earth where an earthquake originates from is called the ________________. (focus/epicentre)

Keywords

Electric discharge: The flow of charges through gases, liquids and solids occurs when there is a huge difference of charges between two objects in close proximity

Lightning: A flash of light produced due to the electric discharge between the clouds and the Earth

Seismograph: A device used to measure the intensity of an earthquake

Richter scale: The scale used to express the magnitude of an earthquake

Focus: The point within the Earth where an earthquake originates from

Epicentre: The point on the Earth's surface which is vertically above the focus

Summary

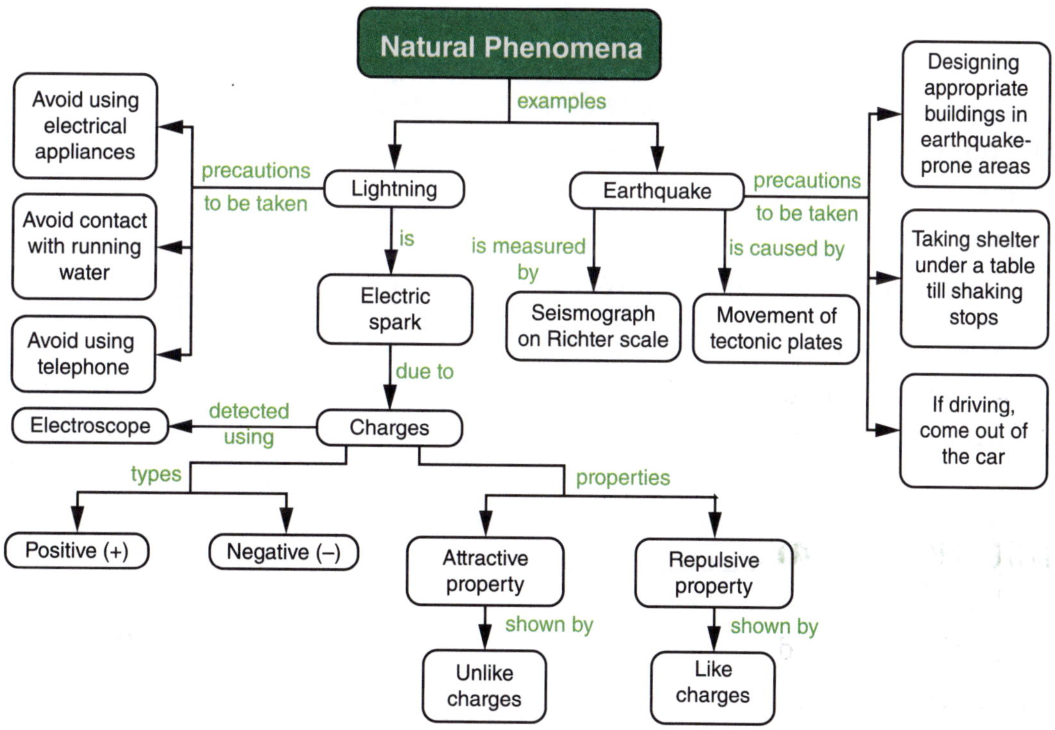

Exercise

A. Choose the correct option.

1. The device used to detect electric charges is called ______________.
   (a) electroscope (b) voltmeter (c) electric cell (d) ammeter
2. Which of the following is the most appropriate for the phenomenon of lightning?
   (a) Lightning is caused due to an electric discharge between the clouds only.
   (b) Lightning is caused due to an electric discharge between the clouds and the Earth only.
   (c) Lightning is not caused by electric discharge between clouds.
   (d) None of these
3. Choose the correct precaution to be taken during an earthquake.
   (a) Do not come out from buildings if you are inside them.
   (b) Rush to an open place if you are inside a building.
   (c) Be under a tree if you are outside.
   (d) Do not stand in the corner of a room.
4. An epicentre is
   (a) the point of origin of an earthquake.
   (b) the point on the Earth's surface directly above the origin of the earthquake.
   (c) the point directly below the origin of the earthquake.
   (d) None of these
5. The waves transmitted during an earthquake are called ______________.
   (a) seismic waves (b) earth waves (c) plate waves (d) all of these

B. State whether the following statements are true (T) or false (F).

1. Unlike charges repel each other. ☐
2. Two glass rods separately rubbed with a piece of silk cloth attract each other. ☐
3. It is not possible to predict the occurrence of an earthquake. ☐
4. It is safe to be under a tall tree during lightning. ☐
5. Staying inside a house or a building is safe at the time of lightning. ☐

C. Fill in the blanks.

1. The point of origin of an earthquake is called __________. (focus/epicentre)
2. The fragmented pieces of the outermost layers of the Earth are called __________ plates. (tectonic/seismic)
3. The magnitude of an earthquake is measured on the __________. scale (Richter/Plank)
4. A material that allows the flow of charges through it is a __________. (conductor/insulator)
5. The waves generated in an earthquake are called __________ waves. (seismic/cosmic)

D. Answer the following questions in one sentence each.

1. What is an electroscope?
2. What are the two types of charges?
3. What are tectonic plates?
4. What is a lightning conductor?
5. What is the Richter scale?

E. Give reasons for the following.

1. During a thunderstorm, contact with electrical wires and metal pipes should be avoided.
2. Provision of earthing is mandatory in domestic electric circuits.
3. Carrying an umbrella is not at all a good idea during thunderstorms.
4. In highly seismic areas, the use of mud or timber is better than using heavy construction materials.
5. On a dry day, we get a slight shock on touching the screen of a television or computer monitor.

F. Answer the following questions briefly.

1. What is an electric discharge?
2. What causes lightning?
3. Mention two precautions to be taken during earthquakes.
4. Mention the different ways in which an uncharged object can be charged.
5. Mention any two safety measures to be taken during an earthquake.

G. Answer the following questions in detail.

1. What is a lightning conductor? Explain its construction and working.
2. Explain how an object can be charged by induction.
3. Explain the principle of the gold-leaf electroscope with a schematic diagram.
4. Explain the method of charging an object by friction.
5. Explain the method of charging an object by conduction.

Cognitive Corner

Critical Thinking

1. In a forest, where there are trees of different heights, which trees would be more prone to lightning? Why?
2. Which of these—amber, plastic straw, hacksaw blade, PVC pipe—cannot be electrified by friction? Why?
3. Why do clothes stick to our body during winter and crackle while they are taken off?

Picture Study

What is the charge on the gold leaf of the electroscope shown here?

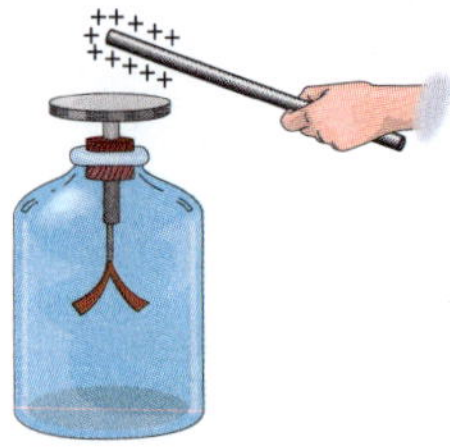

Project

As a part of Science Club activity, make a simple electroscope and demonstrate the behaviour of charges.

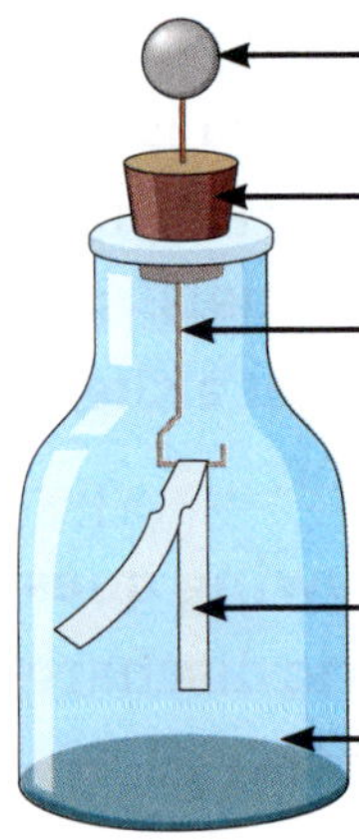

Materials required: Glass bottle, rubber cork, thick copper wire, thin aluminium foil

Procedure: Bend one end of the copper wire at the right angle as shown in the figure. Insert the other end through the rubber cork. Take a small rectangular piece of thin aluminium foil of dimensions 4 cm × 1 cm. Fold the aluminium foil in the middle and place it on the copper wire along the fold. Now, insert the copper wire along with the aluminium foil on it into the bottle and tighten the rubber cork to the neck of the bottle. Make a small ball of aluminium foil and fix it on the other end of the copper wire outside the bottle. Now, bring a charged ebonite rod near the aluminium foil ball. You can see that the two leaves of the aluminium foil hung on the copper wire move apart. This indicates that the ebonite rod is a charged object. **(C-7.2)**

In the Library

Do all buildings need lightning conductors? Find out how earthing is effectively done on lightning conductors and how their maintenance is carried out. **(C-7.1)**

Life Skills

In an event of a natural disaster, what must one do? Are you self-aware of the precautions and safety measures? Can you make quick decisions to combat any disaster? How would you communicate during such difficult times? Create a flowchart on the things you would do in case an earthquake occurs. Share with your family and friends. **(C-7.1)**

Worksheet

Urbanization is one of the important factors that leads to a country's growth. It leads to new jobs and opportunities to millions of people and helps in reducing poverty. However, rapid urbanization adds pressure to the resources available at that place and increases the demand for energy, water, sanitation, as well as for public services, education and health care.

Rapid urbanization has also made the world more vulnerable to natural disasters. Many of the world's largest cities are situated in earthquake, storm or flood-prone areas. Land development in natural barriers such as wetlands and mangroves may have further increased this vulnerability to natural disasters.

A. Is rapid urbanization making us more exposed to natural disasters? Give reasons for your answer.

B. What approaches can be followed to reduce exposure of urban population to natural disasters? Mention any three approaches.

C. Do you live in a city, town or a village? Has any natural disaster affected your life or the life of someone close to you? Share your story in a few sentences.

15 Light

Curricular Goals

- Explore the physical world in scientific and mathematical terms **(CG-2)**
- Communicate questions, observations and conclusions related to science **(CG-7)**

Competencies

- Demonstrate rectilinear propagation of light from different sources and verify the laws of reflection through manipulation of light sources and objects, and the use of apparatus and artefacts (plane mirrors, kaleidoscope, periscope) **(C-2.4)**
- Use scientific vocabulary to communicate science accurately in oral and written forms, and through visual representation **(C-7.1)**
- Design and build simple models to demonstrate scientific concepts **(C-7.2)**

Let's Get Started

The figures given below show a man standing in front of three different surfaces. Which of the three surfaces would be the most smooth and polished? Which one will be the least smooth? Which of these surfaces do you think will produce a clear image of the man?

(1)

(2)

(3)

REFLECTION OF LIGHT

When light falls on any surface, a part of it bounces back to the medium it came from. This phenomenon is known as **reflection of light**. A highly polished surface, such as a mirror, reflects most of the light that falls on it.

Can all surfaces reflect all of the light falling on them? Why are some surfaces given above unable to form images? Why are images diffusely seen or not seen at all from some surfaces? Let us find out about all these and more in this chapter.

Look at Figure 15.1. It is called a ray diagram as it shows the path followed by a ray of light. In this case, the ray of light is falling on a plane mirror.

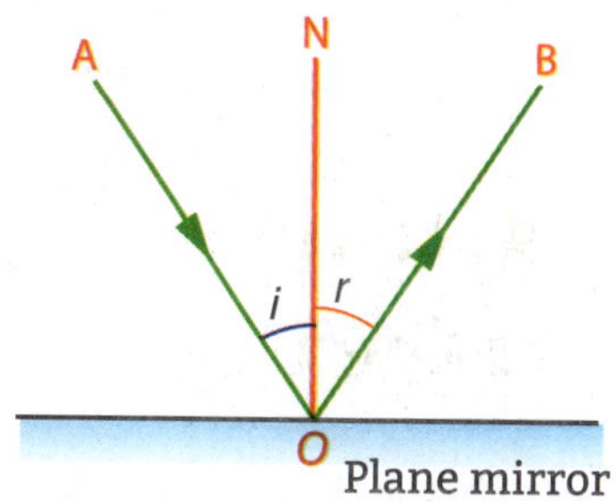

Fig. 15.1: Reflection of light

- The ray of light (A) approaching or falling on the mirror is called the **incident ray**. The point where the incident ray strikes the mirror is called the **point of incidence**. The ray of light reflected by the mirror at the point of incidence and travels away from the mirror is called the **reflected ray** (B).
- A line drawn perpendicular to the plane of the mirror at the point of incidence of light is called **normal** (N) to the reflecting surface.
- The angle between the incident ray and the normal is called the **angle of incidence (i)** and the angle between reflected ray and the normal is called the **angle of reflection (r)**.

Laws of Reflection

When a ray of light falls on a surface, it reflects from the surface following the **laws of reflection** (Fig. 15.2).

First law of reflection: *The incident ray, the reflected ray and the normal, all lie in the same plane.*

Second law of reflection: *The angle of incidence is equal to the angle of reflection.*

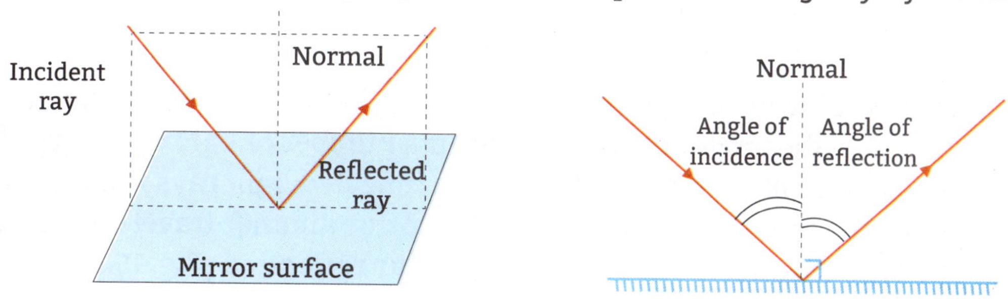

Fig. 15.2: Laws of reflection

Activity 1

Aim: To study the laws of reflection

Materials required: Mirror, three pins or small objects, white paper and protractor

Procedure:

1. Fix the mirror on a white sheet as shown in the figure. Draw a line perpendicular to the plane of the mirror. The perpendicular line is called the normal. Label it N. The normal will be reflected clearly on the mirror. Label the point it touches the mirror as O.

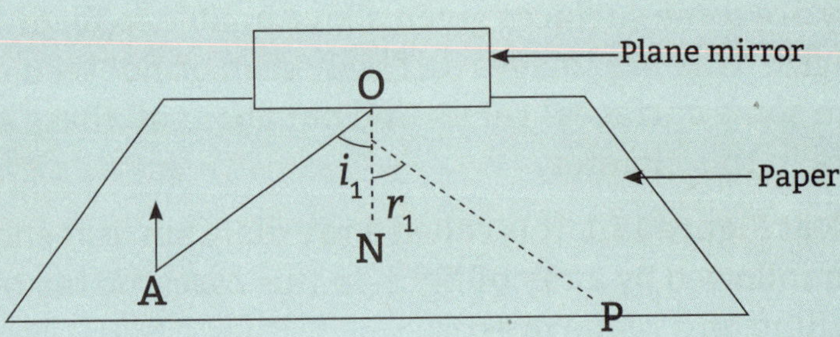

2. Place the three pins/objects at different distances from the normal, (one example shown in the figure). Mark their positions as A, B and C.
3. Observe the images of the objects on the mirror. Mark the positions of the images of the pins at A, B and C as P, Q and R, respectively.
4. Draw lines joining AO, BO and CO for the three pins. These form your incident rays.
5. Draw lines joining OP, OQ and OR for the three images. These form your reflected rays.
6. Measure the angles AON, BON and CON. These are the angles of incidence i_1, i_2 and i_3. Measure angles NOP, NOQ and NOR. These are the angles of reflection r_1, r_2 and r_3. Record the values in the table given below.
7. Compare the values of the angles of incidence and reflection in each case.

Observation:

Angle of Incidence	Angle of Reflection	Inference
$i_1 =$	$r_1 =$	
$i_2 =$	$r_2 =$	
$i_3 =$	$r_3 =$	

Conclusion: The angle of incidence is equal to the angle of reflection.

Regular and Diffused Reflection

We have learned that when a ray of light is reflected from a surface, the angle of incidence is equal to the angle of reflection. So, if a number of light rays parallel to each other fall on a smooth plane surface, then all the reflected light rays will also be parallel to each other. All the reflected light rays parallel to one another travel only in one direction. This type of reflection is known as **regular reflection** [Fig. 15.3(a)]. Reflection of light from a plane mirror is an example of regular reflection.

For parallel rays of light falling on a rough or an irregular surface, the angle of incidence for each ray of light will be different. Therefore, each of these light rays will be reflected from the surface at different angles, that is, in different directions. The reflected light rays will not be parallel to each other. This type of reflection is called **diffused reflection** [Fig. 15.3(b)].

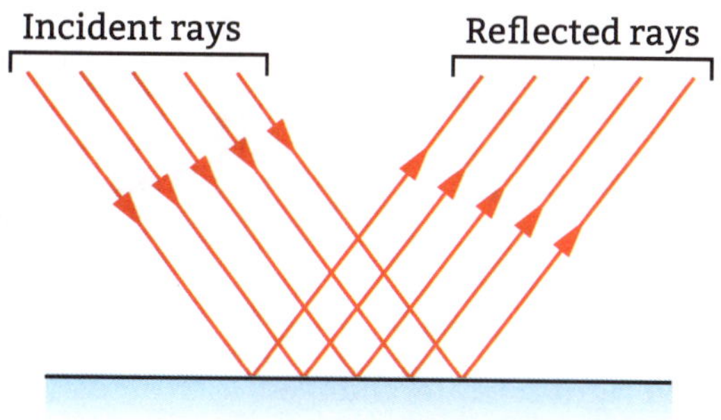

(a) Regular reflection

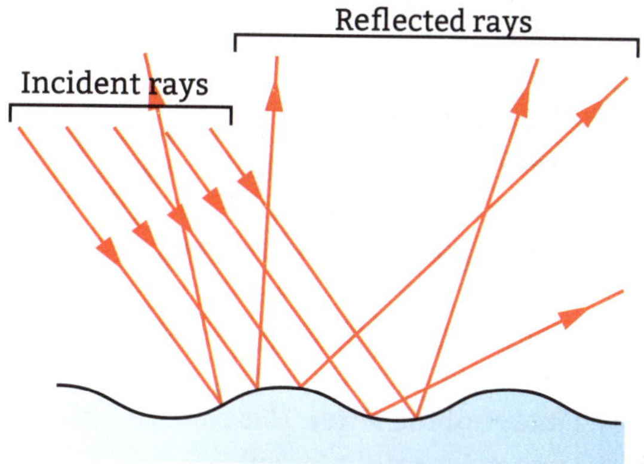

(b) Diffused reflection

Fig. 15.3: Regular and diffused reflections

Try It!

Distinguish between regular and diffused reflections based on the type of surface and laws of reflection.

The properties of reflection of light from different surfaces have certain practical applications. For example, photographers make use of regular reflection from the calm water surface of lakes, rivers, etc. to capture photographs of scenery (Fig. 15.4). If the water surface is turbulent, it creates diffused reflection and the photographs of images are unclear, and the overall effect of the photo is less attractive.

Fig. 15.4: Regular reflection in nature

Images Formed by a Plane Mirror

We have studied that when light rays from an object are reflected by a mirror, an image of the object is formed. Let us study more about the characteristics of the image formed by a plane mirror.

Activity 2

Aim: To show that the image formed by a plane mirror is upright, virtual and reversed (left and right interchanged)

Materials required: A plane mirror and cardboard-cutting of the letter 'L'

Procedure:

1. Keep the mirror vertically on the table.
2. Place the cardboard-cutting 'L' in front of the mirror.
3. Look at the image formed in the mirror. Try to project the image on the screen.
4. Observe and record the nature and size of the image.

Observation:

1. The image formed by the mirror cannot be projected on a screen.
2. The image of the letter 'L' is reversed (that is, left and right are interchanged).
3. The image is upright (erect).
4. The image is of the same size as the object.

Conclusion: The image formed by a plane mirror is always virtual, upright, of the same size and appears reversed (left and right interchanged).

In the above activity, we saw that the left and right sides of the image have reversed their positions. The phenomenon in which the image of an object appears to have left–right inversion is called **lateral inversion**. When we see our image in a plane mirror, we observe that our right side becomes the left side of the image and vice versa. You may have seen that the word '**AMBULANCE**' is written on the vehicle in a laterally inverted way (Fig. 15.5). This helps the person driving a vehicle in front of the ambulance to read it correctly on their rear-view mirror and give way to the ambulance.

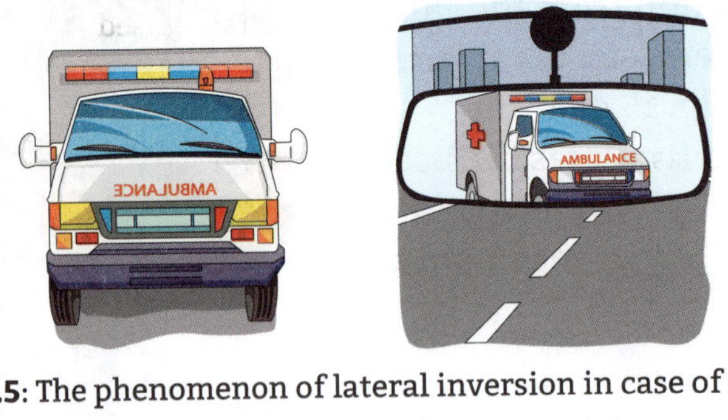

Fig. 15.5: The phenomenon of lateral inversion in case of an ambulance

Characteristics of the image formed by a plane mirror:

- The image formed by a plane mirror is always virtual and upright.
- The image undergoes lateral inversion.
- The size of the image formed by a plane mirror is the same as that of the object.
- The distance of the object from the mirror is equal to the distance of the image from the mirror.

Multiple Reflection

Have you seen places where a number of plane mirrors are used? In textile shops, dressing rooms, hair salons, etc. we can see two or more plane mirrors. Why do we use more number of mirrors in these places? When two or more mirrors are used, light undergoes reflections many times from the different mirrors and we can see many images. This phenomenon is called **multiple reflection of light**.

If we place two plane mirrors parallel to each other, we can see infinite number of images in the mirror. The number of images formed by two plane mirrors depends on the angle between the mirrors. You can do an activity to find the number of images formed when an object is placed between a hinged mirror, as shown in Figure 15.6. The number of images increases as we decrease the angle between the two mirrors.

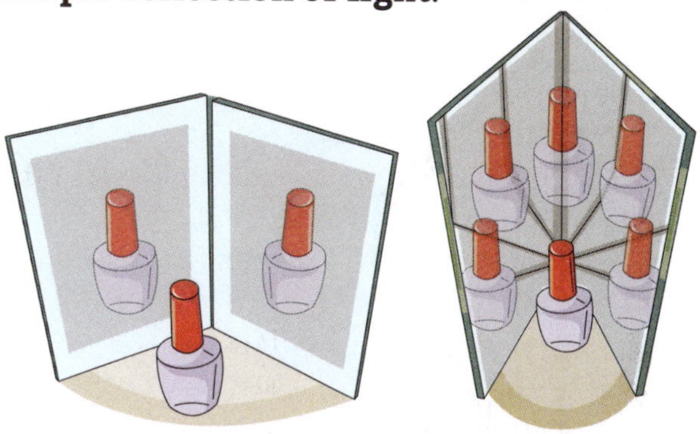

Fig. 15.6: Multiple reflection

The relationship between the number of images and the angle between the mirrors is:
$N = \frac{360}{\alpha} - 1$, where N = number of images and α = angle between the two mirrors

Activity 3

Aim: To study the number of images formed when two mirrors are used

Materials required: Plane mirrors (2), protractor and a white sheet

Procedure:

1. Using a protractor, draw lines aligned at 30°, 45°, 60° and 75° on a white sheet.
2. Arrange the two mirrors so that the angle between them is 30° and place an object between them.
3. Observe the number of images formed.
4. Then, keep the mirrors at the different angles you had marked earlier.
5. Observe the images formed when the angle is increased.

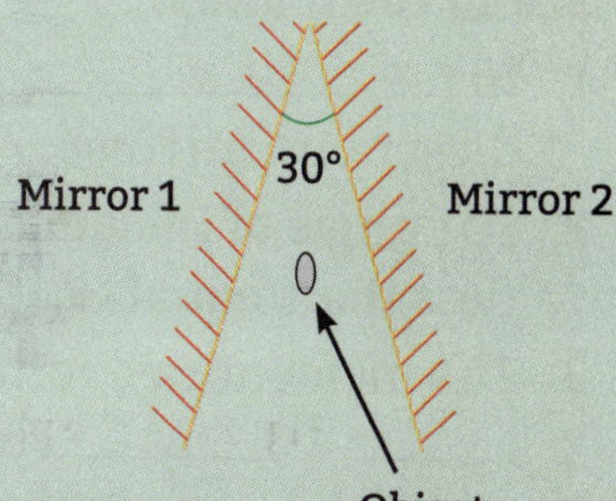

Conclusion: As the angle between the two mirrors increases, the number of images decreases.

Multiple reflection of light by mirrors is used in many optical devices such as periscope and kaleidoscope. A **periscope** [Fig. 15.7(a)] is used to see objects situated at a higher level. Submarines use periscopes to keep a watch on the threats above the water level while still staying underwater.

Kaleidoscope [Fig. 15.7(b)] is used by fabric designers to create beautiful patterns. Many optical illusions such as endless tunnel and well of infinite depth can be created using multiple reflections.

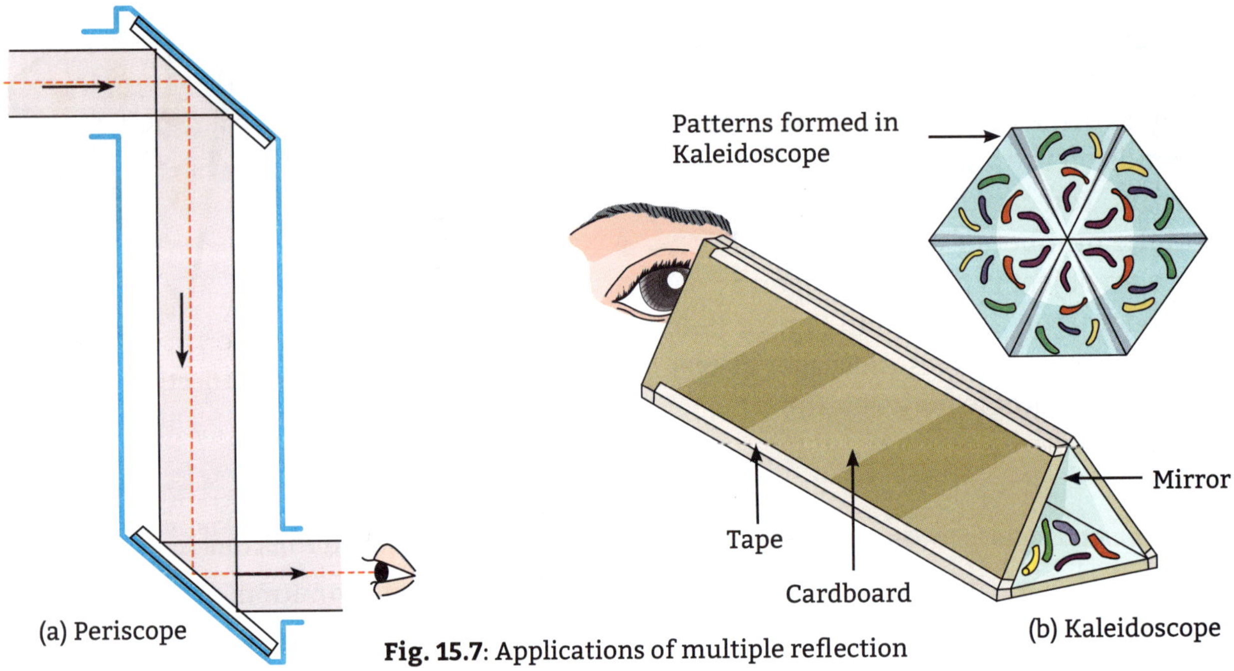

Fig. 15.7: Applications of multiple reflection

Revise and Recall

Fill in the blanks.

1. In ________________ reflection, the rays of light are reflected in different directions. (diffused/regular)
2. The angle of incidence is ________________ the angle of reflection. (less than/equal to)
3. The incident ray, reflected ray and the normal all lie in the ________________ plane. (different/same)
4. Reflection of light from an object by a mirror forms ________________ of the object. (image/shadow)
5. Kaleidoscope works on the principle of ________________ reflection of light. (multiple/diffused)
6. Plane mirror always produces a ________________ image. (real/virtual)

REFRACTION OF LIGHT

You may have noticed that a stick immersed into water appears to be bent or broken at an angle where it enters water. This is because of a phenomenon called refraction of light. **Refraction** is the phenomenon in which a light ray passing obliquely from one medium to another medium of different density, changes the direction of its path. Refraction occurs because light travels with different speeds in different medium.

Activity 4

Aim: To understand the property of refraction of light

Materials required: Beaker, a small piece of mirror, water, hypo (sodium thiosulphate), dilute hydrochloric acid and laser torch

Procedure:

1. Fill water in a beaker and keep it on a table.
2. Add a few pieces of hypo into the water and stir well.
3. Add a few drops of dilute hydrochloric acid into it.
4. Direct the light beam from the torch onto the water, as shown in image (a). Observe the path of light.
5. Now, place the mirror at the centre of the bottom of the beaker.
6. Direct the light beam from the torch onto the mirror, as shown in image (b).
7. Observe the path of light again. Do you see any difference?

Observation: We see that the light ray bends from its path as it passes from one medium to another medium of different density. It bends at the surface of water as it enters from air to water and again bends as it emerges from water to air.

We can see in the above activity that the ray of light bends towards the normal to the surface when the light passes from air to water. This happens because air is optically less dense than water, or we can say that air is optically a **rarer medium** and water is optically a **denser medium** (Fig. 15.8). If we consider water and glass, then water becomes the optically rarer medium and glass becomes the optically denser medium.

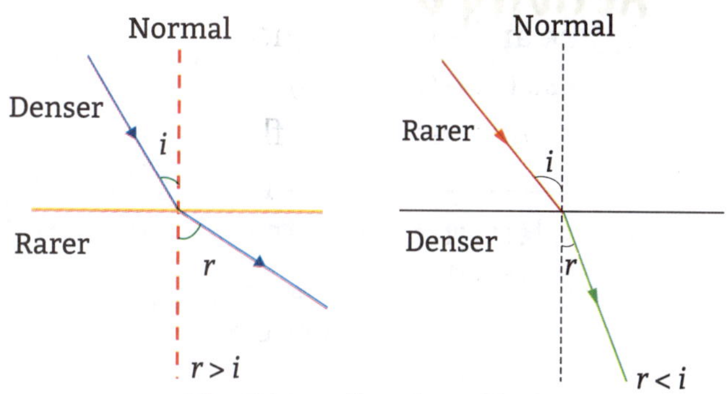

Fig. 15.8: Refraction of light

When light passes from an optically rarer medium to an optically denser medium, it bends towards the normal and when light passes from an optically denser medium to an optically rarer medium, it bends away from the normal.

An example of the **effect of refraction** is that a pencil dipped in a glass of water appears to be broken (Fig. 15.9).

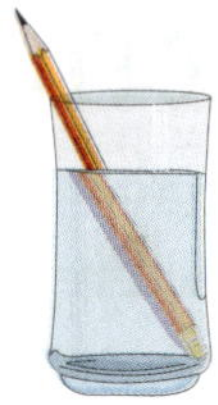

Fig. 15.9: Effect of refraction

We can also perform the following activity to understand refraction.

Activity 5

Aim: To understand refraction

Materials required: A bowl, a coin and water (You will need the help of a friend for this activity.)

Procedure:

1. Put the coin in the bowl.
2. Look at the coin and move backwards till the coin becomes invisible to you.
3. Now ask your friend to slowly pour water in the bowl.
4. Observe what happens.

Observation: If all goes well, the coin will become visible to you.

Conclusion: When your friend pours water into the bowl, the light rays from the coin travel through the water first and then through the air. This change of medium causes the light rays to bend. When these light rays reach your eyes, the coin seems to be raised and becomes visible to you.

DISPERSION OF LIGHT

If we bring a compact disc in sunlight, we can see different colours on it. Why do we see different colours on the disc? It was Sir Isaac Newton who observed that sunlight is composed of different colours of light. He demonstrated that sunlight consists of seven colours by using a small prism and a screen.

Activity 6

Aim: To show that white light consists of seven colours

Materials required: Sun, cardboard with a slit (opening), prism and screen

Procedure:

1. Adjust the cardboard slit in front of the sun such that the light rays can pass through the slit.
2. Arrange the prism and the screen such that the light from the sun coming through the slit passes through the prism and then falls on the screen.
3. Observe the pattern of the light on the screen.

Dispersion of white light

Observation: When passed through a prism, white light splits into its constituent colours and falls as a band of seven colours on the screen.

Conclusion: White light consists of seven colours.

From Activity 6, we can see that a beam of white light passing through a prism splits into its constituent colours. *This process of splitting of white light into its constituent colours is called* ***dispersion of light***. White light is a combination of seven colours: violet, indigo, blue, green, yellow, orange and red (in short, VIBGYOR). When white light passes through a prism, these seven colours are separated from each other. The band of colours obtained on the screen due to the splitting of white light is called **spectrum**.

Rainbow

We all have seen a rainbow. Why are there different colours in a rainbow? The different colours in a rainbow (Fig. 15.10) are formed due to the dispersion of sunlight as it passes through small water droplets in the air after rain. The small water droplets act as a prism splitting the white light into its constituent colours. The different colours thus formed appear in the form of a large curve across the sky as a rainbow.

Fig. 15.10: Rainbow: dispersion of light

Human Eye

The eye is an organ that gives us the sense of vision. It help us to see and interpret the shapes and colours of objects around us. The human eye is a slightly asymmetrical sphere of nearly 2.5 cm diameter. The structure of the human eye and its different parts are shown in Figure 15.11.

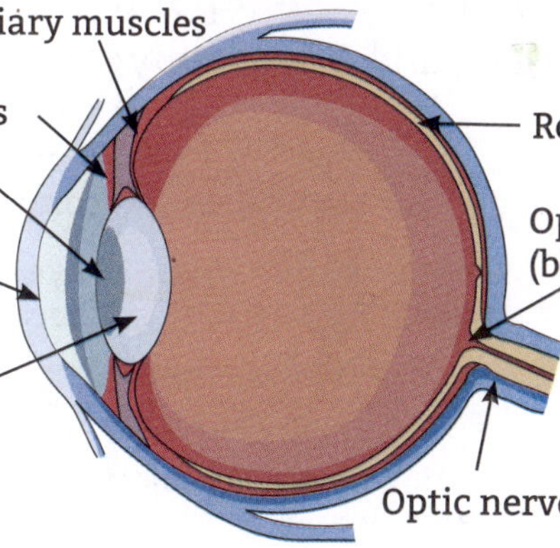

Fig. 15.11: Parts of the human eye

Following are the different parts of an eye:

Cornea: It is the thin transparent tissue which covers the front of the eye.

Pupil: It is the hole located at the centre of iris through which light enters the eye.

Iris: It is the coloured part of the eye and is involved mainly in regulating the amount of light that enters the eye. It consists of radial muscles that control the size of the pupil.

Lens: It is a transparent structure that helps to focus the light rays on the retina.

Ciliary muscles: They control the focal length of the lens by changing the thickness of the lens. The ability of the eye to alter the focal length of its lens to clearly see close and far away objects is known as **accommodation**.

Retina: It is the sensitive screen inside the eye where the light rays fall. It has light receptors called cones and rods. **Rods** are not colour-sensitive, but **cones** are and they enable us to see colour. These light receptors absorb light falling on the retina and convert the message into electrical impulse that can be read by the brain.

Optic nerve: It connects the retina of the eye with the brain and carries impulses to the brain. Jelly-like fluids fill the space behind and in front of the lens, respectively. These fluids give shape to the eye and protect the eye against any damage.

Formation of image in the eye: The light falls on the lens entering via the cornea and pupil, and the ciliary muscles help the lens focus the light on the retina. The inverted image formed on the retina is converted to electrical signal by the sensory cells (rods and cones) present in the retina. These electrical signals are transmitted to the brain through the optic nerve. The brain interprets the signals and renders the image as erect.

Power of Accommodation

Ideally, a normal human eye can see objects clearly from 25 cm up to infinity. Our eye has the ability to adjust the focal length of its lens with the distance of the object from the eyes so that a clear image of the object is formed on the retina. This ability of the eye to adjust its focal length is called the **power of accommodation** of the eye (Fig. 15.12). Eye lens can adjust its focal length to obtain a clear image of an object at a distance of 25 cm and above. This is the minimum distance required for clear vision and is called the **near point**. The maximum distance of clear vision is called **far point** of the eye, and it is usually infinity for a normal human eye.

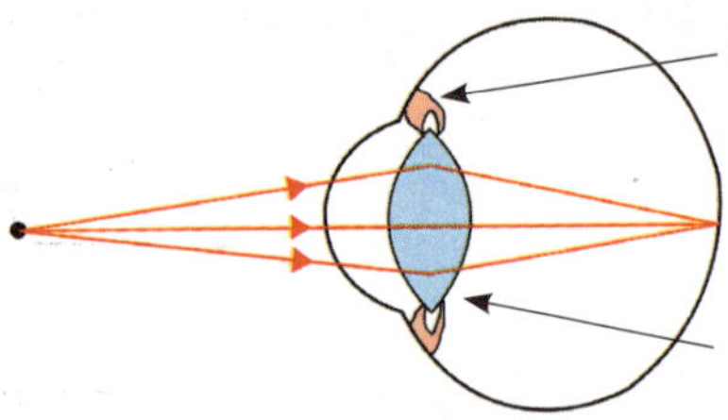

Accommodation for a near object

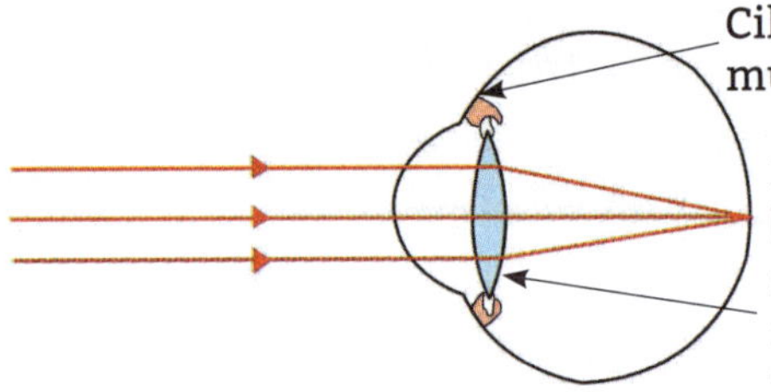

Accommodation for a far object

Fig. 15.12: Accommodation of eye

Science in Context

Blind spot is a region on the retina where the optic nerve exits the back of the eyes. There are no sensory cells at this spot. So, light falling on this region cannot produce any image.

Persistence of Vision

The phenomenon of the human eye by which the image of an object formed on the retina of the eye persists on the retina for one-sixteenth of a second is called **persistence of vision**. This phenomena is used in creating live action film and animations. More than 16 still images of a motion of an object are projected on the screen in quick succession and we interpret it as a continuously moving object. This illusion of movement is possible due to the persistence of vision.

Defects of Eye

Myopia, hypermetropia, presbyopia and astigmatism are commonly encountered defects of the eye.

Myopia or short-sightedness is a defect of the eye in which objects close by are clear but those at a distance are not (Fig. 15.13). This is because the image from distant objects do not reach the retina. Instead they fall in front of it. This defect can be corrected by using a concave lens.

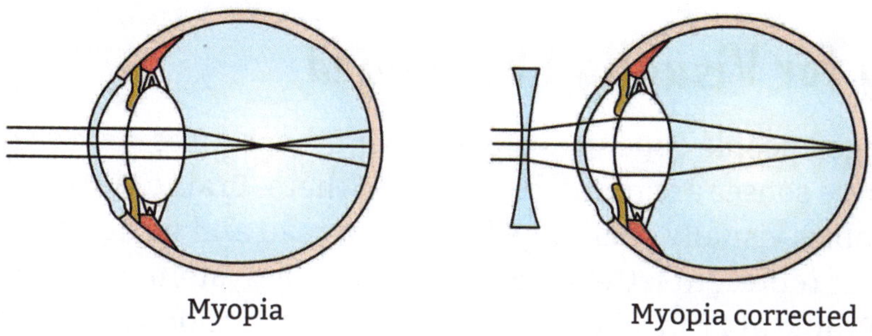

Fig. 15.13: Myopia and its correction using a concave lens

Hypermetropia or far-sightedness is a defect of the eye in which the vision of distant objects are seen clearly but those nearby are not. This is because the image from near objects are formed somewhere behind the retina instead of on it. This defect can be corrected by using a convex lens (Fig. 15.14).

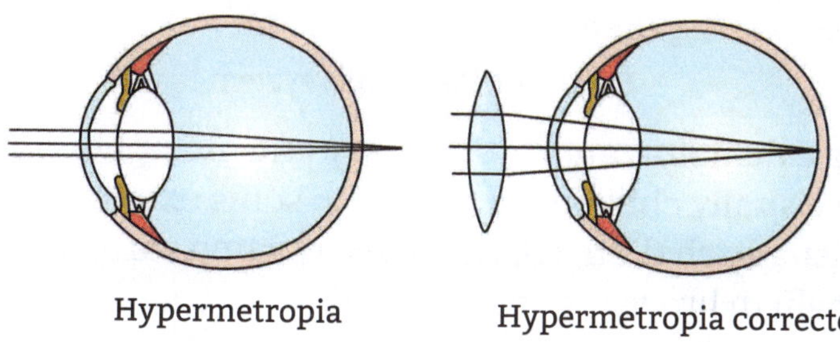

Fig. 15.14: Hypermetropia and its correction using a convex lens

Presbyopia is the gradual loss of the eyes' ability to focus on nearby objects due to the hardness and reduced flexibility of the lens of the eye. It is corrected using reading glasses with convex lenses of appropriate power.

People aged 40 and above may suffer from both myopia and presbyopia at the same time. In such cases, they require a bifocal lens, in which the upper part is a concave lens and the lower part is a convex lens (Fig. 15.15).

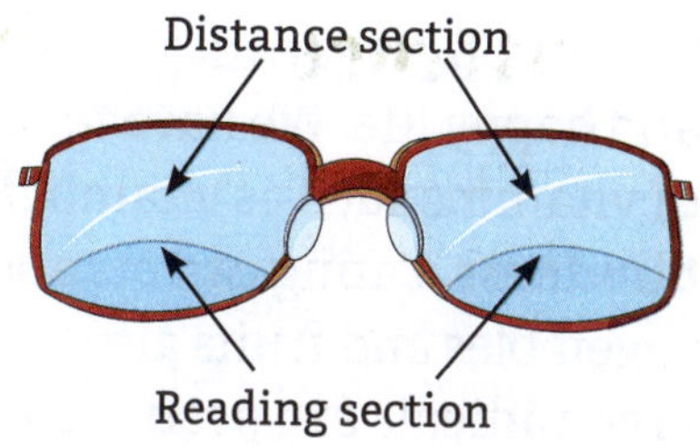

Fig. 15.15: Bifocal spectacle

Astigmatism is the defect in the eye caused due to the defects in cornea or lens. The surface of either the cornea or the lens or sometimes both are irregular and not smoothly curved. The light rays falling on them cannot, therefore, form a clear image on the retina. This results in a blurred vision. It can be corrected by using a cylindrical lens.

When the lens becomes opaque or cloudy, then it is unable to focus the light on the retina and the image appears blurred. This condition is called **cataract**. Mild conditions can be corrected using spectacles or contact lens. Severe condition can be corrected only through surgery where the clouded lens is replaced by an artificial one. Technology has made cataract surgery an easy procedure.

Technology for Visually Challenged

Visually challenged people depend more on their other senses such as hearing and touch. Often, these senses are more developed in them. Braille system (Fig. 15.16) is a method that enables visually challenged people to read and write. It uses some patterns of raised dots that represent letters and numerals. The system has been named after its inventor Louis Braille of France who lost sight after an accident during childhood.

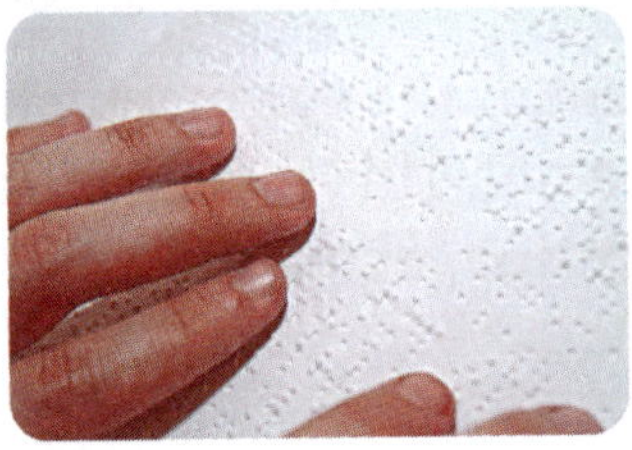

A person using the Braille system

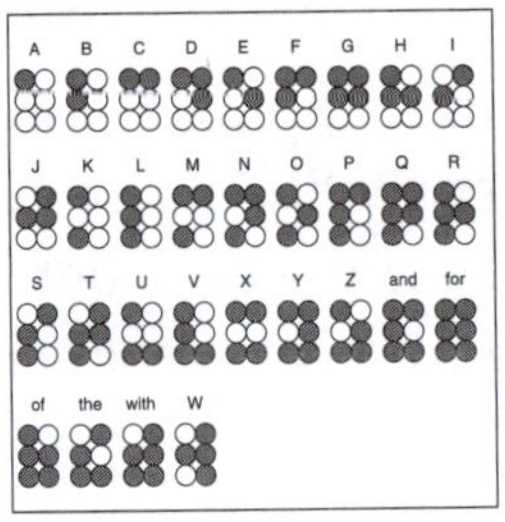

Fig. 15.16: The Braille system

Talking clock, talking calculator, audio dictionary and dictaphone are some of the devices that help the visually challenged person to some extent. There are also computers, for the visually challenged, that have reading software such as JAWS and Kurzweil 3000 that help in browsing the Internet.

Eye Care

Our vision plays a major role in our life. Caring for our eyes is very important for a healthy and happy life. We have to maintain a nutritious diet to keep our vision healthy. Deficiency of vitamins such as vitamin A leads to a disease called **xerophthalmia** also called **night blindness**. Eating carrots and food items rich in vitamin A prevents this disease. Fresh vegetables and fruits also help in preventing age-related disorder of the eyes.

Free radicals are produced in our bodies during the process of respiration. These free radicals are harmful for the skin and eyes. Hence, we should eat food rich in antioxidants, which take care of the free radicals.

Keywords

Rectilinear propagation of light: Travelling of light in a straight line

Refraction: The phenomenon in which a light ray passing obliquely from one medium to another medium of different density, changes the direction of its path

Dispersion: The process of splitting of light into its constituent colours

Spectrum: The band of colours obtained on the screen due to the dispersion of light

Near point: Minimum distance required for clear vision

Far point: Maximum distance for clear vision

Myopia: A defect in which a person can see the near objects clearly and cannot see the distant objects clearly

Hypermetropia: A defect in which a person can see the distant objects clearly and cannot see the near objects clearly

Summary

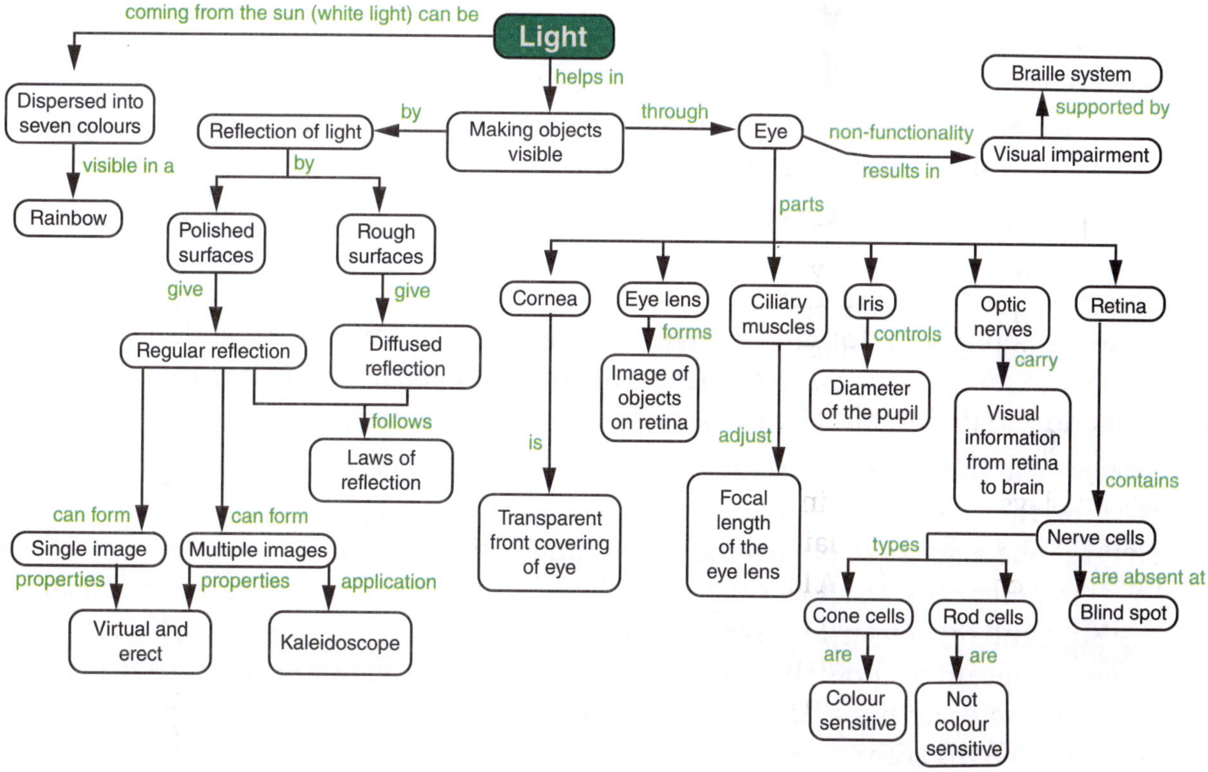

Exercise

A. Choose the correct option.

1. The law of reflection states that
   (a) all rays incident on a mirror are reflected.
   (b) rays incident on a mirror are partially reflected.
   (c) the angle at which a ray is reflected from a mirror is random.
   (d) the angle of reflection is equal to the angle of incidence.
2. The image formed by a plane mirror is ________________.
   (a) virtual (b) real (c) diminished (d) magnified
3. The splitting of light into its constituent colours is called ________________.
   (a) reflection (b) refraction (c) dispersion (d) spectrum
4. When light passes from a rarer medium to a denser medium, it
   (a) bends away from the normal. (b) bends towards the normal.
   (c) always passes undeviated. (d) is shifted laterally.
5. Among the following, which device works on the principle of multiple reflections of light from plane mirrors?
   (a) Periscope (b) Spectroscope (c) Microscope (d) Camera

B. Give reasons for the following.

1. When we look at the mirror in our car, we feel that the driver in the car behind us is sitting on the left side of the car.
2. A rainbow has colours in it.
3. To construct a simple periscope, we need two mirrors.
4. A convex lens of suitable power is used to correct hypermetropia.
5. Cataract cannot be corrected using lenses.

C. Answer the following questions briefly.

1. What are regular and diffused reflections?
2. Give an example where diffused reflection is useful.
3. Give one application for lateral inversion produced by mirror reflection.
4. Give two examples to show the effects of refraction observed in nature.
5. What do you understand by the terms near point and far point?

D. Answer the following questions in detail.

1. Mention the characteristics of an image formed by a plane mirror.
2. Suggest one activity to obtain the spectrum of white light.
3. Draw ray diagrams to show the refraction of a light ray from (a) rarer to denser medium and (b) denser to rarer medium.
4. Draw a diagram to show the dispersion of white light passing through a prism.
5. Describe the structure and the different parts of a human eye with the help of a well-labelled diagram.
6. Explain the major defects of vision and suggest how to correct them.

Cognitive Corner

Critical Thinking

1. A light ray of green colour is passed through a prism. Will it undergo dispersion? Explain.
2. When we enter a room from outside, after being in the sun, it appears dark. Explain the reason.

Picture Study

Which phenomena are shown in the figures given below?

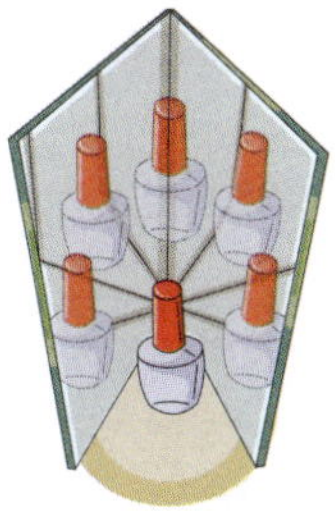

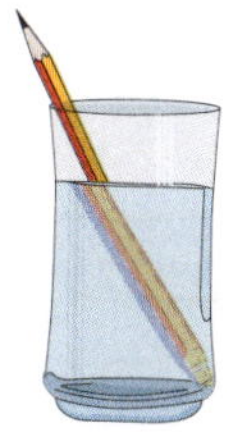

Project

As a part of the Science Club activity, make a periscope to demonstrate the multiple reflection of light. Use a cardboard box and two plain mirrors. Cut two windows on opposite ends and corners of a box. One window is for you to look into, while the other is to look at the objects to be seen. Then, slide each mirror through the windows at a 45 degree angle. Adjust the position of the mirrors so that when you look through the bottom window, you should be able to see out of the top mirror. Then, glue or tape two mirrors in place and your periscope is ready! **(C-7.2)**

In the Library

Collect information about different theories of light and the scientists who proposed those theories. Make a poster about the same. **(C-7.1)**

Life Skills

1. Cataracts and glaucoma are a few of the common age-related eye problems. If you come across any elderly suffering from these problems, what advice would you give to help them? Find out the advances and limitations in this field of study/research. Make a presentation based on your findings. **(C-9.2)**
2. You may have noticed that swimmers and sea divers wear goggles. Have you ever thought how goggles help protect their eyes and also help them see things clearly? Find out how goggles help them to see things clearly under water. **(C-9.1)**

Worksheet

We can see the world through our eyes. Light enters our eyes and allows us to see what is happening around us.

One of the very few organs that can be donated after death are the eyes. It is the corneas from the donor's eyes that are transplanted to patients. With new technology, each cornea can be split into two. Thus, one person's eyes can help four visually impaired eyes restore vision.

A. The cornea lacks blood vessels and requires transparency for clear vision. How does its unique structure contribute to its transparency and function in vision?

____

____

____

B. How can organ donation systems, such as for cornea transplants, be improved to help us reach the goal of making global healthcare better (SDG 3)? List any two steps.

____

____

____

C. Design a poster to inform people about the importance of eye donation, urging them to pledge their eyes for donation after death. There are many centres who can be contacted to make a pledge. Include this information in your poster.

16 The Universe

Curricular Goals

- Explore the physical world in scientific and mathematical terms **(CG-2)**
- Communicate questions, observations and conclusions related to science **(CG-7)**

Competencies

- Observe and identify celestial objects (stars, planets, natural and artificial satellites, constellations, comets) in the night sky using a simple telescope and images/photographs, and explain their role in navigation, calendars and other phenomena (phases of the moon, eclipse, life on earth) **(C-2.5)**
- Use scientific vocabulary to communicate science accurately in oral and written forms, and through visual representation **(C-7.1)**

Let's Get Started

Identify these objects that are visible in the night sky.

____

____

____

When we look up at the clear night sky, we can see a lot of objects. How big are the objects in the universe? How far are they from the Earth? Are they stationary or moving? **Astronomy** is the branch of science that asks these fundamental questions about the universe and tries to find answers to them.

The objects seen in the sky are generally known as **celestial objects.** The sun, planets, stars and objects such as comets and asteroids are all celestial objects. Celestial objects are also known as **heavenly bodies.** Let us find out more about these.

STARS

A **star** is a huge sphere of gases (mostly hydrogen and helium) that is self-luminous. Stars emit energy due to nuclear fusion of hydrogen (hydrogen atoms combine to form helium atoms). During this process, tremendous amount of energy is released. The released energy contains a whole spectrum of electromagnetic radiation such as the infrared, visible and the ultraviolet rays. The visible light part of the spectrum is what we see as sunlight and it makes up about 44% of the solar radiation. The infrared rays are responsible for the heat that reaches the earth.

Sun is a medium-sized star. Since it is very close to the Earth as compared to other stars, it appears very big and bright in the sky. Some stars are several times bigger than the sun and some are smaller. **Sirius** is the brightest star visible in the night sky. We can see a star in the north which appears to be stationary all the time. This is because the position of this star is along the axis on which the Earth rotates. This star is known as the **Pole Star** or North Star. The Indian name of this star is ***Dhruva Nakshathra***. Before the invention of the magnetic compass, sailors used the Pole Star as a reference for navigation. Table 16.1 gives the differences between stars and planets.

Science in Context

Have you observed that some objects twinkle in the night sky while some others have a constant glow? The objects that twinkle are stars and those that do not twinkle are either planets or satellites.

Table 16.1: Differences between stars and planets

Stars	Planets
Stars appear to be twinkling in the sky.	Planets do not twinkle in the sky.
Stars emit their own light.	Planets reflect the sunlight falling on them.
Stars are massive and very large in size.	Planets are much smaller in comparison.

Measuring Distances of Celestial Objects

The distance between celestial objects and their respective distances from the Earth is very large. It is not convenient to measure these distances in kilometres or miles. For example, the sun is the star nearest to the Earth, it is at a distance of 150 million kilometres (1 million = 10,00,000). The second nearest star, Proxima Centauri, is about 40 trillion kilometres away (1 trillion = 10,00,00,00,00,000). Therefore, bigger units of distance are required when dealing with the distance between celestial objects. One such commonly used unit is a **light year**. *A light year is defined as the distance travelled by light in one year with a speed of 3,00,000 km/s.*

One light year = Speed of light × Time of one year expressed in seconds

= 3,00,000 × 365 × 24 × 60 × 60 kilometres = 95,00,00,00,00,000 kilometres = 9.5×10^{12} km

Proxima Centauri is 4.3 light years away from the Earth. This means that the light from the star Proxima Centauri takes 4.3 years to reach the Earth and its distance will be $4.3 \times 9.5 \times 10^{12}$ km from the Earth.

CONSTELLATIONS

Ancient astronomers looked at the stars visible in the sky and observed certain patterns or shapes, which helped them to identify the stars easily. *A group of stars that makes a certain recognizable pattern in the sky is called a* ***constellation***. The shape of the constellation is named after objects, animals and people. The shape of the constellation remains the same at all times. It is important to note that all the stars in a constellation are not at the same distance from the Earth. They only appear to be at the same distance in the sky when observed from the Earth. The International Astronomical Union recognizes 88 constellations, which cover the entire northern and southern sky. Some of the common constellations are discussed below.

Orion

Orion (*pronounced*: Oh·rye·on) is a constellation of seven bright stars. It also has many other faint stars. Its name is based on the Greek mythological hunter, Orion. It is visible from January–March in the evening sky. The three bright stars in the middle of this constellation form the belt of the hunter. Four bright stars Rigel, Betelgeuse, Bellatrix and Saiph together form the shoulders and the legs, a rough rectangular shape (Fig. 16.1). The brightest star in the night sky, **Sirius** (*pronounced*: Sir·i·us), can be easily located with the help of this constellation. If an imaginary line drawn through the three stars in the belt is extended towards the south-west, it will meet the star Sirius. Orion is referred to as *Mriga* (the deer) in the Rig Veda.

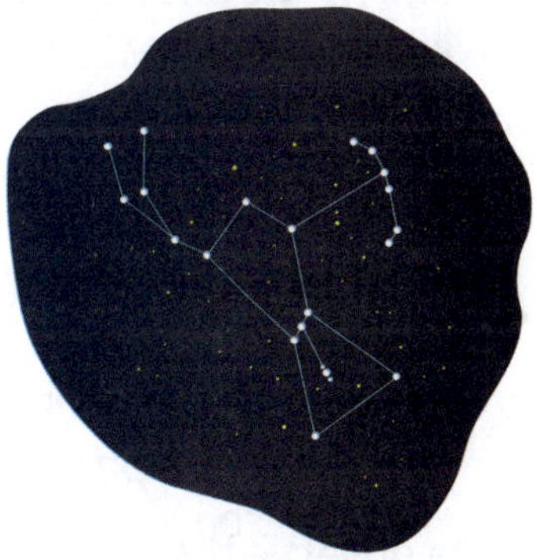

Fig. 16.1: Orion

Ursa Major

Ursa Major (*pronounced*: Oor·sa·may·jor) constellation is visible in the northern hemisphere in the month of April. It is also known as the **Great Bear** and **Big Dipper**. It consists of seven bright stars in the shape of a big spoon and many other faint stars, which together form the shape of a bear (Fig. 16.2). We can easily locate the pole star (*Dhruva Nakshathra*) with the help of this constellation. Ancient Indians called this constellation *Saptarshi*.

Fig. 16.2: Ursa Major

Ursa Minor

The Ursa Minor constellation is also known as **Little Bear**. Ursa Minor (Fig. 16.3) is helpful in locating the celestial North Pole. The well-known North Star or Pole Star belongs to the Ursa Minor and it is the brightest star in this constellation. It appears in the northern sky. Indian name of this constellation is *Laghu Saptarshi*.

Fig. 16.3: Ursa Minor

Cassiopeia

Cassiopeia (*pronounced*: kas·ee·oh·pee·uh) is a constellation of five prominent stars visible in the northern sky. The five stars form the shape of a distorted W or M (Fig. 16.4). It is named after Queen Cassiopeia in Greek mythology.

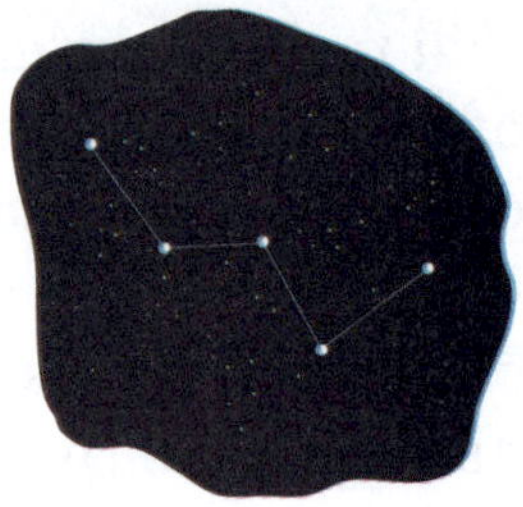

Fig. 16.4: Cassiopeia

Scorpius

Scorpius (*pronounced*: Skor·pi·us), also known as Scorpio, is a constellation of several bright and many other faint stars which appear in the shape of a scorpion (Fig. 16.5). It is located almost at the centre of the Milky Way. It appears in the sky in the summer season.

Fig. 16.5: Scorpius

MOVEMENT OF CELESTIAL OBJECTS IN THE SKY

Is the position of an object in the sky the same at all times? If they are in motion, are they moving in a particular direction or in different directions?

If we observe the objects in the sky at different times on the same night, we will see that they appear to be moving from east to west. Why do all the objects appear to be moving towards the west and none of them moving towards east? This is due to the rotation of the Earth about its own axis. As the Earth rotates from west to east, the objects in the sky appear to be moving from east to west. The sun rises in the east and sets in the west. This is also due to the rotation of the Earth.

Science in Context

Calendars that we follow are based either on the movement of the sun or the moon. A solar calendar uses the year as a solar year. The time for the Earth to complete one revolution around the Sun is one solar year. A lunar calendar uses the phases of the moon to measure time. The time interval between one new moon to the next new moon is considered as one month.

GALAXIES

A galaxy is a huge collection of stars, dust and smoke. There are billions of stars in a galaxy. Our solar system belongs to the **Milky Way** galaxy. There are different types of galaxies. They are named according to their shapes, for example, spiral galaxy, elliptical galaxy and irregular galaxy. Milky Way is a spiral galaxy (Fig. 16.6). The nearest spiral galaxy to the Milky Way is the Andromeda galaxy.

Fig. 16.6: Spiral galaxy

THE SOLAR SYSTEM

a

The sun, the planets that revolve around the sun, the satellites of these planets and other celestial objects such as asteroids together form the **solar system** (Fig. 16.7).

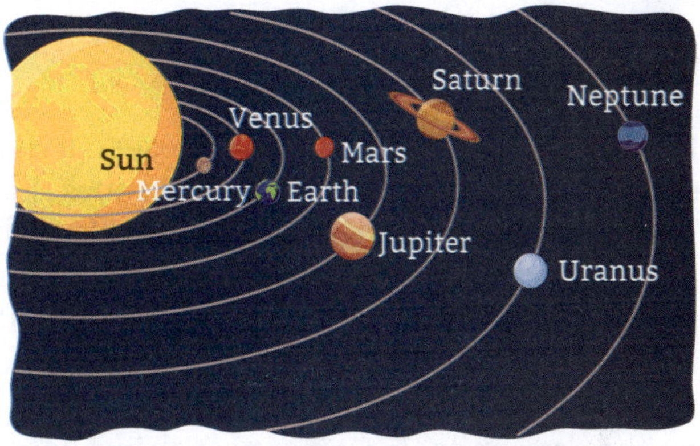

Fig. 16.7: The solar system (not to scale)

Sun

The sun (Fig. 16.8) is a star at the centre of the solar system around which other planets and their moons revolve. It is a huge, self-luminous sphere of gases, mostly hydrogen and helium. Its mass is nearly 3,33,000 times that of the Earth and its volume is about 13,00,000 times the Earth's volume. Gravity on the sun is nearly 28 times that of the Earth. Its average distance from the Earth is about 150 million kilometres. Light from the sun takes about 8 minutes to reach the surface of the Earth.

The average distance between the Earth and the sun is called **one astronomical unit (AU)**, which is used as a unit to express very large distances such as distance between celestial objects. The surface temperature of the sun is about 6000 °C and its interior is very hot.

The temperature at its centre is nearly 15 million degree Celsius. The sun is the main source of energy on Earth. All forms of energy available on Earth are basically derived from solar energy.

Fig. 16.8: Sun

Planets

The solar system consists of **eight** planets revolving around the sun. These planets, in the order of their distances from the sun, are **Mercury, Venus, Earth, Mars, Jupiter, Saturn, Uranus** and **Neptune.** Pluto, once considered the ninth and most distant planet from the sun, is now a dwarf planet in the solar system. Planets revolve around the sun, along concentric elliptical orbits, with the sun at the centre. The movement of the planets around the sun along their orbits is called **revolution**. The time taken by a planet to complete one revolution around the sun is called its **time period of revolution.** While moving around the sun, planets also rotate about their own axis. The spinning of the planet on its own axis is called **rotation**. The time taken by a planet to complete one rotation about its own axis is known as the **time period of rotation.**

The first four planets: Mercury, Venus, Earth and Mars are called the **inner planets**; the remaining planets: Jupiter, Saturn, Uranus and Neptune are called the **outer planets.**

Mercury

Mercury (Fig. 16.9) is the planet closest to the sun. It is the smallest planet in the solar system. Its mass is about 0.55 times that of the Earth. Since its gravitational force is comparatively weak, it is unable to hold gases and so it does not have an atmosphere. During daytime, its surface gets heated to extremely high temperatures (nearly 400 °C), and at night, it cools down to very low temperatures (about –200 °C). Given its proximity to the sun, Mercury is always hidden in the glare of the sun's bright light. It can be seen low on the horizon soon after sunset or just before sunrise to the right of the planet Venus. The Planetary Society of India is a good source that puts out information about the days when planets can be seen in the night sky.

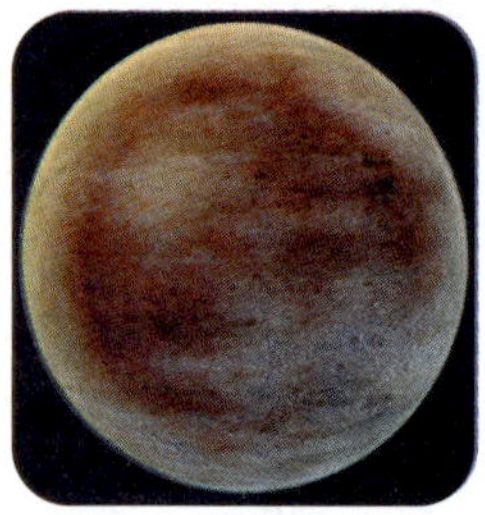

Fig. 16.9: Mercury

Venus

Venus (Fig. 16.10) is the second planet from the sun and the planet closest to the Earth. Also known as the evening star/morning star, it is the brightest planet visible in the sky. Venus is slightly smaller than the Earth. Chemical composition and density of Venus is similar to that of the Earth. Due to its similarities to the Earth, it is also referred to as the Earth's sister planet. Venus has a thick atmosphere mainly composed of carbon dioxide and nitrogen and clouds made up of sulphuric acid. There is no evidence of life on Venus reported so far. Venus is the hottest planet in the solar system with temperatures reaching nearly 480 °C. Venus rotates about its own axis in a direction opposite to that of the other planets, that is, while all planets rotate from west to east, Venus rotates from east to west.

Fig. 16.10: Venus

Earth

Earth is the third planet from the sun. It is the densest planet and fifth biggest in the solar system. It is the largest among the four inner planets in the solar system. Earth is the only planet in the solar system on which life is known to exist. The atmosphere of the Earth contains nitrogen (78%), oxygen (20.9%), carbon dioxide (0.035%), argon (0.90%) and other gases (0.165%) such as krypton, neon, water vapour, etc (Fig. 16.11). Earth's atmosphere has a thin layer of **ozone,** which protects the living things from the harmful radiation of the sun.

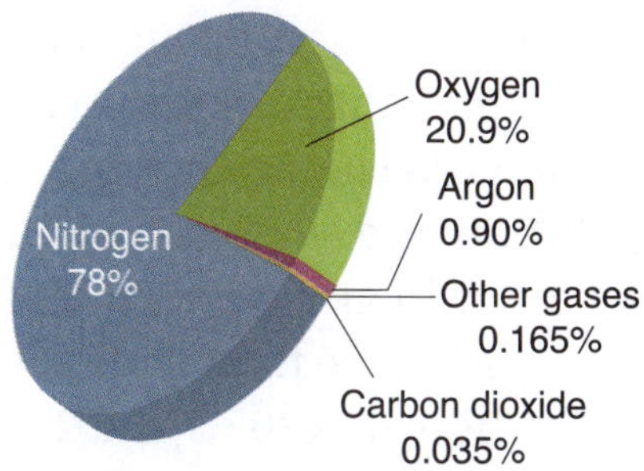

Fig. 16.11: Constituents of the atmosphere

Earth (Fig. 16.12) has water in liquid form on its surface. The presence of water, composition of the gases in the atmosphere, its distance from the sun, etc. make the Earth a suitable planet for the survival of life on its surface.

Fig. 16.12: The Earth

Earth completes one revolution (Fig. 16.13) around the sun in 365¼ days. Its period of rotation about its own axis is 24 hours or one day. Earth's rotation about its axis causes day and night to occur. Its axis of rotation is tilted at an angle of 23.4° from the perpendicular to its orbital plane, which is responsible for the seasonal changes on the surface of the Earth. The moon is the only natural satellite of the Earth.

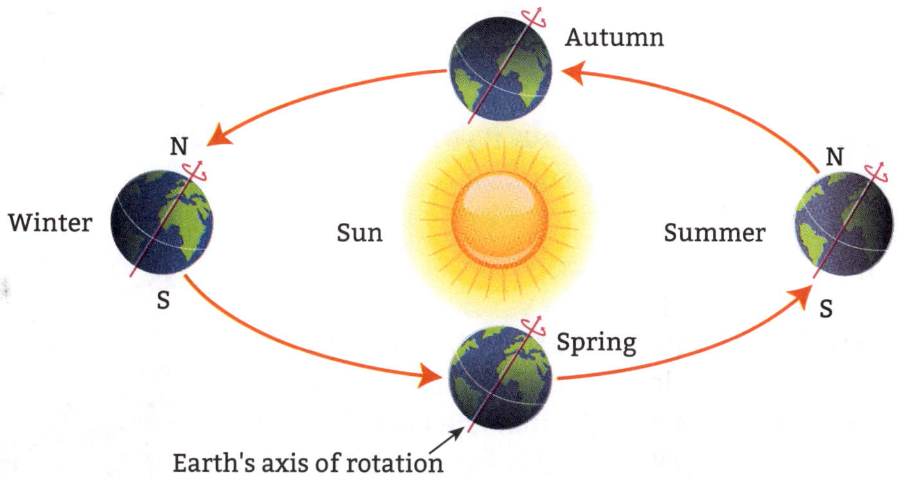

Fig. 16.13: Revolution of the Earth

Mars

Fig. 16.14: Mars

Mars (Fig. 16.14) is the fourth planet in the solar system from the sun. It is the second smallest planet and appears reddish due to the presence of iron oxide on its surface. Hence, it is also called the **red planet**. Its surface has many craters and mountains. The period of rotation and seasons on Mars are similar to that on Earth. Mars has a very thin atmosphere. Its size is nearly half that of the Earth and it is less dense than the Earth. Mars is a cold planet with temperatures varying within the range of –120 °C and 25 °C. It has two moons known as Phobos and Deimos.

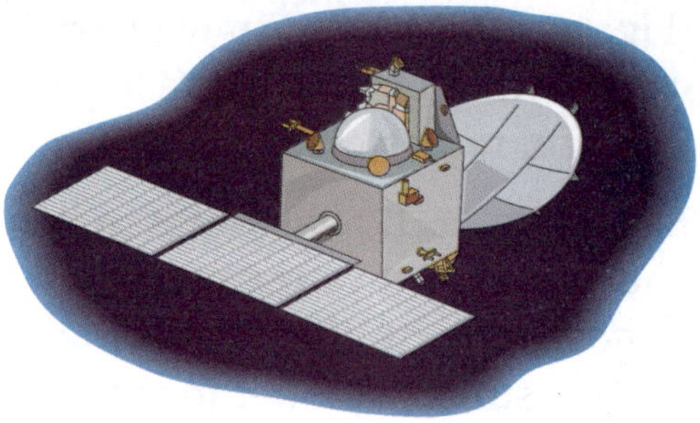

Fig. 16.15: Mangalyaan

Mangalyaan Mission: Mangalyaan (Fig. 16.15) is India's Mars Orbiter Mission (MOM), which was successfully launched into the Earth's orbit on November 5, 2013 by the Indian Space Research Organization (ISRO). The primary objective of the mission was to develop the technologies required to design and plan interplanetary missions. It was launched from the first launchpad at the Satish Dhawan Space Centre, Sriharikota, Andhra Pradesh using a polar satellite launch vehicle (PSLV C25).

Jupiter

Fig. 16.16: Jupiter

Jupiter (Fig. 16.16) is the fifth planet from the sun and the largest planet in the solar system. Its mass is nearly 318 times that of the Earth, and its volume is nearly 1300 times the volume of the Earth. It is the fourth brightest object visible in the sky. The three brighter objects visible are the sun, the moon and Venus. Jupiter has 79 known moons. Jupiter is the fastest spinning planet in the solar system. It completes one rotation about its own axis in 10 hours. Its period of revolution around the sun is about 12 years.

Saturn

Fig. 16.17: Saturn

Saturn (Fig. 16.17) is the sixth planet from the sun and appears yellowish in colour. It is the second largest planet in the solar system and is nearly 95 times heavier than the Earth. Its radius is about nine times the Earth's radius. The density of Saturn is low. It has a prominent ring system around it that can be seen through a small telescope as well. These rings are spectacular to look at and are actually rocky material, ice and dust.

Uranus

Uranus (Fig. 16.18) is the seventh planet from the sun in the solar system. Uranus' atmosphere is the coldest in the solar system. It rotates from east to west, just like Venus. Its axis of rotation is highly tilted from the perpendicular to the orbital plane. Uranus has a ring system around it (13 rings) and has 27 known moons revolving around the planet. Uranus completes one revolution around the sun in 84 years.

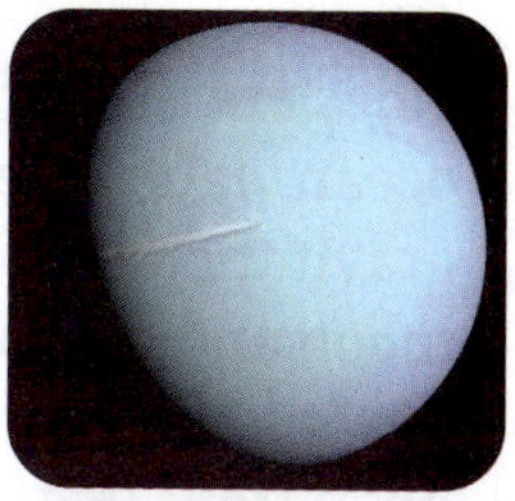

Fig. 16.18: Uranus

Neptune

Neptune (Fig. 16.19) is the eighth and the farthest planet from the sun in the solar system. It is nearly 17 times heavier than the Earth and the third-most massive planet in the solar system. Its volume is about 58 times that of the Earth. The composition of Neptune is similar to that of Uranus. It has 6 rings and 14 known moons revolving around it. Since it is so far from the Earth, it is not visible to the naked eye.

Fig. 16.19: Neptune

Moon

A celestial object that is orbiting a planet in the solar system is known as the **moon** or the **natural satellite** of that planet. We have seen that all the outer planets have numerous moons revolving around them while the inner planets have only a few moons orbiting them.

Science in Context

On January 19, 2006, New Horizons, a NASA space probe was launched to study the planet Pluto, its moons and one or two other Kuiper belt objects, depending on which are in a position to be explored. Pluto was earlier considered as the ninth planet of the solar system but due to its small size, it is now called a dwarf planet.

Moon of the Earth

Earth has one natural satellite, **the Moon** (Fig. 16.20), revolving around it. It is the fifth largest known moon in the solar system. It appears to be shining in the sky because it reflects the sunlight that falls on its surface. It does not have an atmosphere and its surface has several craters and mountains. Its mass is 7.3477×10^{22} kg, which is about one-hundredth (1/100th) the mass of the Earth. The average distance of the moon from the Earth is about 3,84,400 kilometres. The moon takes 27.3 days to complete one revolution around the Earth. Moon's gravitational force has great influence on Earth in the form of ocean tides. Apart from the Earth, the moon is the only celestial object on which humans have set foot on.

Fig. 16.20: Moon

Ocean Tides

Tides are the periodic rise and fall of the ocean water level due to the combined gravitational pull of the sun and the moon and the rotation of the Earth. There are two types of tides, **spring tides** and **neap tides** (Fig. 16.21). Spring tides occur when the Earth comes in between the moon and the sun or when the moon comes between the sun and the Earth. Spring tides are high tides. They are not related with the spring season at all. Neap tides or low tides occur when the sun and the moon are at right angles to each other.

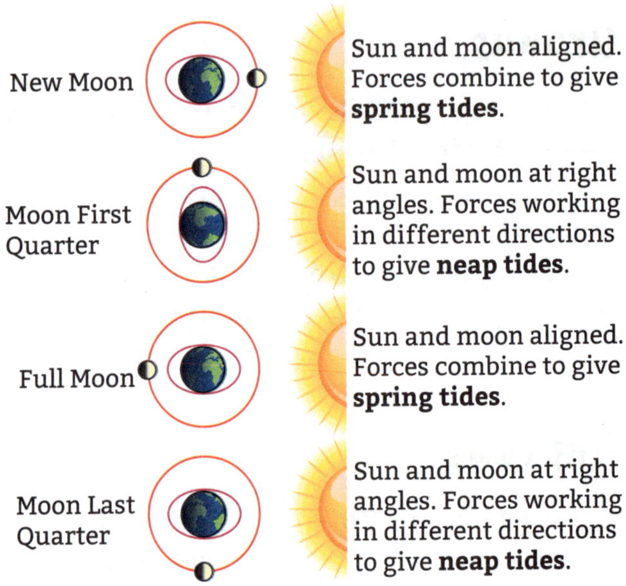

Fig. 16.21: Spring tides and neap tides

A rare phenomenon called **proxigean spring tide** is a very high tide that occurs when the moon comes very close to the Earth while orbiting it. It happens once in 1.5 years.

Phases of the Moon

The moon orbits the Earth in such a way that only one face of it is visible to us; the other side is not visible. Size and shape of the moon's faces visible to us vary from time to time. These variations depend on the relative positions of the sun, the Earth and the moon. The shapes of the bright part of the moon that is visible to us at different times are called the **phases of the moon** (Fig. 16.22). The different phases of the moon occur periodically as the moon revolves around the earth. A lunar calendar is based on these lunar phases and a lunar month has 29.5 days.

Fig. 16.22: Phases of the moon

Know the Scientist

Galileo Galilei (1564–1642) was an Italian physicist and mathematician. In 1610, Galileo was the first to discover Jupiter's four large moons, namely Io, Europa, Ganymede and Callisto, using his telescope. These four moons of Jupiter are known as the **Galilean moons**.

For his remarkable contributions in astronomy, Galileo has been named the father of modern observational astronomy.

Case Study: Chandrayaan-3 Mission

The Indian Space Research Organisation (ISRO) launched its third lunar mission, Chandrayaan-3 on July 14 from Sriharikota, Andhra Pradesh. Chandrayaan-3 is a follow-up mission of the Chandrayaan-2 that failed to land on the moon's surface in September 2019. It is aimed to conduct a study of the lunar soil, explore the moon's surface and record moon quakes. Its propulsion module carried a lander and a rover.

The Vikram lander of Chandrayaan-3 landed on the lunar south pole on August 23, 2023. This made India the fourth country after the United States, Russia and China to land successfully on the lunar surface. The Vikram lander is named after Dr Vikram A Sarabhai, the father of the Indian Space Programme. The Pragyan rover carried India's flag and ISRO's logo, etching the nation's identity on the lunar surface.

Revise and Recall

Fill in the blanks.

1. The brightest star visible in the night is ______________. (Sirius/Pole Star)
2. The Ursa Minor constellation is also known as ______________. (Great Bear/ Little Bear)
3. The moon takes _____________ days to complete one revolution around the Earth. (365/27.3)
4. ______________ occur when the Earth comes in between the moon and the sun. (Spring tides/Neap tides)
5. The farthest planet from the sun in the solar system is ______________. (Mercury/Uranus)

Other Celestial Objects in the Solar System

Asteroids

Fig. 16.23: Asteroids

The rocky remains from the formation of the solar system 4.5 billion years ago are referred to as **asteroids**. Many of these are found in a large ring or band (asteroid belt) between the orbits of Mars and Jupiter. Asteroids (Fig. 16.23) are mainly made up of rocks and are too small to be called planets, although some astronomers sometimes refer to them as **planetoids** or minor planets.

The size of the asteroids may vary from less than a kilometre to a few hundred kilometres. The largest asteroid known is Ceres with a diameter of 950 km. Metis is another asteroid whose diameter is 174 km.

Comets

Comets are small celestial objects made up of ice, dust and small rocks. Comets revolve around the sun in very long orbits. A comet (Fig. 16.24) appears like a glowing ball with a long tail when it comes close to the sun. Halley's comet is a famous comet which takes 76 Earth years to orbit around the sun once. Its last appearance in the solar system was in 1986 and will be visible again in the middle of 2061.

Fig. 16.24: A comet

Know the Scientist

Edmond Halley (1656–1742) was an English astronomer, geophysicist, mathematician, meteorologist, and physicist. Halley's comet was named after him. He examined the reports of three comets approaching the solar system in 1531, 1607 and 1682 and found that it is a single comet. He predicted that it would appear again in the solar system in the year 1758.

Meteors and Meteorites

The small pieces of debris moving in space that are usually parts of asteroids or comets are called **meteoroids**. When they enter the atmosphere of the Earth they are known as **meteors**. While falling to the surface, they get heated up due to friction with the air in the atmosphere. That is why many of these objects are burned and appear as bright streaks of light in the sky. These bright streaks are called **shooting stars**.

If the size of a meteor is very large, it will not be burnt completely in the air and will reach the Earth's surface. These objects that fall on the surface of the Earth are called **meteorites**. They may vary in size from a small grain to large boulders. Large meteorites hitting the Earth's surface create craters.

Artificial Satellites

Artificial satellites (Fig. 16.25) are human-made objects revolving around the Earth that are launched into the orbit by rockets. Sputnik-1 was the world's first artificial satellite launched by the Soviet Union in 1957. Aryabhatta was the first artificial satellite launched by India in 1975. As of April 2014, India has launched 74 artificial satellites. Rohini, INSAT, IRS, EDUSAT, etc. are some of the important series of satellites launched by India.

Fig. 16.25: An early artificial satellite

Some of the important applications of artificial satellites are:

- Telecommunication, radio and television transmission
- Weather forecasting, studying the atmosphere of the Earth
- Remote-sensing, that is, to study the Earth's surface, locating mineral deposits, studying land structures for agricultural purposes, etc. (Fig. 16.26).
- To explore outer space and to study about other celestial objects such as the moon, other planets, asteroids, etc.

Fig. 16.26: NASA's Earth Observation System

The Universe

The universe is the sum total of everything that exists. It includes the Earth and its satellites, other planets and their satellites, billions of stars and billions of galaxies. The sun is just a star among the billions of stars present in our galaxy. Also, there are billions of galaxies other than ours. It is very difficult to comprehend the vastness of the universe.

Activity

Aim: To understand the expansion of the universe

Materials required: Balloon (big) and sketch pen

Procedure:

1. Blow the balloon a little.
2. Mark several dots on the blown balloon almost at equal distances.
3. Now, blow the balloon further and see the dots.

Observation: The distance between the dots on the balloon increases as it expands.

In the above activity, we saw the dots on the balloon move apart as it expands. In a similar manner, the objects in the universe move apart from each other as the universe expands. In other words, the objects in the universe are continuously moving away from each other.

It has been theoretically calculated that the universe would have originated from a single mass about 13.798 ± 0.037 billion years ago. This single mass suddenly exploded, and the fragmented particles flying in all directions as a result of this explosion formed stars, planets and galaxies. This theory explains the formation of the universe due to the explosion of a single mass and is known as the **Big Bang theory**.

Keywords

Celestial object: The common name for all the objects visible in the sky

Star: A huge self-luminous object made up of hot gases

Constellation: A group of stars in the sky that form a recognizable pattern

Galaxy: Huge collection of stars, smoke and dust

Light year: Distance travelled by light in one year with a speed of 3 lakh kilometres per second

Planet: A celestial object in the solar system that revolves around the sun

Satellite: A celestial object in the solar system that revolves around a planet

Asteroids: The rocky remains from the formation of solar system

Comets: Small celestial objects made up of ice, dust and rock that revolve around the sun in very long orbits

Meteors: Shooting stars, or meteors, are bits of interplanetary material falling through the Earth's atmosphere

Meteorite: A meteor that survives the journey through the atmosphere and falls on the surface of the Earth

Artificial satellite: A human-made satellite launched into the space to explore outer space

Summary

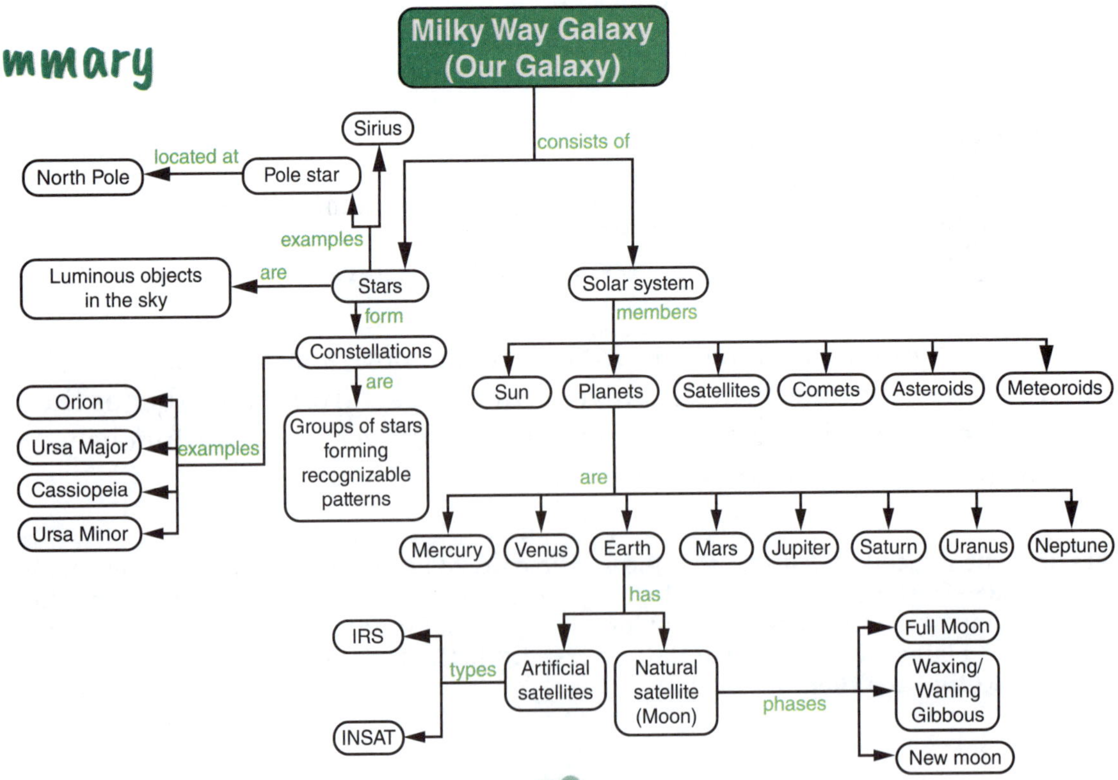

Exercise

A. Choose the correct option.

1. Which of the following is not considered as a planet?
   (a) Saturn (b) Neptune (c) Uranus (d) Moon
2. Day and night occur due to
   (a) the Earth's rotation on its axis.
   (b) the Earth's revolution around the sun.
   (c) the moon's revolution around the Earth.
   (d) the moon's revolution around the sun.
3. Which is the brightest planet visible in the sky?
   (a) Jupiter (b) Mars (c) Mercury (d) Venus
4. Which is the farthest planet from the sun?
   (a) Mercury (b) Saturn (c) Uranus (d) Neptune
5. Which of the following constellations can be used to locate the pole star easily?
   (a) Orion (b) Scorpio (c) Ursa Major (d) Cassiopeia

B. State whether the following statements are true (T) or false (F).

1. Any celestial body revolving around the sun is called a satellite. ☐
2. Venus rotates about its own axis from east to west. ☐
3. All stars belonging to a constellation are at the same distance from the Earth. ☐
4. Mercury is the brightest planet observed in the night sky. ☐
5. Uranus is the farthest planet from the sun in the solar system. ☐

C. Answer the following questions in one sentence each.

1. Which was the first artificial satellite of the Earth?
2. What are asteroids?
3. What is a galaxy?
4. Which is the brightest star in the night sky?
5. Which is the comet that appears in the solar system every 76 years?

D. Give reasons for the following.

1. Mars is called a red planet.
2. Earth appears blue from the space.
3. Sun is also called a star.
4. Meteors are not visible during daytime.
5. The pole star appears to be stationary in the sky.

E. Answer the following questions in brief.

1. Define one light year.
2. Why does the pole star appear to be stationary in the sky?
3. How can you find the star Sirius with the help of the constellation Orion?
4. What are artificial satellites? Mention two applications of them.
5. Differentiate between asteroids, comets and meteors.

F. Answer the following questions in detail.

1. All the stars in a constellation may not be at the same distance from the Earth. Explain.
2. Explain the different phases of the moon with a labelled diagram.
3. How are ocean tides formed? Explain.

Cognitive Corner

Critical Thinking

If you step on Venus, from which side would you expect the sun to rise? How will it be different from what you see on Earth?

Picture Study

Label the given diagram.

Project

Prior to Chandrayaan-3, India had launched two lunar missions, Chandrayaan-1 in 2008 and Chandrayaan-2 in 2019. As a part of the Science Club activity, find out more about India's different lunar missions till date. Make a detailed poster highlighting their important milestones and achievements and comparing their infrastructures, budgets and time taken for completion. **(C-6.1)**

In the Library

You might be familiar with the term GPS that we use to navigate even while travelling in a car. What does the term GPS stand for? Find out more about it and make a report on it. Include how it is used. **(C-7.1)**

Life Skills

Prepare a questionnaire to conduct a quiz programme on astronomy in such a way that the following are the answers. **(C-7.1)**

1. Ozone
2. Milky Way
3. Light year
4. Sirius
5. Jupiter
6. Spring tide
7. Comets
8. Shooting stars
9. Sputnik-1
10. Satellite

Worksheet

India has been sending out satellites to space since 19 April 1975 when it launched Aryabhatta. On 14 July 2023, at 14:35 Indian Standard Time (IST), Chandrayaan-3 was launched from the Satish Dhawan Space Centre in Sriharikota and accomplished its successful lunar landing on 23 August 2023 at 18:05 IST. Its primary scientific goal is to chart the distribution and prevalence of water on the Moon's surface.

Satellites also provide information on weather, images of soil patterns and in predicting cyclones and other natural hazards. They also help in tracking pollution levels and the condition of the ozone layer. We can, in fact, say that satellites help us in every step of our lives, directly or indirectly.

Observe the picture given below and identify how our lives are being helped by satellites today. Write any five points.

1. ______________________________

2. ______________________________

3. ______________________________

4. ______________________________

5. ______________________________

17 Pollution of Air and Water

Curricular Goals

- Explore the world of matter, and its constituents, properties and behaviour **(CG-1)**
- Understand the interface of science, technology and society **(CG-5)**
- Communicate questions, observations and conclusions related to science **(CG-7)**

Competencies

- Classify matter based on observable physical and chemical characteristics **(C-1.1)**
- Illustrate how science and technology can help to improve the quality of human life as well as some of the harmful uses of science in history **(C-5.1)**
- Use scientific vocabulary to communicate science accurately in oral and written forms, and through visual representation **(C-7.1)**

Let's Get Started

Fresh air and clean water are some of our basic necessities. But over the years, human beings and their activities have dirtied air and water on a large scale.

The given pictures show air and water getting dirtied. Can you identify the causes?

____

____

____

The addition of waste or undesirable substances in large amounts to the environment around us such that it becomes unsuitable for all living beings is called ***pollution****.*

Let us learn more about the causes, effects and prevention of air and water pollution.

POLLUTION AND POLLUTANTS

Human activities directly or indirectly affect the environment in some way or the other.

- Construction activities add a lot of suspended particulate matter and noise to the atmosphere.
- Automobiles emit oxides of nitrogen, sulphur dioxide, carbon dioxide, carbon monoxide and a complex mixture of unburnt hydrocarbons and black soot which pollute the atmosphere.
- Domestic sewage and runoff from agricultural fields, loaded with pesticides and fertilizers pollute water bodies.
- Effluents from tanneries contain many harmful chemicals and emit foul smell.

These are only a few examples which show how human activities pollute the environment. **Pollution** may be defined as the addition of undesirable and harmful substances into the environment. The agents which cause environmental pollution are called pollutants. A **pollutant** may be defined as a physical, chemical or biological substance released into the environment which is directly or indirectly harmful to humans and other living organisms.

There are different kinds of pollution. They are air pollution, water pollution, soil pollution and noise pollution.

AIR POLLUTION

Due to rapid industrialization and human activities, the quality of air is declining. Harmful and undesirable substances get added to the air leading to **air pollution**. Such harmful and undesirable substances are called **air pollutants**. The most common air pollutants are dust particles, carbon monoxide, carbon dioxide, sulphur dioxide, nitrogen dioxide, particulates and lead compounds.

Sources of Air Pollution

The main contributors to air pollution are discussed below.

- The increasing population in our country is leading to high usage of fuels for cooking. There are millions of homes in rural India where stoves are used for heating water and cooking food. The fuels used for these purposes are usually firewood or fuel wood and biomass cakes made from animal dung. Pollutants added due to burning of fuels are carbon monoxide, carbon dioxide, sulphur dioxide and nitrogen dioxide.

- The number of vehicles has been steadily increasing along with a rapidly increasing population of the country. Automobile fumes, containing carbon monoxide, are the main source of gaseous pollutants in cities.
- Industrial emissions from chimneys, oil refineries and factories are one of the main causes of air pollution. Oil refineries are the main source of nitrogen oxides released in the atmosphere.
- **Chlorofluorocarbons (CFCs)** are used in refrigerators, air-conditioning systems and aerosol cans. CFCs deplete the ozone layer.
- Forest fires (wild fires, Fig. 17.1) and volcanoes are two natural calamities that can cause air pollution. Along with these sources, the dust cloud formed by the winds from the areas where there is no vegetation also causes air pollution.

Fig. 17.1: Forest fire causing air pollution

EFFECTS OF AIR POLLUTION

Some of the major adverse effects of air pollution are discussed below.

Suspended Particulate Matter

The minute particles of carbon and other pollutants are suspended in the air to form **Suspended Particulate Matter (SPM)**. SPM causes many lung diseases. You must have seen dust deposited on the leaves and stems of plants and trees in the cities. This leads to a disturbance in the process of photosynthesis in plants.

Global Warming

a

Due to air pollution (Fig. 17.2), the amount of carbon dioxide is increasing day-by-day.

Carbon dioxide in the atmosphere traps the heat reflected from the surface of the Earth, which then increases the temperature during the day. This is called the **greenhouse effect**. Gases such as methane, nitrous oxide and water vapour in the air act like carbon dioxide and trap sunlight, leading to greenhouse effect. These gases are called **greenhouse gases.**

Fig. 17.2: Industries giving out fumes

The temperature of the Earth is increasing due to the release of high amounts of carbon dioxide and other greenhouse gases into the atmosphere. This phenomenon is known as **global warming**. This results in the melting of ice caps and glaciers in the polar regions. If global warming continues, it can lead to floods and submergence of land in the coastal regions due to a rise in the seawater level.

Science in Context

The greenhouse effect is somewhat similar to a condition seen in the greenhouses used to cultivate plants by commercial gardeners or horticulturists, etc. A greenhouse is a building facility made of glass or plastic to allow the required amount of sunlight to pass through it for photosynthesis in plants. The heat produced due to the sunlight cannot escape from the greenhouse. Traditionally, greenhouses were maintained by gardeners in temperate areas during winters.

Acid Rain

a

Pollutants such as oxides of sulphur and nitrogen react with water vapour to form acids such as sulphuric acid and nitric acid in the atmosphere. Sulphuric acid and nitric acid mix with the rain to form acid rain. Acid rain changes the composition of soil, affecting plant life. It is more frequent in cities where the pollution levels are high. It damages buildings, limestone and marble structures by corroding them.

Chemical Contamination

The term 'chemical contamination' is used to indicate situations where chemicals either are present where they shouldn't be or are at higher concentrations than they would have occurred naturally. Major outdoor sources of toxic air pollutants include emissions from thermal power plants, industries, refineries and automobiles such as cars, trucks and buses.

Indoor air can also contain hazardous air pollutants from sources that include tobacco smoke, building materials such as asbestos, and chemicals such as solvents. **Indoor Air Quality** (IAQ) refers to the air quality within and around buildings and structures. Understanding and controlling common pollutants indoors can help reduce risk of indoor health concerns.

Depletion of the Ozone Layer

Ozone layer is the layer of ozone gas that prevents ultraviolet (UV) rays of the sun from entering the Earth's atmosphere. It protects living organisms from the harmful effects of ultraviolet radiations. Substances such as chlorofluorocarbons (CFCs) enter the atmosphere and cause thinning of the ozone layer. Due to the thinning of the ozone layer, a hole has been created in this layer called the ozone hole. As a result, UV rays can easily enter the Earth's atmosphere through the thin ozone layer. These rays can cause damage to the eyes and skin causing skin cancer. Therefore, CFCs are being replaced by new and safer compounds.

Effects of Air Pollution on Human Beings, Plants and Animals

Pollution of air causes many respiratory problems.

- SPMs cannot be filtered by the hair in our nostrils. So, they are a major cause of many lung diseases.
- Carbon monoxide is a gas that mixes with blood and prevents it from carrying oxygen, leading to carbon monoxide poisoning.
- Smoke, soot particles, oxides of carbon, sulphur and nitrogen present in the air along with fog and sunlight form complex compounds that get trapped in the fog to form **photochemical smog** (Fig. 17.3).

Fig. 17.3: Smog covered streets in a polluted city

- Lead is added to petrol to prevent knocking during the burning of fuel in the engines. After the burning of fuel, fumes of gases are released that contain lead. These are absorbed by living beings while breathing. Lead poisoning may result in brain damage and mental disorders.
- Pollutants in the air can cause irritation to the nose, throat, eyes and lungs. Long-term exposure to a polluted environment can cause severe respiratory problems such as asthma, bronchitis and lung cancer.

PREVENTION OF AIR POLLUTION

Deforestation, increase in population, usage of fossil fuels and other human activities, all these contribute to air pollution. We should start thinking about preventing it further. The following are some of the ways that can help us in preventing air pollution:

- **Prevent deforestation** and **encourage afforestation**: Trees and plants need carbon dioxide for the process of photosynthesis. It is the best way to reduce the amount of carbon dioxide in the air. So, planting more trees and conserving the forestland are effective ways to decrease air pollution.
- Use of **alternative fuels** such as Liquefied Petroleum Gas (LPG) and Compressed Natural Gas (CNG) in vehicles reduces the emission of carbon compounds into the atmosphere. In many cities of India, autorickshaws and buses have been converted to alternative fuels to reduce air pollution.

- Solar water heaters, Gujarat water boilers, efficient stoves and LPG can be used for cooking and heating water to save energy and reduce air pollution.
- Use of **catalytic converters** in the exhaust of motor vehicles converts harmful gases such as carbon monoxide and nitrogen dioxide into less harmful pollutants such as carbon dioxide, nitrogen and water. This helps in minimizing the effects of air pollution caused by the emission of exhaust gases from vehicles.

Case Study: Air Pollution in Delhi

According to a report in early 2020, Delhi is the 10th most populated city in India. The air in the city is polluted due to the high amount of pollutants released from automobile emissions, industrial effluents, power-plant emissions and other domestic sources.

The population of Delhi is facing a lot of health issues linked to air pollution. It is causing diseases such as asthma, damage to the lungs, eyes, skins, retarded development of the brain and cancer.

Air pollutants have also shown a significant effect on the vegetation in the city. Many sensitive plants and trees are getting affected due to the smoke and deposition of dust on leaves. The authorities in Delhi have taken measures to reduce the amount of pollutants being released into the air. Heavy vehicles have been converted to run on CNG fuels, unleaded petrol and adhere to emission norms.

Revise and Recall

Fill in the blanks.

1. Harmful and undesirable substances that degrade the quality of air are called ____________. (pollutants/pollution)
2. Gases that trap sunlight and increase the temperature of the Earth are called ____________ gases. (ultraviolet/greenhouse)
3. ____________ cause depletion of the ozone layer. (CFCs/Volcanoes)
4. Oxides of sulphur and ____________ can cause acid rain. (iron/nitrogen)

WATER POLLUTION

Fig. 17.4: Sewage being let off into a river

Water is needed for drinking, bathing, washing and many other purposes. Due to an increased population and industrial use, the demand for water has gone up. However, the availability of clean water for consumption is a problem due to the increased level of pollution in water bodies such as rivers, lakes, ponds and groundwater. The impurities present in polluted water make it harmful for humans, animals and plants. Many kinds of fish, tortoise and water plants live in water, which is their only habitat. This is being destroyed by letting wastewater or sewage disposal into them (Fig. 17.4).

The amount of pollutants that are being released into water bodies are increasing due to an increasing population; the amount of wastewater let out from homes and industries has also increased. For example, the river Ganga is termed dead because of the high pollution levels and has become uninhabitable[1] for aquatic organisms.

Word Web

[1]**Uninhabitable:** not capable of being lived in

Sources and Effects of Water Pollution

Pollution of water is caused by many sources that release wastewater into nearby water sources. This affects the life in and around the water sources, by causing diseases and bad odour. A few sources of water pollution are sewage, industrial effluents, fertilizers and pesticides.

Sewage

Sewage from homes, hotels, shopping malls, etc. is disposed of without treatment or without proper management. It contains many microorganisms such as bacteria, virus, fungi and parasites. These give rise to many diseases when water from these sources is used for human activities. These microorganisms may cause harmful diseases such as diarrhoea, dysentery, cholera, typhoid and jaundice.

Industrial effluents

The waste and toxic substances produced by industries are called industrial effluents. The government has made rules for industries, not to dispose untreated water into rivers. Industries such as leather tanning, textile and chemicals produce effluents with compounds containing lead, mercury, arsenic, etc. These pollute rivers and oceans. Paper industry, sugar mills and oil refineries also use water for various purposes.

Nuclear power plants and manufacturers use water as a coolant in various processes. This produces hot water that is released into the water bodies. This changes the temperature of the water bodies that affects all aquatic organisms. This type of pollution is known as **thermal pollution**. The sudden variation of temperature in the water bodies kills many fish and other aquatic organisms, and this is called **thermal shock**.

Fertilizers and pesticides

Chemical fertilizers and pesticides are used by farmers to increase the yield and protect the crops. When it rains, these chemical-based products are washed off into the rivers, lakes and streams. A part of these may percolate into the groundwater, thus polluting it. Pesticides such as DDT are commonly used by farmers. These pesticides can get into the bodies of fish through the water. When these fishes are consumed by human beings, DDT gets accumulated and causes health disorders.

The runoff water carrying fertilizers from the field are rich in nutrients. They get accumulated in the water bodies increasing the growth of algae, which use up the dissolved oxygen in the water. When these algae die, the decomposer bacteria multiply in water, reducing the oxygen levels further. The increase of nutrients in the water leads to excessive growth of aquatic plants on the surface of the water body and depletes the dissolved oxygen levels. This is called **eutrophication** (Fig. 17.5). Hence, nowadays, biodegradable fertilizers such as compost, *Rhizobium* and *Azotobacter*-based fertilizers are used. Extracts of neem tree and natural enemies of pests are used as pesticides for the biocontrol of pests.

Fig. 17.5: Eutrophication of a lake

Case Study: Water Pollution in Mutha River in Pune, Maharashtra

Mutha River in Pune, Maharashtra, plays a major role in the economy of the place. Previously, only agricultural lands were found near this river. However, the riverbank attracted developers for residential, commercial and industrial developments. These developments on the banks of the river resulted in the pollution of the river water. The main sources of river water pollution are:

- The wastewater from the agricultural lands containing pesticides and chemical fertilizers flows directly into the river.
- On both the sides of the river, there are several big- and small-scale industries. The effluents from these industries are let out in the river directly or with improper treatment.
- The domestic wastewater from municipal sewer lines is also directly connected to the river.

The wastewater containing rainwater or storm water, domestic sewage and industrial waste is directly discharged or without proper processing.

Water of the Mutha River is also the source of water for domestic purposes. Consumption of this water has led to many diseases of the skin, cancer, eye irritation, allergies, etc. Even the cattle used for dairy purpose are falling sick and the milk quality is getting affected because of the intake of polluted water. The Government of Maharashtra, in 2014, announced that the Pune Municipal Corporation would build new sewage treatment plants and ensure that no sewage water is mixed with the river water. The Union government had approved a ₹990-crore project in 2016 to abate pollution in Mula-Mutha river under the National River Conservation Plan (NRCP). However, there has been a delay in the implementation of the project.

Prevention of Water Pollution

Prevention of water pollution includes the conservation of water available for the ever-increasing human population. A few methods that are being followed to decrease water pollution are as follows:

Treatment of sewage water from the cities before being released into the water sources.

Biodegradable fertilizers and pesticides to be used to avoid the accumulation of harmful chemicals in both soil and water.

Modern irrigation methods such as drip irrigation should be used instead of flooding the fields with water. This prevents the water to run off along with fertilizers causing losses to farmers and polluting the nearby water sources with chemical fertilizers.

Water recycling is one method that can be used to clean up wastewater, and use it for watering the plants and for washing purposes in the industries.

Avoiding wastage of water at homes due to leaking taps. The water lost in this way goes to the sewage.

Potable Water

Water that is free of pollutants and suitable for human consumption is called **potable water**. Potable water should be free from germs and harmful chemicals that can cause diseases.

To make the water potable, different techniques are used. **Water filters** have ceramic porous filters that separate solid substances from the water. The filtered water may be colourless, but it may have microorganisms. The best way to purify water is by **boiling** it for 15 minutes (Fig. 17.6). Though simple, this method kills most of the harmful microorganisms.

A number of water-purifying technologies are available in the market. One is the **ultraviolet light water filter** (Fig. 17.7). UV light has the capacity to kill harmful microorganisms to make the water potable.

Fig. 17.6: Boiling

Fig. 17.7: UV light water purification device

Reverse osmosis (RO) is a technique used for making the water potable by using a semipermeable[1] membrane. This process removes most of the harmful microorganisms and solid impurities. Many water filters available in the market use this technology.

Word Web

[1]**semipermeable:** allowing only certain molecules to pass through

Purification of Water

In cities and towns, we get water purified by a water purification facility (often called a water treatment plant) owned by a civic authority. The steps involved in the purification of water at a water treatment plant are shown in Figure 17.8.

1. The water from rivers or lakes **(source)** is pumped into the water treatment facility and passed through a bar screen to remove plant material and solids.
2. **Coagulation** is a process in which the dirt particles and large objects that are dissolved in water are removed. Alum is added to the water. All the dirt particles stick to the alum. This is called **floc**. The floc (short form of the word 'flocculent') is heavy because of a combination of alum and dirt particles.
3. **Sedimentation** is that stage of water purification where water is allowed to stand in a big tank. This allows the large suspended particles of impurities or floc to settle at the bottom. This unit is also called flocculator.
4. This water is then passed through filters made of sand and gravel that removes the solid impurities. This process is called **filtration**. This unit is also called clarifier.
5. **Disinfection** is the removal or killing of harmful microorganisms. It is done by passing chlorine gas through water. It can kill all kinds of microorganisms present in the water, and this process is called **chlorination**.

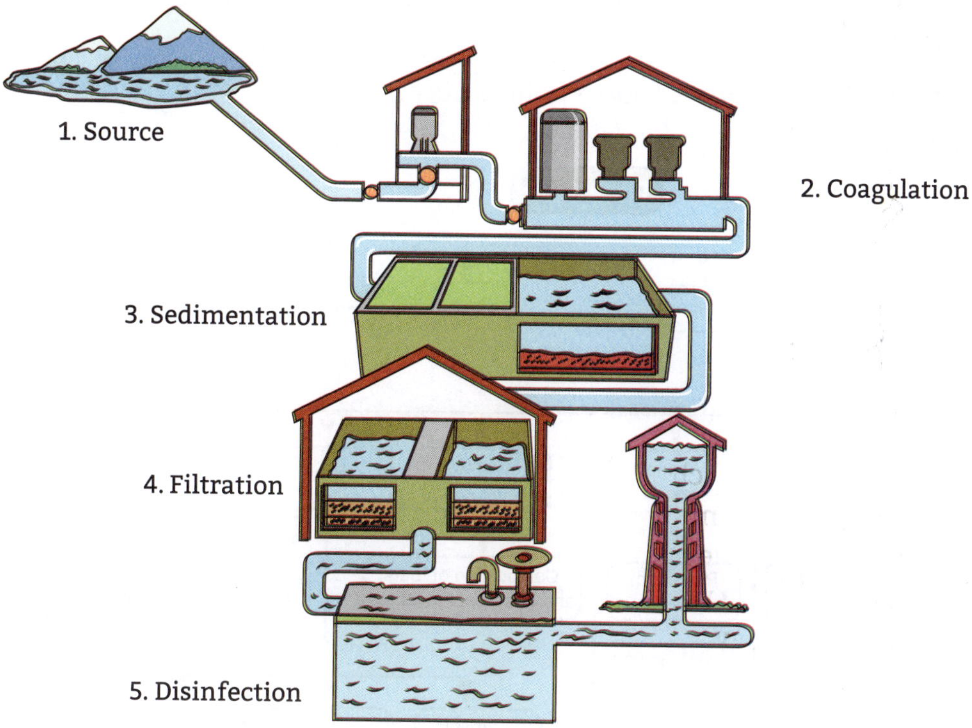

Fig. 17.8: Water treatment plant

Revise and Recall

Fill in the blanks.

1. The pollutants contributing to the depletion of the ozone layer are ________. (chlorofluorocarbons/methyl mercury)
2. The method used for disinfection of water is called _______. (chlorination/alum)
3. The depletion of ozone at certain parts of the atmosphere is called ________. (ozone hole/greenhouse effect)
4. Water that is free from pollutants and suitable for drinking is called _______. (potable water/groundwater)
5. The increase in temperature due to the release of hot water from the industries into water sources is called ________. (thermal shock/water pollution)

Keywords

Greenhouse effect: The process in which carbon dioxide in the atmosphere traps the heat from sunlight and increases the temperature during the day

Eutrophication: The increase of nutrients in water leading to excessive growth of aquatic plants on the surface of a water body and depleting the dissolved oxygen levels

Potable water: Water that is free of pollutants and suitable for human consumption

Summary

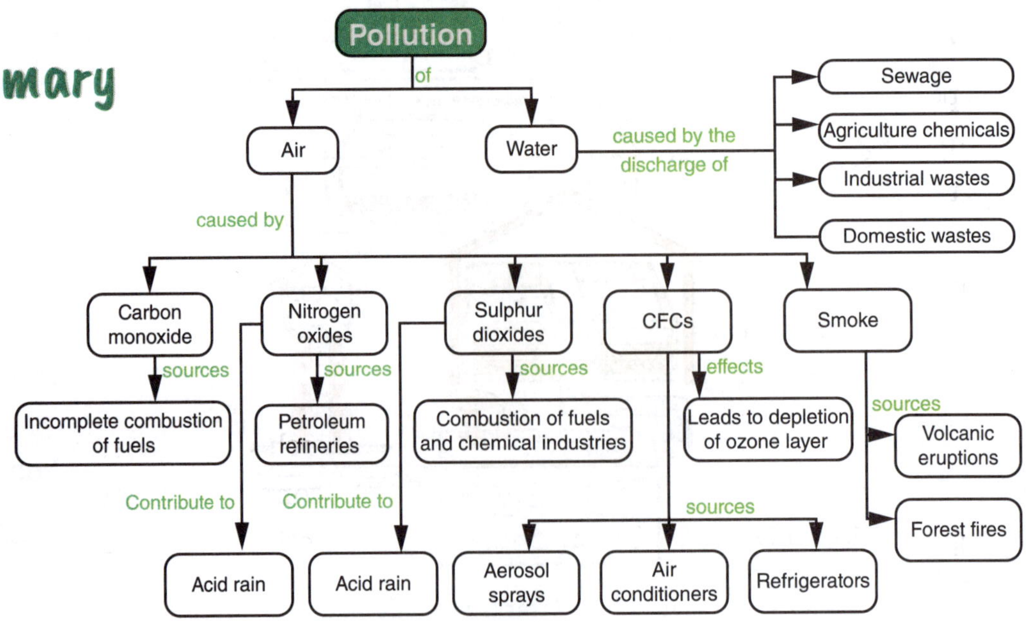

Exercise

w

ia

A. Choose the correct option.

1. The source of air pollution is
   (a) smoke from factories and automobiles. (b) industrial waste discharge into rivers.
   (c) sound produced from factories. (d) oil spills.
2. Which of the following is a greenhouse gas?
   (a) Nitrogen (b) Oxygen (c) Carbon dioxide (d) Argon
3. Deforestation leads to an increase in the amount of
   (a) carbon dioxide (b) carbon monoxide (c) oxygen (d) nitrogen
4. Which of the following is not an alternative fuel choice for automobiles?
   (a) CNG (b) LPG (c) Hydrogen fuel (d) None
5. Which of the following is a disease caused due to air pollution?
   (a) Cholera (b) Bronchitis (c) Typhoid (d) Jaundice

B. State whether the following statements are true (T) or false (F).

ia

1. Volcanic eruption is a natural source of air pollution. ☐
2. Fertilizers and pesticides in the runoff water from the fields lead to water pollution. ☐
3. Increase in the growth of bacteria in water bodies decreases the oxygen level in that water. ☐
4. Discharge of hot water into water bodies does not affect aquatic animals. ☐
5. Air pollution can be minimized by afforestation. ☐

C. Answer the following questions in one line each.

1. What is pollution?
2. Name any two greenhouse gases.
3. What is the function of ozone in the atmosphere?
4. What is SPM?
5. Name any two pollutants found in industrial effluents.

D. Give reasons for the following.

1. Planting and nurturing of trees is essential.
2. Government of India advised to switch over to fuels such as CNG instead of petrol.
3. Incomplete combustion of fuel is more harmful than complete combustion of fuel.
4. Drinking water supplied from the municipalities sometimes smells of chlorine.
5. During water purification, alum is added to water.

E. Answer the following questions briefly.

1. What is greenhouse effect?
2. What is acid rain?
3. How is photochemical smog formed?
4. What is reverse osmosis?
5. What are the sources of water pollution?
6. How does global warming affect seawater level?

F. Answer the following questions in detail.

1. Explain the process of eutrophication of a water source.
2. Suggest some ways to reduce air pollution.
3. Write a note on the effects of air pollution on human beings, plants and animals.
4. Explain the steps involved in the purification of water.

Cognitive Corner

Critical Thinking

Electric vehicles are considered less polluting but they use nickel and cadmium compounds in their batteries. Mining for these elements need energy and leads to deforestation and pollution. Can you suggest a solution for this problem?

Picture Study

The given picture is of a water treatment plant. Label the various stages in which purification of water takes place.

Collins

ADHERES TO National Curriculum Framework 2023 MIDDLE STAGE

SUPPLEMENTARY BOOKLET 8

Enhanced

Science Now

Revised Edition

Series Editor | Geetha Iyer

About the STEAM Activities

In the 21st century where the world is rapidly changing with sudden disruptions and unexpected real-world problems, being skilled in just one stream may not be enough. Many real-world problems can be solved only through interdisciplinary approach. Moreover, educationists have been emphasizing on the importance of subject integration and cross-curricular links. **Science**, **technology**, **engineering**, **arts** and **maths** (**STEAM**) education is one such approach where the integration of these five disciplines is utilized to solve real-world problems. Through this approach, a variety of skills such as critical thinking, creativity, innovation, communication, collaboration and entrepreneurship can be applied to make the students ready for the future, where these skills would be applicable in any field of study.

Students need to be introduced to STEAM education early on in life while their mind is still full of curiosity and imagination. STEAM education would not only help in producing tomorrow's designers and engineers, it would also help develop innovative mindsets and the ability to solve real-world problems. This would bring the students one step closer to becoming innovators or creators, not just passive consumers.

This supplementary booklet which comes along with the ***Enhanced Science Now, Revised Edition*** series, aims to introduce STEAM education to students from classes 1 to 8. There are two problems, based on ***real-world contexts***, in each booklet. The contexts have been carefully designed and mapped directly with the syllabus of each class. The students would be applying interdisciplinary concepts they have learnt in a class to find solution to the given problems. With each problem, research tips have been given to help in the initiation of idea. Clear directives have been given for students to identify the problem, research and record data, record their thinking, sketch their ideas, make observations and improve their designs or solutions as they work through creating the design or solving the problem.

This ***booklet*** is an attempt to give some form of exposure to STEAM education and its importance and benefits. We hope the students, while applying the concepts they have learnt to solve the real-world problems, would find their learning meaningful and thus be inspired to become future problem-solvers, critical thinkers, innovators or inventors.

Content Developed by Excelsoft Technologies Pvt Ltd.

Hazel went to a car service station with her father to get their car washed. She wondered about the set-up used to lift the car. She watched the machine lifting vehicles with a lot of curiosity and wanted to know more about it. She thought that a similar lift can be used to move heavy objects to the upper floors of a building. She wants to learn more about the hydraulic lift and make a prototype to demonstrate its working principle.

Help Hazel collect some information on hydraulic lifts. Also, help her design and construct a model to demonstrate the working principle of hydraulic lifts.

Statement of the problem:

____

____

____

____

____

Research tips:

1. Hydraulic lift
2. Pressure
3. Pascal's law
4. Applications of Pascal's law
5. Working of a hydraulic lift

Gather information relevant for this problem.

1. ______________________________
2. ______________________________
3. ______________________________
4. ______________________________

Draw/Sketch your design.

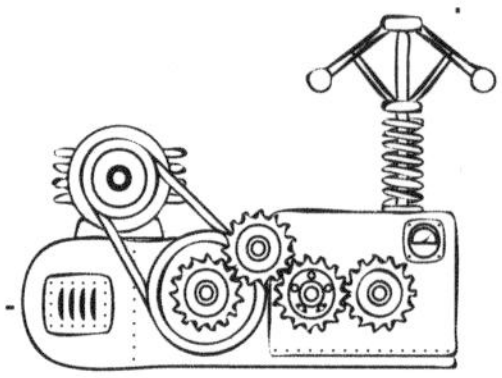

Materials required:

____

____

____

____

____

Construction (Write down the steps to build your design):

1. ______________________________

   ____

2. ______________________________

   ____

3. ______________________________

   ____

4. ______________________________

   ____

Implementation of the prototype (Try out your model):

Step 1: ____________________

Step 2: ____________________

Step 3: ____________________

Step 4: ____________________

Observation (What worked? What did not work?):

____

____

____

____

____

Scope for improvement (How can you make it better?):

In a science magazine, Bala read about a project on making a simple battery using lemons, zinc and copper. He thought, if a disaster ever happens and there is no light, he could make this battery and use it as a survival kit.

He wants to know more about batteries and cells and collect information on primary cells. He wants to make some simple cells, to study about the electric current produced by simple voltaic cells, using zinc, copper and dilute sulphuric acid. He also wants to check what happens to the voltage if the size of the cell is increased.

Help Bala design a simple voltaic cell and study the voltage of these cells.

Statement of the problem:

____

____

____

____

____

Research tips:

1. Voltaic cells
2. Components of a cell
3. Voltage of a cell
4. Zinc–copper cells

Gather information relevant for this problem.

1. ____
   ____
2. ____
   ____
3. ____
   ____
4. ____
   ____

Draw/Sketch your design.

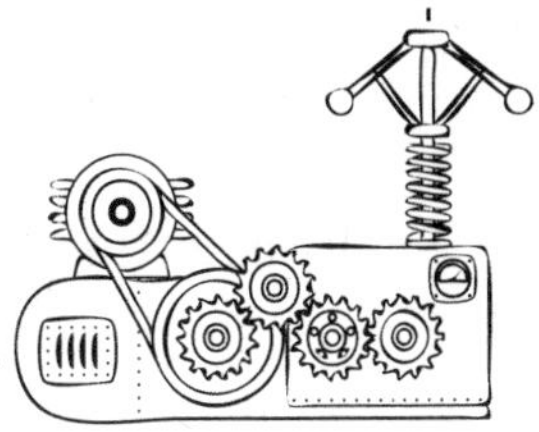

Materials required:

____

____

____

____

____

Construction (Write down the steps to build your design):

1. ______________________________

____

2. ______________________________

____

3. ______________________________

____

4. ______________________________

____

Implementation of the prototype (Try out your model):

Step 1: ____________________

Step 2: ____________________

Step 3: ____________________

Step 4: ____________________

Observation (What worked? What did not work?):

____

____

____

____

____

Scope for improvement (How can you make it better?):

STEAM Vocabulary

Construction: The way in which a thing is built or put together

Implementation: Trying out/carrying out/experimenting

Prototype: A working model of a new product or a new version of an old product

Scope: Possibility

Assessment 1

CHAPTERS 1-5

(Maximum Marks = 10)

Choose the correct option. **(10 × 1 = 10)**

1. Which of the following statements is true about vermicompost?
   (a) It is a type of fertilizer made from synthetic chemicals.
   (b) It is produced by the action of red worms.
   (c) It is a form of compost made by burning organic materials.
   (d) It is made by mixing animal manure with chemical additives.
2. In which of the given situations would farmers most likely choose to raise seedlings in nurseries and then transplant them in the fields instead of broadcasting seeds?
   (a) In an arid region with limited water supply and low annual rainfall
   (b) In a region with less than 100 mm of annual rainfall
   (c) In a region with 1000-1500 mm of annual rainfall
   (d) In a region with abundant rainfall and no need for water management
3. Which of the following completes the given analogy?
   Corrosion of iron : Rust :: Corrosion of silver : ___________
   (a) Silver chloride
   (b) Silver sulphate
   (c) Silver nitrate
   (d) Silver sulphide
4. **Assertion (A):** Only few metals react with strong bases such as sodium hydroxide and release hydrogen.
   Reason (R): Displacement reactions are based on the reactivity strength of metals.
   (a) A is true, but R is false.
   (b) Both A and R are true, but R is not the correct explanation of A.
   (c) Both A and R are true, and R is the correct explanation of A.
   (d) A is false, but R is true.
5. Which of the following actions contributes to the conservation of fossil fuels?
   (a) Using plastic containers made from petroleum by-products
   (b) Using natural fibres such as cotton for clothing
   (c) Using a motor vehicle for all our needs
   (d) Relying solely on fossil fuels for energy needs

6. Match the following.

i. Petroleum gas	(a) Used as a fuel for heavy motor vehicles
ii. Paraffin wax	(b) Used in construction of roads
iii. Bitumen	(c) Used in making ointments and vaseline
iv. Diesel	(d) Used as a fuel for domestic use

(a) (i)-(c), (ii)-(a), (iii)-(b), (iv)-(a)
(b) (i)-(a), (ii)-(d), (iii)-(c), (iv)-(b)
(c) (i)-(d), (ii)-(c), (iii)-(b), (iv)-(a)
(d) (i)-(a), (ii)-(b), (iii)-(d), (iv)-(c)

7. Which of the following completes the given analogy?
Trekking rope : Nylon :: Bathroom brush : ___________
(a) Lycra (b) Coir
(c) Rayon (d) Silk

8. **Assertion (A):** It is not advisable to wear synthetic clothes while working in the kitchen.
Reason (R): Synthetic clothes do not absorb sweat.
(a) A is true, but R is false.
(b) Both A and R are true, but R is not the correct explanation of A.
(c) Both A and R are true, and R is the correct explanation of A.
(d) A is false, but R is true.

9. Which of the following completes the given analogy?
Protozoa : Amoeba :: Virus : ___________
(a) Paramecium (b) Rhizopus
(c) Bacteriophage (d) Volvox

10. **Assertion (A):** Fungal infections in humans are caused due to consumption of contaminated water.
Reason (R): Ringworm is a fungal disease.
(a) A is true, but R is false.
(b) Both A and R are true, but R is not the correct explanation of A.
(c) Both A and R are true, and R is the correct explanation of A.
(d) A is false, but R is true.

How many questions did you answer correctly? Score yourself.

easy ☐ average ☐ advanced ☐ remembering ☐ understanding ☐ applying ☐
analysing ☐ evaluating ☐ creating ☐ justify ☐ associate ☐ analyse ☐
interpret/account for ☐ identification ☐ recognize ☐ select ☐ recall ☐

Assessment 2

CHAPTERS 6-9

(Maximum Marks = 10)

Choose the correct option. **(10 × 1 = 10)**

1. Which of the following completes the given analogy?
   Plant cell : Centrioles :: Animal cell : ____________________
   (a) Cell membrane
   (b) Nucleus
   (c) Chloroplast
   (d) Mitochondria
2. Rajesh suffered an injury to his spinal cord in an accident. His doctor explained him that the damage is permanent because the cells in the spinal cord ____________________
   (a) lack the necessary nutrients to heal.
   (b) are insufficient in number.
   (c) have lost the ability to communicate with surrounding cells.
   (d) cannot undergo cell division to replace the damaged cells.
3. Match the following.

i. Pancreas	(a) Progesterone
ii. Ovaries	(b) Fright, flight and fight hormone
iii. Adrenal gland	(c) Growth hormone
iv. Pituitary gland	(d) Insulin

   (a) (i)-(d), (ii)-(a), (iii)-(b), (iv)-(c)
   (b) (i)-(c), (ii)-(a), (iii)-(b), (iv)-(a)
   (c) (i)-(a), (ii)-(d), (iii)-(c), (iv)-(b)
   (d) (i)-(a), (ii)-(b), (iii)-(d), (iv)-(c)
4. What could be a consequence of sharing of needles among drug addicts?
   (a) Increased risk of addiction
   (b) Damage to mental health
   (c) Exposure to HIV infection
   (d) Increased ability to work
5. Which of the following completes the given analogy?
   Internal fertilization : Reptiles :: External fertilization : ____________________
   (a) Fish
   (b) Birds
   (c) Blue whales
   (d) Human beings

6. All human beings have 23 pairs of chromosomes in the nuclei of their cells. Out of these, the __________ pair of chromosomes are called the sex chromosomes.
   (a) 23rd
   (b) 22nd
   (c) 1st
   (d) 12th
7. The sex of a baby is determined by ________________
   (a) the mother's egg.
   (b) the father's sperm.
   (c) both the mother's egg and the father's sperm.
   (d) the environmental factors.
8. Which type of cells can change their shape?
   (a) Nerve cells
   (b) Muscle cells
   (c) Skin cells
   (d) White blood cells
9. Species found exclusively in a particular area are called ______________ species.
   (a) endangered
   (b) endemic
   (c) migrating
   (d) extinct
10. Which of the following completes the given analogy?
    Dinosaur : __________ :: Lemur : Endemic
    (a) Endangered
    (b) Threatened
    (c) Extinct
    (d) Vulnerable

How many questions did you answer correctly? Score yourself.

easy	average	advanced	remembering	understanding	applying
analysing	evaluating	creating	justify	associate	analyse
interpret/account for	identification	recognize	select	recall	

Assessment 3

CHAPTERS 10–13

(Maximum Marks = 10)

Choose the correct option. **(10 × 1 = 10)**

1. Which of the following forces is only attractive in nature?
   (a) Magnetic force
   (b) Electrostatic force
   (c) Gravitational force
   (d) Muscular force
2. A car is moving on an asphalt road towards North direction. What can be inferred about the direction of the kinetic friction between the tyres of the car and the asphalt road?
   (a) It is towards East.
   (b) It is towards West.
   (c) It is towards North.
   (d) It is towards South.
3. A table sits on a sloping surface. Which of the following methods would help increase the friction between the surface and the table?
   (a) Application of lubricants between the two surfaces in contact
   (b) Polishing the two surfaces in contact
   (c) Increasing the mass of the table
   (d) Decreasing the mass of the table
4. A car weighs 1600 N in total. Each of the tyres has a contact area of 75 cm^2 with the road. What is the pressure exerted by each of the tyres on the road? Assume the load is equally distributed on all the tyres.
   (a) 5.3 Pa
   (b) 21.3 Pa
   (c) 213.3 Pa
   (d) 53.3 kPa
5. Which of the following is not true with respect to fluid pressure?
   (a) Liquid exerts pressure in all directions.
   (b) As the depth in a liquid column increases, the pressure decreases.
   (c) As the depth in a liquid column increases, the pressure increases.
   (d) Pressure at a certain depth would be same in all places.
6. Which of the following characteristics represents the number of vibrations a body undergoes?
   (a) Amplitude
   (b) Frequency
   (c) Time period
   (d) Pitch

7. An auditorium is being prepared for a music concert. The music artist has requested that she needs the sound to echo to produce a certain type of effect in her music. Which of the following conditions would allow for an echo to be produced in the auditorium?
   (a) Increase the speed of the sound waves to 400 m/s.
   (b) Increase the amplitude of the sound waves to twice.
   (c) Place the speakers such that there is a minimum of 17 m distance from the walls.
   (d) Place the speakers such that there is a minimum of 8.5 m distance from the walls.
8. A strong salt solution is being used as an electrolyte. Which of the following is true?
   (a) Negative ions move towards anode.
   (b) Negative ions move towards cathode.
   (c) Positive ions move towards anode.
   (d) The movement of ions depend on the salt.
9. Which of the following is true during the electrolysis of water?
   (a) Hydrogen is released at the anode.
   (b) Oxygen is released at the anode.
   (c) Hydrogen is released at the positive electrode.
   (d) Oxygen is released at the negative electrode.
10. Cochlea is present in which part of the human ear?
    1. Outer ear
    2. Middle ear
    3. Inner ear
    4. Middle ear and outer ear

How many questions did you answer correctly? Score yourself.

easy	average	advanced	remembering	understanding	applying
analysing	evaluating	creating	justify	associate	analyse
interpret/account for	identification	recognize	select	recall	

Assessment 4

CHAPTERS 14-17

(Maximum Marks = 10)

Choose the correct option. **(10 × 1 = 10)**

1. Which of the following is not a natural phenomenon?
   (a) Lightning
   (b) Earthing
   (c) Earthquakes
   (d) Cyclones
2. Where is a lightning conductor installed to protect the building from lightning?
   (a) In the middle of the building
   (b) At the bottom of the building
   (c) At the top of the building
   (d) Underneath the building
3. When two bodies are rubbed against each other, they acquire ________
   (a) equal and unlike charges.
   (b) equal and like charges.
   (c) unequal and unlike charges.
   (d) unequal and like charges.
4. The part of the eye which controls the amount of light entering the eyes is ________.
   (a) cornea
   (b) retina
   (c) lens
   (d) iris
5. As the angle between two plane mirrors is increased gradually, the number of images of an object placed between them ________
   (a) increases gradually.
   (b) decreases gradually.
   (c) first increases then decreases.
   (d) first decreases then increases.
6. The angle between an incident ray and the plane mirror is 50°. The total angle between the incident ray and the reflected ray will be ________.
   (a) 50°
   (b) 80°
   (c) 90°
   (d) 100°

7. The unit used to measure astronomical distances is __________.
   (a) second
   (b) century
   (c) leap year
   (d) light year
8. During a clear night, bright streaks of light are visible in the sky. These are called shooting stars. Identify the shooting stars from the following.
   (a) Meteors
   (b) Comets
   (c) Asteroids
   (d) Satellites
9. **Assertion (A):** Carbon dioxide is one of the important greenhouse gases.
   Reason (R): Carbon dioxide is released due to exhalation by animals and plants.
   (a) A is true, but R is false.
   (b) Both A and R are true, but R is not the correct explanation of A.
   (c) Both A and R are true, and R is the correct explanation of A.
   (d) A is false, but R is true.
10. Which of the following fuels is described as a clean fuel?
   (a) CNG
   (b) Petrol
   (c) Diesel
   (d) Gasoline

How many questions did you answer correctly? Score yourself.

easy ☐	average ☐	advanced ☐	remembering ☐	understanding ☐	applying ☐
analysing ☐	evaluating ☐	creating ☐	justify ☐	associate ☐	analyse ☐
interpret/account for ☐	identification ☐	recognize ☐	select ☐	recall ☐	

Global Citizenship Education (GCED)

CHALLENGING ENVIRONMENTAL INJUSTICE

Social injustice refers to the unfair distribution of resources, opportunities and privileges within a society, leading to disparities and disadvantages for certain groups of people. Environmental injustice is one of the root causes of social injustice. Environmental injustice refers to the unequal distribution of environmental benefits and burdens among different communities, often along racial, ethnic or socioeconomic lines.

Look at the picture. Can you explain the message hidden in this picture?

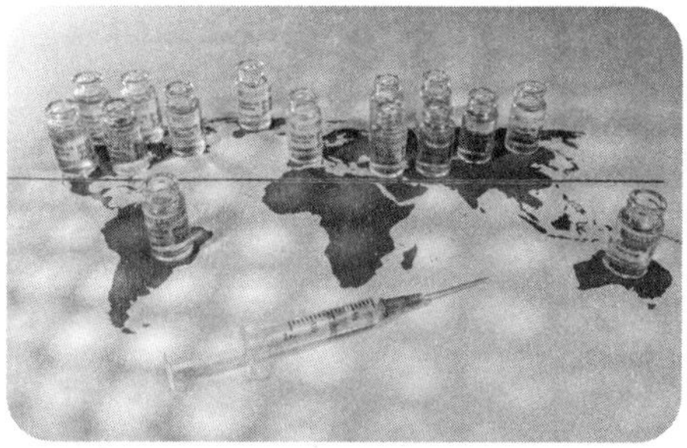

Look at the picture. It shows an underdeveloped country on the left side and a developed country on the right side. Why do you think there is more pollution in underdeveloped countries? Give one example to support your answer.

What is shown in the above picture is called **environmental disparity** between the rich and poor countries. This happens when the environment is harmed, but the developed countries get away with the consequences using their resources, while the poor countries suffer because of lesser resources available to them.

GLOBAL ENVIRONMENTAL INJUSTICE

What do you understand by the term "global environmental injustice"?

Complete the chart given below to find out the consequences of global environmental injustice on developing and underdeveloped countries.

Consequences of Global Environmental Injustice

Occupational Hazards

Environmental Racism

Climate Change

Poor Access to Clean Resources

Can you think of a few more ways in which developing countries suffer from environmental inequalities?

My Global Actions!

My Thought Bubble!

Write a few words that come to your mind when you think of environmental injustice.

My Thinking Circle!

Discuss with your classmates the ways you can contribute to reduce pollution. Write the major points in the given space.

My Action Plan!

As a science student, what would you recommend to reduce the suffering of marginalized communities in developing countries?

Skills You Need

ARTIFICIAL INTELLIGENCE

Have you ever done online shopping of books? After a purchase, has the website ever recommended you books similar to the one you purchased? How and who do you think predicted your choice? This is possible through **artificial intelligence** (**AI**), which has studied your user data and shopping patterns and predicted the recommendation.

Artificial intelligence *(AI) is a type of computer technology which is concerned with making machines work in an intelligent way, similar to the way that the human mind works.*

For this, computers are programmed to mimic certain aspects of human intelligence such as:

- Learning
- Planning
- Problem solving
- Recognizing speech and faces

You will learn more on this in your computer science classes.

Artificial Intelligence

Daily Uses of AI

AI is a part of our lives in one way or another. Some examples where you can see artificial intelligence around you are:

- Google Maps
- Auto suggestions while searching the Internet
- Voice assistants on mobile devices such as Siri, Cortona and Google Assistant
- Video games
- Smart speakers
- Streaming recommendations on apps and streaming sites
- Remote-controlled drones
- Smart homes

Can you think of other examples?

Benefits of AI

AI is beneficial for us in the following ways:

- It does not get tired or wear out easily.
- It has huge applications in many industries such as banking, healthcare, manufacturing, e-commerce, transport and finance.
- It can make decisions accurately.
- It does not need to take breaks.

Would there be any disadvantages of AI? Do some research on the topic and discuss with your classmates.

Career Exploration

- Data Analysts and Scientists
- AI and Machine Learning Specialists
- Big Data Engineer/Architect
- New Technology Specialists
- Business Intelligence Developer

AI DETECTIVES!

Activity: Talking with a voice assistant on a mobile device

We need: A mobile device, Internet connection

Procedure:

1. Make a list of interesting questions that you would like to ask the personal assistant. (Example, are you intelligent?)
2. Get hold of a mobile device.
3. Check and confirm that it is connected to the Internet.
4. Start asking the questions. Does it understand all your questions?
5. Note down the answers.
6. How would a person have answered your questions? Try asking your friends and compare the answer. Would there be any differences?
7. Analyse and note down what you understood about the way the mobile personal assistant responded to your questions.

Try It!

Read about the 17 Sustainable Development Goals adopted by all United Nations Member States to transform the world. Write an article on how AI can help in achieving these goals.

Happiness Activity Sheets

SELF-ESTEEM!

Have you ever felt moody and avoided meeting your friends? Have you ever felt low on confidence or suddenly very confident? These feelings may be due to the onset of puberty and the hormonal changes you are experiencing during your adolescent years. Thus, growth hormones and the onset of puberty affect your self-esteem.

Your ***self-esteem*** is how you feel about yourself. If you have high self-esteem, you will see yourself in a positive light and feel good and confident. If you have low self-esteem, you do not behave confidently because you do not like yourself or you do not think of yourself as a valuable person. A healthy self-esteem would create confidence, self-reliance and happiness in yourself.

You can build your self-esteem in the following ways:

- Eat healthy food.
- Get moving and exercise daily.
- Practice daily hygiene.
- Keep your curiosity alive.
- Learn, try and create new things.
- Be positive and look at the brighter side of things.
- Focus on solutions instead of problems.
- See mistakes as learning opportunities.
- Surround yourself with supportive friends.
- Ask for help and support.
- Avoid comparing yourself with others.
- Remember that no one is perfect.

Are you aware of your feelings?

How do you feel when your self-esteem is low? How do you feel when your self-esteem is high? Write 3–4 words that best describe your feelings in this thought bubble.

How mindful are you?

Completing your study or assignments would give you a good feeling. Getting things done even when you do not want to, because it is too difficult or too boring, can give you a sense of achievement. However, there are some things which you can control and cannot control.

Identify the things you can and cannot control. How would you take advantage of the things you can control?

What about a reflective conversation!

Many unrealistic images of people, that you see on magazine covers, movies, advertisements, etc., with very slim figure, crystal clear skin, very fair skin, etc., are edited and photoshopped.

Having a healthy body image is more important than an ideal body image. Reflect on this topic and have a conversation with your classmates. Note down some role models in the space provided to start your conversation.

Too much of anything is not good! So, take care as overconfidence, due to very high self-esteem, could lead to vanity.

Vernacular Names

Amoeba • Assamese: *Amiiba* • Bengali: *Jibanubisesa* • Hindi: *Amiba* • Kannada: *Amiba* • Malayalam: *Amiba* • Marathi: *Amiba* • Mizo: *Thil hrik* • Tamil: *Amipa* • Telugu: *Amiba*

Barley
• Bengali: *Barli*
• Hindi: *Jau*
• Kannada: *Barli*
• Marathi: *Barli*
• Malayalam: *Barli*
• Tamil: *Parli*
• Telugu: *Barli*
• Urdu: *Jo*

Earth • Assamese: *Prithiwi* • Bengali: *Prthibi* • Hindi: *Prthevee* • Kannada: *Bhumi, Pruthvi* • Meiteilon: *Malem* • Marathi: *Prthvi* • Malayalam: *Bhumi* • Mizo: *Lei pum* • Tamil: *Pumi* • Telugu: *Bhumi* • Urdu: *Zameen*

Kelp • Bengali: *Kelapa* • Hindi: *Samundree ghass* • Kannada: *Kadala hullu* • Meiteilon: *Nung-sam* • Marathi: *Kelpa* • Malayalam: *Kelpp* • Urdu: *Samundari ghas*

Lemon • Assamese: *Nemu tenga*
• Bengali: *Lebu*
• Hindi: *Nimboo*
• Kannada: *Nimbe*
• Meiteilon: *Champra*
• Marathi: *Limbace*
• Malayalam: *Cerunaranna*
• Mizo: *Ser*
• Tamil: *Elumiccai*
• Telugu: *Nimmakaya*
• Urdu: *Limun*

Lemur
• Bengali: *Lemura*
• Kannada: *Lemur*
• Marathi: *Lemara*
• Malayalam: *Lemur*
• Mizo: *Sahuai*
• Tamil: *Lemur*
• Telugu: *Lemar*

Mars • Assamese: *Mongol* • Bengali: *Mangala* • Hindi: *Mangal grah* • Kannada: *Mangala* • Marathi: *Mangala* • Mizo: *Indona pathian* • Tamil: *Cevvay kirakam* • Telugu: *Angaraka* • Urdu: *Mareekh*

Mustard plant• Assamese: *Methiguti*
• Bengali: *Sarisa gacha*
• Hindi: *Sarson ka paudha*
• Kannada: *Sasive sasya*
• Meiteilon: *Hang-gam*
• Marathi: *Moharica ropa*
• Malayalam: *Katuk ceti* • Tamil: *Katuku alai* • Telugu: *Avalu mokka*
• Urdu: *Sarson ka paudha*

Penguin• Bengali: *Penguina* • Hindi: *Penguin* • Kannada: *Pengvin* • Malayalam: *Pengin paksi* • Marathi: *Pengvina* • Tamil: *Penkuyin* • Telugu: *Pengvin*

Spotted deer • Assamese: *Phutuki horin*
• Bengali: *Dayayukta harina*
• Hindi: *Chitteedaar hiran*
• Kannada: *Macheyulla jinke*
• Meiteilon: *Saji*
• Marathi: *Klankita harana*
• Malayalam: *Pulli man*
• Tamil: *Pulliyitappatta man*
• Telugu: *Maccala jinka*
• Urdu: *Hiran*

Tomato • Assamese: *Bilahi*
• Bengali: *Tameto*
• Hindi: *Tamatar*
• Kannada: *Tometo*
• Malayalam: *Takkali*
• Meiteilon: *Khamen asinba*
• Marathi: *Tometo*
• Mizo: *Sap bawkbawn*
• Tamil: *Takkali*
• Telugu: *Tametokai*
• Urdu: *Tamatar*

What do you call these plants and animals in your language? Share the names with us at schoolsupport@harpercollins.co.in

Project

1. Visit a Pollution Control Board office in your region to know more about the regulations to control industrial effluents. Know more about the norms to follow to build a chimney that emits fumes and the wastewater treatment conditions to be followed in a factory. Make a report on the measures taken by the Board to reduce the pollution of air and water. **(C-7.1)**
2. Write slogans about the prevention of pollution of air and water. Organize a rally for environmental protection in your school locality to spread awareness among people about the dangers of pollution and the prevention methods. **(C-7.1)**
3. As a student, how can you help in reducing the pollution of air and water? Discuss the ways that can be followed at home and in your residential area. **(C-7.1)**

In the Library

1. Read more about the 'Carbon footprint' and methods of 'carbon offsetting' to reduce the carbon emission levels in the atmosphere to reduce pollution. Find out how India has contributed in this area. Prepare a presentation based on your findings. **(C-8.1)**
2. Read about the Ganga Action Plan. Prepare a comprehensive report on the aim, its plan of action, the results and the conclusion to be drawn from them. Suggest ways in which the plan can be made better. **(C-7.3)**

Life Skills

Does your school perform any environment-related activities? Make groups of 5 students and find out the following.

1. Is there an environment club in your school?
2. What are its objectives?
3. What events does it perform in a year?
4. How can one become a member?

If there is no such club in your school, would you form a club?

How would you do it? Sketch your plan in consultation with your friends. **(C-7.1)**

Worksheet

Even though three-fourths of the Earth's surface is covered with water, potable water or drinking water resources are very limited. As the population of the world increases, the amount of water required also increases.

Ancient Indians, like many other ancient civilizations, developed various methods to preserve and manage their water resources. India's diverse geography and climate, which include arid regions and monsoon-dominated areas, required the implementation of different water conservation techniques. Ancient Indians had a profound understanding of their local ecosystems and water resources. They developed community-based water management systems, incorporating traditional knowledge and customs to ensure sustainable water use.

Across different regions of India, ancient communities followed various water conservation practices, including fixing leakages in water structures, using water wisely, and respecting water bodies as sacred places.

A. How can lessons from ancient Indian water management practices be applied to address modern-day water challenges in India and beyond?

B. Identify and document existing ancient water preservation structures, such as stepwells, tanks, and reservoirs, in India. Propose strategies for preserving and safeguarding these ancient water structures for future generations.

C. Examine how water preservation techniques varied in different ecological regions of ancient India. How did the choice of water preservation methods correlate with the specific environmental challenges faced in each region? What lessons can be learned from these historical practices to address contemporary water resource management in diverse ecological settings?